TEACHER'S BOOK

with Digital Pack

3

CEFR B1+

AMERICAN TH!NK

SECOND EDITION

Zoltan Rezmuves

CAMBRIDGE UNIVERSITY PRESS

CONTENTS

Welcome to **AMERICAN TH!NK**, the course that develops your students' communication and critical thinking skills, values, and life competencies so they can successfully meet the challenges ahead.

Have you ever asked yourself: "how can I be expected to prepare my students to succeed in a world that's changing so fast?" While it's impossible to predict what specific skills will be in demand by the time our students enter the workforce, there are some things that we as educators can do to ensure our students are as well prepared for their futures as they can be. We know there is an ever-increasing need for individuals to be able to work together effectively with others around the world, and to be able to think creatively and solve problems collaboratively. They also need to be able to analyze and process sources of information more critically, communicate, and support their views more effectively, and they need to maintain a positive mindset in challenging environments.

With **AMERICAN TH!NK** you can be certain you're giving your learners the tools they need to build a brighter future for themselves and a better world for us all.

What's new in the Second Edition?

We've kept everything that teachers loved about AMERICAN TH!NK First Edition:

The high-interest, relevant, and thought-provoking topics	The development of critical thinking, positive values, and self-esteem	A syllabus built on the Cambridge English Learner Corpus and English Profile	The inclusion of Cambridge Exams practice sections

The second edition builds and expands on these strengths:

- The **globally focused content** will appeal to teens' natural curiosities and interests, and feed their growing sense of the world around them.
- The **Life Competencies** strand, supported by entertaining student vlogs and correlated to the Cambridge Life Competencies Framework, will help them develop the vital capabilities they'll need to be successful throughout their lives.
- The authentic, **real-world documentary-style videos** will captivate student interest and provoke meaningful thought and lively classroom discussion.
- Powerful, all-in-one digital tools and support will empower teachers to deliver dynamic and effective lessons.

The story of AMERICAN TH!NK

AMERICAN TH!NK Second Edition was developed using the latest research into teen cognitive science and best practices and methodologies for the secondary classroom. To learn more, visit **cambridge.org/americanthink2e** or scan this QR code with your smartphone or tablet.

Cambridge Life Competencies

A framework to develop skills for life

There have been many initiatives to address the skills and competencies our students need for the 21st century – each relating to different contexts. At Cambridge, we are responding to educators who have asked for a way to understand how all these different approaches to life competencies relate to English language programs.

The Cambridge Framework sets out to have three dimensions:

BREADTH	DEVELOPMENT	DEPTH
Complete view of transferable skills within one system	How the skills develop across stages of the learning journey	Enough detail to guide teaching and assessment in practical ways

We have grouped the different competencies into six main areas.

- **Creative Thinking**
- **Critical Thinking**
- **Learning to Learn**
- **Communication**
- **Collaboration**
- **Social Responsibilities**

These are supported by three foundation layers that underpin the Framework:

- **Emotional Development**
- **Digital Literacy**
- **Discipline Knowledge**

What Are "Competencies"?

We call these "competencies" rather than "skills," because competencies are more than just skills. The competencies in this Framework are complex and require development in three areas:

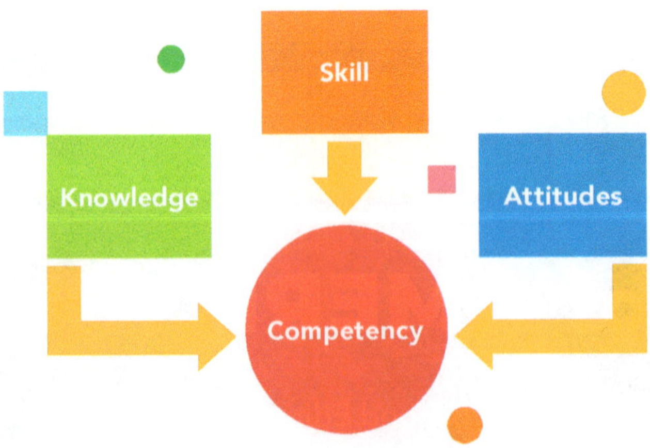

Competencies are defined as a combination of knowledge, skills, and attitudes, where:

a) knowledge is composed of the facts and figures, concepts, ideas, and theories which are already established and support the understanding of a certain area or subject;

b) skills are defined as the ability and capacity to carry out processes and use the existing knowledge to achieve results;

c) attitudes describe the disposition and mindsets to act or react to ideas, persons, or situations.

Council of the European Union, 2018, p14.

Core areas

Core area				
Creative Thinking	Participating in creative activities	Creating new content from own ideas or other resources	Using newly created content to solve problems and make decisions	
Critical Thinking	Understanding and analyzing links between ideas	Evaluating ideas, arguments, and options	Synthesizing ideas and information	
Learning to Learn	Practical skills for participating in learning	Taking control of own learning	Reflecting on and evaluating own learning success	
Communication	Using appropriate language and register for context	Managing conversations	Participating with appropriate confidence and clarity	
Collaboration	Taking personal responsibility for own contribution to a group task	Listening respectfully and responding constructively to others' contributions	Managing the sharing of tasks in a project	Working towards a resolution related to a task
Social Responsibilities	Understanding personal responsibilities as part of a group and in society – including citizenship	Taking active roles including leadership	Understanding and describing own and others' cultures	Understanding and discussing global issues – environmental, political, financial, and social

Foundational layers

- Emotional Development
- Digital Literacy
- Discipline Knowledge

cambridge.org/clcf

For a full correlation to the Cambridge Life Competencies Framework, visit **cambridge.org/americanthink2e**

AMERICAN TH!NK and the Cambridge Life Competencies Framework

Although **AMERICAN TH!NK** focuses on both the *Social Responsibilities* and the *Emotional Development* competencies in the *Cambridge Life Competencies Framework*, all of the six Life Competencies are explored throughout the course.

The table below shows, at a glance, where you can find an activity which concentrates on a particular Core Area.

The following table shows which *competencies* are developed in this level.

Competency	Core Area	U1	U2	U3	U4	U5	U6	U7	U8	U9	U10	U11	U12
Social Responsibilities	Understanding personal responsibilities as part of a group and in society – including citizenship								✔				
	Understanding and discussing global issues – environmental, political, financial, and social		✔		✔							✔	
	Understanding and describing own and others' cultures					✔		✔					
	Taking active roles including leadership												✔
Emotional Development	Identifying and understanding emotions										✔		
	Empathy and relationship skills				✔			✔	✔				
	Managing own emotions	✔			✔								
Critical Thinking	Evaluating ideas, arguments, and options	✔						✔		✔		✔	✔
	Understanding and analyzing links between ideas		✔	✔				✔					
Learning to Learn	Practical skills for participating in learning	✔	✔	✔	✔	✔	✔	✔	✔	✔	✔	✔	✔
Communication	Using appropriate language and register for context					✔					✔		
Creative Thinking	Participating in creative activities							✔	✔				
Collaboration	Listening respectfully and responding constructively to others' contributions	✔	✔	✔	✔	✔	✔	✔	✔	✔	✔	✔	✔
	Taking personal responsibility for own contribution to a group task						✔						
	Setting measurable objectives					✔	✔						

Here are a few examples of how activities can help your students develop particular Can Do Statements:

BIG DECISIONS UNIT 1

What next?

John *posted 2 hours ago*

My time at school is almost up and of course I'm thinking about the big question: what next? Maybe I've waited too long to start thinking about it, but that's how I am. I think I'll do well in my exams, so maybe I'll go to college and get more qualifications – but I've been asking myself if it's better to just find a job and start a career that way. On the other hand, if I do go on to study further, should I do it right away or maybe take a year off – a "gap year"? Helpful comments and ideas, please! Thanks.

Like Share Reply

Amy *posted 5 minutes ago*

Hi, John. I'm doing a gap year right now. I saved up some money and went to Thailand, but after two months of vacation, I got bored and the money was running out. Then I learned about a volunteer medical organization working in poor parts of the country and they let me join as a driver. Now I'm working, struggling with the Thai language (I spend up to an hour a day practicing with friends), and learning lots about myself. I've made a resolution, too – when I go home, I'm going to study medicine to be a doctor or a nurse. So my advice? Do a gap year, but don't just travel around – do some volunteer work somewhere. For me, it's been life-changing.

Like Share Reply

Mark *posted 28 minutes ago*

Hey! I finished high school three months ago and I didn't want to go to college or travel. So I'm doing a course. I'm studying to become a yoga teacher. I took up yoga a couple of years ago and I've loved it ever since. I was very lazy at school, but I've changed my ways and now I study really hard. The class starts every day at 7:00, so I've had to get into the habit of waking up early. But that's fine – I love what I'm doing. That's the important thing – do what you love, if you can.

Like Share Reply

Pauline *posted 1 hour ago*

Hi there! Here's my advice. Do what feels right for you now, but keep an open mind and be prepared to change. Some of my friends went traveling after school, but I didn't have the courage; I just went to college. It was OK and I was having a good time. Then one day, an old friend from school called me and said he was going to start an online company and asked me to join him. So, I quit college and went to work with him. It was the best thing I've ever done. I wasn't planning on dropping out of college, but I took the chance to try something different and I don't regret it.

Like Share Reply

Train to TH!NK

Reading between the lines

Sometimes a writer doesn't tell us everything directly: we need to draw conclusions from the information the writer gives. We call this "reading between the lines."

6 **Answer the questions and give reasons for your answers.**

0 Is John worried about his abilities as a student?
No, he says he'll do well on his exams and he's thinking about university.
1 Has Amy been enjoying her work with a medical organization?
2 Is Mark different now than when he was at school?
3 Did Pauline want to travel after leaving school?

SPEAKING

7 **Work in pairs. Discuss these questions.**

1 What resolutions are you going to make for this school year?
2 What do you think is the secret of changing your life for the better?

Plan carefully. *Do work first, play later.* *Listen to your parents.*

Competency: Critical Thinking

Core Area: Evaluating ideas, arguments, and options

Can Do Statement: Identifies assumptions and inferences in an argument.

In this Train to ***TH!NK*** *section, students are asked to draw their own conclusions from texts in which the writer does not give direct information.*

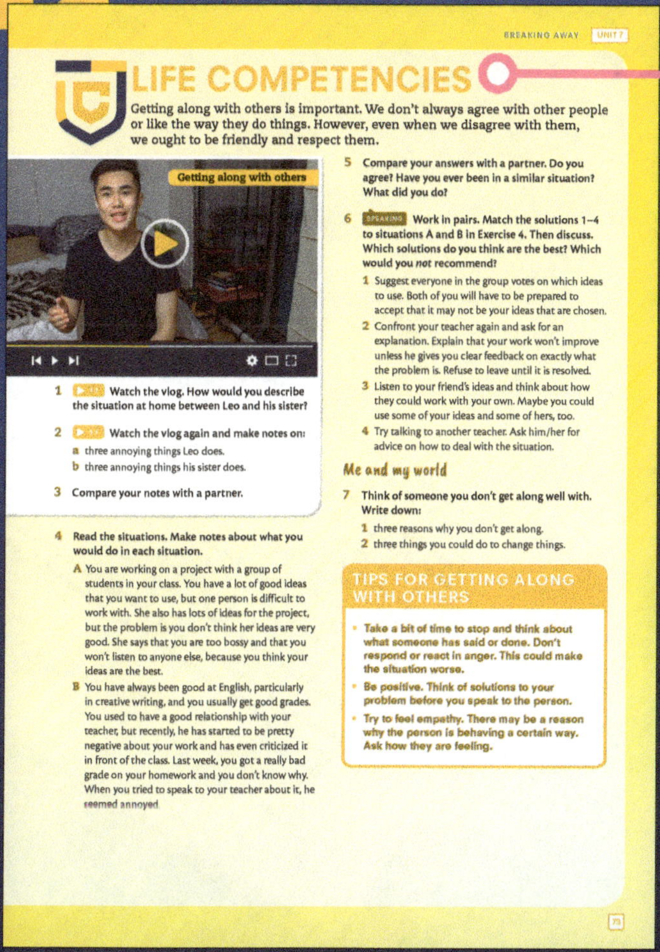

BREAKING AWAY UNIT 7

LIFE COMPETENCIES

Getting along with others is important. We don't always agree with other people or like the way they do things. However, even when we disagree with them, we ought to be friendly and respect them.

Getting along with others

1 **Watch the vlog. How would you describe the situation at home between Leo and his sister?**

2 **Watch the vlog again and make notes on:**

a three annoying things Leo does.
b three annoying things his sister does.

3 **Compare your notes with a partner.**

4 **Read the situations. Make notes about what you would do in each situation.**

A You are working on a project with a group of students in your class. You have a lot of good ideas that you want to use, but one person is difficult to work with. She also has lots of ideas for the project, but the problem is you don't think her ideas are very good. She says that you are too bossy and that you won't listen to anyone else, because you think your ideas are the best.

B You have always been good at English, particularly in creative writing, and you usually get good grades. You used to have a good relationship with your teacher, but recently, he has started to be pretty negative about your work and has even criticized it in front of the class. Last week, you got a really bad grade on your homework and you don't know why. When you tried to speak to your teacher about it, he seemed annoyed.

5 **Compare your answers with a partner. Do you agree? Have you ever been in a similar situation? What did you do?**

6 SPEAKING **Work in pairs. Match the solutions 1–4 to situations A and B in Exercise 4. Then discuss. Which solutions do you think are the best? Which would you *not* recommend?**

1 Suggest everyone in the group votes on which ideas to use. Both of you will have to be prepared to accept that it may not be your ideas that are chosen.
2 Confront your teacher again and ask for an explanation. Explain that your work won't improve unless he gives you clear feedback on exactly what the problem is. Refuse to leave until it is resolved.
3 Listen to your friend's ideas and think about how they could work with your own. Maybe you could use some of your ideas and some of hers, too.
4 Try talking to another teacher. Ask him/her for advice on how to deal with the situation.

Me and my world

7 **Think of someone you don't get along well with. Write down:**

1 three reasons why you don't get along.
2 three things you could do to change things.

TIPS FOR GETTING ALONG WITH OTHERS

- Take a bit of time to stop and think about what someone has said or done. Don't respond or react in anger. This could make the situation worse.
- Be positive. Think of solutions to your problem before you speak to the person.
- Try to feel empathy. There may be a reason why the person is behaving a certain way. Ask how they are feeling.

Competency: Emotional Development

Core Area: Empathy and relationship skills

Can Do Statement: Negotiating conflict constructively.

The following exercises encourage students to put themselves in the position of others during times of conflict. They also practice stating opposing opinions in a constructive way.

Student's Book

Each unit of AMERICAN TH!NK builds students' knowledge and skills through a series of carefully constructed learning inputs and activities. Units begin with a thought-provoking question and introductory video, followed by a series of high-interest readings and abundant opportunities for personalized speaking practice.

Each sequence of exercises helps students unlock the text, while contextualized vocabulary and grammar concepts recycle and build throughout the unit, sharpening students' language proficiency.

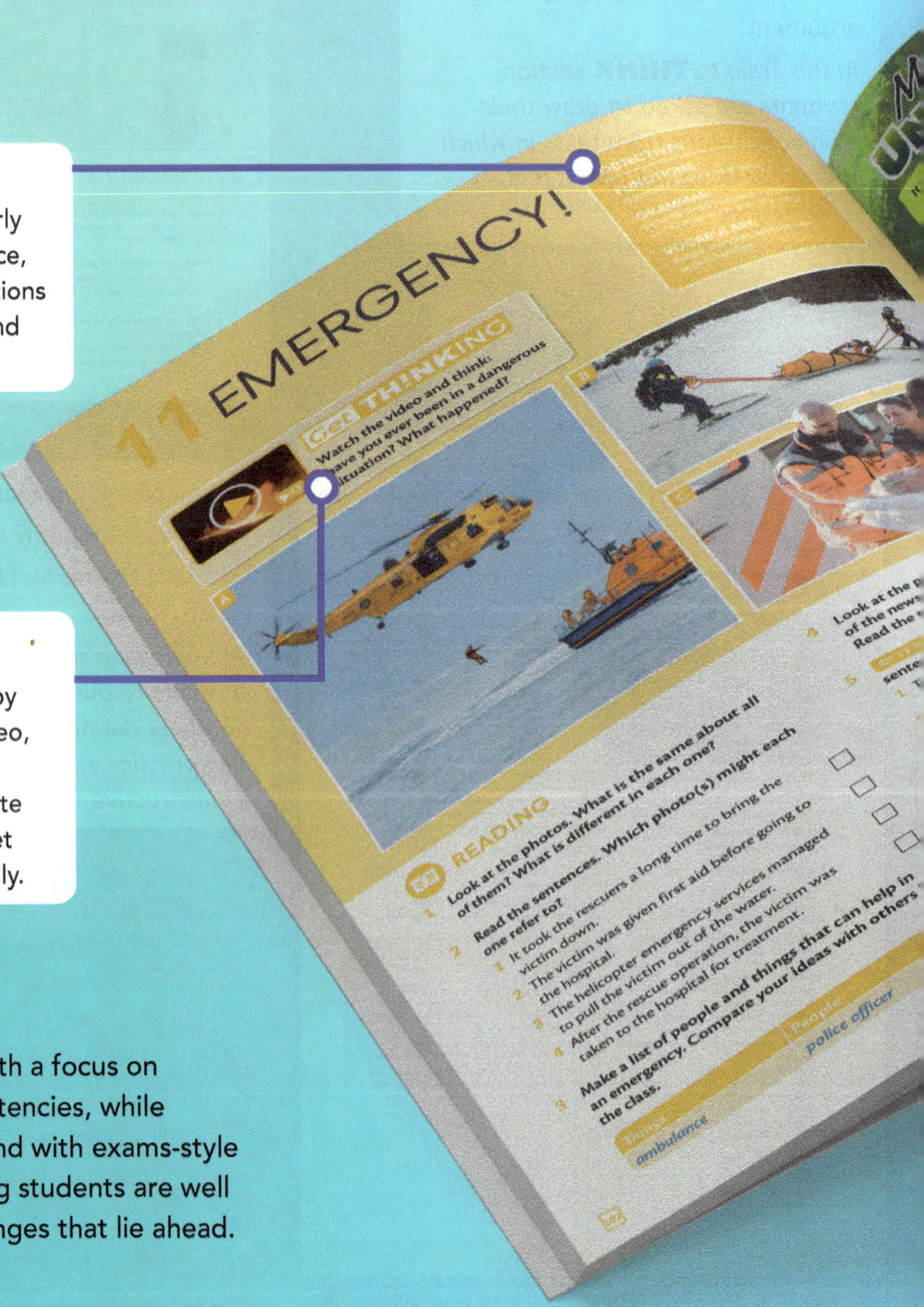

Objectives

Learning objectives clearly show unit aims at a glance, including language functions and target vocabulary and grammar concepts.

Get TH!NKING

Each unit is introduced by a documentary-style video, with questions designed to pique curiosity, activate prior knowledge, and get students thinking critically.

Some units conclude with a focus on developing Life Competencies, while even-numbered units end with exams-style practice pages, ensuring students are well prepared for the challenges that lie ahead.

SPEAKING

Frequent opportunities for speaking practice build on students' prior knowledge and encourage them to relate the text to their own experience, personalizing the speaking tasks.

Train to TH!NK

Train to **TH!NK** sections encourage students to reflect on the topics presented in the readings and to express their opinions on meaningful issues, as well as require them to work together to achieve consensus or to solve a problem.

GRAMMAR

Grammar presentations use a scaffolded inductive approach to help students understand the features and structures of English grammar.

GRAMMAR and VOCABULARY

Each unit includes grammar and vocabulary sections that are presented in context and supported by additional practice in the Workbook.

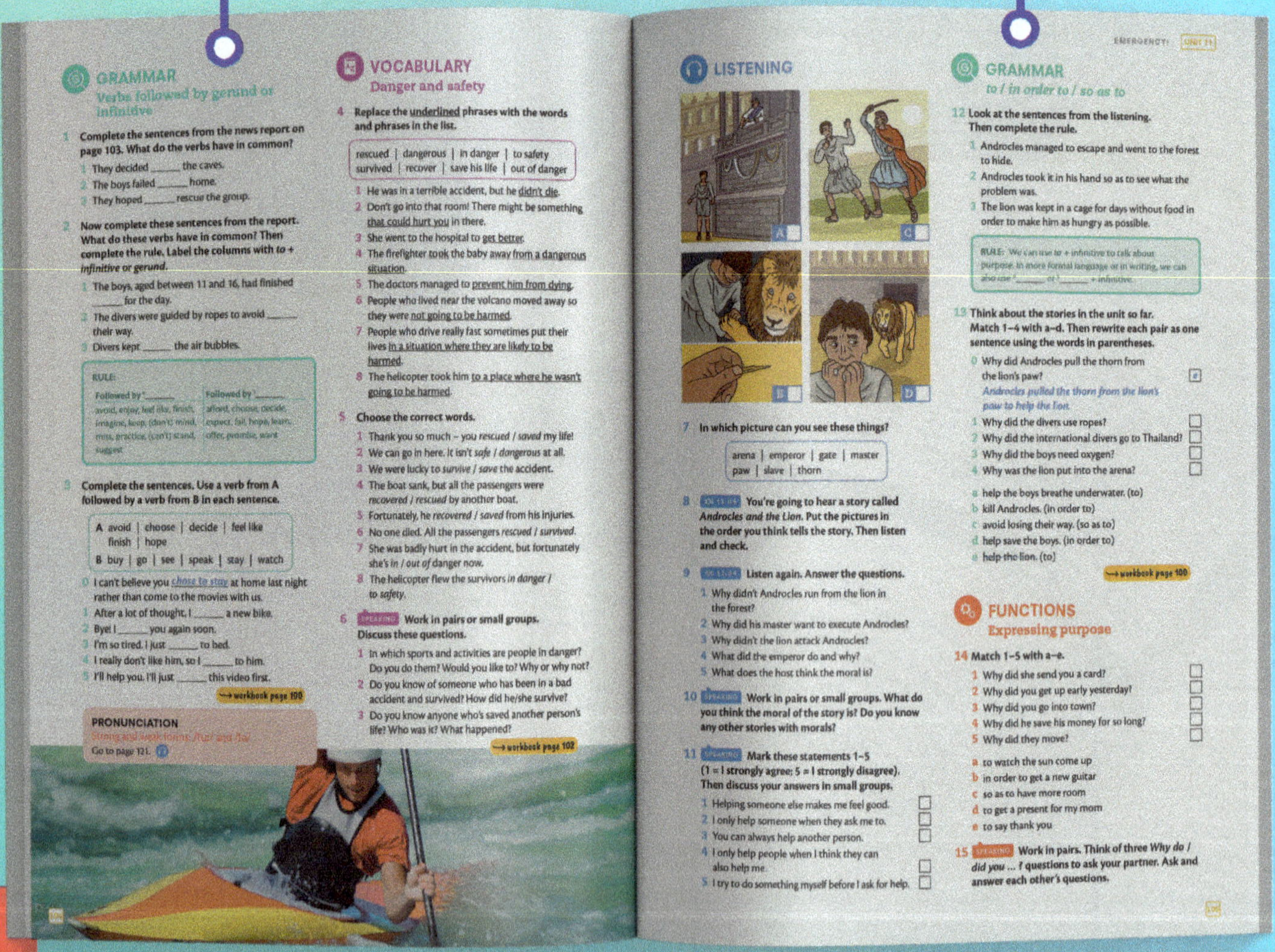

Grammar rap!

These short but catchy videos help illustrate and explain grammar concepts in an innovative and memorable way.

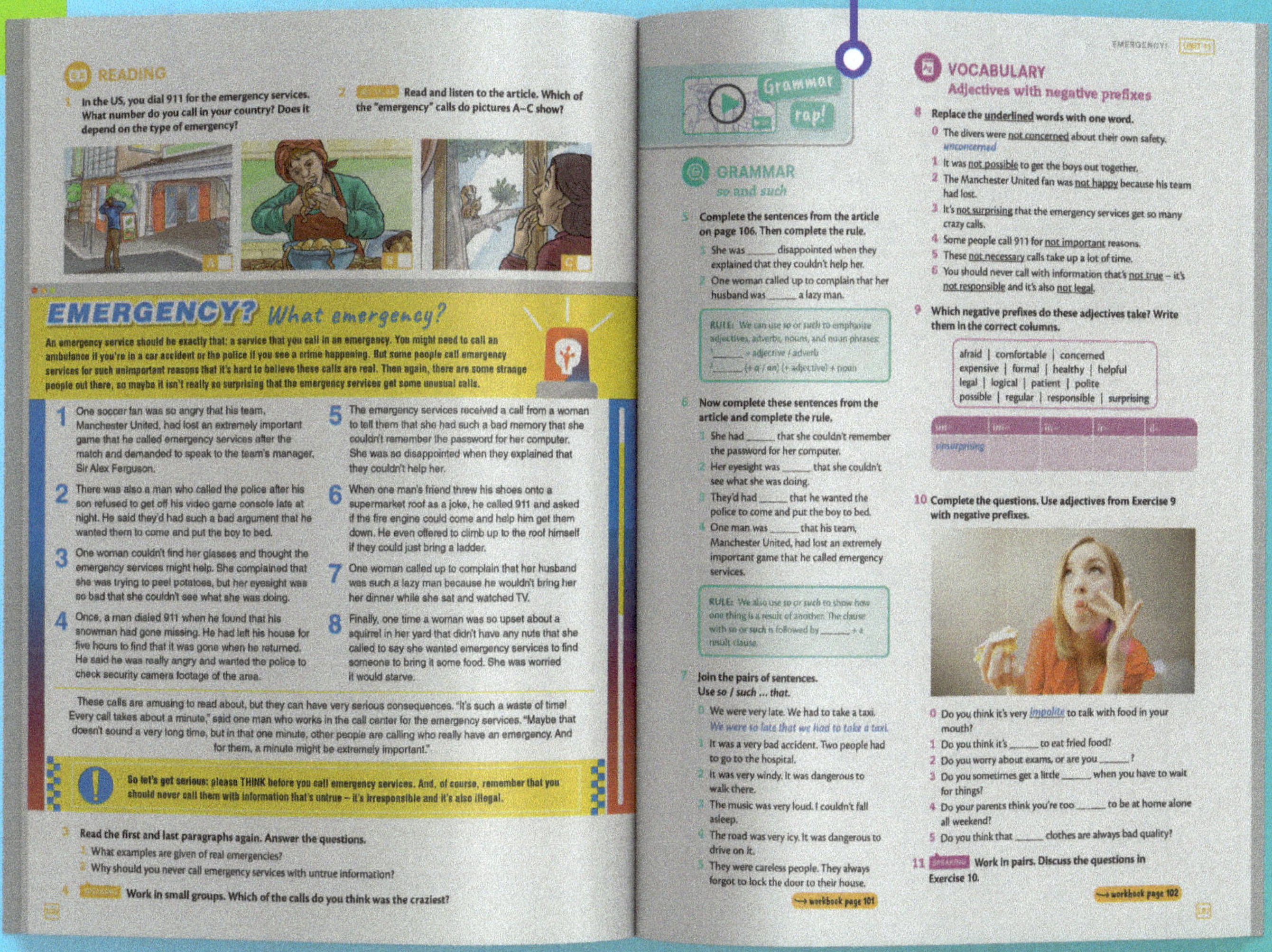

DEVELOPING SPEAKING

These modeled speaking activities provide abundant practice to help students build their speaking confidence while Phrases for Fluency tips focus on authentic language to help them sound more natural.

LIFE COMPETENCIES

These lessons focus on developing a key competency area from the Cambridge Life Competencies Framework. The competencies that students develop throughout **AMERICAN TH!NK** will serve them throughout their lives within their communities and in the world at large.

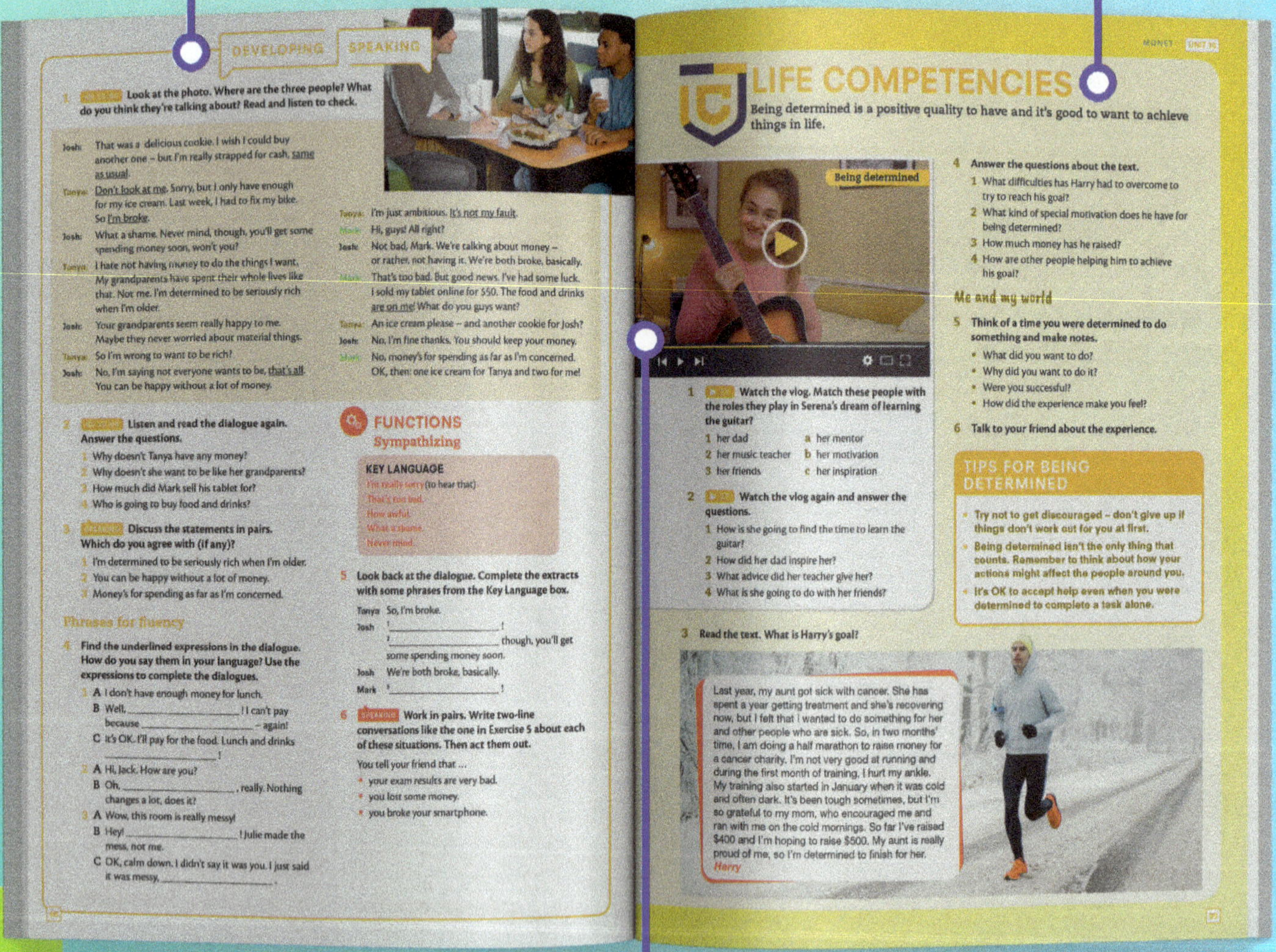

DEVELOPING SPEAKING

1 Look at the photo. Where are the three people? What do you think they're talking about? Read and listen to check.

Josh: That was a delicious cookie. I wish I could buy another one – but I'm really strapped for cash, same as usual.
Tanya: Don't look at me. Sorry, but I only have enough for my ice cream. Last week, I had to fix my bike. So I'm broke.
Josh: What a shame. Never mind, though, you'll get some spending money soon, won't you?
Tanya: I hate not having money to do the things I want. My grandparents have spent their whole lives like that. Not me. I'm determined to be seriously rich when I'm older.
Josh: Your grandparents seem really happy to me. Maybe they never worried about material things.
Tanya: So I'm wrong to want to be rich?
Josh: No, I'm saying not everyone wants to be, that's all. You can be happy without a lot of money.
Tanya: I'm just ambitious. It's not my fault.
Mark: Hi, guys! All right?
Josh: Not bad, Mark. We're talking about money – or rather, not having it. We're both broke, basically.
Mark: That's too bad. But good news. I've had some luck. I sold my tablet online for $50. The food and drinks are on me! What do you guys want?
Tanya: An ice cream please – and another cookie for Josh?
Josh: No, I'm fine thanks. You should keep your money.
Mark: No, money's for spending as far as I'm concerned. OK, then: one ice cream for Tanya and two for me!

2 Listen and read the dialogue again. Answer the questions.
1 Why doesn't Tanya have any money?
2 Why doesn't she want to be like her grandparents?
3 How much did Mark sell his tablet for?
4 Who is going to buy food and drinks?

3 Discuss the statements in pairs. Which do you agree with (if any)?
1 I'm determined to be seriously rich when I'm older.
2 You can be happy without a lot of money.
3 Money's for spending as far as I'm concerned.

Phrases for fluency

4 Find the underlined expressions in the dialogue. How do you say them in your language? Use the expressions to complete the dialogues.
1 A I don't have enough money for lunch.
B Well, __________! I can't pay because __________ – again!
C It's OK. I'll pay for the food. Lunch and drinks __________!
2 A Hi, Jack. How are you?
B Oh, __________, really. Nothing changes a lot, does it?
3 A Wow, this room is really messy!
B Hey! __________! Julie made the mess, not me.
C OK, calm down. I didn't say it was you. I just said it was messy, __________.

FUNCTIONS
Sympathizing

KEY LANGUAGE
I'm really sorry (to hear that).
That's too bad.
How awful.
What a shame.
Never mind.

5 Look back at the dialogue. Complete the extracts with some phrases from the Key Language box.
Tanya So, I'm broke.
Josh 1 __________! 2 __________ though, you'll get some spending money soon.
Josh We're both broke, basically.
Mark 3 __________!

6 SPEAKING Work in pairs. Write two-line conversations like the one in Exercise 5 about each of these situations. Then act them out.
You tell your friend that …
- your exam results are very bad.
- you lost some money.
- you broke your smartphone.

LIFE COMPETENCIES
Being determined is a positive quality to have and it's good to want to achieve things in life.

Being determined

1 Watch the vlog. Match these people with the roles they play in Serena's dream of learning the guitar?
1 her dad a her mentor
2 her music teacher b her motivation
3 her friends c her inspiration

2 Watch the vlog again and answer the questions.
1 How is she going to find the time to learn the guitar?
2 How did her dad inspire her?
3 What advice did her teacher give her?
4 What is she going to do with her friends?

3 Read the text. What is Harry's goal?

Last year, my aunt got sick with cancer. She has spent a year getting treatment and she's recovering now, but I felt that I wanted to do something for her and other people who are sick. So, in two months' time, I am doing a half marathon to raise money for a cancer charity. I'm not very good at running and during the first month of training, I hurt my ankle. My training also started in January when it was cold and often dark. It's been tough sometimes, but I'm so grateful to my mom, who encouraged me and ran with me on the cold mornings. So far I've raised $400 and I'm hoping to raise $500. My aunt is really proud of me, so I'm determined to finish for her.
Harry

4 Answer the questions about the text.
1 What difficulties has Harry had to overcome to try to reach his goal?
2 What kind of special motivation does he have for being determined?
3 How much money has he raised?
4 How are other people helping him to achieve his goal?

Me and my world

5 Think of a time you were determined to do something and make notes.
- What did you want to do?
- Why did you want to do it?
- Were you successful?
- How did the experience make you feel?

6 Talk to your friend about the experience.

TIPS FOR BEING DETERMINED
- Try not to get discouraged – don't give up if things don't work out for you at first.
- Being determined isn't the only thing that counts. Remember to think about how your actions might affect the people around you.
- It's OK to accept help even when you were determined to complete a task alone.

Life Lessons videos

Each Life Competency is introduced by a Life Lessons vlog recorded by a student. These videos help introduce the competency area in a natural and accessible way and serve as a springboard to the activities that follow.

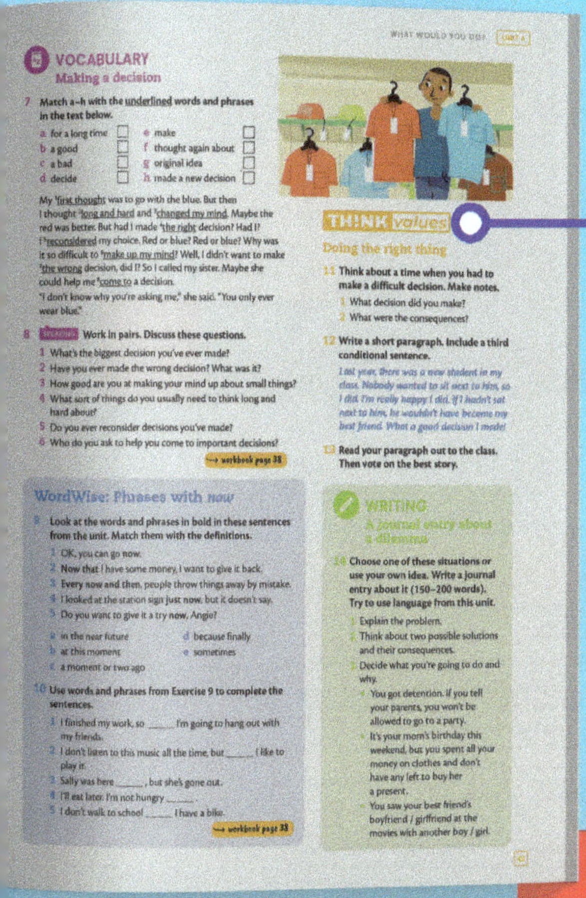

TH!NK values

This feature encourages students to reflect on and discuss a wide range of important values, helping to develop their character as well as their sensitivity to others.

Culture

The Culture sections introduce interesting topics and information about people and places around the world and spark discussion in a speaking task that requires students to make use of the information presented in the text.

WRITING

An extended writing section guides students through the writing process for a variety of text types. Students are presented with a model text for analysis of the task and purpose, and to practice the useful language they will need, before they move on to produce and share their own compositions.

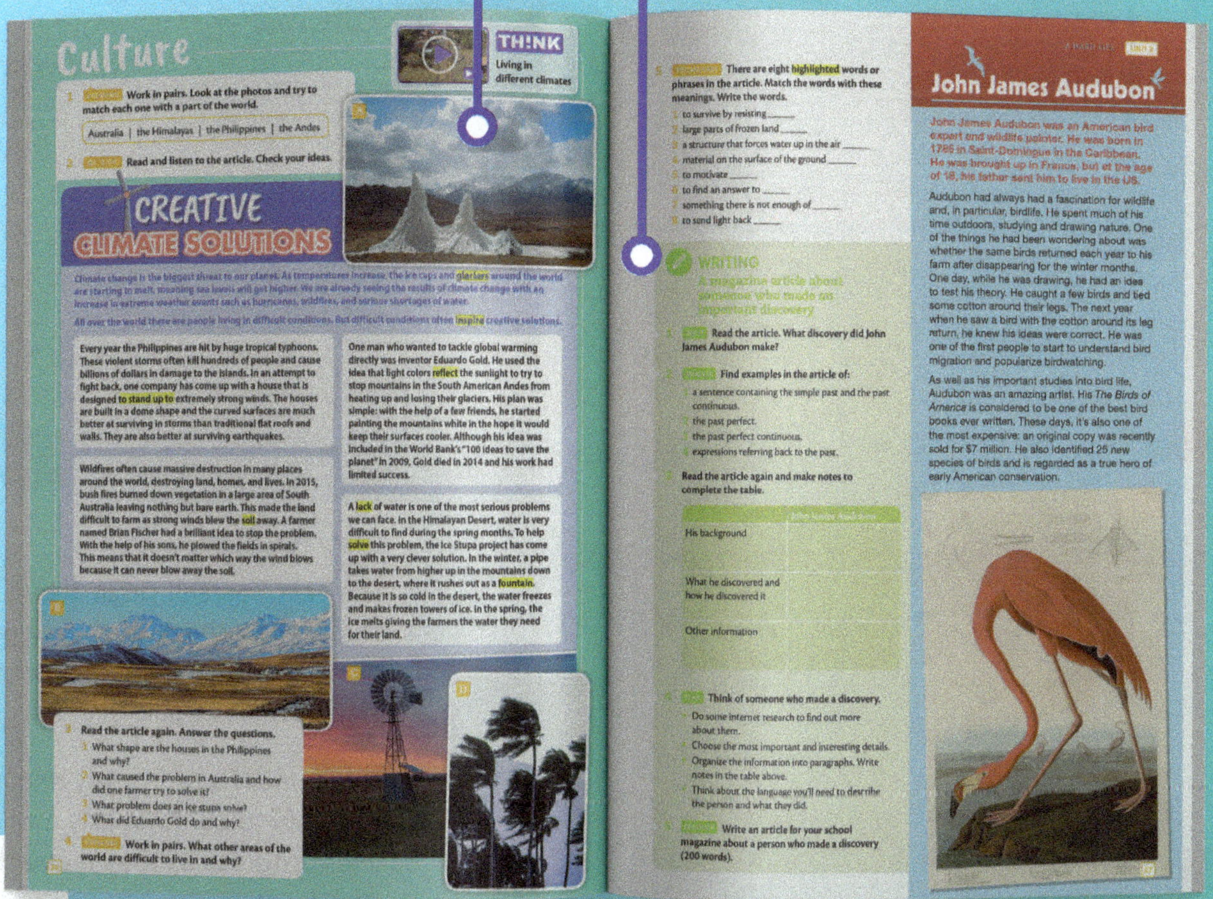

Exams

Exercises on these pages replicate the format of tasks from the Cambridge English Exams.

Cross-references to the Workbook lead to additional exams practice and useful test-taking tips.

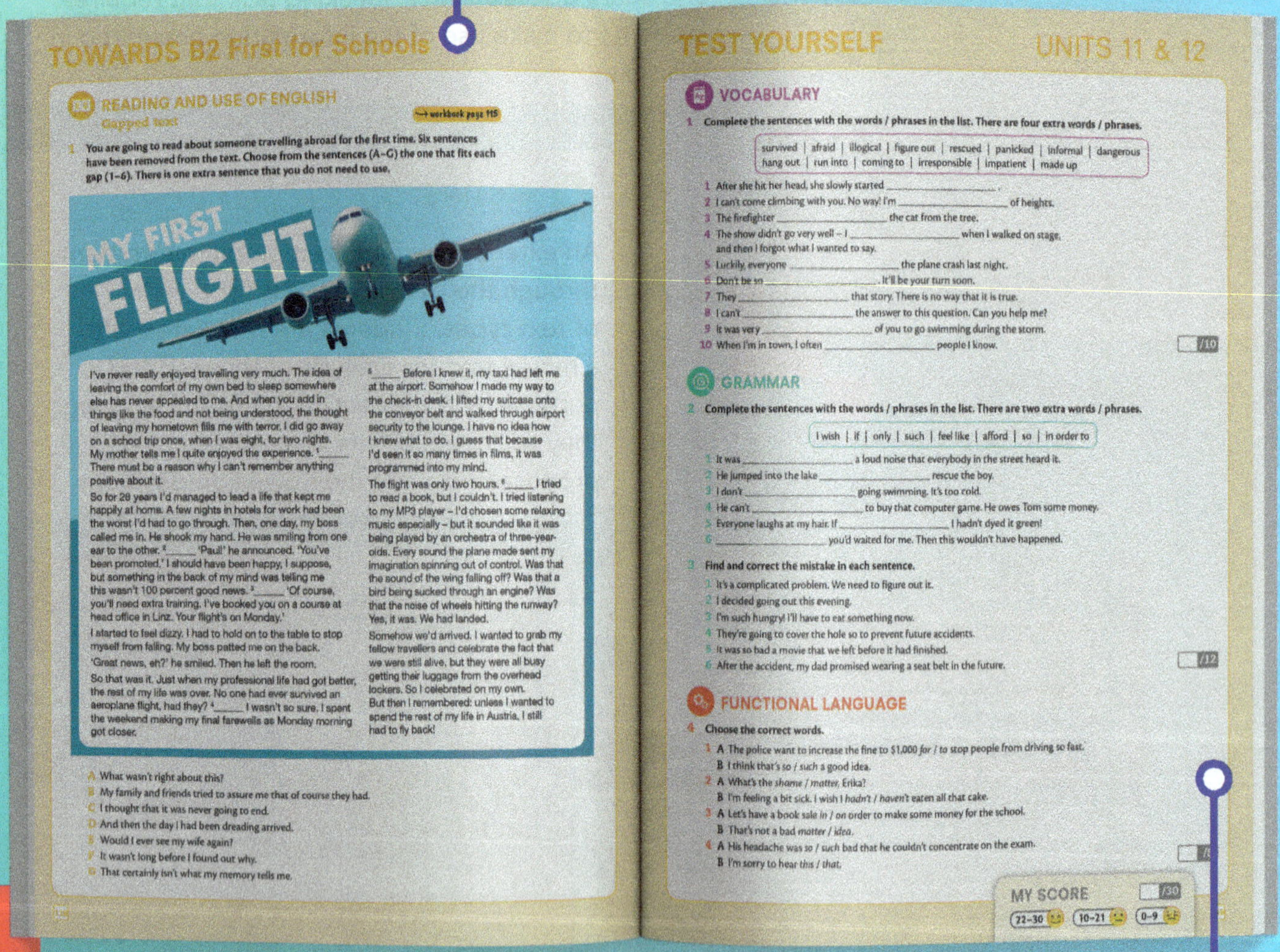

Test Yourself

The Test Yourself page allows students to check their progress and is based on the language presented in the previous pair of units.

The "emoji" scoring key encourages students to continuously monitor their progress as they move through each level.

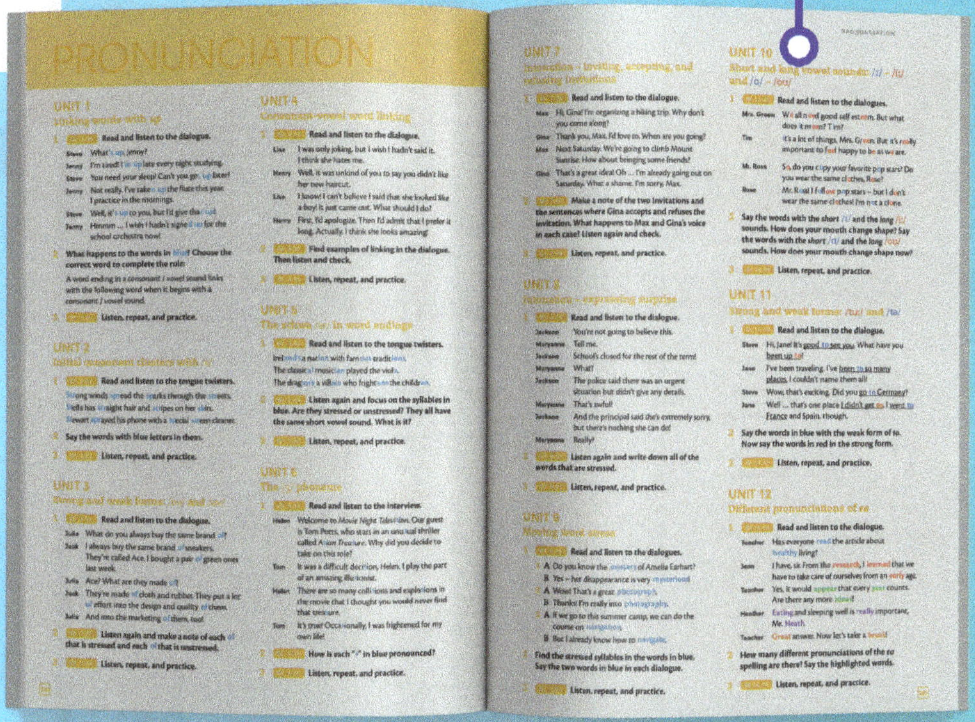

Pronunciation

This handy reference at the back of the Student's Book covers sounds that are likely to pose a challenge for English learners and provides additional practice and support via the classroom audio program.

Get it Right!

Cross-references in the Teacher's Book indicate appropriate points within the unit to direct students to this section in the back of the Student's Book. Get it Right! activities help students avoid common errors as identified by the Cambridge English Learner Corpus*.

Cambridge English Corpus

*What is the Cambridge English Learner Corpus?

The Corpus comprises a 50 million-word collection of real-life learners' written and spoken English, derived from actual students taking the Cambridge English exams. We use this information to determine which word structures are more easy or more difficult for English learners, and ultimately, to determine how best to support students when they encounter them.

Workbook

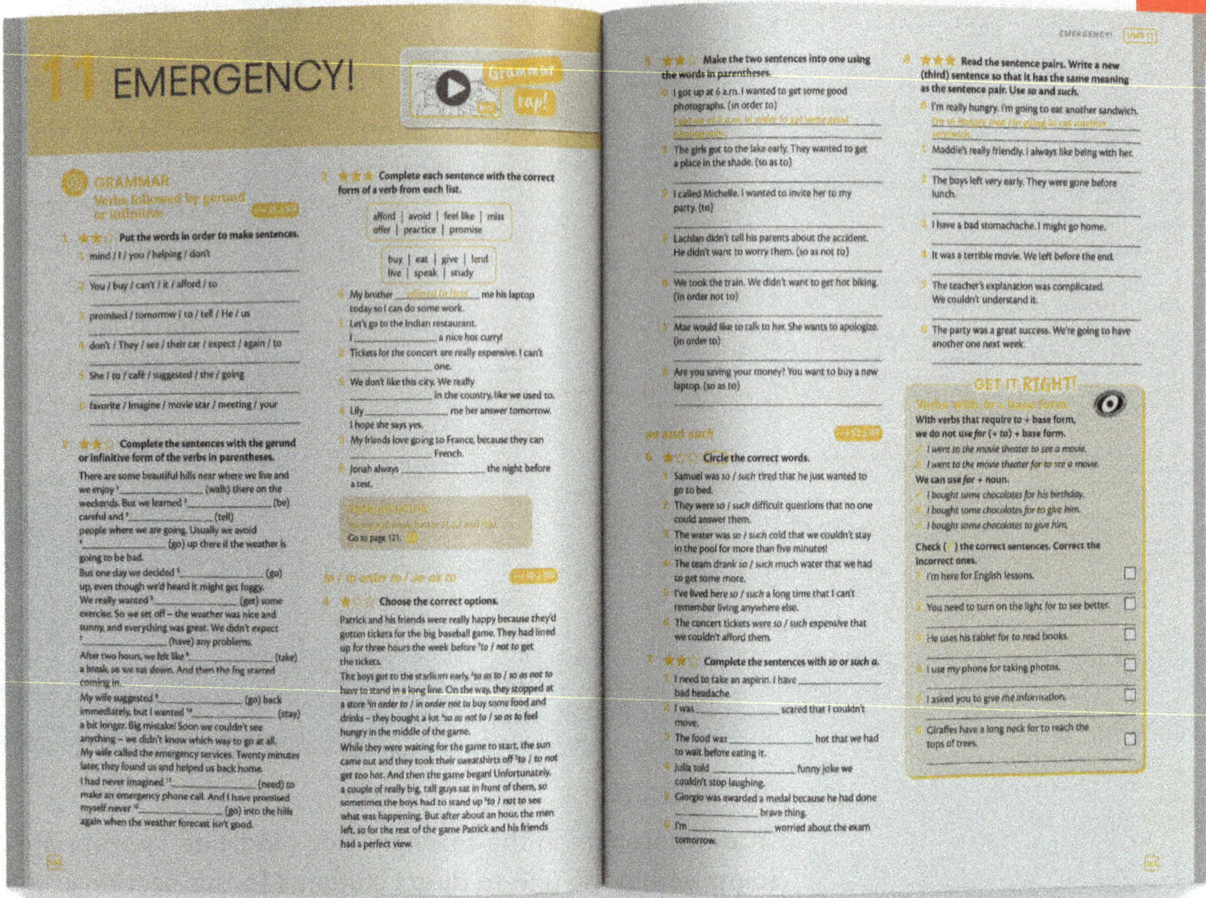

The Workbook offers extra practice of the language and skills presented in the Student's Book. Handy cross-references immediately following activities in the Student's Book direct students to corresponding pages in the Workbook, where they can get additional practice.

Cambridge Exams Practice

The Cambridge Exams sections provide useful tips and practice to help students prepare for Cambridge English as well as other high-stakes international exams.

AMERICAN TH!NK
Digital Support

Presenting all your digital tools together in one place!

With **AMERICAN TH!NK**, everything you need is at your fingertips, including Presentation Plus, the powerful front-of-class presentation tool with complete course content, the entire classroom audio and video programs, Teacher's Resource Bank, and Test Generators.

Presentation Plus

- Student's Book and Workbook with interactive exercises
- Embedded links to classroom audio and video
- Additional games and activities
- Accessible online and offline.

Teacher's Resource Bank

- Online teacher resource area with support for projects, graded grammar and vocabulary practice worksheets, video worksheets, writing templates, extra speaking activities, and more!
- Test Generator: an easy-to-use tool to customize and create end of unit, end of term, and end of year tests, as well as exam practice tests.

Collaboration Plus

- Students can work together on digital projects online using the Collaboration Plus tools and teachers can set, view, support, and grade the work.
- Teachers can share students' project work with the class in the Showcase area.

Practice Extra

- Mobile-friendly platform and content
- Bite-sized learning activities with audio and video
- Performance tracking.

For updated information on **AMERICAN TH!NK**'s Digital Tools, visit **cambridge.org/americanthink2e** or scan this QR code.

How to use the Teacher's Book

The **AMERICAN TH!NK** wraparound Teacher's Book is designed to help you plan and deliver highly effective lessons easily and seamlessly.

White panel side notes provide guided lesson support and include model student responses in activities and answers to questions.

Light blue panel notes provide additional background information and optional suggestions for building and expanding on lessons.

Purple panels identify lesson objectives and assist with unit navigation.

Yellow panels identify potential homework and flipped-classroom ideas.

Red panels alert teachers to available teaching resources and point out areas where students are likely to struggle.

Warmer

Ideas to introduce students to the unit's topic help activate their prior knowledge and experience and encourage classroom discussion.

Get TH!NKing

Strategies to help teachers get the best use out of the Get **TH!NK**ing videos and activities ensure students are primed to discuss the unit topic.

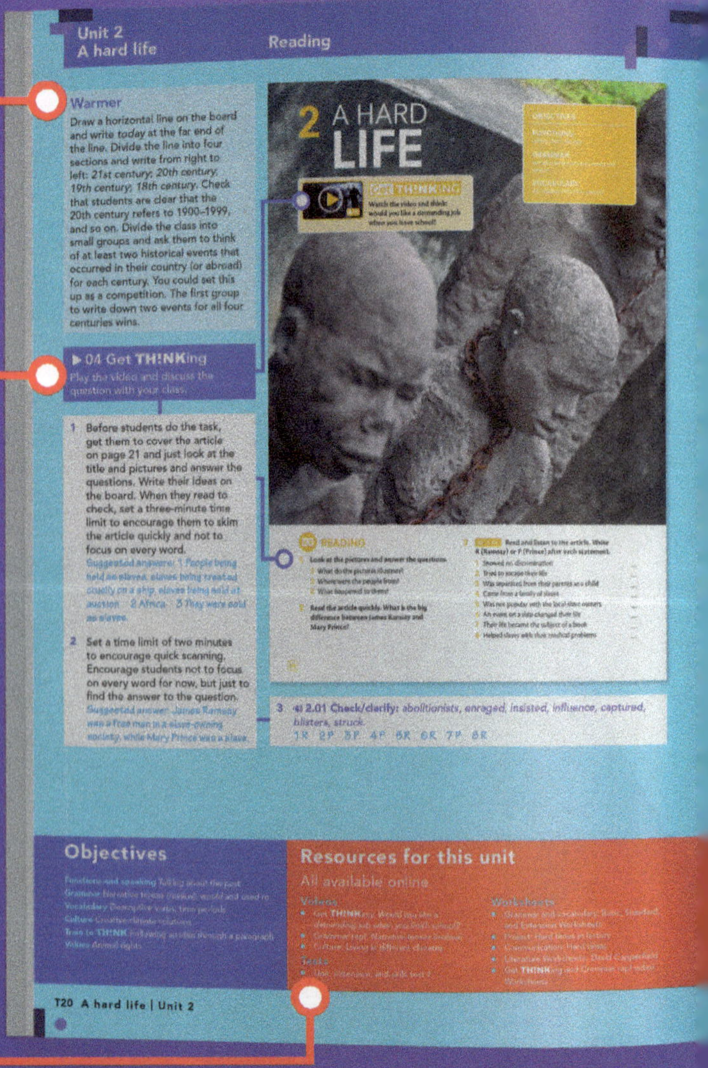

Resources for this unit

An at-a-glance listing of all the lesson support available for the unit appears in the bottom panel, including available teaching resources, video, digital support, and assessment tools.

Cambridge Framework for Life Competencies

This icon identifies which Life Competency is being developed and what teachers should expect students at this level to be able to do via a Can-Do statement.

Alternative Activities

Ideas for alternative classroom activities give teachers additional flexibility and freedom to dive deeper into rich language-building opportunities.

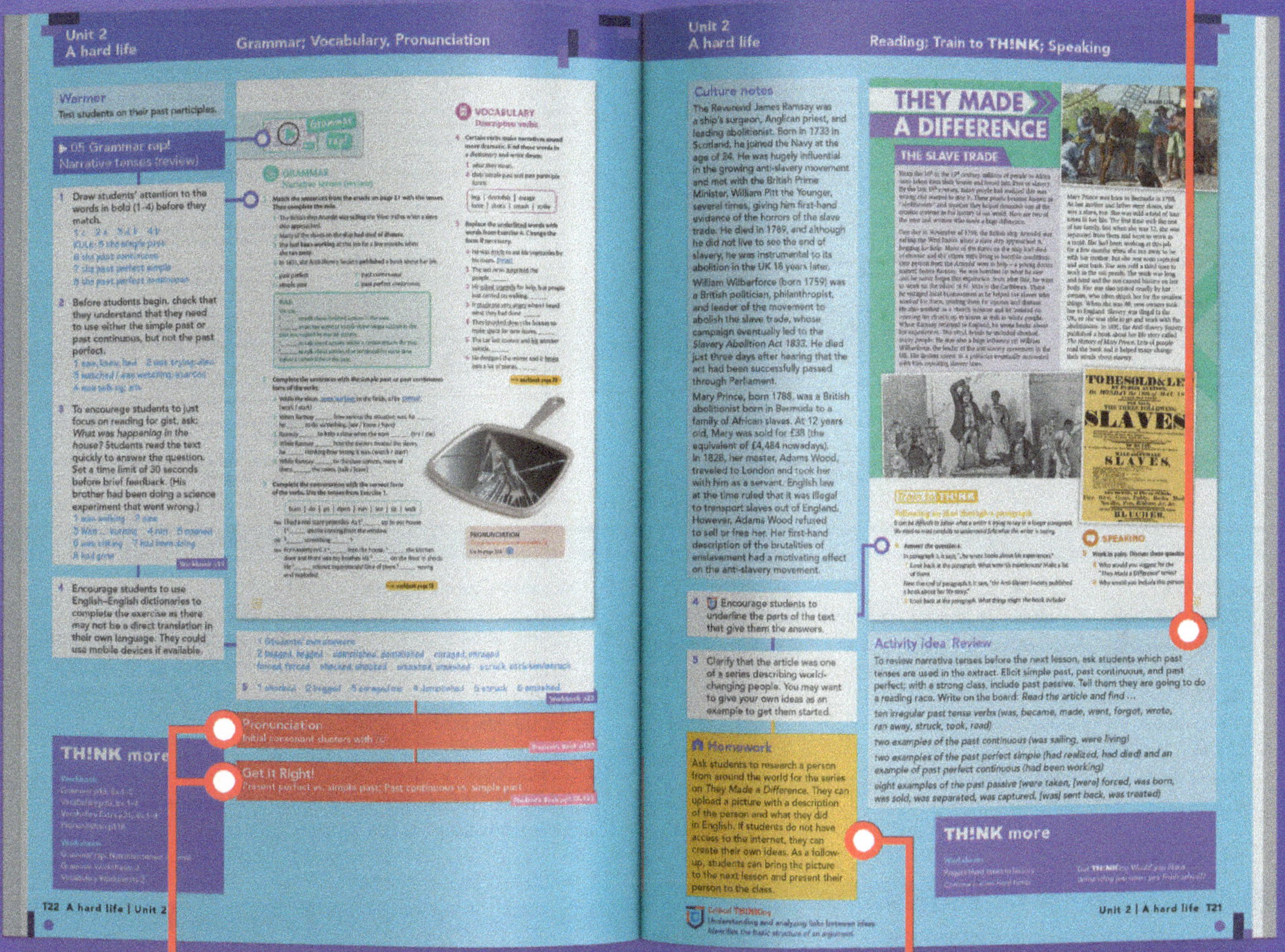

Get it Right! and Pronunciation

These notes help alert teachers to potential problem areas for English learners and offer mitigation and/or remediation strategies and tools.

Homework

Useful ideas for activities that students could do at home to consolidate in-class learning and encourage independent study.

WELCOME

A THAT'S ENTERTAINMENT!

let and *allow*

1 W.01 **Complete the conversation with the words. Then listen and check.**

allowed | angry | feel | get
guitar | let | look | ~~looking~~
makes | songs | sound | talent show

Sara Hey, Karl, what are you [0]*looking* at?
Karl My history book. Can't you see I'm busy?
Sara I'm just asking. Sorry.
Karl No, I'm sorry. I don't [1]_____ great today.
Sara You don't [2]_____ very happy. What's the matter?
Karl My dad [3]_____ me so [4]_____ .
Sara That doesn't [5]_____ so good. Why?
Karl He says I'm not [6]_____ to be in the band.
Sara What?! So he won't allow you to play in the [7]_____ on the weekend?
Karl No. He says no music until after my exams.
Sara But that's four weeks from now!
Karl I know. He wants me to study and forget about writing [8]_____ . He won't even [9]_____ me practice the [10]_____ .
Sara But you need some time to relax.
Karl I know. I [11]_____ so angry when I think about it. It just isn't fair.

2 W.01 **Listen again. Answer the questions.**

1 Why is Karl angry?
2 How long is it until the exams finish?
3 What does Sara think about the situation?
4 Who do you agree with: Karl or his dad? Why?

3 SPEAKING **What do your parents allow you to do during exam time? What don't they let you do? Make lists. Then compare with a partner.**

Music

4 **Sort the words into two groups. Label the groups. Then think of four more items for each one.**

classical | drums | guitar | jazz
piano | pop | rap | violin

Verbs of perception

5 **Complete the sentences from the conversation with the correct forms of (*not*) *look*. Then match them with the rules.**

1 You ______________ very happy.
2 Hey, Karl, what ______________ at?

RULE: We use verbs of perception (*look, smell, feel, taste*) ...
- in the present continuous to talk about actions. ☐
- in the simple present to talk about states. ☐

6 **Complete the mini-dialogues with the correct forms of the verbs.**

1 taste
A What are you doing?
B I _____ the soup ... It _____ great.

2 smell
A My socks _____ really bad!
B Then why _____ you _____ them?

3 feel
A Why _____ you _____ that sweater?
B Because it's so soft. I like the way it _____ .

7 SPEAKING **Work in pairs. Karl tries to persuade his dad to let him play in the talent show. Write a conversation of eight lines. Then read it out loud.**

4

The big screen

8 SPEAKING **Work in pairs. For each movie genre, think of an example that you have both seen.**

action | animated | comedy
drama | horror | romantic comedy
science fiction | thriller

9 **Read the article. What movie genres does it mention?**

10 **Read the article again and answer the questions.**

1 When did Columbus start making movies?
2 Who are his movies especially popular with?
3 Where did he learn about filmmaking?
4 What does he do apart from direct movies?
5 Who started a company with him?

11 SPEAKING **Work in pairs. Think of your favorite movie director and discuss these questions.**

1 What movies has this director made?
2 What do you like about his/her movies?

Present perfect tenses

12 **Complete the sentences. Use the present perfect simple or continuous form of the verbs and choose the correct words.**

1 They ______________ (play) *for / since* 87 minutes and neither side has scored yet.
2 I *yet / still* ______________ (not see) the finale, so please don't tell me which singer won.
3 ______________ you ______________ (see) last night's show *still / yet*? Bradley Cooper and Lady Gaga were guests.
4 The children ______________ (sit) in front of the TV watching *SpongeBob for / since* seven o'clock this morning.
5 It's the funniest show on TV. I ______________ (not miss) an episode *still / yet*.
6 The President ______________ (say) the same thing *for / since* weeks now. No one believes her.

BEHIND THE CAMERA
CHRIS COLUMBUS

A 12-year-old who gets left behind when his family goes on vacation, a teenage magician fighting to save his world, and the troubled son of a Greek god living in modern-day America: these are just three of the characters brought to life on the big screen by director Chris Columbus. With movies like *Home Alone, Harry Potter and the Chamber of Secrets*, and *Percy Jackson: Sea of Monsters*, Columbus has certainly shown that he knows how to get teenagers into movie theaters.

Columbus, who studied film at New York University, has been making movies for more than 30 years and has become one of the most successful movie directors of all time. Since he directed his first movie, *Adventures in Babysitting* in 1987, Columbus has been involved in some of the biggest movies as both a director and a producer.

But Columbus doesn't only make action movies for the teenage market. He's also made a number of successful movies for adults. Comedies such as *Mrs. Doubtfire*, dramas such as *The Help*, and science fiction movies such as *Bicentennial Man* have all helped make Columbus one of Hollywood's most popular filmmakers. And in 2014, he formed a production company with his daughter Eleanor.

TV shows

13 SPEAKING **Work in pairs. Look at the sentences in the previous exercise. Match them with the types of TV show.**

cartoon | talk show | sitcom
sports show | talent show | the news

14 **Choose a type of TV show from the list below. Write a sentence about it using the present perfect simple and/or continuous. Don't include the type of TV show in your sentence!**

drama series | game show
reality TV show | soap (opera)

I've been watching it for weeks, but no one has won the million-dollar prize yet.

15 SPEAKING **Read out your sentence. Can the rest of the class guess the type of TV show?**

5

---

1 W.01
1 feel 2 look 3 makes 4 angry 5 sound 6 allowed
7 talent show 8 songs 9 let 10 guitar 11 get

2 W.01
1 His dad says no music until after exams.
2 Four weeks from now.
3 She disagrees with Karl's dad because Karl needs to relax.
4 Students' own answers

3 Students' own answers

4 Instruments: drums, guitar, piano, violin
Types of music: classical, jazz, pop, rap
Students' own answers

5 1 don't look 2 are you looking RULE: 2, 1

6 1 'm tasting; tastes 2 smell; are, smelling
3 are, feeling; feels

7 Students' own answers

8 Students' own answers

9 Action, comedy, drama, science fiction movies: *Home Alone, Harry Potter and the Chamber of Secrets, Percy Jackson: Sea of Monsters, Adventures in Babysitting, Mrs. Doubtfire, The Help, Bicentennial Man*

10 Check/clarify: *magician.*
1 1987 2 teenagers 3 New York University
4 He produces. 5 His daughter, Eleanor

11 Students' own answers

12 1 have been playing; for 2 still; haven't seen
3 Have, seen; yet 4 have been sitting; since
5 haven't missed; yet 6 has been saying; for

13 1 sports show 2 talent show 3 talk show 4 cartoon
5 sitcom 6 the news

14 Students' own answers

15 Students' own answers

Culture notes

Chris Columbus is an American film director, producer, and writer who is best known for his family and sentimental movies. His greatest commercial successes have been *Harry Potter and the Sorcerer's Stone* and its sequel *Harry Potter and the Chamber of Secrets*.

TH!NK more

Workbook
A That's entertainment! pp4–5, Ex. 1–9

B TIME TO ACT

Our endangered planet

1 SPEAKING Work in pairs. Describe the photos. What problems do they show?

A

B

C

2 W.02 Listen to three conversations. Match them with the photos.

3 W.02 Listen again. In which conversation do you hear these words? Write the number.

a trash ☐
b climate change ☐
c litter ☐
d pollution ☐
e fumes ☐
f smog ☐
g flooding ☐

Question tags

4 Complete these sentences from the recording with the question tags.

are they? | aren't they? | does it? | did they? | is it? | isn't it? | weren't they? | doesn't it?

1 I guess they're just lazy, ____________
2 But it only takes a few people to spoil everything, ____________
3 Yes, it's all those fumes from the factory, ____________
4 They didn't ask us if we wanted it here, ____________
5 Even if they do, it doesn't make our lives any better, ____________
6 Hundreds of homes were damaged, ____________
7 And the politicians aren't really doing anything to help, ____________
8 It isn't the sort of thing you'd expect to see here, ____________

5 Complete the sentences with question tags.

1 You haven't told Ron, ________ ?
2 You're going to do something about it, ________ ?
3 It sounds pretty dangerous, ________ ?
4 It didn't work, ________ ?
5 It won't be easy, ________ ?
6 She wrote to her local politician, ________ ?

So do I / Neither do I

6 Look at the questions and complete the answers with *so* or *neither*.

1 A I don't really believe in all that.
B ____________ do I.
2 A I think we should do something.
B ____________ do I.

7 SPEAKING Complete the sentences so that they are true for you and read them out. Agree (or disagree!) with your partner's sentences.

1 I really like ____________.
2 I don't like ____________.
3 I believe ____________.
4 I don't believe ____________.

Accepting and refusing invitations

8 W.03 Put the sentences in order to make a conversation. Then listen and check.

[1] **Mandy** Marco and I want to do something to help the flood victims.
☐ **Mandy** Yes – 20 km! Want to join us?
☐ **Mandy** That's a shame. But you will sponsor us, won't you?
☐ **Mandy** We're going to do a sponsored walk next Sunday.
☐ **Jamal** Of course I will.
☐ **Jamal** Are you going to walk a long way?
☐ **Jamal** What are you going to do?
☐ **Jamal** I'd love to, but I can't. I'm busy.

9 SPEAKING Work in pairs. Write a conversation using the underlined phrases from Exercise 8.

You and your friend are tired of all the trash in the street and have decided to do something about it. What are you going to do? Invite another friend to join you.

Party time

10 Work in pairs. Imagine you're organizing a party. Make a list of important things to do.

11 Read the article. Does it mention the things on your list?

HOW TO PLAN A PARTY

The first question to ask is, "Why am I having a party?" (It's someone's birthday; it's the end of term; your team won a big championship; just to have fun with friends.)

A really good party has a theme. What's going to be the theme for yours? Beach party? 1970s disco? Something else? Then you have to find [1]______ to have your party. Wherever you decide to have it, it's always a good idea to [2]______ permission from your parents first.

Now, it's time to [3]______ the guest list. Are you going to invite [4]______ you know, or just some of your friends? It's important to think hard about how many people you can afford to invite. Once your list is ready, you can [5]______ the invitations. A good time is about two weeks before the party. Any sooner, and people might forget about it; any later, and some of the people on your list might already have other plans.

OK, so now you have two weeks to get everything ready. Don't panic – it's plenty of time: just don't leave [6]______ until the last minute. If you want to [7]______ a DJ, start looking now. Remember that they might ask you to [8]______ a deposit, so make sure you have money for that. Then you need to [9]______ the food and [10]______ the room, although these things can be left until the day before.

Last but not least, keep cool, get some sleep, and in the afternoon before the party, just check it's all ready. Then – have fun!

12 Read the article again and complete it with the missing words.

decorate | draw up | everyone | everything | get | hire | organize | pay | send out | somewhere

Indefinite pronouns

13 W.04 Complete the conversation with suitable indefinite pronouns (*everyone, somewhere, nothing,* etc.). Then listen and check.

David Do you have [1]____________ ready for the party?
Joanna No, [2]____________ is ready. We haven't found [3]____________ to have it, for a start. We've looked [4]____________.
David Have you invited [5]____________ yet?
Joanna Yes, we've invited 50 people and [6]____________ is coming!
David So you have 50 people coming, but [7]____________ for them to come to?
Joanna That's right.
David Well, we have to do [8]____________. How about using my house?
Joanna What about your parents?
David They won't mind. They're going [9]____________ for the weekend. I'll make sure [10]____________ is nice and clean when they get home.

14 Read the next part of the story and continue the conversation. Write four more lines. Use at least one indefinite pronoun.

It's the day after the party. David's mom and dad arrive home and open the door ...

Mom What's happened? Look at our house!
Dad David! DAVID!
David Oh, hi, Mom. Hi, Dad. You're home early. Did you have a good time?

Arranging a party

15 SPEAKING Work in pairs to organize a party. Be creative! Think about:

- what it's for
- the theme
- who to invite
- where it will be
- food and drink
- music

1 Students' own answers

2 W.02
A 3 B 2 C 1

3 W.02
a 1 b 3 c 1 d 2 e 2 f 2 g 3

4 1 aren't they? 2 doesn't it? 3 isn't it? 4 did they? 5 does it? 6 weren't they? 7 are they? 8 is it?

5 1 have you 2 aren't you 3 doesn't it 4 did it 5 will it 6 didn't she

6 1 Neither 2 So

7 Students' own answers

8 W.03
1, 5, 7, 3, 8, 4, 2, 6

9 Students' own answers

10 Students' own answers

11 Students' own answers

12 1 somewhere 2 get 3 draw up 4 everyone 5 send out 6 everything 7 hire 8 pay 9 organize 10 decorate

13 W.04
1 everything 2 nothing 3 anywhere 4 everywhere 5 anyone 6 everyone 7 nowhere 8 something 9 somewhere 10 everything

14 Students' own answers

15 Students' own answers

Language notes *So do I / Neither do I*

Students may think that *neither* makes a verb negative and say A: *I love going to concerts.* B: *Neither do I.* (meaning *I don't*) To disagree with a statement, we repeat the auxiliary verb in the negative: A: *I love going to concerts.* B: *I don't.* or in the positive: A: *I don't like swimming.* B: *I do.*

Indefinite pronouns

Students might say sentences such as **Everybody are tired.* Indefinite pronouns are singular and are therefore followed by the singular form of a verb: *Everybody is tired.* A common mistake is the use of double negatives (**I don't know nothing.*) instead of a negative verb with an indefinite pronoun (*I don't know anything*).

TH!NK more

Workbook
B Time to act pp5–6, Ex. 1–7

C IN MY OPINION, ...

Feeling under the weather

1 W.05 Listen to the conversation. What's the matter with Angie?

2 Complete the conversation with the words.

appointment | better
energy | get | operation
physically | should | took

Mom You don't look well, Angie. What's up?
Angie I'm just tired all the time, Mom. You know, I don't have any [1]______.
Mom Are you sleeping OK?
Angie Not great, no. I often wake up in the night.
Mom Well, you know, Angie, you [2]______ get more exercise. That would help.
Angie Really?
Mom Yes. I mean, if you [3]______ more exercise, you'd be more tired [4]______ and then you'd sleep better.
Angie You're joking, right? I run, I go swimming, I go for long walks. My problem isn't exercise.
Mom Yes, you're right, of course. Well, perhaps you'd [5]______ see a doctor. I can call and make an [6]______ for you if you like.
Angie A doctor? I don't think so. I don't feel sick – just tired. I'm sure I'll [7]______ better soon.
Mom OK, well, we can talk about it later. I'm going out to see a friend of mine who had an [8]______ last week.
Angie OK, Mom. Hope your friend's all right. And don't worry about me. I'll be fine.

3 Match the verbs (1–5) with the nouns and adjectives (a–e) to make phrases. Sometimes there's more than one possible combination.

1 feel — a an appointment
2 get — b an operation
3 have — c a doctor
4 make — d better
5 see — e sick

4 Write down as many words related to health as you can think of. Then compare with a partner.
sick
nurse
hospital
...

Giving advice

5 Complete the sentences with *better, should,* or *ought.*
1 It's late – you'd ______ go.
2 If you don't feel well, you ______ to see a doctor.
3 Jane's in the hospital. We ______ go and visit her.
4 The doctor is very busy, so you ______ make an appointment. Don't just show up.
5 Your knee hurts? Well, you'd ______ not play soccer today, then.
6 If you want to get better, you ______ to rest as much as possible.

6 Match the problems (1–3) with the advice (a–c). Then write one more piece of advice for each problem. Use *had better, should,* and *ought to.*
1 My hand really hurts. ☐
2 I think I'm going to be late for school. ☐
3 I can't do this homework. ☐

a You'd better hurry.
b Maybe you should call a friend.
c You ought to see a doctor.

7 SPEAKING Work in pairs. Write mini-dialogues including the problems and advice in Exercise 6. Add two or three lines to each. Then act them out.

Better or worse?

8 Read the blog entry. Mark the sentences T (true) or F (false).
1 The writer likes awards ceremonies. ☐
2 *A Star is Born* won Best Picture at the 2019 Oscars. ☐
3 The writer thinks the song in *A Star is Born* is the coolest he's ever heard. ☐
4 Dave thinks the writer is very intelligent. ☐

9 SPEAKING Work in pairs. Discuss these questions.
1 What other awards ceremonies do you know of?
2 Do you like awards ceremonies? Why or why not?
3 Do you think it's fair to compare different movies, actors, music, etc. and choose one as the best?

Comparisons

10 Complete the sentences with the correct form of the adjectives and adverbs. Add any other necessary words.
1 The weather tomorrow won't be ______ (cold) as today.
2 This is the ______ (good) pizza I've ever eaten.
3 Do you think this is ______ (difficult) than the other test?
4 This book's OK, but it isn't the ______ (interesting) one I've ever read.
5 She learns things ______ (easy) than I do.
6 I'm not very good at tennis, but I'm ______ (bad) as Janice!
7 Hurry up! Can't you walk ______ (quick) than that?
8 Do you speak ______ (loud) as your sister?

11 SPEAKING Work in pairs or small groups. Discuss these statements. Do you agree or disagree with them? Why?
1 The best things in life are free.
2 If something is more expensive, it's always better.
3 It's more important to work hard than to play hard.
4 Exercise isn't as important as good sleep.

12 Choose two things or people from one of these categories. Write a paragraph comparing them.

sports that you like | actors that you like
towns or cities that you know
school subjects | books that you have read

WHY ALL THESE awards?

I'm really tired of awards ceremonies and prizes. Why do we have to compare things? Everywhere you look, there's something going on about who or what is "the best" or "the most comfortable" or "the biggest," and so on. And sometimes the prize winners aren't the best anyway!

Here's an example: the Oscars in 2019. I saw the movie *A Star is Born* and it was the most wonderful movie I'd ever seen. But did it win the Oscar for Best Picture? No! They gave the award to *Green Book*! Can you believe it? It wasn't as good as *A Star is Born*.

OK, *A Star is Born* got lots of nominations – seven, I think – but I don't think that's enough. Lady Gaga was fantastic as Ally Maine. In my opinion, I think she's much better than Olivia Colman, who won Best Actress. But the good thing is that *A Star is Born* won Best Original Song for *Shallow* – I've never heard anything as cool. And was the acting good? It was great! No other movie had acting as good as that.

I said all these things to my friend Dave the day after the Oscars. I told him I thought the judges were the craziest people in the world. Dave asked me how many movies I'd seen in 2018. I said, "One – *A Star is Born*." Dave says he doesn't know anyone as silly as me.

1 W.05
She's tired because she hasn't been sleeping well.

2 1 energy 2 should 3 took 4 physically 5 better 6 appointment 7 get 8 operation

3 1 d, e 2 a, d, e 3 a, b 4 a 5 c

4 Students' own answers

5 1 better 2 ought 3 should 4 should 5 better 6 ought

6 1 c 2 a 3 b

7 Students' own answers

8 **Check/clarify:** *nominations.*
1 F The writer's really tired of them. 2 F *Green Book* won Best Picture at the 2019 Oscars. 3 T
4 F He says he doesn't know anyone as silly as the writer.

9 Students' own answers

10 1 as cold 2 best 3 more difficult 4 most interesting 5 more easily 6 not as bad 7 more quickly 8 as loudly

11 Students' own answers

12 Students' own answers

Culture notes

The Oscars is the popular name for the Academy Awards, an American annual movie awards ceremony, which has taken place in Hollywood every year since 1929.

A Star is Born is a 2018 American romantic musical drama and is the third remake of a movie from 1937. It features Bradley Cooper and Lady Gaga. It was nominated for eight Oscars, but only won one for Best Original Song.

Green Book is a 2018 American biographical comedy drama. Set in 1962, the movie is based on a true story of a jazz pianist and his driver. It stars Mahershala Ali and Viggo Mortensen. *Green Book* won three Oscars in 2019.

Stefani Germanotta, known professionally as Lady Gaga, is a singer/songwriter and actress from New York. Her debut album, *The Fame*, was released in 2008.

Sarah Caroline Olivia Sinclair, known as Olivia Colman, is a British actress. In 2019, she won an Oscar for her leading role as Queen Anne in *The Favourite*.

TH!NK more

Workbook
C In my opinion, ... pp7–8, Ex. 1–7

D HELP!
Reported speech

1 **Read the story and answer the questions.**

1 What had happened to the caller's computer screen?
2 What three things did Vicky ask the caller to do?
3 Why couldn't the caller turn on the lights?
4 What did Vicky finally say to the caller?
5 What happened to Vicky in the end?

We asked readers to tell us about a time when they tried to help someone. Here's one from Vicky Hastings.

I used to work in IT for a big company, but I was fired because I got angry with a manager. Here's what happened.

I answered the phone one day and said, "Hi. Can I help you?" A voice said, "Hi. I'm a manager in the Sales Department and I have an IT problem. I need your help." "What's the problem?" I asked and he told me his computer screen had suddenly gone black.

[1]______ , I couldn't think why it had happened. I asked him to check that the screen was still connected. He said it was. [2]______ I asked him if he'd pressed any buttons by mistake. He said, "No, I was downloading a program when, suddenly, it went 'poof.'"

[3]______ a few seconds, I said, "OK, please check that your computer is still plugged in at the wall. Sometimes it gets disconnected accidentally." The manager asked me to wait a bit. Then he came back and said, "I can't see behind my desk where the plug is. It's very dark." So I told him to turn the light on. Do you know what he said? "Oh, I can't do that, the electricity went off five minutes ago."

I tried to keep quiet. But [4]______ , I had to say something. I warned him never to waste my time again, ever. He complained to my boss and I got fired. How fair is that, do you think?

2 **Rewrite the sentences in reported speech.**

0 "I need your help."
He said that *he needed my help.*
1 "What's the problem?"
I asked him ______
2 "I can't see here because it's very dark."
He said that ______
3 "Please check that your computer is still plugged in."
I asked him to ______
4 "I can't turn the light on because the electricity went off five minutes ago."
He said that ______

Sequencing words

3 **Match these words with spaces 1–4 in the story.**

a After ☐ c finally ☐
b Then ☐ d At first ☐

Asking for and offering help

4 **Put the words in order to make questions.**

1 I / you / Can / help / ?
2 help / something / you / me / Could / with / ?
3 me / you / Can / a / lend / hand / ?
4 you / Do / help / any / need / ?
5 you / minutes / have / a / Do / few / ?

5 **Look at the sentences in Exercise 4 again. Mark them A (asking for help) or O (offering help).**

6 SPEAKING **Work in pairs. Choose a situation and write a conversation in which A asks B for help. Use expressions from Exercise 4. Then act it out.**

- A has a problem with some homework.
- A isn't feeling well.
- A's computer isn't working.
- A wants to have a party, but doesn't know where to hold it.

IT problems

7 SPEAKING **Work in pairs. What do the pictures show?**

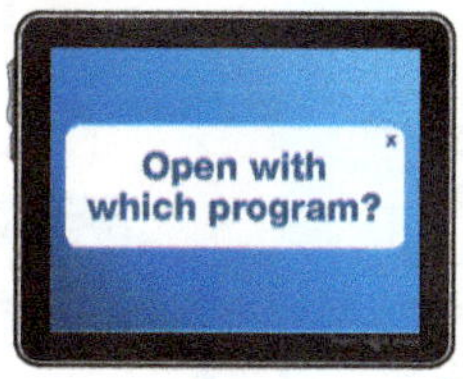

A ☐

B ☐

C ☐

8 W.06 **Listen to three conversations. Match them with the pictures in Exercise 7.**

9 W.06 **Listen again. In which conversation do you hear these words? Write the number.**

a attachment ☐ e install ☐
b coverage ☐ f online ☐
c downloaded ☐ g program ☐
d file ☐ h upload ☐

IT vocabulary

10 **Choose the correct words.**

1 *go / have* online
2 *post / file* a comment
3 *install / key in* your password
4 *install / go* a program
5 *attach / activate* a file
6 *go / download* a file
7 *upload / key* a photo
8 *key / delete* a message
9 *open / install* an attachment
10 *post / buy* an app
11 *upload / activate* flight mode
12 *have / go* cell phone service

11 **Match the verbs with the nouns. Make as many combinations as you can.**

a message | a photo | flight mode | a password | an attachment | a program | a file | an app

0 install *install a program / an app*
1 attach ______
2 download ______
3 upload ______
4 open ______
5 post ______
6 delete ______
7 activate ______
8 key in ______

Passive tenses

12 **Complete the sentences from the conversations with the verb forms.**

is being repaired | was taken | is installed

1 The photo ______ on a safari trip.
2 Just click on it and the program ______ automatically.
3 The network ______ out here.

13 **Rewrite the sentences in the passive.**

0 Someone posted a message.
A message was posted.
1 Someone is downloading a program.
______
2 Someone has installed a new program.
______
3 Someone has entered the password.
______
4 Someone is repairing the anti-virus software.
______
5 Someone deleted the message.
______

14 **Describe one of these processes using the passive.**

- downloading an app to your cell phone
- uploading a photo to a social networking site
- installing a program on your computer

1 Check/clarify: *disconnected, to get fired.*
1 The caller's screen had suddenly gone black.
2 Vicky asked the caller to check that the screen was still connected, to check that the computer was still plugged in at the wall, and to turn the light on.
3 He couldn't turn the light on because the electricity had gone off five minutes before.
4 She told him to never waste her time again.
5 She got fired.

2 1 what the problem was. 2 he couldn't see (there) because it was very dark. 3 check that his computer was still plugged in. 4 he couldn't turn on the light on because the electricity had gone out five minutes before.

3 1 d 2 b 3 a 4 c

4 1 Can I help you? 2 Could you help me with something? 3 Can you lend me a hand? 4 Do you need any help? 5 Do you have a few minutes?

5 1 O 2 A 3 A 4 O 5 A

6 Students' own answers

7 Students' own answers

8 W.06
A 3 B 1 C 2

9 W.06
a 2 b 1 c 3 d 3 e 3 f 2 g 3 h 2

10 1 go 2 post 3 key in 4 install 5 attach 6 download 7 upload 8 delete 9 open 10 buy 11 activate 12 have

11 1 a photo; a file
2 a photo; an attachment; a program; a file; an app
3 a photo; a file
4 a message; an attachment; a program; a file; an app
5 a message; a photo
6 a message; a photo; an attachment; a program; a file; an app
7 flight mode
8 a password

12 1 was taken 2 is installed 3 is being repaired

13 1 A program is being downloaded.
2 A new program has been installed.
3 The password has been entered.
4 The antivirus software is being repaired.
5 The message was deleted.

14 Students' own answers

THINK more

Workbook
D Help! pp8–9, Ex. 1–8

Warmer

Write on the board: *play*, *eat*, *read*, *text*, *talk*, *watch*, *drink*. In pairs, students use the verbs to discuss what they do in their free time. They should find three things they have in common with their partners. Monitor and encourage them to use the simple present to describe their habits and routines. Nominate one or two pairs to share what they have in common with the class.

▶ 01 Get TH!NKing

Play the video and discuss the question with your class.

1 You may like to give an example from your own experience to get students started on this exercise.
Possible answers: A backpacking B studying C driving D doing yoga E working

2 Ask students to rank this list in order of things they'd like to do, from most to least. At the end of the exercise, listen to some of the students' ideas and encourage open class discussion.

3 If space allows, encourage students to walk around the classroom to find someone who would like to do the same things. Ask students to report their findings back to the class and encourage them to use the phrase *So does he/she*.

4 Give students two minutes to scan the blog post quickly. Encourage them not to focus on every word for now, but just to match the people with the photos.
Amy C Mark D Pauline E

1 BIG DECISIONS

OBJECTIVES

FUNCTIONS: talking about the future; complaining

GRAMMAR: present tenses (review); future tenses (review)

VOCABULARY: making changes; life plans; phrases with *up*

Get TH!NKING
Watch the video and think: are you good at making decisions?

READING

1 What are the people doing in the photos? Are these things you do or would like to do? Why?

2 Check (✓) the things you would like to do when you finish school. Then add two more ideas of your own.

- ☐ travel to other countries
- ☐ go to college
- ☐ go into business
- ☐ get any job you can find
- ☐ do any job you can and spend time on your hobbies
- ☐ find work that provides training on the job
- ☐ do volunteer work

3 SPEAKING Work in pairs. Compare your ideas from Exercise 2. Give reasons for your choices.

4 Read John's blog post on the next page and the replies to it quickly. Which three photos show activities that these people do now?

Amy ☐ Mark ☐ Pauline ☐

5 1.01 Read the article again and listen. Mark the sentences T (true) or F (false).

1 John is unsure what to do when he leaves school. ☐
2 John is worried about his exam results. ☐
3 Amy went to Thailand to learn the language. ☐
4 Amy has plans for when she leaves Thailand. ☐
5 Mark's advice is to do a course. ☐
6 Pauline got a job before she finished her university course. ☐

12

5 1.01 **Check/clarify:** *volunteer*, *resolution*, *habit*.
During feedback, ask students to say why the false statements are incorrect.
1 T 2 F 3 F 4 T 5 F 6 T

Objectives

Functions and speaking Talking about the future; complaining
Grammar Present tenses (review); future tenses (review)
Vocabulary Making changes; life plans; **WordWise:** Phrases with *up*
Life Competencies Managing stress
Train to TH!NK Reading between the lines

Resources for this unit

All available online

Videos
- Get **TH!NK**ing: *Are you good at making decisions?*
- Grammar rap!: Future tenses (review)
- Vlog: Managing stress

Tests
- Unit, extension, and skills test 1

Worksheets
- Grammar and vocabulary: Basic, Standard, and Extension Worksheets
- Project: My bucket list
- Communication worksheets: Life plans
- Get **TH!NK**ing, Grammar rap!, and Life Lessons video Worksheets

6 Encourage students to underline key information in the article that supports their answers. Remind them that the answer is not written directly in the text, but needs to be inferred. Encourage them to challenge each other and voice different answers, as this will help develop their critical thinking skills.

1 Yes, it's led to a decision to study medicine and become a doctor or nurse.

2 Yes, he isn't as lazy as when he was in school and is working hard in his yoga course.

3 Yes, she says it was a lack of courage that stopped her from traveling and "I just went to college" implies that this was a less interesting option.

7 Allow students time for pairs to discuss. At the end of the exercise, listen to some of the students' ideas and write them on the board. Ask students to put the items in order of how effective they are likely to be. Hold a class vote to decide which they feel are the most and the least effective ways to change your life for the better.

Homework

Ask students to interview members of their family, friends, or neighbors using the questions in Exercise 7 and to write a short text. As a follow-up, students can present any good ideas for how to change your life for the better in class.

BIG DECISIONS UNIT 1

What next?

John *posted 2 hours ago*

My time at school is almost up and of course I'm thinking about the big question: what next? Maybe I've waited too long to start thinking about it, but that's how I am. I think I'll do well in my exams, so maybe I'll go to college and get more qualifications – but I've been asking myself if it's better to just find a job and start a career that way. On the other hand, if I do go on to study further, should I do it right away or maybe take a year off – a "gap year"? Helpful comments and ideas, please! Thanks.

Like Share Reply

Amy *posted 5 minutes ago*

Hi, John. I'm doing a gap year right now. I saved up some money and went to Thailand, but after two months of vacation, I got bored and the money was running out. Then I learned about a volunteer medical organization working in poor parts of the country and they let me join as a driver. Now I'm working, struggling with the Thai language (I spend up to an hour a day practicing with friends), and learning lots about myself. I've made a resolution, too – when I go home, I'm going to study medicine to be a doctor or a nurse. So my advice? Do a gap year, but don't just travel around – do some volunteer work somewhere. For me, it's been life-changing.

Like Share Reply

Mark *posted 28 minutes ago*

Hey! I finished high school three months ago and I didn't want to go to college or travel. So I'm doing a course. I'm studying to become a yoga teacher. I took up yoga a couple of years ago and I've loved it ever since. I was very lazy at school, but I've changed my ways and now I study really hard. The class starts every day at 7:00, so I've had to get into the habit of waking up early. But that's fine – I love what I'm doing. That's the important thing – do what you love, if you can.

Like Share Reply

Pauline *posted 1 hour ago*

Hi there! Here's my advice. Do what feels right for you now, but keep an open mind and be prepared to change. Some of my friends went traveling after school, but I didn't have the courage; I just went to college. It was OK and I was having a good time. Then one day, an old friend from school called me and said he was going to start an online company and asked me to join him. So, I quit college and went to work with him. It was the best thing I've ever done. I wasn't planning on dropping out of college, but I took the chance to try something different and I don't regret it.

Like Share Reply

Train to TH!NK

Reading between the lines

Sometimes a writer doesn't tell us everything directly: we need to draw conclusions from the information the writer gives. We call this "reading between the lines."

6 **Answer the questions and give reasons for your answers.**

0 Is John worried about his abilities as a student?
No, he says he'll do well on his exams and he's thinking about university.
1 Has Amy been enjoying her work with a medical organization?
2 Is Mark different now than when he was at school?
3 Did Pauline want to travel after leaving school?

SPEAKING

7 **Work in pairs. Discuss these questions.**

1 What resolutions are you going to make for this school year?
2 What do you think is the secret of changing your life for the better?

Plan carefully.
Do work first, play later.
Listen to your parents.

13

Activity idea Fast finishers

To give students extended speaking practice on the themes in the reading text, write these questions on the board:

In what ways are you good/bad at planning your time? When was the last time you left homework until the last minute? What are your bad habits? Do they make life difficult for you? What was the last good habit that you formed?

Give students two minutes to think about their answers and make notes. Divide the class into small groups for students to compare answers and decide who is the most organized. Monitor but, as the focus is on fluency, avoid correcting errors.

TH!NK more

Worksheets
Project My bucket list
Communication Life plans
Get TH!NKing *Are you good at making decisions?*

Critical THINKing
Competency: Evaluating ideas, arguments, and options
Identifies assumptions and inferences in an argument.

Warmer

Challenge the students to try to make you say *Yes, I do*. Tell them to ask you *Do you …?* questions. They get one point for each positive answer, but no points for *No, I don't*.

After demonstrating a few examples, students can play the game in pairs.

1 Write sentences 1–4 on the board. Nominate a student to underline all the verbs in the sentences in red. Give students one minute to work with a partner and name the four tenses.
1 c 2 a 3 b 4 d
RULE: 5 simple present 6 present continuous 7 present perfect 8 present perfect continuous

2 Before students complete the text, ask them to read it quickly and find out why the writer is having trouble sleeping (they're worrying about exams and the future).
1 am ('m) lying
2 am ('m) trying / have ('ve) tried / have ('ve) been trying
3 have ('ve) been having
4 have ('ve) tried / have ('ve) been trying
5 has worked / works / is working
6 doesn't want
7 is happening
8 have ('ve) been studying / am ('m) studying
9 have ('ve) been thinking
10 want

3 Encourage students to think about possible solutions, too. Monitor students' use of present tenses and make a note of common errors. Write these on the board, ensuring anonymity, and ask students to correct them as part of whole-class feedback.

Workbook p10

GRAMMAR
Present tenses (review)

1 Match sentences (1–4) with the tenses (a–d) and then complete the rule with the names of the tenses.

1 I'm thinking about the big question: what next?
2 I've been asking myself if it's perhaps better to just find a job.
3 I spend up to an hour a day practicing with friends.
4 I've made a resolution.

a present perfect continuous
b simple present
c present continuous
d present perfect

RULE:
We use the [5]______ to talk about something that happens regularly.
We use the [6]______ to talk about what's happening at or around the time of speaking.
We use the [7]______ to talk about past actions without saying when they happened.
We use the [8]______ to talk about actions that started in the past and are still happening.

Look

We can use the present continuous with *always* to complain about behavior that we don't like and find annoying.

My dad's always telling me what to do.

2 Complete the text with the correct present tense forms of the verbs. Sometimes more than one tense is possible.

It's 2 a.m. and I [1]________ (lie) in bed. I [2]________ (try) to get to sleep, but I can't. I [3]________ (have) trouble sleeping for about a month now. I [4]________ (try) different things to help me sleep, but nothing [5]________ (work). My mind [6]________ (not want) to stop. A lot [7]________ (happen) in my life right now. It's exam season, so I [8]________ (study) a lot. There's also the question of next year. I [9]________ (think) about it for ages. Mom and Dad [10]________ (want) me to go to college, but I'm just not sure what to do.

3 SPEAKING Work in pairs. Think about a problem you've been having and tell your partner.

I've been fighting a lot with my little brother recently. I've tried to ignore him, but it's impossible.

workbook page 10

VOCABULARY
Making changes

4 Match the phrases with the definitions.

0 make a resolution *f*
1 give something up
2 do well
3 struggle with something
4 take something up
5 take the chance (*to do something*)
6 get into the habit (*of doing something*)
7 make some changes

a stop doing something
b start doing something regularly
c use an opportunity
d find something difficult
e start a new hobby or interest
f decide to make a positive change
g do things differently (usually for the better)
h be successful

5 Complete the email with the missing verbs.

Sam
Sam@thinkmail.com
New Year's resolutions?

Last year, I [1]______ a lot of resolutions and decided to [2]______ some changes. I tried to [3]______ the habit of getting up early. For two months, I got up at 8 a.m., and I even [4]______ running before going to school. But I started falling asleep in the afternoon, so I soon [5]______ that idea! Then I stopped eating meat. I was [6]______ well until Mom made roast beef. I just had to eat it. I also [7]______ the chance to start learning the piano when my school offered extra classes. But I [8]______ with finding time to practice, so I stopped. This year I've only made one resolution: not to make any resolutions!

6 SPEAKING Work in pairs. Discuss these questions.

1 What subjects are you doing well in at school?
2 What subjects do you struggle with?
3 What was the last thing you gave up doing? Why?

workbook page 12

14

4 Ask students to try to match the definitions from memory before referring back to the text to check. Encourage them to underline the phrases in the reading text.
1 a 2 h 3 d 4 e 5 c 6 b 7 g

5 Point out that students need to put the verbs in the correct tense.
1 made 2 make 3 get into 4 took up 5 gave up 6 doing 7 took 8 struggled

6 Invite students to share their answers with the rest of the class during feedback.

Workbook p12

TH!NK more

Workbook
Grammar p10, Ex.1–5
Vocabulary p12, Ex.1–2
Vocabulary Extra p13, Ex.1–3

Worksheets
Grammar Worksheets 1
Vocabulary Worksheets 1

Get it Right!
Simple present vs. present continuous

Student's Book p122

7 Invite students to share their ideas with the rest of the class, but do not give the answers yet.

8 🔊 **1.02** Tell students to check their answers to Exercise 7 and not to worry about understanding every word. If students struggle with the spelling of the names, write them on the board.
A Vincent van Gogh B Carey Mulligan C Walt Disney

9 🔊 **1.02** Ask students to answer the questions from memory before listening again to check.
1 He's worried because he really wants to be an actor, but is finding it very difficult to get into a drama school.
2 Because she was also rejected by drama schools, but she's now a big star.
3 His first businesses failed.
4 The fact that he was poor and unhappy.
5 He compares the encouragement he is getting from Becky to the encouragement that Van Gogh got from his friends.

10 Invite students to share their answers with the rest of the class.

▶ 02 Grammar rap! Future tenses (review)

11 *1 're having 2 going to apply 3 will say RULE: 4 present continuous 5 will 6 going to*

12 *1 We're going 2 I'll finish 3 I'm not going 4 I'm seeing 5 She's going to be 6 going to eat 7 will win 8 We're flying*

13 If space allows, encourage students to walk around the classroom to find someone who has the same arrangements, intentions, and predictions. Ask students to make notes and report their findings back to the class. Encourage them to use the phrase *So does he/she.*

Workbook p11

Homework

Ask students to use the notes they made in Exercise 13 to write ten sentences describing similarities between themselves and their friends' arrangements, intentions, and predictions using *So do I* and *Neither do I.*

LISTENING

7 SPEAKING **Work in pairs. Discuss these questions.**
1 What do you know about these people?
2 Can you match the information with each person?

A ____________ was a famous painter.
B ____________ is an actress.
C ____________ started a movie studio.

8 🔊 1.02 **Listen and check.**

9 🔊 1.02 **Read the questions carefully. Listen again and make notes.**
1 What is Alan worried about?
2 Why does Becky tell Alan about Carey Mulligan?
3 Why was Walt Disney unsuccessful at first?
4 What does Alan not like about the example of Van Gogh?
5 How does Alan compare himself to Van Gogh?

10 SPEAKING **Work in pairs. Compare your answers to Exercise 9.**

Grammar rap!

GRAMMAR
Future tenses (review)

11 **Look at the sentences from the listening. Complete them with the correct future forms of the verbs. Then complete the rule with the present continuous, *going to*, or *will*.**
1 We ____________ (have) a party at our place.
2 Are you ____________ (apply) to other drama schools?
3 I'm sure one of them ____________ (say) yes.

RULE:
- To talk about future arrangements, we often use the [4] ______.
- To make predictions, we often use [5] ______.
- To talk about intentions, we often use [6] ______.

12 **Choose the best tense.**
1 *We'll go / We're going* to the beach this Friday. Do you want to come?
2 I don't think *I'll finish / I'm finishing* this homework.
3 *I won't go / I'm not going* to college this year. I want to take a year off.
4 I have an appointment with the dentist tomorrow. *I'm seeing / I'll see* her at 10 a.m.
5 Daisy's learning to fly. *She'll be / She's going to be* a pilot.
6 I'm not *eating / going to eat* chocolate. That's my resolution for next year.
7 Argentina *will win / is winning* the next World Cup. That's what I think.
8 *We're flying / We'll fly* on Friday. I'm so excited.

13 **Write down:**
1 two arrangements you've made for this week.
2 two intentions you have for this year.
3 two predictions for your life.

→ workbook page 11

Culture notes

Carey Mulligan, born 1985, is a British actor. She is known for her role in *An Education*, for which she won a BAFTA Award for Best Actress.

Vincent van Gogh (1853–1890) was one of the greatest post-impressionist painters. His works include *Sunflowers* and self-portraits. Virtually unknown at the time of his death, his works are now among the world's most famous paintings.

Walt Disney (1901–1966) was an American entrepreneur, animator, and film producer. As a film producer, he held the record for the most Oscars.

Activity idea Extension

Divide the class into AB pairs. Students test each other on the phrases in Exercise 4. B closes their book. A says the first part of the phrase, and B tries to remember the rest of it.

TH!NK more

Workbook
Listening p16, Ex.1–3 Grammar p11, Ex.6–10

Worksheets
Grammar rap! Future tenses (review)
Grammar Worksheets 1

Reading

Warmer

Write *Life Plans* on the board and tell the class your own plans for your life, some of which should be true; others, made up. Students decide in pairs which are false. Listen to some of their ideas before revealing which are true.

1 **Check/clarify:** *settle down.*
Allow students time for pairs to discuss. Ask them to put the items in order of importance. As a follow-up, discuss as a class and hold a class vote to decide which they feel are the most and the least important.

2 **1.03 Check/clarify:** *billionaire, marathon.*
Encourage students to underline the parts of the text that helped them as they complete the matching task.
1 e 2 a 3 f 4 b 5 d

3 Give students some time to discuss the questions in small groups. At the end of the exercise, listen to some of the students' ideas and encourage open class discussion. Then hold a class vote to find out which activity is the most popular.

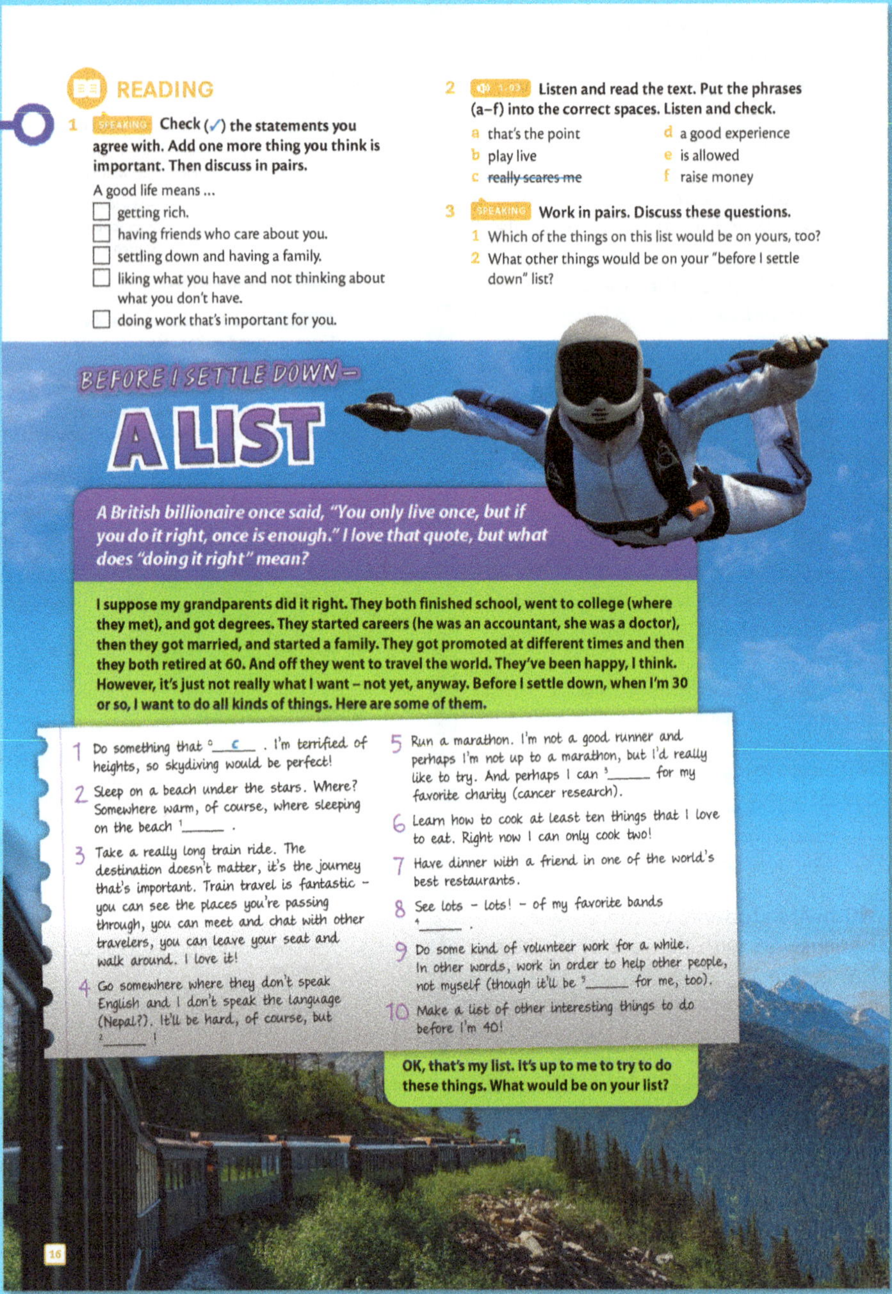

READING

1 SPEAKING Check (✓) the statements you agree with. Add one more thing you think is important. Then discuss in pairs.

A good life means ...

- [ ] getting rich.
- [ ] having friends who care about you.
- [ ] settling down and having a family.
- [ ] liking what you have and not thinking about what you don't have.
- [ ] doing work that's important for you.

2 1.03 Listen and read the text. Put the phrases (a–f) into the correct spaces. Listen and check.

a that's the point
b play live
c ~~really scares me~~
d a good experience
e is allowed
f raise money

3 SPEAKING Work in pairs. Discuss these questions.

1 Which of the things on this list would be on yours, too?
2 What other things would be on your "before I settle down" list?

BEFORE I SETTLE DOWN – A LIST

A British billionaire once said, "You only live once, but if you do it right, once is enough." I love that quote, but what does "doing it right" mean?

I suppose my grandparents did it right. They both finished school, went to college (where they met), and got degrees. They started careers (he was an accountant, she was a doctor), then they got married, and started a family. They got promoted at different times and then they both retired at 60. And off they went to travel the world. They've been happy, I think. However, it's just not really what I want – not yet, anyway. Before I settle down, when I'm 30 or so, I want to do all kinds of things. Here are some of them.

1 Do something that [0] c . I'm terrified of heights, so skydiving would be perfect!
2 Sleep on a beach under the stars. Where? Somewhere warm, of course, where sleeping on the beach [1] ______ .
3 Take a really long train ride. The destination doesn't matter, it's the journey that's important. Train travel is fantastic – you can see the places you're passing through, you can meet and chat with other travelers, you can leave your seat and walk around. I love it!
4 Go somewhere where they don't speak English and I don't speak the language (Nepal?). It'll be hard, of course, but [2] ______ !
5 Run a marathon. I'm not a good runner and perhaps I'm not up to a marathon, but I'd really like to try. And perhaps I can [3] ______ for my favorite charity (cancer research).
6 Learn how to cook at least ten things that I love to eat. Right now I can only cook two!
7 Have dinner with a friend in one of the world's best restaurants.
8 See lots – lots! – of my favorite bands [4] ______ .
9 Do some kind of volunteer work for a while. In other words, work in order to help other people, not myself (though it'll be [5] ______ for me, too).
10 Make a list of other interesting things to do before I'm 40!

OK, that's my list. It's up to me to try to do these things. What would be on your list?

16

TH!NK more

Workbook
Reading p14, Ex.1–5

4 **Check/clarify:** *start a career, retire, get a degree, get promoted.*
Say the phrases for students to repeat and provide a focus on pronunciation. Point out the linking of the verb and *a* in *start a career*, *get a degree*, and *start a family*; also the stress on the second syllable and /ɪd/ ending in *promoted*.
A4 B6 C2 D3 E1 F5 G7 H8

5 Ask students to read the text quickly and answer the question: *In what way has the writer's uncle always done things differently?* (He's experienced several life events at unconventional ages; for example, he went to college in his 40s.)
1 finished school 2 traveling the world 3 got a degree 4 started a career 5 got promoted 6 settle down 7 start a family 8 to retire

Workbook p12

6 1c 2e 3b 4a 5f 6d

7 If you're short on time, you could assign this exercise for homework.
1 up to 2 up 3 What's up 4 up to 5 up to 6 up to

Workbook p12

Pronunciation
Linking words with *up*

Student's Book p120

8 With weaker classes, divide the students into small groups so that they can share ideas before writing individually. Students make notes in preparation for writing their email. Encourage students to use future forms when describing their future plans.

Homework

Students could do Exercise 8 for homework. If they have access to mobile devices, you could ask them to write an email about themselves and send it to another member of the class. When students have received their email, ask them to check that all the points in the task have been covered. Finally, ask students to write a short response encouraging the sender to stick to their resolutions.

VOCABULARY
Life plans

4 **Match the phrases with the pictures. Write 1–8 in the boxes.**

1 retire
2 travel the world
3 start a career
4 get a degree
5 start a family
6 settle down
7 get promoted
8 finish school

5 **Complete the text with phrases from Exercise 4. Use the correct forms of the verbs.**

My uncle has always done things differently. He [1]__________ when he was 18 because he wanted to see other places. He spent the next 20 years [2]__________, working in restaurants and hotels in many different countries. When he was in his early forties, he decided to return to the UK. He went to college and [3]__________. He did really well, and when he finished, he [4]__________ as a translator. Because he was good at his job, he [5]__________ very quickly and he soon became Head Translator. When he was 48, he met the love of his life and they decided to [6]__________ and [7]__________. Now he's 55, with three young children. He says he wants [8]__________ soon. He wants to stop working and take the whole family around the world with him. I wouldn't be surprised if he does.

→ workbook page 12

WordWise: Phrases with *up*

6 **Match the phrases in bold with the definitions.**

1 **What's up**, Alan?
2 I spend **up to** an hour a day practicing with friends.
3 What are you **up to** tomorrow night?
4 My **time** at school is almost **up**.
5 It's **up to me** now to try to do some of the things.
6 Perhaps I'm not **up to** a marathon.

a finished
b doing
c what's the matter?
d capable of
e as long as / to a maximum of
f my responsibility

7 **Use words and phrases from Exercise 6 to complete the sentences.**

1 What have you been _____ recently?
2 The time is almost _____. Two more minutes!
3 Oh, no! You look really unhappy. _____ ?
4 It isn't my decision. It's _____ you to decide.
5 He's 75 now, so he isn't _____ long walks.
6 This car can carry _____ six people.

→ workbook page 12

PRONUNCIATION
Linking words with *up* Go to page 120.

WRITING
An email about resolutions

8 **Write an email to an English-speaking friend in another country. Describe your resolutions for the coming school year. Write about:**

- bad habits you're changing
- new classes you're taking
- activities you plan to take up
- why you're doing all of this

Activity idea Extension

Give students three minutes to decide at what age (if any) they are planning to do the things in Exercise 4. Next, students describe their plans to a partner. Encourage them to not look at their books and to try to recall the target phrases. Monitor and prompt strong students to add as much detail as possible.

TH!NK more

Practice Extra
Unit 1 Practice it!

Workbook
Vocabulary p12, Ex.3–4
WordWise p12, Ex.5–6
Pronunciation p118
Developing Writing p15

Worksheets
Vocabulary Worksheets 1

Developing Speaking; Phrases for fluency; Functions

Warmer

Review phrases with *up* by giving students a definition and eliciting a phrase with *up*. For example, *What's the matter?* = *What's up?*

1 **1.06** Tell students to cover the dialogue and discuss the question in pairs before listening to check their answers.
She's feeling stressed.

2 **1.06** Have students highlight the answers in the dialogue.
1 She's changed her diet, her sleep patterns, and her attitude.
2 Seven hours a night.
3 Look at the big picture and don't worry about things that aren't very important.
4 He's getting stressed about being a person who can't stop worrying.

3 At the end of the exercise, listen to some of the students' ideas and encourage open class discussion.

4 Write the sentences on the board. Ask students for an L1 translation before they complete the sentences in English.
1 Where do I start; You're awesome
2 Where have you been hiding; Now that you mention it 3 Here we go; Don't be silly

5 As an alternative, you could ask students to cover the Key Language box and try to guess what phrases start sentences a–d.
1 d 2 c 3 b 4 a

ROLE-PLAY Allow students six to eight minutes to prepare their dialogues. Monitor to make sure all students are on task. Encourage them to use the key language.

DEVELOPING SPEAKING

1 1.06 **Look at the photo. How does the girl feel? Listen and read to check.**

Martin: Hi, Sandra. I haven't seen you for ages. Where have you been hiding?
Sandra: Hi, Martin. Hiding? Nowhere. I've just changed some of my routines. I was feeling so stressed a few months ago that I thought, "Sandra, you have to make some changes." So I did!
Martin: What kind of changes? Exercise? Sleep?
Sandra: Well, where do I start? I'm eating better. And now that you mention it, I'm trying to get seven hours sleep a night, minimum. But the big thing is my attitude.
Martin: And how has that changed?
Sandra: Well, I read an article about stress and it said something like, "Look at the big picture. How important is this problem? Is it going to matter in three months' time?" And I thought, that's right – the problem is, I worry about little things too much. So I'm trying to worry less.
Martin: But can you do that? If I'm honest, I'm a terrible worrier, too. But I can't stop.
Sandra: Don't be silly. Anyone can stop worrying – not overnight, but you can do it little by little.
Martin: Now I'm getting stressed about being someone who can't stop worrying.
Sandra: Let's go have ice cream and talk more.
Martin: Thanks, Sandra. You're awesome.
Sandra: Here we go! Ice cream coming up! And don't worry, I'll pay!

2 1.06 **Read and listen again to the dialogue. Answer the questions.**
1 What areas of her life does Sandra say she's changed?
2 How much sleep is she trying to get?
3 What advice did she get from the article?
4 What is Martin getting stressed about?

3 SPEAKING **Discuss the questions in pairs. What do you think?**
1 Do things like diet and sleep help with stress?
2 Does the article give good advice? Why or why not?
3 Is it possible to slowly reduce how much you worry?

Phrases for fluency

4 **Find the underlined expressions in the dialogue. How do you say them in your language? Use the expressions to complete the conversations.**

1 **A** You look tired. Has it been a busy day?
B Busy? ________________ ? First, I had a math test. Then I had drama club at lunchtime. Then it was a five-kilometer run in PE …
A Well, you just sit down and I'll get you something to eat.
B Thanks, Mom. ________________ .

2 **A** ________________ , Annie? I haven't seen you for days.
B I haven't been anywhere. You're the one who disappeared.
A ________________ , I have been really busy.

3 **A** It's ten o'clock. Time for the test.
B ________________ ! I'm really not ready for this.
A Me neither. I have a feeling I'm not going to pass.
B ________________ . You always pass.

FUNCTIONS
Expressing dissatisfaction

KEY LANGUAGE
I'm not happy with (my attitude).
The thing / problem is, (I worry too much).
If I'm honest, (I'm a terrible worrier, too).
My parents are always (telling me to work harder).

5 **Match the parts of the sentences.**
1 I'm not happy with ☐
2 He's always ☐
3 If I'm honest, ☐
4 The problem is, ☐

a he just laughs when I complain about it.
b I don't like his attitude.
c borrowing my things without asking me.
d the things my brother does.

ROLE PLAY **Work in pairs. Student A: go to page 127. Student B: go to page 128.**

18

Activity idea Mixed ability

Stronger students practice the role-play on pages 127 and 128 and then try to think of their own situations and create further dialogues. Weaker students might benefit from preparation time. Divide them into pairs of As and Bs and give them three minutes to prepare ideas for their side of the conversation before making A/B pairs.

Life Competencies

Warmer

Write *managing stress* on the board and elicit the meaning. Encourage students to try and clarify through examples or explanation, rather than through translation. Elicit examples of people managing their stress in Unit 1.

▶ 03 Life Lessons: Managing stress

1 ▶03 Ask students to compare their ideas with a partner.
He's stressed because it's exam time. Also, his parents are insisting that he tidy his room, and his phone broke.

2 ▶03 Ask students to try to answer the questions from memory before watching the video again to check.
a Possible answers: lack of energy, sadness, bad moods, difficulty concentrating
b Possible answers: stop worrying about things you can't control; keep a diary; get regular sleep; go swimming once a week; prepare in advance for stressful events; talk to friends/parents about problems; turn off phone.

3 As a follow-up, ask students to rank their list in Exercise 2, Part b from the best piece of advice to the worst. Discuss as a class and come up with a definitive list.

4 **Check/clarify:** *cavemen.*
Give students one minute to read the article and find the answer. Encourage them not to focus on every word.
It can be useful in a difficult situation / when you have to perform under pressure or need to avoid danger.

5 At the end of the exercise, listen to some of the students' ideas and encourage open class discussion.
1 When it reaches high levels and continues for a long period of time.
2 Because we worry (often unnecessarily) about money, and we spend a lot of time using technology rather than relaxing or exercising.
3 Students' own answers
4 Students' own answers

LIFE COMPETENCIES

Stress can cause health problems, emotional problems, and relationship problems. Finding ways to reduce or manage stress helps you feel healthier and happier, and be a better friend.

1 ▶03 Watch the vlog. Why is Leo feeling stressed?

2 ▶03 Watch the vlog again and make notes about:
a three symptoms of stress.
b three things you can do to deal with stress.

3 Compare your notes with a partner.

4 Read this online article about stress. When can stress be useful?

ALL ABOUT STRESS

We tend to think of stress as negative, but in fact it's something normal. Stress is our body's natural way of reacting to a difficult situation. Stress improves our ability to perform under pressure and to avoid danger. Cavemen hunting dangerous animals for food felt stress and famous singers perform better on stage because of stress. However, stress becomes a problem when it reaches high levels and continues for a long period of time.

People seem to feel more stress these days. Money is one source of stress. Not having any money at all is very stressful, but for most of us, the problem is that we always want something better or newer. And we worry unnecessarily about things we can't afford.

Things like cell phones can be a problem, too. We spend our lives moving from screen to screen, responding to a huge number of messages and images instead of really relaxing. Exercise is great for reducing stress, but technology in the form of smartphones and computers also means that we do much less exercise now than people did in the past.

The level of stress in our daily lives means that when we have to face really challenging situations, like taking exams or performing in public, our bodies are often less able to cope with them in a positive way.

5 SPEAKING Work in pairs. Answer the questions.
1 When does stress have a negative effect on us?
2 Why does the writer think people are more stressed these days?
3 Do you agree that the things mentioned in the article cause stress?
4 Can you think of any other reasons why people feel stressed?

Me and my world

6 Make notes under the headings to show how your *family, friends,* and *school* might cause stress.

FAMILY

FRIENDS

SCHOOL

7 SPEAKING Think of a time when you were stressed. Talk to your partner about:
- how you felt.
- what you did.
- what you would do differently in the future.

TIPS FOR MANAGING STRESS

- Tell people how you are feeling. Being strong means sharing, not hiding feelings.
- Be patient – try not to worry about things you can't control.
- Get enough sleep and exercise, and eat well.

6 You may like to give your own example to get students started. If you think this might be a sensitive subject, suggest the class make up some exaggerated ideas about you.

7 Set pairs up into close friendships to avoid any awkward over-sharing. Monitor to help with any difficulties, but do not interrupt as this is a fluency activity.

Homework

Have the students keep a journal for two or three days, with a record of what made them stressed, how stressed they were, how long they were stressed, and what they did or could have done about it. If this is too sensitive a topic, they could make up some ideas.

TH!NK more

Practice Extra
Unit 1 Master it!

Worksheets
Life Lessons: Managing stress

Tests
Unit, extension, and skills test 1

Emotional Development
Managing own emotions
Managing stress by employing strategies.

Reading

Warmer

Draw a horizontal line on the board and write *today* at the far end of the line. Divide the line into four sections and write from right to left: *21st century*; *20th century*; *19th century*; *18th century*. Check that students are clear that the 20th century refers to 1900–1999, and so on. Divide the class into small groups and ask them to think of at least two historical events that occurred in their country (or abroad) for each century. You could set this up as a competition. The first group to write down two events for all four centuries wins.

▶ 04 Get THINKing

Play the video and discuss the question with your class.

1 Before students do the task, get them to cover the article on page 21 and just look at the title and pictures and answer the questions. Write their ideas on the board. When they read to check, set a three-minute time limit to encourage them to skim the article quickly and not to focus on every word.
Suggested answers: 1 People being held as slaves, slaves being treated cruelly on a ship, slaves being sold at auction 2 Africa 3 They were sold as slaves.

2 Set a time limit of two minutes to encourage quick scanning. Encourage students not to focus on every word for now, but just to find the answer to the question.
Suggested answer: James Ramsay was a free man in a slave-owning society, while Mary Prince was a slave.

READING

1 Look at the pictures and answer the questions.
1 What do the pictures illustrate?
2 Where were the people from?
3 What happened to them?

2 Read the article quickly. What is the big difference between James Ramsay and Mary Prince?

3 2.01 Read and listen to the article. Write R (Ramsay) or P (Prince) after each statement.
1 Showed no discrimination _
2 Tried to escape their life _
3 Was separated from their parents as a child _
4 Came from a family of slaves _
5 Was not popular with the local slave owners _
6 An event on a ship changed their life _
7 Their life became the subject of a book _
8 Helped slaves with their medical problems _

20

3 🔊 2.01 **Check/clarify:** *abolitionists, enraged, insisted, influence, captured, blisters, struck.*
1 R 2 P 3 P 4 P 5 R 6 R 7 P 8 R

Objectives

Functions and speaking Talking about the past
Grammar Narrative tenses (review); *would* and *used to*
Vocabulary Descriptive verbs; time periods
Culture Creative climate solutions
Train to THINK Following an idea through a paragraph
Values Animal rights

Resources for this unit

All available online

Videos
- Get THINKing: *Would you like a demanding job when you finish school?*
- Grammar rap!: Narrative tenses (review)
- Culture: Living in different climates

Tests
- Unit, extension, and skills test 2

Worksheets
- Grammar and vocabulary: Basic, Standard, and Extension Worksheets
- Project: Hard times in history
- Communication: Hard times
- Literature Worksheets: *David Copperfield*
- Get THINKing and Grammar rap! video Worksheets

Culture notes

The Reverend James Ramsay was a ship's surgeon, Anglican priest, and leading abolitionist. Born in 1733 in Scotland, he joined the Navy at the age of 24. He was hugely influential in the growing anti-slavery movement and met with the British Prime Minister, William Pitt the Younger, several times, giving him first-hand evidence of the horrors of the slave trade. He died in 1789, and although he did not live to see the end of slavery, he was instrumental to its abolition in the UK 18 years later.

William Wilberforce (born 1759) was a British politician, philanthropist, and leader of the movement to abolish the slave trade, whose campaign eventually led to the *Slavery Abolition Act 1833*. He died just three days after hearing that the act had been successfully passed through Parliament.

Mary Prince, born 1788, was a British abolitionist born in Bermuda to a family of African slaves. At 12 years old, Mary was sold for £38 (the equivalent of £4,484 nowadays). In 1828, her master, Adams Wood, traveled to London and took her with him as a servant. English law at the time ruled that it was illegal to transport slaves out of England. However, Adams Wood refused to sell or free her. Her first-hand description of the brutalities of enslavement had a motivating effect on the anti-slavery movement.

THEY MADE A DIFFERENCE

THE SLAVE TRADE

From the 16th to the 19th century, millions of people in Africa were taken from their homes and forced into lives of slavery. By the late 18th century, many people had realized this was wrong and wanted to stop it. These people became known as "abolitionists" and together they helped demolish one of the cruelist systems in the history of our world. Here are two of the men and women who made a huge difference.

One day in November of 1759, the British ship *Arundel* was sailing the West Indies when a slave ship approached it, begging for help. Many of the slaves on the ship had died of disease and the others were living in horrible conditions. One person from the *Arundel* went to help – a young doctor named James Ramsay. He was horrified by what he saw and he never forgot this experience. Soon after this, he went to work on the island of St. Kitts in the Caribbean. There he enraged local businessmen as he helped the slaves who worked for them, treating them for injuries and disease. He also worked as a church minister and he insisted on opening his church up to slaves as well as white people. When Ramsay returned to England, he wrote books about his experiences. The vivid details he included shocked many people. He was also a huge influence on William Wilberforce, the leader of the anti-slavery movement in the UK. His tireless career as a politician eventually succeeded with him repealing slavery laws.

Mary Prince was born in Bermuda in 1788. As her mother and father were slaves, she was a slave, too. She was sold a total of four times in her life. The first time with the rest of her family, but when she was 12, she was separated from them and went to work as a maid. She had been working at this job for a few months when she ran away to be with her mother, but she was soon captured and sent back. She was sold a third time to work in the salt ponds. The work was long and hard and the sun caused blisters on her body. She was also treated cruelly by her owners, who often struck her for the smallest things. When she was 40, new owners took her to England. Slavery was illegal in the UK, so she was able to go and work with the abolitionists. In 1831, the Anti-Slavery Society published a book about her life story called *The History of Mary Prince*. Lots of people read the book and it helped many change their minds about slavery.

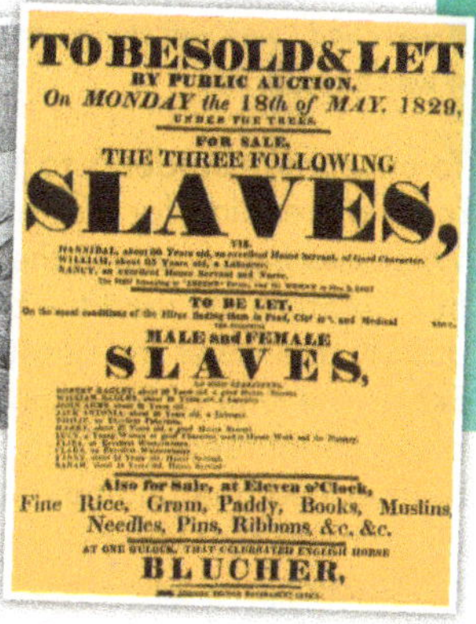

Train to TH!NK

Following an idea through a paragraph

It can be difficult to follow what a writer is trying to say in a longer paragraph. We need to read carefully to understand fully what the writer is saying.

4 **Answer the questions.**

In paragraph 2, it says, "...he wrote books about his experiences."

1 Look back at the paragraph. What were his experiences? Make a list of them.

Near the end of paragraph 3, it says, "the Anti-Slavery Society published a book about her life story."

2 Look back at the paragraph. What things might the book include?

SPEAKING

5 **Work in pairs. Discuss these questions.**

1 Who would you suggest for the "They Made a Difference" series?

2 Why would you include this person?

21

4 Encourage students to underline the parts of the text that give them the answers.

5 Clarify that the article was one of a series describing world-changing people. You may want to give your own ideas as an example to get them started.

Activity idea Review

To review narrative tenses before the next lesson, ask students which past tenses are used in the extract. Elicit simple past, past continuous, and past perfect; with a strong class, include past passive. Tell them they are going to do a reading race. Write on the board: *Read the article and find ...*

ten irregular past tense verbs (was, became, made, went, forgot, wrote, ran away, struck, took, read)

two examples of the past continuous (was sailing, were living)

two examples of the past perfect simple (had realized, had died) and an example of past perfect continuous (had been working)

eight examples of the past passive (were taken, [were] forced, was born, was sold, was separated, was captured, [was] sent back, was treated)

Homework

Ask students to research a person from around the world for the series on *They Made a Difference*. They can upload a picture with a description of the person and what they did in English. If students do not have access to the internet, they can create their own ideas. As a follow-up, students can bring the picture to the next lesson and present their person to the class.

TH!NK more

Worksheets

Project Hard times in history

Communication Hard times

Get **TH!NK**ing *Would you like a demanding job when you finish school?*

Critical THINKing

Understanding and analyzing links between ideas

Identifies the basic structure of an argument.

Grammar; Vocabulary, Pronunciation

Warmer

Test students on their past participles.

▶ 05 Grammar rap!
Narrative tenses (review)

1 Draw students' attention to the words in bold (1–4) before they match.
1 c 2 a 3 d, b 4 b
RULE: 5 the simple past
6 the past continuous
7 the past perfect simple
8 the past perfect continuous

2 Before students begin, check that they understand that they need to use either the simple past or past continuous, but not the past perfect.
1 saw; knew; had 2 was trying; died
3 watched / was watching; started
4 was talking; left

3 To encourage students to just focus on reading for gist, ask: *What was happening in the house?* Students read the text quickly to answer the question. Set a time limit of 30 seconds before brief feedback. (His brother had been doing a science experiment that went wrong.)
1 was walking 2 saw
3 Was … burning 4 ran 5 opened
6 was sitting 7 had been doing
8 had gone

Workbook p18

4 Encourage students to use English–English dictionaries to complete the exercise as there may not be a direct translation in their own language. They could use mobile devices if available.

Grammar rap!

GRAMMAR
Narrative tenses (review)

1 Match the sentences from the article on page 21 with the tenses. Then complete the rule.

1 The British ship *Arundel* **was sailing** the West Indies when a slave ship approached.
2 Many of the slaves on the ship **had died of disease**.
3 She **had been working** at this job for a few months when she **ran away**.
4 In 1831, the Anti-Slavery Society **published** a book about her life.

a past perfect c past continuous
b simple past d past perfect continuous

RULE:
We use …
[5]_____ to talk about finished actions in the past.
[6]_____ to set the scene or to talk about longer actions in the past interrupted by shorter actions.
[7]_____ to talk about actions before a certain time in the past.
[8]_____ to talk about actions that continued for some time before a certain time in the past.

2 Complete the sentences with the simple past or past continuous form of the verbs.

0 While the slaves *were working* in the fields, a fire *started*. (work / start)
1 When Ramsay _____ how serious the situation was, he _____ he _____ to do something. (see / know / have)
2 Ramsay _____ to help a slave when the man _____. (try / die)
3 While Ramsay _____ how the owners treated the slaves, he _____ thinking how wrong it was. (watch / start)
4 While Ramsay _____ to the slave owners, many of them _____ the room. (talk / leave)

3 Complete the conversation with the correct form of the verbs. Use the tenses from Exercise 1.

burn | do | go | open | run | see | sit | walk

Ian I had a real scare yesterday. As I [1]_____ up to our house, I [2]_____ smoke coming from the window.
Oli [3]_____ something _____?
Ian Fortunately not. I [4]_____ into the house, [5]_____ the kitchen door and there was my brother. He [6]_____ on the floor in shock. He [7]_____ science experiments! One of them [8]_____ wrong and exploded.

→ workbook page 18

VOCABULARY
Descriptive verbs

4 Certain verbs make narratives sound more dramatic. Find these words in a dictionary and write down:

1 what they mean.
2 their simple past and past participle forms.

beg | demolish | enrage | force | shock | smash | strike

5 Replace the underlined words with words from Exercise 4. Change the form if necessary.

0 He was made to eat his vegetables by his mom. *forced*
1 The sad news surprised the people. _____
2 He asked urgently for help, but people just carried on walking. _____
3 It made me very angry when I heard what they had done. _____
4 They knocked down the houses to make space for new stores. _____
5 The car lost control and hit another vehicle. _____
6 He dropped the mirror and it broke into a lot of pieces. _____

→ workbook page 20

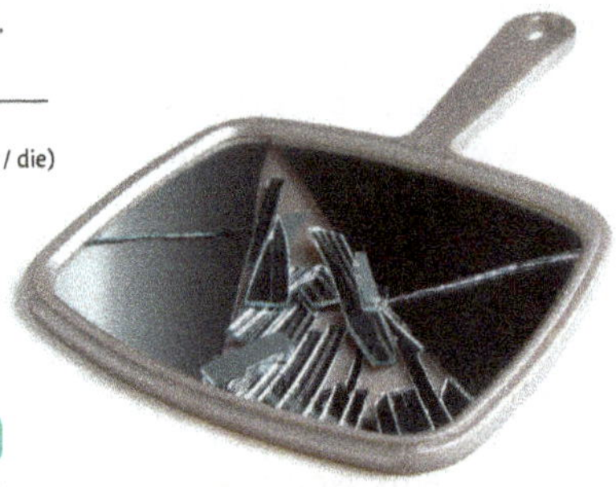

PRONUNCIATION
Initial consonant clusters with /s/
Go to page 120.

1 Students' own answers
2 begged, begged demolished, demolished enraged, enraged forced, forced shocked, shocked smashed, smashed struck, stricken/struck

5 1 shocked 2 begged 3 enraged me 4 demolished 5 struck 6 smashed

Workbook p20

Pronunciation
Initial consonant clusters with /s/

Student's Book p120

Get it Right!
Present perfect vs. simple past; Past continuous vs. simple past

Student's Book pp122–123

TH!NK more

Workbook
Grammar p18, Ex.1–5
Vocabulary p20, Ex.1–4
Vocabulary Extra p21, Ex.1–4
Pronunciation p118

Worksheets
Grammar rap! Narrative tenses (review)
Grammar Worksheets 2
Vocabulary Worksheets 2

6 Invite students to share their ideas with the rest of the class, but do not give the answer yet.
B

7 2.04 Before students listen, explain that they will hear an interview between two people. Tell them not to focus on understanding every word for now, but to focus on listening for the answers.
1 She was the last living passenger pigeon. 2 In 1900.

8 2.04 **Check/clarify:** *19th century.*
Before playing the audio again, ask students to answer as much as they can from memory.
1 C 2 A 3 C 4 B

9 **Check/clarify:** *rare, putting pressure on.*
Do the first one in open class to demonstrate the task.
A 3, 4 B 1, 6 C 2, 5

10 With quieter groups, consider dividing the class into As and Bs. Tell As (animal "indifferents") they need to argue in favor of statements 1, 2, and 5. Tell Bs (animal lovers) they should argue in favor of 3, 4, and 6. Ask groups of As and Bs to plan their arguments and make notes. Regroup students into groups of six (AAABBB). At the end of the exercise, discuss ideas as a class.

Homework

Write the questions from the extension activity on the board. Ask students to write a sentence for each scenario using the past perfect continuous.

LISTENING

6 **Look at the picture. Why is this bird special?**

A It is the rarest bird in the world.
B It was once the most common bird in the world.
C It has a very unusual song.

7 2.04 **Listen to the interview with Chris Oddie. Check your answer to Exercise 6 and answer these questions.**

1 Who or what was Martha?
2 When was the last passenger pigeon seen in the wild?

8 2.04 **Listen again. Choose A, B, or C for each question.**

1 What do we learn about passenger pigeons in Sarah's introduction?
 A They flew in enormous groups at night.
 B They lived up to the age of 50.
 C Their numbers dropped dramatically in the 19th century.
2 Which of these did not help lead to the extinction of the passenger pigeon?
 A a shortage of food
 B a big increase in hunting
 C better communication systems
3 Why did the US government law fail to help the passenger pigeon?
 A because people didn't respect the law
 B because no one cared about passenger pigeons
 C because they introduced the law too late
4 What does Chris hope we have learned from the extinction of the passenger pigeon?
 A All animals are equal.
 B Humans need to make sure animals are protected.
 C We need better programs in zoos to help species in danger.

TH!NK values

Animal rights

9 **Read the scenarios. Match them with statements 1–6. There are two statements for each scenario.**

Scenario A: ☐ / ☐
Work on a huge multi-million-dollar shopping mall has been stopped because nests of an extremely rare frog have been found in the area. It is one of only five places where this frog breeds. The property developers are putting pressure on the local government, saying it will be a disaster for the economy if they aren't allowed to finish the job.

Scenario B: ☐ / ☐
An elderly woman lives on her own. She has family, but they all live far away. A relative suggested buying her a parrot for her 80th birthday. Other family members are against the idea of keeping an animal in a cage.

Scenario C: ☐ / ☐
There is a hotel that's very popular with tourists because it's close to a beautiful forest. The forest is home to a species of large spider. Although it's harmless, people working in the hotel have been given strict orders to kill any spiders that get into the guest rooms.

1 A bird in a cage can be a great companion for a person who lives alone, so it's the right present.
2 Creating places where people can relax is more important than worrying about a few animals.
3 We can't afford to lose any species of animal.
4 Places where endangered animals have their natural habitat belong to them, and not to people.
5 Spiders are ugly and disgusting. Many people are scared of them; of course they should be killed.
6 Birds need to fly and they need space to be able to do that. Cages should be forbidden.

10 SPEAKING **Which of the statements 1–6 do you agree and disagree with? Why? Make notes of your answers. Then compare your ideas in pairs or small groups.**

Activity idea Extension

Divide the class into small groups. Write on the board: *1 Why was Tony's face wet? 2 Why did Bill's feet hurt? 3 Why was Kate carrying two heavy bags? 4 Why were Josh's knees dirty? 5 Why did Sue have blue fingers?*

Give students a short time to think of a reason for the situations. Example: *Why was Sally standing at the bus stop looking angry? She had been waiting for twenty minutes.* Their reason must include the past perfect continuous. Encourage them to use their imagination and give a point for the best idea.

Social Responsibilities
Understanding and discussing global issues – environmental, political, financial, and social
Understands how personal habits and behavior have the capacity to affect others and the environment.

TH!NK more

Workbook
Listening p24, Ex.1–4

Reading

Warmer

Write on the board: *What do you know about life in your country in the 17th century? How was it different from life today? Where did people live? What did they eat? What did they wear?* Ask students to discuss in pairs or small groups. After five minutes, bring the class together and listen to some of their ideas.

1 Before students read the article, get them to cover it, just look at the pictures, and answer the question.

2 🔊 **2.05** Read the article or play the audio. Then discuss the question as a class.

3 🔊 **2.05 Check/clarify:** *medieval, perfumes, petals, bakeries, public baths, concerns, hygiene, saltwater, rural.*
Ask students to underline the key parts of the text which give them their answers.
1 T 2 F 3 F 4 T 5 F 6 T 7 F

4 Monitor and prompt students to keep talking, but as this is a fluency activity, do not interrupt to correct mistakes. While monitoring, note down any common errors, to review as a class at the end. At the end of the exercise, listen to some of the students' ideas and encourage open class discussion.

READING

1 SPEAKING Work in pairs. Look at the pictures. What are the problems with baths like these?

2 🔊 2.05 Read and listen to the article. Then check your answers.

A short history of bathing in the UK

These days, most people in the UK have access to hot water by simply turning on the tap. People know how important it is to keep clean and take baths and showers daily. But of course, it wasn't always so easy.

In medieval times, most people knew that washing your body with water was a good thing to do and there were instruction books that explained the importance of keeping your body clean. Some, though, offered strange advice, such as to avoid taking a bath in the summer or not to take long baths because they would make you fat.

In the palaces and houses of the rich, people enjoyed bathing in a wooden bathtub that servants filled with hot water. They would often add perfumes and flower petals to make the water smell nice. Having your own private bath was a sign of importance. King John, for example, used to take his bathtub with him whenever he traveled.

Most people had no bath of their own, but they might visit one of the many public baths that started to appear in most cities by then. These were often beside bakeries and the heat from baking the bread was used to warm up the water.

People with no access to public baths would wash using only cold water and a cloth. When the weather was warm enough, they would jump in the nearest river for a bath.

By the early 1800s, there were serious concerns about the dreadful conditions in crowded cities and people started to recognize the importance of hygiene. Some now bought metal bathtubs for their homes, although for most people, there was no bathroom and the water still had to be carried in from outside and heated up. Many people still didn't use to have baths in their homes, but some could afford to make a weekly visit to the new public baths that opened in the 19th century. At the same time, bathing in the ocean became popular as people looked to saltwater to help cure skin problems.

Bathing habits changed for good in the late 19th century, when pipes could carry water directly into homes. Bathing became a lot easier and people started taking many more baths. However, many homes in the UK, especially those in rural areas, had to wait until as late as the 1960s before they had running water directly connected to them.

3 🔊 2.05 **Read and listen to the article again. Mark the sentences T (true) or F (false).**

1 In medieval England, many people believed water was important for your health. ☐
2 Flower petals helped to keep people clean. ☐
3 King John had a bathtub made for him everywhere he went. ☐
4 Bathing in rivers was common in medieval times. ☐
5 By the early 1800s, some people had hot water in their homes. ☐
6 In the early 1800s, bathing in the ocean was thought to help skin problems. ☐
7 Most homes in the UK had running water by the 1940s. ☐

4 SPEAKING **Work in pairs. Discuss these questions.**

1 How do medieval bathing habits compare with those of today?
2 How might bathing habits change in the future? Why do you think this?

24

TH!NK more

Workbook
Reading p22, Ex.1–4

Grammar; Vocabulary; Functions

5 Ask students to try to answer the questions from memory before referring back to page 24 to check.
1 used to 2 would 3 didn't use to
RULE: 4 used to / didn't use to
5 would(n't)

6 1 would / used to 2 used to
3 used to 4 used to 5 would / used to 6 used to

7 1 Did … use to; used to 2 didn't use to 3 Did … use to; used to
4 didn't use to 5 Did … use to; used to 6 didn't use to

Workbook p19

8 As an extension, encourage students to underline any time periods vocabulary in the reading text and then decide if they are a, b, or c.
1 b 2 c 3 a 4 a 5 c 6 b 7 a 8 b 9 b

Workbook p20

9 You may like to give an example from your own experience to get students started on this exercise.

Homework

Ask students to choose a topic from the list in Exercise 9 and a time period, e.g., food in the 1970s. Ask them to research information on their topic and prepare a short presentation. In the following lesson, put the students into small groups for them to present their information. During feedback, ask students which things were better in the past.

Language note *would* and *used to*

Students may produce questions like: *Would you like Mickey Mouse when you were little? We cannot use *would* with state verbs to describe a repeated past action: we use the question form *did* + *use to*. Students may find it helpful to translate examples into L1 and compare the two.

GRAMMAR
would and *used to*

5 **Complete these sentences from the article on page 24. Then complete the rule with *used to / didn't use to* and *would(n't)*.**

1 King John ______ take his bathtub with him whenever he traveled.
2 People … ______ wash using only cold water and a cloth.
3 Many people still ______ have baths in their homes.

RULE:
To talk about habits and repeated actions in the past, we can use *used to / didn't use to* or *would(n't)*.
- We use [4]______ with both action and stative verbs.
- We use [5]______ only with action verbs.

6 **Choose the correct words. Sometimes both options are possible.**

1 When I was a child, I *would / used to* play a lot with my sister.
2 We *would / used to* have a cat, Tubby.
3 We *would / used to* like her a lot and play with her all the time.
4 It's funny, but I *would / used to* think I'd never learn to read.
5 I *would / used to* sit and talk to my grandmother for hours.
6 My sister and I *would / used to* be such good friends!

7 **Complete the sentences and conversations with the correct form of *used to*.**

1 A ___________ you ___________ have a pet when you were a child?
B Yes, I ___________ have a cat.
2 We ___________ have a car. We used to walk everywhere.
3 A ___________ you ___________ watch a lot of TV when you were younger?
B Yes, I ___________ watch it every day when I got home from school.
4 I ___________ like vegetables, but I love them now.
5 A ___________ your dad ___________ read you books before you went to bed?
B No, he didn't, but my mom ___________.
6 I ___________ like having birthday parties. I was a really shy child.

→ workbook page 19

VOCABULARY
Time periods

8 **Look at phrases (1–9) and match them with categories (a–c).**

a the present
b the recent past
c a long, long time ago in history

1 from 1995 until 2004 ☐
2 in medieval times ☐
3 in this day and age ☐
4 these days ☐
5 in the olden days ☐
6 in the last century ☐
7 nowadays ☐
8 a decade ago ☐
9 not so long ago ☐

→ workbook page 20

FUNCTIONS
Talking about the past

9 SPEAKING **Work in pairs. Choose a topic for your partner and a period in the past. Your partner makes a comparison between the present and that time period. Take turns.**

food | games | home | school | technology | travel

games in the 1930s

Well, children would play with teddy bears or dolls. These days, many children have electronic games.

Activity idea Extension

Ask students to think of things they used to play with when they were young children. Elicit one or two examples in open class and prompt students to use *used to / would*. Students continue discussing in pairs. Nominate one or two pairs to share their ideas during feedback. You could even hold a class vote to find out which were the most popular childhood toys.

TH!NK more

Practice Extra
Unit 2 Practice it!

Workbook
Grammar p19, Ex.6–9
Vocabulary p20, Ex.5–6

Worksheets
Grammar Worksheets 2
Vocabulary Worksheets 2

Warmer

Write these questions on the board: *In which countries do you think it snows every year? How do you imagine life changes when it snows? What becomes more difficult? How can we use the snow in a positive way?* Discuss in pairs or small groups.

▶ 06 TH!NK
Living in different climates

1 Ask students to describe what they can see in the photos before looking at the words in the box and completing the exercise.

2 🔊 **2.06** Tell students not to try to understand every word, but to focus on checking their answers to Exercise 1.
A the Himalayas B the Andes
C Australia D the Philippines

3 **Check/clarify:** *melt, hurricanes, wildfires, destruction, bushfires, shortages of water, inspire, creative solutions, tropical typhoons, dome shape, curved surfaces, plowed, spirals.* Before students read the article again, get them to read through the questions.
1 They are dome shaped because curved surfaces can survive storms and strong winds better than flat ones.
2 Fires and winds caused the problem. He plowed the fields in spirals.
3 A lack of water in the spring.
4 He painted some of the mountains in the Andes white to try to stop them from heating up and losing their glaciers.

4 At the end of the exercise, listen to some of the students' ideas and encourage open class discussion.

Culture

TH!NK Living in different climates

1 SPEAKING Work in pairs. Look at the photos and try to match each one with a part of the world.

Australia | the Himalayas | the Philippines | the Andes

2 🔊 2.06 Read and listen to the article. Check your ideas.

A

CREATIVE CLIMATE SOLUTIONS

Climate change is the biggest threat to our planet. As temperatures increase, the ice caps and **glaciers** around the world are starting to melt, meaning sea levels will get higher. We are already seeing the results of climate change with an increase in extreme weather events such as hurricanes, wildfires, and serious shortages of water.

All over the world there are people living in difficult conditions. But difficult conditions often **inspire** creative solutions.

Every year the Philippines are hit by huge tropical typhoons. These violent storms often kill hundreds of people and cause billions of dollars in damage to the islands. In an attempt to fight back, one company has come up with a house that is designed **to stand up to** extremely strong winds. The houses are built in a dome shape and the curved surfaces are much better at surviving in storms than traditional flat roofs and walls. They are also better at surviving earthquakes.

Wildfires often cause massive destruction in many places around the world, destroying land, homes, and lives. In 2015, bush fires burned down vegetation in a large area of South Australia leaving nothing but bare earth. This made the land difficult to farm as strong winds blew the **soil** away. A farmer named Brian Fischer had a brilliant idea to stop the problem. With the help of his sons, he plowed the fields in spirals. This means that it doesn't matter which way the wind blows because it can never blow away the soil.

One man who wanted to tackle global warming directly was inventor Eduardo Gold. He used the idea that light colors **reflect** the sunlight to try to stop mountains in the South American Andes from heating up and losing their glaciers. His plan was simple: with the help of a few friends, he started painting the mountains white in the hope it would keep their surfaces cooler. Although his idea was included in the World Bank's "100 ideas to save the planet" in 2009, Gold died in 2014 and his work had limited success.

A **lack** of water is one of the most serious problems we can face. In the Himalayan Desert, water is very difficult to find during the spring months. To help **solve** this problem, the Ice Stupa project has come up with a very clever solution. In the winter, a pipe takes water from higher up in the mountains down to the desert, where it rushes out as a **fountain**. Because it is so cold in the desert, the water freezes and makes frozen towers of ice. In the spring, the ice melts giving the farmers the water they need for their land.

B

C

D

3 Read the article again. Answer the questions.
1 What shape are the houses in the Philippines and why?
2 What caused the problem in Australia and how did one farmer try to solve it?
3 What problem does an ice stupa solve?
4 What did Eduardo Gold do and why?

4 SPEAKING Work in pairs. What other areas of the world are difficult to live in and why?

26

Culture notes

The Philippines (officially, the Republic of the Philippines) is a country in Southeast Asia, made up of about 7,641 islands in the western Pacific Ocean. The capital city is Manila.

Australia (officially, the Commonwealth of Australia) is a country comprising the mainland of the Australian continent, the island of Tasmania, and lots of smaller islands. It is the world's sixth largest country by area. The capital city is Canberra, and the biggest city is Sydney.

The Andes mountains are the longest mountain range in the world, running 7,000 km through Venezuela, Colombia, Ecuador, Peru, Bolivia, Chile, and Argentina. At the highest point, Mount Aconcagua in Argentina reaches about 6,961 meters above sea level.

The Himalayas is a mountain range in Asia, running 2,400 km across Bhutan, China, India, Nepal, and Pakistan. It has many of the Earth's highest peaks, including Mount Everest at 8,848 meters.

Social Responsibilities
Understanding and discussing global issues – environmental, political, financial, and social
Is aware of different global issues (e.g., global warming).

5 Check/clarify: *resist.*
Ask students to try to match the definitions from memory before referring back to the article to check.
1 to stand up to 2 glaciers 3 fountain 4 soil 5 inspire 6 solve 7 lack 8 reflect

1 Give students just two minutes to scan the article quickly to find the answer to the question. Encourage them not to focus on every word for now.
He discovered that migrating birds return to the same place each year.

2 Encourage students to underline the language in the article.
1 One day, while he was drawing, he had an idea to test his theory.
2 had (always) had
3 had been wondering
4 in 1785, One day, The next year

3 Students can check their answers in pairs.
Suggested answers:
Background: Born 1785 in Saint-Domingue, brought up in France, moved to the US at age 18
Discovery: Tied cotton around the legs of birds, discovered that they return to same place the following year
Other information: Popularized bird watching, amazing artist, wrote very famous book *The Birds of America*, identified 25 new bird species, hero in American conservation

4 If students are struggling to think of someone, give them some ideas. You could divide the class into small groups so that they can share ideas before writing individually (they could do this for homework).

5 Encourage students to organize their writing as outlined in Exercise 3 and to use narrative tenses.

Homework

If you are short on time, students can do Writing Exercise 5 for homework. If you did this in the class, ask students to exchange their articles with another student for them to read and give feedback on content and structure. Students could check if the article uses the same structure as the template. They should also decide which is the most/least interesting part of the article.

5 VOCABULARY There are eight **highlighted** words or phrases in the article. Match the words with these meanings. Write the words.

1 to survive by resisting ______
2 large parts of frozen land ______
3 a structure that forces water up in the air ______
4 material on the surface of the ground ______
5 to motivate ______
6 to find an answer to ______
7 something there is not enough of ______
8 to send light back ______

WRITING
A magazine article about someone who made an important discovery

1 INPUT **Read the article. What discovery did John James Audubon make?**

2 ANALYZE **Find examples in the article of:**
1 a sentence containing the simple past and the past continuous.
2 the past perfect.
3 the past perfect continuous.
4 expressions referring back to the past.

3 **Read the article again and make notes to complete the table.**

	John James Audubon
His background	
What he discovered and how he discovered it	
Other information	

4 PLAN **Think of someone who made a discovery.**
- Do some internet research to find out more about them.
- Choose the most important and interesting details.
- Organize the information into paragraphs. Write notes in the table above.
- Think about the language you'll need to describe the person and what they did.

5 PRODUCE **Write an article for your school magazine about a person who made a discovery (200 words).**

A HARD LIFE UNIT 2

John James Audubon

John James Audubon was an American bird expert and wildlife painter. He was born in 1785 in Saint-Domingue in the Caribbean. He was brought up in France, but at the age of 18, his father sent him to live in the US.

Audubon had always had a fascination for wildlife and, in particular, birdlife. He spent much of his time outdoors, studying and drawing nature. One of the things he had been wondering about was whether the same birds returned each year to his farm after disappearing for the winter months. One day, while he was drawing, he had an idea to test his theory. He caught a few birds and tied some cotton around their legs. The next year when he saw a bird with the cotton around its leg return, he knew his ideas were correct. He was one of the first people to start to understand bird migration and popularize birdwatching.

As well as his important studies into bird life, Audubon was an amazing artist. His *The Birds of America* is considered to be one of the best bird books ever written. These days, it's also one of the most expensive: an original copy was recently sold for $7 million. He also identified 25 new species of birds and is regarded as a true hero of early American conservation.

27

Activity idea Mixed ability

Ask stronger students to not look at the definitions in Culture/Vocabulary Exercise 5 and to just use the context provided by the article to try to work out meaning of the highlighted words. They then refer to the definitions to check their ideas. Weaker students work in pairs to match definitions and words from the article directly.

TH!NK more

Practice Extra
Unit 2 Master it!

Workbook
Developing Writing p23

Tests
Unit, extension, and skills test 2

1 In B2 First for Schools Reading and Use of English Part 1, candidates have to read a short text with eight numbered spaces, then decide which of the four words provided belongs in each blank space. This part of the exam tests understanding of words within a context.

Encourage your students to do the following when they approach this task:

- Skim the text to find out the topic and general meaning.
- Work through the eight questions, reading the whole sentence to choose the correct word to complete each space.
- After choosing an answer, check the other three options and decide why they are wrong.
- Read the completed text again to make sure it makes sense.

1D 2D 3A 4B 5A 6D 7C 8B

Workbook p17

2 In B2 First for Schools Speaking Part 1, candidates will be asked a range of questions about their everyday lives, like sports they enjoy, travel and vacations, work experience, and so on. Encourage your students to do the following when they approach this task:

- Respond promptly, with answers that are complete and spontaneous.
- Rehearsed speeches should be avoided as these might be inappropriate for the question asked.
- Brainstorm possible questions from the categories above and practice.
- Look for opportunities to socialize with English speakers.

Workbook p25

TOWARDS B2 First for Schools

READING AND USE OF ENGLISH

Multiple-choice cloze

→ workbook page 17

1 **For questions 1–8, read the text below and decide which answer (A, B, C or D) best fits each gap. There is an example at the beginning (0).**

0 A (stopped) B finished C ended D not

Do you ever stop and think about how easy the internet has made our lives? I know there are times when it's slow or has [0] _A_ working altogether, times when maybe you feel like [1]_____ your computer into pieces. But just think of all those things you use it for. You want to buy a new book – you can [2]_____ online and buy it. You need to [3]_____ some research for your homework – you can find it all there on the web. You feel like a [4]_____ with your best friend, so you Skype them. You just want a [5]_____ from your homework, so you start up Minecraft or whatever game it is you prefer and start playing. These [6]_____, everything we need is just a click of a button away.

Of course, it wasn't always like this. Only a few decades [7]_____, people had to do things like go to the shops if they wanted to buy something and often those shops were closed! They had to look in very large, heavy books called encyclopedias to find information. They had to [8]_____ up the telephone if they wanted to talk, and if their best friend wasn't at home, they simply couldn't talk to them. That's how tough life was! And these poor people who had to suffer such hardships were … our parents! Makes you feel sorry for them, doesn't it?

	A	B	C	D
1	begging	striking	forcing	smashing
2	come	enter	click	go
3	do	make	find	ask
4	talking	chat	question	speak
5	break	stop	end	fix
6	times	ages	years	days
7	after	since	ago	past
8	take	pick	grab	hold

SPEAKING

Interview

→ workbook page 25

2 **In pairs, ask and answer the questions.**

1 Who do you spend the most time with at the weekends, and what do you do with them?
2 What kind of films do you like best? What do you like about them?
3 Where did you go for your last holiday? What was it like?
4 What's your favourite sport to play? What do you like about it?
5 What things do you enjoy doing the most with your parents?
6 What is your favourite room in your home and why do you like it?
7 If you could be anywhere now, where would it be and why?
8 What things do you like to do at home on a rainy day?
9 Who is your best friend and what do you like the most about him/her?

28

1 1 travel 2 got into 3 changes 4 do 5 make 6 got promoted 7 retire 8 give up 9 demolished 10 forced

2 1 see 2 are going to 3 'll love 4 used to love 5 'm seeing 6 was looking

3 1 ~~reading~~ read 2 ~~finished~~ had finished 3 ~~am running~~ run 4 ~~will go~~ are going / 're going 5 ~~had been running~~ had run 6 ~~was falling~~ fell

4 1 always; I don't like 2 olden; these days 3 are having; I'll see 4 uses; this day and age

TEST YOURSELF UNITS 1 & 2

VOCABULARY

1 Complete the sentences with the words in the list. There are four extra words.

changes | demolished | do | forced | form | give up | got into | got promoted | make | retire | settle | strike | struggle | travel

1 It would be wonderful to __________ the world one day.
2 I'm happy I __________ the habit of exercising every day.
3 After the principal talked to him about being late, he's going to make some __________ .
4 Good luck with the test – I'm sure you'll __________ really well.
5 Every December 31st, I __________ a resolution to do something, but I usually break it!
6 Mom makes more money now because she __________ .
7 On her 65th birthday, she decided to __________ and never work again.
8 I need more time to study for my exams, so I'm going to __________ my judo classes for a while.
9 The hurricane __________ more than 50 homes in the town.
10 As the flames got closer, many people were __________ to leave their homes.

/10

GRAMMAR

2 Complete the sentences with the phrases in the list. There are two extra phrases.

was looking | would look | 'm seeing | are going to | go to | used to love | see | 'll love

1 I __________ my aunt and uncle once a month.
2 Four or five of us __________ eat curry tonight.
3 Have fun at the concert – I'm sure you __________ it!
4 When I was a kid, I __________ going to the river to swim.
5 I don't feel very well, so I __________ the doctor tomorrow.
6 When I saw her, she __________ in a store window.

3 Find and correct the mistake in each sentence.

1 When he was young, my dad used to reading books about nature.
2 When I got to the house, there was no one there. The party finished!
3 I am running in the park every morning before school.
4 We're really excited because we will go on a vacation next week.
5 He was tired because he had been running two kilometers.
6 While I was cycling in the park, I was falling off my bicycle.

/12

FUNCTIONAL LANGUAGE

4 Choose the correct words.

1 A I'm angry with Mike. He's *always* / *often* making jokes about me.
B I know. He's horrible. *I don't like* / *I'm not liking* him at all.
2 A You know, in the *past* / *olden* days, people didn't have the Internet.
B I know! But *these days* / *not so long ago* we can get information so quickly!
3 A Gina and I *have* / *are having* lunch tomorrow. Why don't you come, too?
B Great – thank you! *I see* / *I'll see* you at the restaurant!
4 A No one *uses* / *is using* typewriters any more.
B Not in *nowadays* / *this day and age*, no!

/8

MY SCORE /30
22–30 | 10–21 | 0–9

29

The Cambridge Life Competencies Framework

Critical THINKing
Using Venn diagrams
Watch this video for a tip on developing your students' critical thinking skills. Scan the QR code here.

Warmer

Ask pairs of students to list as many logos as they can see on clothes, bags, etc. in one minute. Award one point for each logo listed.

▶ 07 Get TH!NKing

Play the video and discuss the question with your class.

1 Swatch sells watches. Jaguar makes cars. WhatsApp provides a messaging service. Pret A Manger sells food and drinks.

2 If your students struggle to think of ideas, you could broaden out the discussion to why brands are important.

3 Jaguar, WhatsApp, Pret A Manger

4 🔊 **3.01 Check/clarify:** *unique, wordplay, targeted, obsessed.*
1 Companies think a lot about brand names because it distinguishes their product from all others, and it's important that they get it right the first time.
2 A good brand name is unique, memorable, and easy to understand.
3 Jaguar was chosen because it makes people think of a beautiful but dangerous wild cat. Pret A Manger was chosen because it's in a foreign language (French) and therefore sounds special and different. WhatsApp was chosen because it uses wordplay (it's based on the English expression What's up?).
4 Because in Spanish no va means "it doesn't go."
5 Because they want to have something with the right brand or logo.

3 WHAT'S IN A NAME?

OBJECTIVES

FUNCTIONS: giving advice; expressing obligation; giving recommendations, warnings, and prohibitions

GRAMMAR: *(don't) have to / ought to / should(n't) / must; had better (not); can('t) / must(n't)*

VOCABULARY: making and selling; expressions with *name*

Get TH!NKING
Watch the video and think:
do you have a favorite logo? Why do you like it?

swatch
WhatsApp
JAGUAR
ORGANIC COFFEE ★ PRET ★ NATURAL FOOD

READING

1 **Look at the names and logos and answer the questions.**
1 These are the names and logos of various companies. What kind of products do they offer?
Jaguar sells cars.
2 Add two more names of companies or products that are famous around the world.

2 SPEAKING **Work in pairs. Some people think the name of a brand is very important. What do you think is the reason for this?**

3 **Read the blog entry on the next page quickly. Which of the brands shown above does it mention?**

4 🔊 3.01 **Read the blog entry again and listen. Answer the questions.**
1 Why do companies think a lot about a brand name?
2 What makes a good brand name?
3 Why were each of these names chosen?
• Jaguar • Pret A Manger • WhatsApp
4 Why was Nova a bad name for a car in Spain?
5 Why do some teenagers choose to buy more expensive products (like clothes)?

Train to TH!NK

Identifying the main topic of a paragraph
Writers use a new paragraph when they want to change the topic. The opening line of a paragraph usually gives you a clue about its topic.

5 **Look at paragraphs 3 and 4. What is the topic of each paragraph? Check (✓) two options.**
A what teenagers wear to school ☐
B brand names are important in the teenage market ☐
C some really bad brand names ☐
D ways to pick a brand name ☐

30

5 Tell students that one technique to help them read a text quickly is to focus only on the first sentences of each paragraph, as this should give a good overview of the main topics of the text.
Paragraph 3: D Paragraph 4: B

Critical TH!NKing
Understanding and analyzing links between ideas
Distinguishes between main and supporting arguments.

Objectives

Functions and speaking Giving advice; expressing obligation; giving recommendations, warnings, and prohibitions
Grammar *(don't) have to / ought to / should(n't) / must; had better (not); can('t) / must(n't)*
Vocabulary Making and selling; expressions with *name*
Fiction *How I Met Myself*
Train to TH!NK *Identifying the main topic of a paragraph*

Resources for this unit

All available online

Videos
- Get TH!NKing: *Do you have a favorite logo? Why do you like it?*
- Grammar rap!: *had better (not)*

Tests
- Unit, extension, and skills test 3
- End of term test 1

Worksheets
- Grammar and vocabulary: Basic, Standard, and Extension Worksheets
- Project: Advertisements
- Communication: What's in a name?
- Literature Worksheets: *David Copperfield*
- Grammar presentation: *(don't) have to / ought to / should(n't) / must / had better (not)*
- Get TH!NKing and Grammar rap! video Worksheets

Culture notes

Swatch is a Swiss watch company founded in 1983. The name refers to "second watch" as the company mostly produces cheaper, more disposable, and often colorful watches.

Jaguar is a British car company, which was first set up in 1922. It is now part of Jaguar Land Rover and produces expensive models such as the XE and the F-Type.

WhatsApp Messenger is an American messaging service that enables users to send text and voice messages, make voice and video calls, and share images and other types of media.

Despite its French name, the sandwich company Pret A Manger was started in London in 1986, by two friends who wanted to produce healthier takeout food. There are now more than 300 Pret stores in the UK.

6 Give a couple of your own ideas as examples before students work in pairs. At the end of the exercise, listen to some of the students' ideas and encourage open class discussion. During feedback, you could extend the discussion by asking students which brands are fashionable right now and which used to be in fashion but aren't now.

Homework

Ask students to invent a brand logo for something generic like sneakers or a soda. They can upload a picture with a description of the logo development in English. If students do not have access to the internet, they can create their own ideas. As a follow-up, students can bring the picture to the next class and present their logos to the class.

Brand names

1 OK, so imagine you've thought of a great idea for a product to make and sell – a game, an app, or clothes, for example. You know you can sell millions of them, but first of all, you must give the product a name – a brand name. And that may not be as easy as you think.

2 The brand name is the thing that distinguishes your product from all others and it's really important that it makes an impact. Businesses spend a lot of time thinking about brand names; when the name has been picked, it's very difficult to change, so companies have to get it right first time.

3 So how do you choose a name? A brand name ought to be unique, memorable, and easy to understand. It should create some kind of emotional connection with people who buy the product – the target market. Some companies use the family name. When Henry Ford started making cars, he just called the company "Ford." But you don't have to use a family name – you can go for an image. Staying with cars, think about the brand name Jaguar, a beautiful but dangerous wild cat. What does that say about the manufacturer's product? Some companies use wordplay. It's a common technique for naming apps, like how WhatsApp got its name from the English expression "What's up?". Others like to use foreign words because they sound special or different. For example, in Britain, in Europe, and in the US, there's a chain of sandwich shops with the French name Pret A Manger, which means "ready to eat." And what do you have to be careful about when choosing a name? Well, you shouldn't choose one that might not work in certain countries or cultures. Many years ago, a car company launched a new car that they called Nova. They thought it suggested something nice and new, but in Spanish it can be read as *no va* ("it doesn't go"). Not a good name for a car in Spain, then!

4 These days, the choice of brand name is particularly important if your product is targeted at the teenage market. Teenage consumers are perhaps more concerned with brand names and company logos than any other group. When a brand, especially a clothing brand, becomes popular with teenagers, there's a lot of pressure to wear those clothes and have the name and/or logo visible. A teacher in an American high school said, "I certainly see that kids are obsessed with brand names. They won't buy something that's almost identical – and cheaper – simply because they feel they must wear something with the right logo." So if you want to get into the teenage market, you have to find a product and a brand name that works with that age group, and create some great advertisements, too.

5 Companies know that the name isn't everything – the product itself has to be good, of course – but it's an essential part of the package.

SPEAKING

6 Work in pairs. Discuss these questions.

1 Can you think of any more brand names that:
   a use a family name?
   b try to create an image?
   c are in another language?
2 Have you ever bought or wanted something just because of the brand? Give examples.

"I'm so glad that we don't have to wear school uniforms any more!"

31

Activity ideas Extension

Write these anagrams on the board: 1 gtrtea *target;* 2 blrmmeeao *memorable;* 3 eqiuun *unique;* 4 ssssbuniee *businesses* 5 laneimoot *emotional;* 6 nishisseugdti *distinguishes;* 7 vremdnaesttei *advertisement;* 8 fctmunarreau *manufacturer;* 9 rmnscoeus *consumers;* 10 srpreeus *pressure*

Before showing the anagrams, divide the class into small mixed-ability groups and tell them that they will compete to solve all of the anagrams. Tell them the words appear in the blog entry. Ask groups to choose one student to be secretary. This student writes the answers. You could choose a weaker student to do this to make sure they're involved. If students are struggling, underline the first letter. Groups race to get the answers.

TH!NK more

Worksheets
Project Advertisements
Communication What's in a name?
Get **TH!NK**ing *Do you have a favorite logo? Why do you like it?*

Warmer

Write on the board: *How often do you see or hear advertisements? Do you think there are too many advertisements? Why? Can you think of any brands or products that you don't see advertising for?* Discuss.

1 Ask students to try to answer the questions from memory before referring back to page 31 to check.
1 must 2 have to 3 ought to 4 don't have to 5 do … have to 6 shouldn't RULE: 7 have to, must 8 don't/doesn't have to 9 should 10 ought to 11 shouldn't

2 Ensuring students are clear on context first will help them decide on the correct form.
1 have to 2 don't have to 3 has to 4 do … have to 5 have to 6 don't have to

3 You may like to do the first item with the whole class as an example.
1 should / ought to 2 shouldn't 3 have to / must / should / ought to 4 don't have to 5 should / ought to 6 should / ought to 7 should / ought to 8 have to / must 9 don't have to 10 have to / must / should / ought to

Workbook p28

Get it Right!
have to vs. *had to*; *don't have to* vs. *mustn't*

Student's Book p123

4 During feedback, check pronunciation. You may like to write the words on the board and elicit and mark stressed syllables (underlined below).
1 products 2 consumers 3 brand 4 chain 5 advertisement 6 logo 7 image 8 manufacturer

GRAMMAR
(don't) have to / ought to / should(n't) / must

1 Complete the sentences from the article on page 31. Then complete the rule with *have to, don't have to, ought to, should, shouldn't,* and *must*.

1 First of all, you ______ give the product a name.
2 Companies ______ get it right the first time.
3 A brand name ______ be unique, memorable, and easy to understand.
4 But you ______ use a family name.
5 And what ______ you ______ be careful about?
6 Well, you ______ choose a name that might not work in certain countries or cultures.

RULE: We use [7]______ or ______ to say, "This is important or necessary." We use [8]______ to say, "This isn't important or necessary." We use [9]______ or [10]______ to tell someone that something is a good idea. We use [11]______ to tell someone that something isn't a good idea. (*Ought to* isn't as frequent as *should*. The negative form is rare.)

2 Complete the conversation with the correct form of *have to*.

Mandy Mom, there's a new cell phone out. It's really good. I [1]______ get one!
Mom No way! Your phone is fine. You [2]______ buy another one.
Mandy But you know what it's like at school. Everyone [3]______ have the latest product!
Mom Yes, and it's terrible. Why [4]______ you all ______ wear the same clothes, for example?
Mandy Because it's what teenagers do. You were young once. Don't you remember?
Mom I see. And I [5]______ go to work to pay for all these things, right?
Mandy Oh, Mom! You [6]______ be difficult!

3 Complete the conversation with suitable modal verbs. There is often more than one possible answer.

Gill The new café is great – you [1]______ go there.
Jack I've heard it's a bit expensive.
Gill Yes, that's true. You [2]______ go there every day. But you [3]______ try the cupcakes – they're delicious!
Jack OK. What's the place called, anyway?
Gill Can you believe it's called The Coffee Shop?!
Jack What a boring name! You [4]______ be a genius to think of that! They [5]______ have a foreign name, like Le Café.
Gill Well, OK. But it [6]______ be easy to pronounce. There's a store in town called Arighi Bianchi and no one knows how to say it.
Jack But the owner is Italian. It's his name!
Gill I guess I [7]______ know that. Anyway, I [8]______ go home and do my homework for tomorrow.
Jack You [9]______ worry about that. It's easy.
Gill Really? OK, so let's go to the movies. There's a new movie that we [10]______ see!

→ workbook page 28

VOCABULARY
Making and selling

4 Complete the sentences with the words.

advertisement | brand | chain | consumers
image | logo | manufacturer | products

1 They make cleaning ______, like washing powder.
2 The prices have gone up a lot, so now ______ have to pay more.
3 I always buy the same ______ of shoes – they're so comfortable.
4 It's a ______ that has stores in every town.
5 That store has a really funny ______ on TV.
6 The Nike ______ is a large checkmark.
7 When the company's director went to prison, it damaged the company's ______.
8 If it doesn't work, send it back to the ______.

5 SPEAKING **Answer the questions. Then work in pairs and compare your answers.**

Can you name …
1 three places where you find advertisements?
2 a manufacturer of cell phones?
3 a chain of stores and a chain of restaurants?
4 one thing you always buy the same brand of?

→ workbook page 30

5 At the end of the exercise, listen to some of the students' ideas and encourage open class discussion.

Workbook p30

THINK more

Workbook
Grammar p28, Ex.1–4
Vocabulary p30, Ex.1–2
Vocabulary Extra p31, Ex.1–3

Worksheets
Grammar Worksheets 3
Grammar presentation: *(don't) have to / ought to / should(n't) / must / had better (not)*
Vocabulary Worksheets 3

Language notes *(don't) have to / ought to / should(n't) / must*

Students are often confused by the difference between *must* and *have to* in both their positive and negative forms. If the obligation comes from the speaker, we use *must*, for example:

Teacher: *You must do your homework today* (because I am telling you to!).
If the speaker is *describing* an obligation, we use *have to* since this obligation is not coming from the speaker, for example:

Student: *I have to do my homework* (because my teacher has told me to!).

Students can also confuse the negatives of *must* and *have to*.

Teacher: *You must do your homework today – the deadline is tomorrow* (obligation).

Teacher: *You don't have to do your homework today* (not necessary – you could do it tomorrow or later since the deadline is a week away).

Teacher: *You mustn't copy your classmate's test!* (prohibition).

6 🔊 **3.02** Ask students to read the question and options before they listen. Encourage them to focus on answering the question and not to worry if they don't understand every word.
B

7 🔊 **3.02** Before listening, ask students to read the questions and underline key information they will need to listen for.
1 T 2 F 3 F 4 F 5 T 6 T

▶ 08 Grammar rap!
had better (not)

8 1 'd better 2 'd better not
RULE: 3 don't do 4 do

9 1 'd better 2 'd better not
3 'd better 4 'd better
5 'd better not

Workbook p29

10 🔊 **3.03** You could extend this activity by getting students to role-play the conversations.
1 – 3, 1, 5, 4, 2 2 – 3, 5, 1, 2, 4

11 Allow students six to eight minutes to prepare their dialogues. Monitor to make sure all students are on task.

12 **Check/clarify:** *feel sorry for.* Encourage students to explain their choices.

13 If space allows, encourage students to walk around the classroom to find someone who agrees with their statements. Ask students to report their findings back to the class and encourage them to use the phrase *So does he/she.*

Homework

Write on the board: *1 I have a hole in my shoe, and it's raining hard. 2 I have an important exam tomorrow. 3 I saw a man stealing a car this morning. 4 I broke my friend's smartphone.*
Ask students to think of responses to the situations. Each response should include *had better*. As a follow-up in the next class, ask students to provide their responses in pairs. Their partner guesses the situations they refer to.

LISTENING

6 🔊 3.02 **Listen to Paul talking to Alexandra. What is their conversation about? Choose the correct option.**

A why it's good to have a nickname
B how people get their nicknames
C why some people don't like their nicknames

7 🔊 3.02 **Listen again. Mark the sentences T (true) or F (false).**

1 There are at least two shortened versions of the name Alexandra. ☐
2 Paul got the nickname Smithy because he lived in a town called Smith. ☐
3 Paul's brother liked his nickname. ☐
4 Sting got his nickname because he liked bees. ☐
5 Miley Cyrus's given name was Destiny. ☐
6 Lady Gaga got her name from a text message. ☐

GRAMMAR
had better (not)

8 **Complete these sentences from the listening. Then choose the correct words to complete the rule.**

1 We _______________ go now.
2 You _______________ tell anyone at school.

RULE: We use *had* ('d) *better* to warn someone that something bad will happen if they [3]*do / don't do* something. We use *had* ('d) *better not* to warn someone that bad things will happen if they [4]*do / don't* do something.

9 **Complete the sentences with *had better (not)*.**

1 The bus leaves in two minutes. You _______________ run.
2 I'll lend you my pen – but you _______________ break it!
3 It's going to rain. We _______________ go inside.
4 You have to get up very early tomorrow, so you _______________ go to bed. It's 1 a.m.
5 You _______________ eat any more candy. You'll get sick.

→ workbook page 29

FUNCTIONS
Giving advice

10 🔊 3.03 **Put the sentences in the correct order to make two conversations. Then listen and check.**

1 ☐ **Liam** Why? What's her name?
☐ **Liam** What's the matter, Jo?
☐ **Liam** Well, you'd better get some help – quickly!
☐ **Jo** It's something like Sharita Wass Ikonor.
☐ **Jo** I have to call someone and I have no idea how to pronounce her name.

2 ☐ **Bob** Well, I wrote the wrong name in my birthday card to her son. I called him Jason, not Jacob.
☐ **Bob** I know. She's really upset.
☐ **Bob** My sister's really angry with me.
☐ **Mia** Why?
☐ **Mia** You'd better not do that again!

11 SPEAKING **Work in pairs. Imagine you forgot your best friend's birthday. Write a conversation using *had better (not)*.**

SPEAKING
People and their names

12 **Complete the questionnaire with 1–5 (1 = I strongly agree; 5 = I strongly disagree).**

1 It's cool to have a nickname. ☐
2 I only remember the names of people I like. ☐
3 I hate it when people forget my name. ☐
4 Your name is an important part of who you are. ☐
5 I feel sorry for people who have unusual names. ☐

13 **Compare your answers in small groups. Which question(s) do you agree on?**

Language notes *had better (not)*

To clarify the meaning of *had better*, write on the board:
***Billy:** It's my mom's birthday tomorrow. I forgot! I haven't bought her a present.*
***Bobby:** Oh no! You _____ buy one, or you'll be in big trouble!*
Elicit answers in open class. If students use *should* or *ought to*, praise them, but elicit that in this situation, something bad will happen if Billy doesn't buy a present, so we would probably use *had better*. Point out that we use subject + *had better* + base form of the verb.

TH!NK more

Workbook
Listening p31, Ex.1–5
Grammar p29, Ex.5–6

Worksheets
Grammar rap! *had better (not)*
Grammar Worksheets 3
Grammar presentation: *(don't) have to / ought to / should(n't) / must / had better (not)*

Warmer

As a class, brainstorm the best/worst/funniest/strangest place names students have heard.

1 1 b 2 a

2 Give students two minutes to read the article and match the names and places. Encourage them not to focus on every word for now.

3 🔊 **3.04**
1 Turkey 2 Scotland 3 the US
4 Austria 5 Belgium
6 the Netherlands 7 the US

4 **Check/clarify:** *provisions.*
1 He sent two teams of engineers to find the best land.
2 A person from Accident.
3 Because it was halfway between two cities (Natchez and Mobile).
4 In the 1920s.
5 The local road signs were often stolen.
6 The town made the signs stronger.
7 The name probably came from the Bati Raman Mountain.
8 Because he thought Nolan had used the name of the city for his movies without getting permission.

Culture notes

The Big Apple is a nickname for New York City. The exact origin is unknown, but it was popularized in the 1920s by John J. Fitz Gerald, a sports writer for the *New York Morning Telegraph.*

The name "Chicago" comes from a French interpretation of the indigenous word *shikaakwa* for a wild relative of the onion. The current city of Chicago was first referenced as "Checagou" in 1679. The city has had several nicknames, including the Windy City, Chi-Town, Second City, and City of the Big Shoulders.

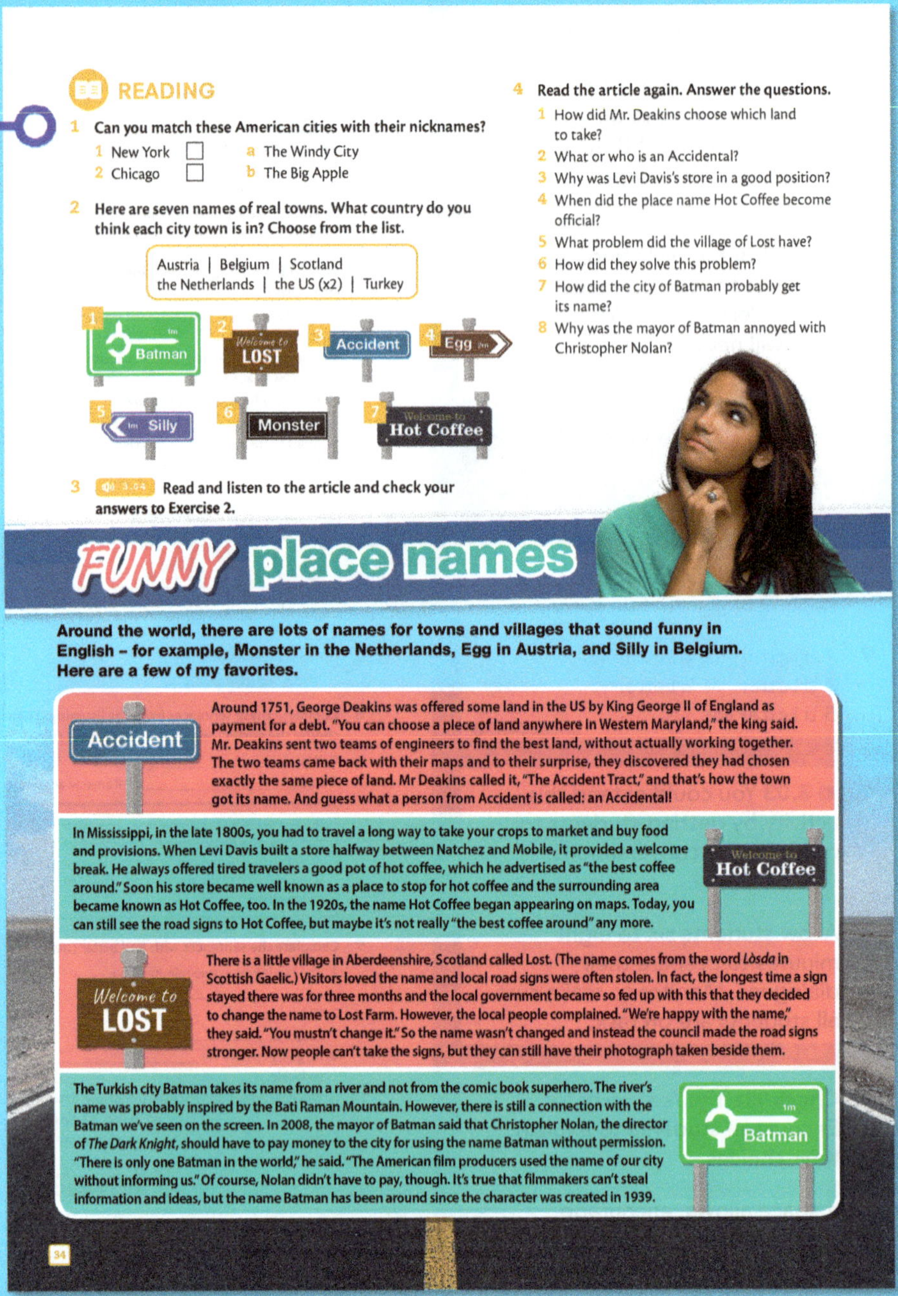

READING

1 Can you match these American cities with their nicknames?
1 New York ☐ a The Windy City
2 Chicago ☐ b The Big Apple

2 Here are seven names of real towns. What country do you think each city town is in? Choose from the list.

Austria | Belgium | Scotland
the Netherlands | the US (x2) | Turkey

1 Batman 2 Welcome to LOST 3 Accident 4 Egg 5 Silly 6 Monster 7 Welcome to Hot Coffee

3 🔊 3.04 Read and listen to the article and check your answers to Exercise 2.

4 Read the article again. Answer the questions.
1 How did Mr. Deakins choose which land to take?
2 What or who is an Accidental?
3 Why was Levi Davis's store in a good position?
4 When did the place name Hot Coffee become official?
5 What problem did the village of Lost have?
6 How did they solve this problem?
7 How did the city of Batman probably get its name?
8 Why was the mayor of Batman annoyed with Christopher Nolan?

FUNNY place names

Around the world, there are lots of names for towns and villages that sound funny in English – for example, Monster in the Netherlands, Egg in Austria, and Silly in Belgium. Here are a few of my favorites.

Accident

Around 1751, George Deakins was offered some land in the US by King George II of England as payment for a debt. "You can choose a piece of land anywhere in Western Maryland," the king said. Mr. Deakins sent two teams of engineers to find the best land, without actually working together. The two teams came back with their maps and to their surprise, they discovered they had chosen exactly the same piece of land. Mr Deakins called it, "The Accident Tract," and that's how the town got its name. And guess what a person from Accident is called: an Accidental!

In Mississippi, in the late 1800s, you had to travel a long way to take your crops to market and buy food and provisions. When Levi Davis built a store halfway between Natchez and Mobile, it provided a welcome break. He always offered tired travelers a good pot of hot coffee, which he advertised as "the best coffee around." Soon his store became well known as a place to stop for hot coffee and the surrounding area became known as Hot Coffee, too. In the 1920s, the name Hot Coffee began appearing on maps. Today, you can still see the road signs to Hot Coffee, but maybe it's not really "the best coffee around" any more.

Welcome to Hot Coffee

Welcome to LOST

There is a little village in Aberdeenshire, Scotland called Lost. (The name comes from the word *Lòsda* in Scottish Gaelic.) Visitors loved the name and local road signs were often stolen. In fact, the longest time a sign stayed there was for three months and the local government became so fed up with this that they decided to change the name to Lost Farm. However, the local people complained. "We're happy with the name," they said. "You mustn't change it." So the name wasn't changed and instead the council made the road signs stronger. Now people can't take the signs, but they can still have their photograph taken beside them.

The Turkish city Batman takes its name from a river and not from the comic book superhero. The river's name was probably inspired by the Bati Raman Mountain. However, there is still a connection with the Batman we've seen on the screen. In 2008, the mayor of Batman said that Christopher Nolan, the director of *The Dark Knight*, should have to pay money to the city for using the name Batman without permission. "There is only one Batman in the world," he said. "The American film producers used the name of our city without informing us." Of course, Nolan didn't have to pay, though. It's true that filmmakers can't steal information and ideas, but the name Batman has been around since the character was created in 1939.

Batman

34

TH!NK more

Workbook
Reading p32, Ex.1–6

5 Discuss as a class. Encourage students to refer back to the article on page 34 for inspiration.

6 Ask students to try to complete the sentences from memory before referring back to the article to check. Encourage them to underline the sentences in the reading text.
1 can 2 mustn't 3 can't
RULE: 4 can 5 can't; mustn't

7 After checking answers, point out that we often use *must* to tell ourselves to (not) do something, for example, *I must do more exercise*, or *I mustn't be late*.
1 mustn't talk, A 2 mustn't be, C
3 mustn't miss, D 4 mustn't run, B

8 Encourage students to use a variety of modal verbs, not just *can('t)* and *must(n't)*.
1 We don't have to wear uniforms.
2 You should / ought to buy a new phone.
3 You can use my laptop.
4 They must / have to work harder.
5 Can we play here?

Workbook p29

9 You could ask students to cover the definitions (a–h) and to work with a partner to try to work out the meanings from context.
1 d 2 f 3 e 4 h 5 b 6 a
7 c 8 g

10 If you're short on time, assign this exercise for homework.
1 name it 2 name … the game
3 big name 4 call … names
5 name the 6 what's … name
7 a name … herself
8 stage

Workbook p30

Pronunciation
Strong and weak forms: /ɒv/ and /əv/

Student's Book p120

Homework
Ask students to use the internet to research another unusual place name from around the world. They make a poster that shows their place, write a short text about it and how it got its name, and if necessary, give a translation. As a follow-up, students can bring the poster to the class and discuss which is the funniest name.

Some ideas include: *Dull* (Scotland) and *Chicken* (Alaska).

SPEAKING

5 **Work in pairs. Discuss these questions.**
1 Do you know how your town or city got its name?
2 What funny or unusual town names are there in your country?

GRAMMAR
can('t) / must(n't)

6 **Complete these sentences from the reading. Then complete the rule with *can*, *can't*, and *mustn't*.**
1 "You ______ choose a piece of land anywhere in Western Maryland."
2 "We're happy with the name. You ______ change it."
3 It's true that filmmakers ______ steal information and ideas.

RULE: To talk or ask about permission, we often use the modal verb [4] ______ . To say what isn't allowed, we often use [5] ______ or ______ .

7 **Complete the sentences with *mustn't* and the verbs. Then match them with the pictures.**

be | miss | run | talk

1 You ______ so loudly!
2 I ______ late.
3 I ______ the goal!
4 You ______ .

8 **Rewrite the sentences using modal verbs from this unit and the pronouns in parentheses. There is often more than one possible answer.**
0 Diving isn't allowed. (you) *You can't dive here.*
1 It isn't necessary for us to wear uniforms. (we)
2 It's a good idea to buy a new phone. (you)
3 It's OK for you to use my laptop. (you)
4 It's necessary for them to work harder. (they)
5 Are we allowed to play here? (we)

→ workbook page 29

VOCABULARY
Expressions with *name*

9 **Match the underlined expressions with the definitions.**
1 Tony Hawk is a big name in skateboarding.
2 He's upset because some of the other kids call him names.
3 Jay-Z isn't his real name – it's his stage name.
4 Fish, meat, vegetables, fruit – you name it, I eat it.
5 Look! It's what's-his-name / what's-her-name.
6 We want to get married, but we haven't named the day yet.
7 I know you don't want to take the exams, but it's the name of the game for college entry.
8 He made a name for himself as a great actor.

a decide the date of an event, often a wedding
b someone whose name I can't remember
c something necessary that you have to accept
d a person who is important or famous in their profession
e a name that an actor or musician uses in their profession
f use rude names about, or to, a person
g become known or respected by many people
h anything you say (or choose)

10 **Complete the missing word(s).**
1 She's been to Europe, Asia, and Australia – you ______ ______ , she's been there!
2 Hard work is the ______ of ______ ______ if you want to do well in your exams.
3 My uncle's a doctor. He's a ______ ______ in the field of cancer research.
4 Some of her classmates ______ her ______ . It's horrible for her.
5 You're engaged? That's great! When are you going to ______ ______ day?
6 Oh look! There's ______ -his- ______ – you know, that boy who lives on your street.
7 She made a ______ for ______ on a reality TV show and became a famous singer.
8 Bruno Mars is the ______ name of Pete Gene Hernandez.

→ workbook page 30

PRONUNCIATION
Strong and weak forms: /ɒv/ and /əv/
Go to page 120.

Language notes *can('t) / must(n't)*
We use *mustn't* or *can't* to describe something that is not allowed. We use *can't* to describe a rule, for example, *I can't speak Spanish in class*. We use *mustn't* when the speaker is setting the rule, for example, *You mustn't eat so much dessert*.

We often use *can* in questions to ask if something is permitted. For example: *Can I go to Matt's party?* However, *must* is rarely used in the question form: ~~*Must I help with the dishes?*~~ *Do I have to help with the dishes?*

Activity idea Extension
Ask students to discuss what the class rules are and elicit sentences with *can*, *can't*, *must*, and *mustn't*; for example, *We must speak in English*; *We mustn't look at our cell phones*; *We can't eat*. Ask students to write a set of rules to display on the classroom wall.

TH!NK more
Practice Extra
Unit 3 Practice it!

Workbook
Grammar p29, Ex.7 Vocabulary p30, Ex.3–5
Pronunciation p118

Worksheets
Grammar Worksheets 3
Vocabulary Worksheets 3

Fiction; Reading

Warmer

In pairs, give students three minutes to brainstorm different genres of books. Write their ideas on the board to refer to later. Then ask students to swap pairs and give them another three minutes to think of a book title for each genre.

1 Check/Clarify: *doppelgänger.* Before reading the introduction, focus attention on the cover of the book and ask students what type of story they think it is and what they think it's about. Ask them to read the introduction to check.

It's a mystery story.

2 3.07 Tell students not to worry about difficult vocabulary at this stage and encourage them just to find the answers to the questions. If students are struggling, go through the first paragraph with them line by line to make sure they understand the significance of Szabó.

Szabó means "tailor." It's important for John because his last name is Taylor.

Fiction

1 Read the introduction. What kind of story is this?

How I Met Myself

by David A. Hill

John Taylor is an Englishman living in Budapest with his wife and daughter. One day, he is knocked over in the street by a man who looks exactly like him – his "doppelgänger."
He starts to look for more information about the man, and learns that he is a Hungarian called János Szabó. But he also learns that Szabo died in the 1956 Hungarian Revolution.

2 3.07 Read and listen to the extract. What does the Hungarian word *szabó* mean in English? Why is this important for John?

The next day, I was walking home from work. [...] As I went along a street, I saw some men putting up a new sign on an old shop. There was the owner's name in red, and below it the word *szabó* in green. In the window, there were suits, jackets, and trousers. *Szabó*. Tailor. The tailor's was getting a new sign. "*Szabó*," I thought. Then I said, "János Szabó" out loud. Then I thought, "Janos the tailor. John the tailor. John Taylor." I stopped in the street. János Szabó was John Taylor! My doppelgänger and I shared a name. John Taylor was the English for the Hungarian János Szabó. My hair stood up. Here was something new and important: we shared the same name!

I [...] thought about what I had discovered. I tried to decide what to do. Should I tell Andrea about this? Perhaps it would help her to believe me? I didn't know. [...] I decided to go and see Mrs. Fischer again. I walked quickly round to [...] her flat.

"Do you remember I came to ask you about János Szabó, Mrs. Fischer?" I asked when she let me in.

"Oh, the poor young man," she said, looking at me sadly. "And do you know something – you look so like him, too."

This was quite a surprise. "Really?" I asked.

"Come here under the light," she said.

I moved under the strong light in the hall.

"Yes," she said, looking at me carefully. "You look very much the same. The eyes, the nose, the mouth. Very much the same. I didn't look at you carefully when you came last time. Oh, the poor young man."

I felt myself getting very hot.

"Mrs. Fischer, I came to ask you something different," I said. Then I went on very slowly, because I was so afraid of her possible answer. "Can you remember the names of the wife and daughter who were killed in the cellar?"

"Well, I know the wife was called Andrea," she started and I felt my face go white, "but as for the little girl ... let's think ..."

I waited for a moment. She didn't seem able to remember.

"It wasn't ..." I waited, and then said, "It wasn't Kati, was it?"

Mrs. Fischer looked at me and smiled. "Yes, that was it," she said. "Quite right. Andrea and Kati. The poor young things."

I thanked her and left as quickly as I could. My head was turning round and round. I felt sick. Outside in the cold street, I stood against the wall of the building. There were too many new things inside my head to understand at once: my doppelgänger had the same name as me – Szabó, or Taylor – I looked like him and his wife and daughter had the same names as mine!

36

Activity idea Extension

In pairs, ask students to think of a famous book that other students are likely to know and ask them to write down five words that are key to describing the plot of the story. Collect these and read some out to the class; for example, "Boy and grandad visit factory." The rest of the class guess which book it is (*Charlie and the Chocolate Factory*). If your students are struggling, you can give them some of these ideas:

"A giant hears Sophie's dreams." *The BFG*

"Spider makes friends with pig." *Charlotte's Web*

"Boys trapped on an island." *Lord of the Flies*

"Doctor plays God, creates monster." *Frankenstein*

"Girl falls in rabbit hole." *Alice in Wonderland*

"Teenager with autism turns detective." *Curious Incident Of The Dog In The Night-Time*

"Poor man fights with windmills." *Don Quixote*

"Oh yikes! A hungry dinosaur." *Jurassic Park*

"Man is huge then tiny." *Gulliver's Travels*

3 1F 2T 3T 4T 5T 6F

4 Encourage students to express themselves in English and to use any vocabulary they have learned from the extract.

1 Suggested answers:
1 Alan's problem is the boy next door because he calls other kids names and makes horrible comments.
2 Susannah suggests that he ask himself if he could be friends with the boy if his behavior was better.

2 During feedback, take the opportunity to review the use of modal verbs.
1 ought to 2 you'd better
3 should definitely 4 had better
5 it's a good idea

3 Encourage students to underline key text in the reply.
1 Paragraph 3 2 Paragraph 1
3 Paragraph 4 4 Paragraph 2

4 You could pair weaker students so that they can write collaboratively. Ask students to write full sentences and to try to include a modal verb in each one.

5 Students should expand on the sentences they wrote in Exercise 4 and follow the same paragraph format as in Exercise 3.

Homework

If you are short on time, students can do Exercise 5 for homework.
If you have done this in class, ask students to exchange their texts with another student for them to read and give feedback on content and structure. Students could check if the reply uses the same structure as the template.

Activity idea Mixed ability

In Exercise 2, weaker students refer to the letter and reply in order to complete the sentences. Stronger students complete the blank spaces from memory before checking in the letter and reply.

3 **Read the extract again. Mark the statements T (true) or F (false).**
1 John Taylor goes into a store to buy a suit. ☐
2 He realizes that János Szabó is a translation of John Taylor. ☐
3 John's wife Andrea doesn't believe something he told her. ☐
4 It is not the first time he has talked to Mrs. Fischer. ☐
5 He is scared to ask Mrs. Fischer about the wife and daughter's names. ☐
6 He is happy when he leaves Mrs. Fischer's apartment. ☐

4 SPEAKING **Work in pairs. Discuss these questions.**
1 Why does Mrs. Fischer call Szabó "the poor young man?"
2 What do you think happened in the cellar?
3 What might happen next to solve this mystery?
4 Would you like to meet someone who looks exactly like you and has the same name? Why or why not?

WRITING
A reply to a letter asking for advice

1 INPUT **Read the letter and the reply. Then answer the questions.**
1 What is Alan's problem?
2 What question does Susannah suggest that Alan asks himself?

2 **Complete the missing words from Susannah's reply.**
1 This is the first question you ______ ______ ask yourself.
2 If the answer is no, then maybe ______ ______ end the friendship now.
3 ... you ______ ______ talk to him about the name-calling ...
4 ... and explain that he ______ ______ stop saying those things.
5 Finally, ______ ______ ______ ______ to talk to your parents.

3 ANALYZE **Read Susannah's reply again. In which paragraph does she ...**
1 offer advice to make the friendship work?
2 outline Alan's problem?
3 tell him to speak to others about his problem?
4 ask Alan to think more carefully about the situation?

4 PLAN **Read another letter to Susannah. Write three pieces of advice for Lara.**

5 PRODUCE **Write a reply to Lara (150–200 words). Say what you think she should do.**

SUSANNAH'S
ADVICE PAGE

Write with your problem and Susannah will give you advice. This week's letters are from Alan in Houston, Texas and Lara in Santa Fe, New Mexico.

Dear Susannah,
Last month, we moved to a new town. My parents quickly made friends with the people who live next door. They have a son about my age. He's friendly and invites me to do things with him. But the thing is, when we see other kids, he calls them names and makes horrible comments. He wants me to join in, but I don't want to.
What can I do? If I tell my parents, it'll be hard because they really like his parents. And to be honest, I don't have many other friends yet. If I stop hanging out with him, maybe he'll start calling me names, too.
What should I do?
Alan, Houston, Texas

Dear Alan,
It's often difficult to make new friends when you move to a new town, so it was almost perfect that your new neighbors had a son your age and that he wanted to be your friend. What a shame that you're finding it difficult to spend time with him.
You don't say in your letter if you think you could be friends if his behavior was better. This is the first question you ought to ask yourself. If the answer is no, then maybe you'd better end the friendship now. Don't worry – I'm sure you'll soon make lots of friends when you start school.
However, if you think you could be friends, then you should definitely talk to him about the name-calling and explain that he had better stop saying those things. If he's going to be a good friend, he'll listen to you. If he ignores you, then this friendship probably isn't going to work.
Finally, it's a good idea to talk to your parents. They're the people who know you best and are often the best people to give you advice.
Good luck!
Susannah

Dear Susannah,
I have very bad eyesight and need to wear glasses. Because of this, some people at school call me names. I tried not to let it bother me too much, but the problem is that it happens a lot. I've always enjoyed school and had lots of friends, but I'm starting to hate going there. My grades are also getting worse and some of the teachers have said they're disappointed with me. I know I should talk to the teachers, but I'm sure this is only going to make things worse. Can you help?
Lara, Santa Fe, New Mexico

37

TH!NK more

Practice Extra
Unit 3 Master it!

Workbook
Developing Writing p33

Tests
Unit, extension, and skills test 3
End of term test 1

Warmer

Tell students an anecdote that features a dilemma. For example: *I go to my friend's house. She's getting ready, so she tells me to wait in the living room. There is a letter under a book on the table, and I can read the first line. It says, "Dear [FRIEND'S NAME]. I can't believe what you did." I don't know what to do. Should I read the rest of the letter?*

Explain that this is a *dilemma*.
Ask students to work with a partner and discuss what they would do in this situation. Elicit their ideas in open class.

▶ 09 Get TH!NKing

Play the video and discuss the question with your class.

1 Explain that there could be more than one possible answer in each case. Invite students to share their ideas with the rest of the class, but do not give the answers yet.

2 Set a two-minute time limit to encourage students to read quickly and focus on the task rather than trying to understand every word.
A4 B5 C6 D2

3 🔊 **4.01 Check/clarify:** *homeless person, legal, referee, dent, principal.*
During feedback, find out how many students got mostly As, Bs, or Cs.

4 a3 b2 c5 d6 e1 f4

4 WHAT WOULD YOU DO?

OBJECTIVES

FUNCTIONS: talking about hypothetical situations; expressing wishes; apologizing and accepting apologies

GRAMMAR: first and second conditional (review); time conjunctions; *wish* and *if only*; third conditional (review)

VOCABULARY: being honest; making a decision; *now*

Get TH!NKING
Watch the video and think:
are you always honest with your friends?

READING

1 Read the definition. Then look at the pictures. What dilemmas do you think they show?

dilemma: a situation in which a difficult choice has to be made between two or more alternatives

2 Read the quiz on the next page quickly. Match each picture with a question.

3 🔊 4.01 Read and listen to the quiz. Then take the quiz and compare with a partner.

4 Match these responses with the quiz questions.

a I'd keep quiet and run back to the middle of the field. ☐
b I'd ask if I could exchange it for another one. ☐
c I wouldn't look because I'd be scared of getting caught. ☐
d I'd tell the person who did it that they should tell the truth. ☐
e I'd put it in my pocket as quickly as I could. ☐
f I'd make the door dirty to try to cover it up. ☐

38

Objectives

Functions and speaking Talking about hypothetical situations; expressing wishes; apologizing and accepting apologies

Grammar First and second conditional (review); time conjunctions; *wish* and *if only*; third conditional (review)

Vocabulary Being honest; making a decision; **WordWise:** Phrases with *now*

Life Competencies Acting on instinct

Train to TH!NK Thinking of consequences

Values Doing the right thing

Resources for this unit

All available online

Videos
- Get **TH!NK**ing: *Are you always honest with your friends?*
- Grammar rap!: *wish* and *if only*
- Vlog: Acting on instinct

Tests
- Unit, extension, and skills test 4

Worksheets
- Grammar and vocabulary: Basic, Standard, and Extension Worksheets
- Project: What would you do?
- Communication: Dilemmas
- Literature Worksheets: *Tom Jones*
- Get **TH!NK**ing, Grammar rap!, and Life Lessons video Worksheets

5 Give a couple of your own ideas as examples before students work in pairs. You could divide the class into two groups (A and B) and ask pairs in group A to think of consequences for situations 1–3 and pairs in group B for situations 4–6 before regrouping As with Bs to report back on the consequences they came up with.

6 Encourage students to express their real opinions, but to use English to do so. Monitor, but avoid correcting mistakes unless these really hinder comprehension. The focus of this task is on fluency, not controlled language practice.

Homework

Ask students to write three more questions for the quiz, each with A, B, and C answer options. They can bring them to the next lesson for partners to read and respond to them.

Activity idea Extension

Ask pairs to rank the situations in the quiz from most to least serious. Students then compare with another pair and try to agree on a ranking in their group of four. To extend fluency practice, write these questions on the board for students to discuss in their groups: *What would you really do in the six situations? Would you do something different from the options in the quiz?*

HOW HONEST ARE YOU?

Take our quiz! For each question choose A, B, or C.

What would you do if ...

1 you gave a $10 bill to buy a $5 item, but the cashier gave you $15 change by mistake?
A I'd take the money and walk out quickly.
B I'd tell the cashier he had made a mistake and give ten dollars back.
C I'd take the money and give it to a homeless person.

2 your grandparents gave you a shirt as a present, but you didn't like it?
A I'd say "thank you" but never wear the shirt.
B I'd say "thank you" but tell them it really wasn't my style.
C I'd say "thank you" but only wear it when I was with them.

3 you scored a goal in a soccer game, but you knew it wasn't legal because the ball had hit your hand without the referee seeing it?
A I'd celebrate my goal in the usual way.
B I'd tell the referee that the ball hit my hand, so it wasn't a goal.
C I'd say sorry to the players on the other team, but tell them it was the referee's mistake, not mine.

4 you kicked a rock outside your house and it made a dent in the neighbor's car door?
A I wouldn't do anything.
B I'd ring my neighbor's doorbell and tell them I'd damaged their car.
C I'd tell the neighbors that their car was damaged, but I didn't know who did it.

5 you couldn't answer a question on a test, but you realized you could see another student's answer?
A I'd try to copy their answer.
B I wouldn't look, but would just try to answer the question myself.
C I'd look a little bit to help myself think more clearly.

6 your school principal wanted to know who broke a classroom window and you knew who the person was?
A I wouldn't say anything.
B I'd go to the principal's office and say who did it.
C I'd write a note to the principal, saying who did it but without putting my name on the note.

RESULTS

MOSTLY A: Sometimes you take the easy way out. Be careful, because it may cause you problems. You don't want people to think of you as dishonest.

MOSTLY B: You're basically an honest person. You understand that if you always tell the truth, people will trust you. But don't forget that the truth can hurt a little, too, sometimes!

MOSTLY C: Maybe you should ask yourself why you are taking this middle path between being dishonest and being completely honest? Maybe you'd feel better if you always acted 100% honestly.

Train to TH!NK

Thinking of consequences

In order to make a good decision, it's important to think of all the possible consequences for others and for yourself.

5 **Choose four of the questions in the quiz. Think of possible consequences for each option.**

Question	Action	Consequence
1	*I tell the man about his mistake.*	*I don't get an extra $10.*
	I take the money.	*Maybe the man loses that money from his wages that week.*

SPEAKING

6 **Work in pairs. Discuss these questions.**
1 Which of the situations in the quiz is the most / least serious?
2 Do you agree with what the results say about you?

39

Social Responsibilities
Understanding and discussing global issues – environmental, political, financial, and social
Understands how personal habits and behavior have the capacity to affect others and the environment.

TH!NK more

Worksheets
Project What would you do?
Communication Dilemmas
Get **TH!NK**ing *Are you always honest with your friends?*

Warmer

Test students on their simple past irregular verbs.

1 Ask students to try to answer the questions from memory before referring back to page 39 to check.
1 would … do; kicked; made
2 tell; will trust RULE: 2, 1

2 During feedback, check students' understanding by asking: *Is this a real or an imaginary situation?* (imaginary – in reality, Jan is mean to me).
1 wasn't/weren't 2 'd want
3 didn't have 4 would care
5 don't invite 6 will come
7 don't have 8 won't get
9 wasn't/weren't 10 wouldn't be
11 knew 12 'd do

Workbook p36

3 Ask pairs to discuss the meaning of each of the conjunctions. Listen to some of their ideas during feedback. Elicit/explain that: *as soon as* = at exactly the same moment; *when* = at or around the same moment; *unless* = if not; *until* = up to a point in time; *if* introduces a condition.
1 if 2 when 3 as soon as
4 unless 5 until

4 If you're short on time, assign this exercise for homework.

Workbook p36

Get it Right!
if vs. *when*

Student's Book p124

5 During feedback, check understanding of the expressions by eliciting example sentences from the students.

GRAMMAR
First and second conditional (review)

1 Complete these sentences from the quiz on page 39 with the correct forms of the verbs. Then match them with the parts of the rule.

1 What ______ you ______ (do) if you ______ (kick) a stone and it ______ (make) a dent in the neighbor's car door?
2 If you always ______ (tell) the truth, people ______ (trust) you.

RULE:
We use the first conditional to talk about real situations and their consequences. We form it with *if* + simple present / future (*will*) clause. ☐
We use the second conditional to talk about hypothetical or very unlikely situations and their outcomes. We form it with *if* + simple present / (*would*) clause. ☐

2 Complete the conditional sentences with the correct forms of the verbs. Think carefully about whether each one is a first or second conditional.

What should I do?

Why is Jan so mean to me? If Jan [1]______ (not be) so mean to me, I [2]______ (want) to invite her to my party. The problem is, she's so popular. If she [3]______ (not have) so many friends, nobody [4]______ (care) if she was at my party or not. I have to invite her. If I [5]______ (not invite) Jan to my party, nobody [6]______ (come) to it.
Maybe I shouldn't have a party. But if I [7]______ (not have) a party, I [8]______ (not get) any presents and I want presents! Why are birthdays always so much trouble? If it [9]______ (not be) my birthday next week, my life [10]______ (not be) so complicated. If I [11]______ (know) what to do, I [12]______ (do) it. But I don't!

→ workbook page 36

Time conjunctions

3 Complete the sentences with the words.

as soon as | if | unless | until | when

1 I don't know where he is, but I'll tell him ______ I see him.
2 I'm meeting him later, so I'll tell him ______ I see him.
3 It's really important. I'm going to tell him ______ I see him.
4 I won't tell him anything ______ he asks.
5 I'll work ______ he arrives and then I'll stop.

4 Complete the sentences so that they are true for you. Tell your partner.

1 As soon as I get home tonight, I …
2 If the weather is good this weekend, I …
3 When I'm 18, I …
4 Unless I get lots of homework this weekend, I …
5 I'm going to save all my money until …

→ workbook page 36

VOCABULARY
Being honest

5 Write the words in the correct columns.

cheat | get away with something | hide the truth | do the right thing | tell a lie | be open about something | tell the truth | own up to something

Positive behavior	Negative behavior
	cheat

6 Compete the conversation with the correct form of the verbs from Exercise 5.

Dan I have a dilemma. The other day I [1]______ on a test. I copied from Ben.
Ana Why?
Dan Well, I thought I could [2]______ away with it, but now the teacher wants to know who copied who. I said it was Ben.
Ana You should [3]______ up to it and say it was you.
Dan I know, but it's too difficult to [4]______ the truth.
Ana But you can't [5]______ the truth now! What about poor Ben? What were you thinking?
Dan It's math. I just find it so difficult.
Ana Well, you need to [6]______ about this. First, say you're sorry for cheating and explain why you [7]______ a lie. Then tell your teacher what the problem is.
Dan You're right, of course. It's just so difficult to [8]______ the right thing sometimes.

→ workbook page 38

40

Positive behavior: do the right thing, be open about something, tell the truth, own up to something
Negative behavior: get away with something, hide the truth, tell a lie

6 Before doing the exercise, ask students the following questions to check general understanding: *What did Dan do?* (He cheated on a test by copying from a classmate's paper.) *What does Ana think he should do now?* (She thinks he should tell the teacher what he did.)
1 cheated 2 get 3 own 4 tell 5 hide 6 be open 7 told 8 do

Workbook p38

THINK more

Workbook
Grammar p36, Ex.1–5
Vocabulary p38, Ex.1–2
Vocabulary Extra p39, Ex.1–3

Worksheets
Grammar Worksheets 4
Vocabulary Worksheets 4

Language note First and second conditional (review)

Write on the board: *If I found a handbag, I'd take it to the police station.* Ask students: *Did I find a handbag?* (no); *Is the situation real or imagined?* (imagined) Elicit that this is an example of the second conditional and that we form it with the simple past and *would* + base form.

Write this first conditional sentence on the board: *If I see John later, I'll buy him a cup of coffee.* Ask students: *Is it possible that I will see John later?* (yes); *What do I plan to do if I see John?* (buy him a cup of coffee).

Point out that in the first conditional, we use *If* + present to talk about the future, and in the second conditional, we use *If* + past to talk about an imaginary situation.

7 Students discuss in pairs, then as a class.

8 4.02
They're waiting for a bus. They decide to play a game.

9 4.02 Before listening, ask students to underline key information in the questions.
1 B 2 B 3 C 4 C 5 A

▶ 10 Grammar rap! *wish* and *if only*

10 Point out that the use of the simple past tense in 1 is similar to its use in the second conditional. It refers to a hypothetical, in this case, a wish about a present situation. When checking answers, write the character names on the board to show correct spelling.
1 R2-D2 2 Gollum 3 Gru RULE: 4 simple past 5 could 6 would

11 1 was/were 2 liked 3 had 4 didn't have 5 could go 6 would knock

12 Invite students to share their answers with the rest of the class during feedback.

Workbook p37

Homework

Ask students to write three wishes of their own.

Culture notes

Gollum is a fictional character in J.R.R. Tolkien's fantasy novels *The Hobbit* and *The Lord of the Rings*. He was corrupted by a malevolent ring of power. Throughout the books, Gollum both loved the Ring and wanted to escape its power.

Felonious Gru is the main character in the *Despicable Me* film series, voiced by Steve Carell. At the beginning of the first film, Gru is a villain but later becomes a father and secret agent.

R2-D2 is a fictional droid in the famous George Lucas *Star Wars* films. He appears at various points throughout the series as a friend to several of the main characters and along with his companion C-3PO, is the only character to appear in all nine of the main *Star Wars* movies.

LISTENING

7 SPEAKING **Work in pairs. Look at the photo. What do you think they are doing?**

8 4.02 **Listen to the conversation. Were you right? What did they decide to do?**

9 4.02 **Listen again. Choose the correct answers.**

1 Why are the teenagers there?
A they are going on a long trip
B they are waiting for a friend
C they are going home

2 What do they decide to play?
A a card game invented by Angie
B a guessing game invented by Stuart
C a traditional children's game

3 Why does Maria say, "a cartoon animal, perhaps"?
A because animals aren't usually tall
B because the game can only have fictional characters
C because Stuart is thinking of a non-human character

4 Why does Angie give three clues at the same time?
A because Jenny's bus is arriving
B because she wants to make the game easier
C because she's bored with the game

5 Why is Angie wrong to make Gru say, "I wish I could steal the Moon"?
A because in the movie, Gru steals the Moon
B because in the movie, Gru doesn't steal the Moon
C because Angie is reading *The Lord of the Rings*

Grammar rap!

GRAMMAR
wish and *if only*

10 **Read the sentences. Which fictional characters might say them? Complete the rule. Use the sentences to help you.**

1 "If only I **spoke** Luke Skywalker's language."
2 "I wish I **could** get the ring back."
3 "I wish those three girls **would** go to sleep."

RULE:
- We use *wish / if only* + the [4] ______ tense to express how we would like our current situation to be different.
- We use *wish / if only* + [5] ______ to say that we'd like the ability to do something.
- We use *wish / if only* + [6] ______ to say that we'd like something to happen or someone (else) to do something.

Look
We can use *was* or *were* after a singular subject (*I, he, she* or *it*) when we express wishes.
I wish I was older. / I wish I were older.

11 **Complete the sentences with the correct forms of the verbs.**

be | go | have | knock | like | not have

1 I wish I ______ taller.
2 I wish you ______ me more.
3 If only I ______ a more interesting book to read.
4 I wish I ______ this awful headache.
5 If only I ______ to sleep.
6 I wish you ______ before you come into my room!

12 SPEAKING **Play "famous wishes" in groups of four.**
- Choose a famous fictional person and write three wishes. (Remember: they should be about the present situation, not the past.)
- Read your sentences out loud. The other students have to guess who you are.

→ workbook page 37

Language note *wish* and *if only*

While we can use *if only* to replace *I wish* with the same meaning, *if only* is more emphatic and can sound rather dramatic – *If only he would call me!*

We use *wish / if only + would(n't)* when we don't like something that another person does, like *I wish my dad would stop calling me Buttercup* or *I wish John wouldn't say bad things about me.* We cannot say *I wish I would …*

We don't normally use *would* with stative verbs, like **If only I would have an interesting book with me.*

TH!NK more

Workbook
Listening p42, Ex.1–4 Grammar p37, Ex.6–7

Worksheets
Grammar rap! *wish* and *if only*
Grammar Worksheets 4

Warmer

Test students on their past participles.

1 4.03 Tell students not to focus on understanding every word for now, but to focus on listening to match.
A 2 B 1 C 3

2 1 Jimmy James 2 The manager of the store in Seattle 3 Luis Lopez's lawyer 4 The family member that Jimmy James gave the card to 5 A guard at the prison in Florida 6 The person who stole $25 from the store in Seattle

3 At the end of the exercise, listen to some of the students' ideas and encourage open class discussion.

4 Ask students to try to answer the questions from memory before referring back to the text to check.
1 hadn't gone; would have had 2 had put; would have grown RULE: 3 past perfect 4 past participle

5 During feedback, point out that the *if* clause and *would* clause can be reversed and that in this case, a comma is not required. Demonstrate using the example sentence:

If the court hadn't made a mistake, Lopez wouldn't have left prison early.

Lopez wouldn't have left prison early if the court hadn't made a mistake.

1 had released; would have known
2 had kept; wouldn't have gotten

6 You may like to give an example from your own experience to get students started on this exercise.

Workbook p37

READING

1 4.03 **Read and listen to the stories. Match the stories (1–3) with the pictures (A–C).**

2 **Read the stories again. Who do you think said these things?**
1 "I found this in your trash."
2 "I was very surprised when I read the letter."
3 "They let you out too soon."
4 "It's incredible that you brought it back to us."
5 "OK, you can go now."
6 "It was a long time ago, but I've always been sorry for what I did."

3 SPEAKING **Work in pairs. Decide what you would have done in each situation. Then compare with other students.**

A

B

C

HOW HONEST IS THAT?

1 MAKING IT RIGHT – MANY YEARS LATER
The manager of a store in Seattle was very surprised one day in 2011 when a man came in, gave him an envelope, and left. The manager opened the envelope and found a $100 bill and a short letter. The letter said, "I stole $25 from this store in 1961. Now that I have some money, I want to give it back. If you had put it in the bank, it would have grown to $100. So here it is."
The newspapers wanted to know who the man was, but the manager didn't release his name.

2 BACK TO PRISON
In 2011, Luis Lopez was sent to prison in Florida for a year. After three months, the prison guards came and told him he could go home. Amazed, Lopez asked the guards if they were sure – they said "yes," so he left. But it didn't feel right to Lopez, so when he got home, he called his lawyer. The lawyer told him that in fact the local court had made a mistake. He advised Lopez to go back and finish his prison sentence – and that's what he did. If he hadn't gone back to prison, he would have had bigger problems.

3 A LITTLE MONEY, A LOT OF HONESTY
Every now and then, people throw things away by mistake. One day, garbage collector Jimmy James found a $50 store gift card in the trash outside a home. He went on working, but later that day, Jimmy went back to the house, rang the doorbell, and gave the family the card. They were very surprised because $50 didn't seem like a lot of money to them. But Jimmy just said he thought it was the right thing to do. The family gave him a $75 reward to say thank you.

42

GRAMMAR
Third conditional (review)

4 **Complete these sentences from the story with the correct forms of the verbs. Then complete the rule.**
1 If Lopez ________ (not go) back to prison, he ________ (have) bigger problems.
2 If you ________ (put) it in the bank, it ________ (grow) to $100.

RULE:
We use the third conditional to talk about imagined situations and their outcomes in the past. We form it with:
if + [3] ______ + *would(n't) have* + [4] ______.

5 **Complete the third conditional sentences.**
0 If the court *hadn't made* a mistake, Lopez *wouldn't have left* prison early.
1 If the store ________ (release) the video, everyone ________ (know) the man's name.
2 If Jimmy James ________ (keep) the card, he ________ (not get) the reward.

6 **Complete the sentences so that they are true for you.**
1 If I hadn't gone to school today, …
2 I'd have been really happy if …
3 If I'd been born 100 years ago, …

→ workbook page 37

Activity idea Extension

Write these sentence endings on the board: … , *my mother wouldn't have made me stay at home.* … , *they would have won the Championship.* … , *I would have been very happy.* … , *they wouldn't have got married.* … , *it wouldn't have broken.*

Elicit that each of these is the consequence of an imaginary past event and that students now need to choose an imagined event. Elicit that students should use *if* + past perfect to complete the sentences.

Language note Third conditional (review)

Would always appears in the main clause, not the *if* clause.

~~*If you would have remembered your list, you would have known what to buy at the store.*~~

If you had remembered your list, you would have known what to buy at the store.

TH!NK more

Workbook
Reading p40, Ex.1–5
Grammar p37, Ex.8–9

Worksheets
Grammar Worksheets 4

7 To give students an overall understanding of the text first, focus on the picture and ask: *What decision is the boy trying to make?* (whether to buy a red or blue T-shirt) Give them only 30 seconds to find the answer.
a 2 b 4 c 7 d 6 e 8 f 5 g 1 h 3

8 At the end of the exercise, listen to some of the students' ideas and encourage open class discussion.

Workbook p38

9 During feedback, elicit or explain the meaning of the five phrases and give further examples.
1 b 2 d 3 e 4 c 5 a

10 Encourage students to refer to the definitions from Exercise 9 to help them choose the correct word or phrase.
1 now 2 every now and then 3 just now 4 now 5 now that

Workbook p38

11 You may like to give an example from your own experience to get students started on this exercise.

12 Check understanding of the paragraph. Ask: *Did the writer sit next to the new student?* (yes); *Does she wish she hadn't?* (no); *Why?* (They're best friends now.) Point out the use of the third conditional.

13 If you feel your students might be demoralized by such a vote, you may want to limit the selection to just five paragraphs. Select paragraphs from your more confident students.

14 **Check/clarify:** *detention.* Encourage students to organize their writing as outlined in points 1, 2, and 3 and use some third conditional sentences.

Homework
Students can complete Exercise 14 for homework.

VOCABULARY
Making a decision

7 **Match a–h with the underlined words and phrases in the text below.**

a for a long time ☐
b a good ☐
c a bad ☐
d decide ☐
e make ☐
f thought again about ☐
g original idea ☐
h made a new decision ☐

My [1]first thought was to go with the blue. But then I thought [2]long and hard and [3]changed my mind. Maybe the red was better. But had I made [4]the right decision? Had I? I [5]reconsidered my choice. Red or blue? Red or blue? Why was it so difficult to [6]make up my mind? Well, I didn't want to make [7]the wrong decision, did I? So I called my sister. Maybe she could help me [8]come to a decision.
"I don't know why you're asking me," she said. "You only ever wear blue."

8 SPEAKING **Work in pairs. Discuss these questions.**
1 What's the biggest decision you've ever made?
2 Have you ever made the wrong decision? What was it?
3 How good are you at making your mind up about small things?
4 What sort of things do you usually need to think long and hard about?
5 Do you ever reconsider decisions you've made?
6 Who do you ask to help you come to important decisions?

→ workbook page 38

WordWise: Phrases with *now*

9 **Look at the words and phrases in bold in these sentences from the unit. Match them with the definitions.**
1 OK, you can go **now**.
2 **Now that** I have some money, I want to give it back.
3 **Every now and then**, people throw things away by mistake.
4 I looked at the station sign **just now**, but it doesn't say.
5 Do you want to give it a try **now**, Angie?

a in the near future
b at this moment
c a moment or two ago
d because finally
e sometimes

10 **Use words and phrases from Exercise 9 to complete the sentences.**
1 I finished my work, so _____ I'm going to hang out with my friends.
2 I don't listen to this music all the time, but _____ I like to play it.
3 Sally was here _____, but she's gone out.
4 I'll eat later. I'm not hungry _____.
5 I don't walk to school _____ I have a bike.

→ workbook page 38

TH!NK values
Doing the right thing

11 **Think about a time when you had to make a difficult decision. Make notes.**
1 What decision did you make?
2 What were the consequences?

12 **Write a short paragraph. Include a third conditional sentence.**
Last year, there was a new student in my class. Nobody wanted to sit next to him, so I did. I'm really happy I did. If I hadn't sat next to him, he wouldn't have become my best friend. What a good decision I made!

13 **Read your paragraph out to the class. Then vote on the best story.**

WRITING
A journal entry about a dilemma

14 **Choose one of these situations or use your own idea. Write a journal entry about it (150–200 words). Try to use language from this unit.**
1 Explain the problem.
2 Think about two possible solutions and their consequences.
3 Decide what you're going to do and why.
- You got detention. If you tell your parents, you won't be allowed to go to a party.
- It's your mom's birthday this weekend, but you spent all your money on clothes and don't have any left to buy her a present.
- You saw your best friend's boyfriend / girlfriend at the movies with another boy / girl.

Activity idea Extension
Ask students to write more third conditional sentences based on the stories, e.g. *If Jimmy had kept the gift certificate, …*

TH!NK more
Practice Extra
Unit 4 Practice it!
Workbook
Vocabulary p38, Ex.3–4
WordWise p38, Ex.5
Developing Writing p41
Worksheets
Vocabulary Worksheets 4

Emotional Development
Empathy and relationship skills
Shows understanding of other people's perspectives and feelings.

Developing Speaking; Phrases for fluency; Functions, Pronunciation

Warmer

Call out either the verb or the noun from the phrases for making a decision in Exercise 7 on page 43 and elicit the whole phrase. For example, you say: *make up* or *mind* and students say: *make up your mind*. Once you've demonstrated this with one or two examples, pairs take turns testing each other in the same way.

1 4.04 Tell students not to focus on understanding every word for now, but to focus on listening for the answer.

2 4.04
1 He can't decide which subject to choose, economics or Spanish.
2 He's worried that he might end up in an office job and isn't sure that's what he wants.
3 He isn't sure that he wants to live far away from home and is worried about what job he would do.
4 He thinks it isn't good.

3 At the end of the exercise, listen to some of the students' ideas and encourage open class discussion.

4 During feedback, say the sentences for students to repeat.
Students' own answers
1 A I was wondering if B Between you and me
2 A What's with B Believe it or not
3 A Any chance B Are you out of your mind

5 During feedback, ask students for an L1 translation.
Apologizing: I'm so ashamed. I feel awful about this. I don't know what to say. I'm so sorry.
Accepting apologies: No problem. That's/It's OK. Don't worry about it. No worries.

DEVELOPING SPEAKING

1 4.04 **Look at the photo. Who do you think the two people are and what are they talking about? Listen and read to check.**

Dad: What's with the sad face, Tom?
Tom: Well, I'm thinking about what to study if I go to college.
Dad: Well, I'd like to help if I can. Any chance?
Tom: Of course, Dad! Believe it or not, I really like it when we talk together.
Dad: Well, me too. OK, so if I remember correctly, you're torn between studying Spanish or economics.
Tom: Exactly. And between you and me, I'm pretty good at both. They just seem to lead in different directions.
Dad: How do you mean?
Tom: Well, if I go with economics, I think I'll end up in an office job. But do I want that?
Dad: And Spanish?
Tom: Well, then I could live in a Spanish-speaking country, like Peru or Ecuador, and that could be exciting. But do I want to live so far away? And what job would I do? Teaching? I don't know. It's a dilemma.
Dad: Listen, don't overthink it. There's no hurry. You have six months before you have to choose. And if you still can't decide – well, just go with your instincts.
Tom: Thanks, Dad. I'll do that. Can we keep talking about this?
Dad: Of course. Now Tom, I was wondering if you could help me with a dilemma. Should I cook dinner or should I ask you to?
Tom: Dad! Are you out of your mind? You're a terrible cook! I'll do it!

2 4.04 **Read and listen to the dialogue again. Answer the questions.**
1 What is Tom's dilemma?
2 What are his worries about studying economics?
3 What are his worries about studying Spanish?
4 What does he think of his father's cooking?

3 SPEAKING **Discuss the statements in pairs. What do you think?**
1 Tom's dilemma is an important one.
2 Tom should probably choose Spanish because then he can travel.
3 His father gives him good advice.

Phrases for fluency

4 **Find the underlined expressions in the dialogue. How do you say them in your language? Use the expressions to complete the mini-dialogues.**
1 A Andy, ______________ you could come and help me choose my next tattoo?
B Sorry, no. ______________, I don't think tattoos look good on you at all.
2 A Hi, Steve. Wow! ______________ those really old soccer cleats?
B They're ancient, aren't they? ______________, my dad used to wear them when he was in school. I need new ones.
3 A Listen, Jane. I love that new necklace of yours. ______________ I could borrow it tonight?
B ______________? It's really expensive! I wouldn't lend it to anyone!

FUNCTIONS
Apologizing and accepting apologies

KEY LANGUAGE
No problem.
That's / It's OK.
Don't worry about it.
I'm so ashamed.
I feel awful about this.
I don't know what to say.
No worries.
I'm so sorry.

5 **Write the expressions from the Key Language box in the correct columns.**

Apologizing	Accepting apologies

6 SPEAKING **Work in pairs. Imagine you're in these situations and act out conversations. Use expressions from the Key Language box.**
- A has spilled a drink on B's pants.
- A has arrived very late for a meeting with B.
- A has bumped into B and B has fallen down.
- A has completely forgotten B's name.

PRONUNCIATION
Consonant–vowel word linking Go to page 120.

44

6 Allow students six to eight minutes to prepare their role-plays. Monitor to make sure all students are on task. If students have access to a recording device (their cell phones, for example), they could record their conversation and play it back to check their own pronunciation and intonation. They can then repeat the exercise and listen for improvements.

Pronunciation
Consonant–vowel word linking

Student's Book p120

THINK more
Workbook
Pronunciation p119

Life Competencies

Warmer

Write *acting on instinct* on the board and elicit what it might mean. Encourage students to try and clarify its meaning through examples or explanation rather than through a translation. For example on page 42, Luis Lopez acted on his instinct when he called his lawyer to check whether or not he was really free to leave prison. Ask students to read the introductory paragraph to check their ideas. Elicit examples of people acting on instinct in Unit 4.

▶ 11 Life Lessons: Acting on instinct

1 **▶ 11 Check/clarify:** *dilemma, the pros and cons, flip a coin.* Ask students to compare their ideas with a partner.
She can't decide which of her two friends to invite on a beach trip.

2 **▶ 11** Ask students to try to answer the questions from memory before watching the video again to check.
1 She's a bit serious and not really into games. 2 She is very funny and makes Serena laugh. 3 She took it home with her. 4 Serena ate it. 5 She doesn't make one.

3 **Check/clarify:** *footpath.* Give students one minute to read the text and think of their answer. Encourage them not to focus on every word.

4 **Check/clarify:** *stranger, insisted, twisted her ankle, upset.*
A Ellie and Marta both got home safely. B Ellie had a frightening and upsetting experience on her own.

5 You may like to give your own example to get students started on this.
1 Students' own answers 2 Her instinct was to act on her anxiety about Ellie's safety by walking home with her. 3 She probably felt sorry/guilty that she hadn't acted on her instinct.

6 Monitor to help with any difficulties, but do not interrupt as this is a fluency activity.

LIFE COMPETENCIES

We all act on instinct at some point in our lives and acting on instinct can have positive or negative consequences.

1 Watch the vlog. What is Serena's dilemma?

2 Watch the vlog again and answer the questions.
1 What are the bad things about Mandy?
2 What are the good things about Nadia?
3 What did Serena do with the kitten on the street?
4 What happened with the cake in the fridge?
5 What is Serena's final decision?

3 Read the start of Marta's story. What do you think she should do?

Over summer vacation, my friends and I met up for a picnic and a game of soccer. We had a great day, the weather was good, and we all had fun. My friend Ellie needed to be home by 9 p.m., and by this time it was getting dark. The bike ride back to her house takes her along a quiet footpath in the woods and across a main road. Ellie was happy to walk back to her house by herself, but I felt worried about her.

TIPS FOR ACTING ON INSTINCT

- If something doesn't feel right, take some more time to think about it.
- If your friends are all doing one thing but you feel it isn't right, don't feel pressured into behaving in a way you don't agree with. If your instinct says "no," don't do it.
- Acting on instinct can be a good thing. If you think your actions will benefit or help someone else, go ahead and do what you feel!

4 Now read endings A and B. What was the result of Marta's actions in each ending?

A
It was nearly dark; what if she met a stranger in the woods or got lost? I said I would walk with her, and then we would call my dad from her house to pick me up. At first, Ellie said she was fine, she didn't want me to have to call my dad. But when I insisted I was worried about her, finally she agreed and we both got home safely.

B
It was getting dark, but I thought she'd think I was being silly if I told her how I felt. I asked her to text me when she got home. At 10 p.m., Ellie's mom called me. She was at the hospital with Ellie. On her way home, she had twisted her ankle, and couldn't walk on it. Because she was on her own, she had been frightened and upset, but she had managed to call her mom on her cell phone.

5 Answer the questions about the story.
1 How would you have acted in the situation?
2 What was Marta's instinct in ending A?
3 How do you think Marta feels in ending B?

Me and my world

6 SPEAKING Work in pairs. What is your instinct in each of the situations? Would you normally act on your instinct? Why or why not?
A You are at the local skate park. Your friend is about to do a dangerous jump. He's not wearing a helmet.
B You are with a group of friends. A few of them are being unkind to another friend in your group.
C You have always wanted to buy a particular thing, but it's very expensive. One day you see it on sale, 40% off the original price – but it's still more than you can really afford. Your friend offers to lend you the money to buy it.

Activity idea An interview

Students could act out an interview with either Marta or Ellie. Divide the class into four groups: A (Marta), B (Ellie), C (Reporter to Marta), and D (Reporter to Ellie). Ask groups C and D to look at the text again and write down five questions to ask Marta/Ellie. Ask group A to look at the texts again and find key information about Marta and group B about Ellie in preparation for an interview. Monitor to make sure all the students are making notes; help with ideas if necessary. Put the students in A/C and B/D pairs and give them time to act out the interview.

TH!NK more

Practice Extra
Unit 4 Master it!

Worksheets
Life Lessons: Acting on instinct

Tests
Unit, extension and skills test 4

Emotional Development
Managing own emotions
Managing and understanding emotions which lead to acting on instinct.

1 4.07 In B2 First for Schools Listening Part 1, there are eight short recordings, each with a question and three answer options. Candidates have to listen, then choose the option which best answers the question. This part of the exam requires candidates to listen for specific information.

Encourage your students to do the following when they approach this task:

- Read the question and the options for each question.
- During the first listening, listen for specific information, choosing the best option.
- During the second listening, check that the answer is correct, focusing on the key information.

1 B 2 B 3 A 4 C 5 B 6 B 7 A 8 C

Workbook p35

TOWARDS B2 First for Schools

LISTENING
Multiple choice

→ workbook page 35

1 4.07 **You will hear people talking in eight different situations. For questions 1–8, choose the best answer (A, B or C).**

1 You hear a boy talking about how he got his name. Why was it hard for his parents to name him?
A They each wanted different names.
B There weren't many possibilities for a name that worked in two languages.
C He was born two weeks early.

2 You hear a girl talking on her phone. What is her problem?
A She doesn't want to invite Lucy to her birthday celebration.
B Her mum said that Lucy can't come for a sleepover.
C She really wants to have a big party.

3 You hear part of an interview with a footballer. What does he find most difficult about his job?
A not being free at weekends
B having to work out every day
C the comments some of the fans make

4 You hear two friends talking about a camping trip. What advice does Alan give Steve?
A to take a comfortable sleeping bag
B to get a lift to the campsite
C not to take things that weigh too much

5 You hear a local news report. What did Clive Roberts think when he found the money?
A I'm £10,000 richer.
B How can I return this to the owner?
C Could I keep this? Would anybody ever know?

6 Two friends are talking about a party. Why did Chloë miss the party?
A Her dad said she had to go cycling with him.
B She fell asleep in the middle of the day.
C She was watching TV and forgot the time.

7 You hear a girl talking about a difficult decision. Why did she find it hard to choose which exams to take?
A She had no idea about what career she wanted to do.
B She didn't want to disappoint her dad.
C She wanted to make sure her exams would help her get a well-paid job.

8 You hear a book review on the radio. What did Carla like best about the book?
A that she was able to understand the story
B that it was a love story
C the way the characters developed during the story

WRITING
Story

→ workbook page 43

2 Your English teacher has asked you to write a short story for the school's new website. The story must begin or end with the following words:

I still don't know why I didn't tell the truth.

Write your story in 140–190 words.

2 In B2 First for Schools Writing Part 2, candidates are given a choice of four tasks, one of which is to write a story of 140–190 words. For the story, they are given a sentence and must use it either at the beginning or the end of their story. This part of the exam tests the candidates' ability to write well-organized texts with a real communicative purpose and good use of narrative tenses.

Encourage your students to do the following when they approach this task:

- Candidates should read all the tasks and consider the topic and the language that is needed in each before choosing the task that best suits them.
- For the chosen task, identify what is required, who it is for, and what kind of information is needed.
- Make a plan, referring closely to the question.
- Look for opportunities to develop ideas and show a range of language.
- Write a rough draft before writing the final answer. Make sure that it is well-organized and has a range of tenses, expressions, and vocabulary.
- Read the work again to check that it makes sense and that all the content points have been included. Check the spelling.

Workbook p43

1 1 make 2 products 3 cheat 4 name 5 get away with 6 call 7 logo 8 tell 9 chain 10 own up to

2 1 go 2 went 3 when 4 until 5 unless 6 better

3 1 ~~shouldn't to talk~~ shouldn't talk 2 ~~wouldn't be~~ weren't 3 ~~don't~~ didn't 4 ~~you~~ you'd 5 ~~had~~ would have 6 ~~can~~ could

4 1 ought; could stay 2 mustn't; I'd better not 3 can't; were 4 wouldn't have; we'd told

TEST YOURSELF UNITS 3 & 4

VOCABULARY

1 Complete the sentences with the words / phrases in the list. There are four extra words / phrases.

brand | call | chain | cheat | consumers | get away with | image | logo | manufacturer | make | name | own up to | products | tell

1 He worked hard for a long time before he started to __________ a name for himself in Hollywood.
2 The company was in trouble until they started making some new __________.
3 If you __________ during the exam, we'll take you out of the exam room and rip up your paper.
4 I like so many different kinds of fruit. Basically, you __________ it, I like it!
5 He tried to look at another boy's test, but the teacher saw him so he didn't __________ it.
6 Other kids used to __________ me names, but it never upset me.
7 Our website has been redesigned – and if you visit it, you'll see that we have a new __________, too.
8 It's not always easy, but it's important always to __________ the truth.
9 We started with just one store, but now we have a __________ of 20.
10 I know you took my things without asking. Why don't you just __________ it?

/10

GRAMMAR

2 Complete the sentences with the words in the list. There are two extra words.

better | go | if | ought | unless | until | went | when

1 It's pretty late – I think I have to __________ now, OK?
2 I really wish we __________ out to eat more often.
3 I'll call you __________ the movie finishes, OK?
4 I'm not going to bed __________ I finish this book – it's amazing!
5 You'll never be his friend __________ you go and talk to him!
6 It's a secret, so you'd __________ not tell anyone else!

3 Find and correct the mistake in each sentence.

1 You shouldn't to talk to a teacher like that. It isn't respectful.
2 If they wouldn't be so expensive, I'd buy those sneakers.
3 I wish you don't live so far away.
4 Your eye looks bad – I think you better go to the doctor.
5 If it hadn't rained, we had gone for a walk yesterday.
6 If only we can see you more often.

/12

FUNCTIONAL LANGUAGE

4 Choose the correct words.

1 **A** I think we *should / ought* to go now.
B That's a shame. If only you *could stay / stayed* a little longer.
2 **A** Listen, we *mustn't / don't have to* miss the last bus tonight.
B You're right. *I'd better not / I don't have to* forget to set an alarm on my phone.
3 **A** Sorry, but you *don't / can't* come in. You're too young!
B I know. But I really want to see the movie. I wish I *would be / were* 18 already!
4 **A** Patrick *wouldn't have / won't have* come to the party if he'd known Sue was going to be there.
B Yeah, it's a shame – if only *we'd told / we've told* him earlier.

/8

MY SCORE /30

22–30 | 10–21 | 0–9

47

The Cambridge Life Competencies Framework

Learning to Learn
Reflecting on learning
Watch this video for tips on how to help your students learn how to learn. Scan the QR code here.

Warmer

Ask the class to stand up. Nominate a student to say the name of a favorite book. Students who have read this book sit down. Keep going until everybody is sitting down.

▶ 12 Get TH!NKing

Play the video and discuss the question with your class.

1 Check/clarify: *thriller, grabbed, anecdote.*
To get students started on Exercise 1, give some examples of your own. Allow students three minutes to think of an example of each of the four things.

2 As a follow-up, students can discuss the statements as a class and come up with a definitive list. Write their ideas on the board.

3 🔊 **5.01** Tell students not to worry about unknown words but to focus on getting an overall understanding of the main points of the article and checking which of their "ingredients" were mentioned.

4 Check/clarify: *novel, self-belief, plot, conflict, struggle, presumably.*
Ask students to try to answer the questions from memory before looking back at the article to check. Encourage them to underline the key parts of the text that gave them their answers.
1 B 2 C 3 C 4 C 5 A

5 STORYTELLING

OBJECTIVES

FUNCTIONS: telling a story

GRAMMAR: relative pronouns; defining and non-defining relative clauses; relative clauses with *which*

VOCABULARY: elements of a story; types of story

Get TH!NKING Watch the video and think: what makes a really good story?

READING

1 SPEAKING **Think of an example of each of these things. Then work in pairs and share one or two of your ideas.**
- a story or a favorite fairy tale from your childhood
- a favorite movie
- a thriller (either a book or a movie) that really grabbed you
- an anecdote or a joke you've heard recently

2 SPEAKING **What are the ingredients of a good story? Discuss with a partner. Then compare your ideas with the rest of the class.**

3 🔊 5.01 **Read and listen to the article on the next page. Were your ideas the same as the writer's?**

4 **Choose the correct answers to the questions.**

1 What advice does the writer give about getting started?
A Think carefully about how all the events in the story will develop.
B Choose your best idea and just start writing.
C Write the first thing that comes into your head.

2 What does the writer say is important for a good plot?
A a happy ending
B a fight between good and bad
C a situation where there is conflict

3 What does the writer suggest about the theme of a novel?
A You should try to make it as clever as possible.
B It is more important than your plot.
C Your reader should work it out for themselves.

4 What does the writer suggest about the characters?
A Get to know them as you write.
B Make sure you tell your reader exactly what they look like.
C Let them make mistakes.

5 What advice does he give about writing style?
A Keep your reader in mind.
B Take your time to think of the right words.
C Try to copy the style that other writers use.

48

Objectives

Functions and speaking Telling a story
Grammar Relative pronouns; defining and non-defining relative clauses; relative clauses with *which*
Vocabulary Elements of a story; types of story
Culture Storytelling in the Caribbean
Train to TH!NK Thinking about different writing styles

Resources for this unit

All available online

Videos
- Get TH!NKing: *What makes a really good story?*
- Grammar rap!: Relative pronouns
- Culture: Storytelling in the Caribbean

Tests
- Unit, extension, and skills test 5

Worksheets
- Grammar and vocabulary: Basic, Standard, and Extension Worksheets
- Project: Great books
- Communication: What a story!
- Literature Worksheets: *Tom Jones*
- Grammar presentation: Defining and non-defining relative clauses
- Get TH!NKing and Grammar rap! video Worksheets

5 **Check/clarify:** *rhetorical question.*
Do the first question in open class. Ask students to look back at the article to find the answers to questions 2 and 3. Encourage students to work in pairs or small groups. Check answers in open class.
Suggested answers: 1 A direct (rhetorical) question to the reader. 2 Six times. 3 To introduce a topic, create a personal connection with the reader and encourage the reader to think.

6 During feedback, if you haven't yet related this concept back to L1, ask: *Do you use rhetorical questions in your language?*
1 B 2 A

7 Put students in pairs for this exercise. Then discuss as a class.

8 You may like to give some examples of your own and perhaps even tell them a story from your childhood.

Homework

Ask students to choose three types of book and write sentences saying why they like / don't like each type. This can be shared in the next lesson.

Activity idea Extension

Ask students to work in pairs and to agree on the overall ideas of each paragraph of the article. Check their ideas in open class. Then ask them to write a rhetorical question for each paragraph. While monitoring, note down some good examples and the students who came up with them. Call on these students to share their ideas during feedback.

Activity idea Mixed ability

Exercise 5 is a challenging activity, so consider introducing the concept of rhetorical questions to weaker students by giving an example in L1 before asking them to find examples in the article and discuss why they are used.

SO YOU WANT TO WRITE A NOVEL, DO YOU?

About Blog Latest posts Archives

What's stopping you? Time? Ideas? Self-belief? Well, let me help you. Time: find half an hour to write every day. You'll be surprised to see how quickly the pages start filling up. Ideas: write down everything and then choose the best. You only need one main idea. Start writing and the rest will soon come. Self-belief: what can I say? You can do it. I know you can. Remember, your novel, which will be fun to write, doesn't need to be 600 pages long. You could start with a short one.

What else do you need to know? Here are a few rules I always follow that might help you:

I always like to start with the plot. That's because I like a novel with a good story. And a good story comes from conflict. Many of the best novels start in a good place where the main character is happy with their life. Then something goes wrong and as the situation gets worse, our hero is thrown into conflict. The plot is then driven by how they can make things better. But in their struggle to right these wrongs, the character should learn something about themselves.

The theme, which is basically the message that the story is trying to get across, is also important. This is something you should never tell your reader directly. No one likes to be told what's right or what's wrong. The best thing to do is to let your reader work out the message on their own. That way your novel will make them feel smart and they'll want to read your next one!

Characters. They're important! Before you start writing, get to know the people whose stories you will be telling. Ask yourself questions about them. Get inside their heads and answer your questions. Don't spend too much time describing what they look like. What's important is what they're like inside. Who are they? What motivates them? Why are they doing those things? And they shouldn't be perfect. They're humans (presumably). They need to make mistakes from time to time and as they try to deal with the conflict in their life, they should develop and change.

Finally, you might want to think about your own writing style – the words you are going to use to write your story. You don't need to use long complex sentences or words that will leave your readers confused (but some variety in words is good!). You can keep your style simple. Think about the people who might want to read your story. Think about how to keep them interested. But be yourself. Write the words that come most naturally. These will always be your best words. So there you have it: plot, theme, characters, and style. Follow these golden rules and you'll never go wrong. Of course, though, don't forget – rules are often there to be broken.

Train to TH!NK

Thinking about different writing styles

Writers use different techniques to bring their texts alive.

5 **Answer the questions.**
1 What technique does the writer use in the title of the article?
2 How many times does he use this technique in the article?
3 Why do you think he does this?

6 **Choose the correct option.**
1 When people ask a rhetorical question, they …
A expect an answer.
B don't really expect an answer.
2 They ask a rhetorical question to …
A introduce a subject they want to talk about.
B find out what you're thinking.

7 **Some of the paragraphs don't contain any rhetorical questions. Think of a rhetorical question that you could add to the final paragraph.**

SPEAKING

8 **Work in pairs. Discuss these questions.**
1 What kind of stories do you enjoy most? Give an example.
2 What kind of story would you like to write most?

TH!NK more

Worksheets
Project Great books
Communication What a story!
Get **TH!NK**ing *What makes a really good story?*

Communication
Using appropriate language and register for context
Uses language for effect (e.g., exaggerations or cleft sentences).

Warmer

Write *Elements of a story* on the board. Give students three minutes to work in pairs and remember the things that all stories contain that were discussed in the last lesson. During feedback, try to elicit some of the words from Exercise 6 for later.

▶ 13 Grammar rap! Relative pronouns

1 Ask students to work in pairs and complete the sentences with different relative pronouns before referring back to page 49 to check.

1 who 2 whose 3 which; that 4 where RULE: 5 who 6 which; that 7 whose 8 where

2 During feedback, draw attention to the use of commas in the sentences.

1 One of the world's greatest storytellers was Roald Dahl, who wrote wonderful books for children.
2 Many people love his children's stories, which are fun for all ages. / Many people love his children's stories that are fun for all ages.
3 The best storyteller I know is my uncle, who lived in India for several years.
4 We love listening to our English teacher, whose stories are fascinating.
5 At our school we have a great library, where we like to relax and read.

Workbook p46

3 After reading the rule, ask students to say which sentence in Exercise 3 is a defining relative clause (sentence 2) and which is non-defining (sentence 1).

1 which 2 that

Grammar rap!

GRAMMAR
Relative pronouns

1 Complete these sentences from the article on page 49. Then complete the rule.

1 Think about the people ______ might want to read your story.
2 Get to know the people ______ stories you will be telling.
3 The theme, ______ is basically the message ______ the story is trying to get across, is also important.
4 Many of the best novels start in a good place ______ the main character is happy with their life.

RULE:
We use relative clauses to include information.
We use ...
5 ______ to refer to people.
6 ______ and ______ to refer to things.
7 ______ to refer to possessions.
8 ______ to refer to places.

2 Combine the sentences by replacing the underlined words with relative pronouns from Exercise 1.

1 One of the world's greatest storytellers was Roald Dahl. He wrote wonderful books for children.
2 Many people love his children's stories. The children's stories are fun for all ages.
3 The best storyteller I know is my uncle. He lived in India for several years.
4 We love listening to our English teacher. Her stories are fascinating.
5 At our school we have a great library. We like to relax and read there.

→ workbook page 46

Defining and non-defining relative clauses

3 Complete these sentences from the article on page 49. Then read the rule.

1 Remember, your novel, ______ will be fun to write, doesn't need to be 600 pages long.
2 You don't need to use long complex sentences or words ______ will leave your readers confused.

RULE:
We use a defining relative clause to identify an object, a person, a place, or a possession. Without this information, it's hard to know who or what we're talking about.
We don't often see the people. (Which people?)
*We don't often see the people **who live next door.***
We use a non-defining relative clause to add extra information. We don't need this information to understand the sentence. We put commas around it.
Roald Dahl was a famous writer.
*Roald Dahl, **who was British,** was a famous writer.*
(Extra information: he was British.)

4 Complete these defining relative clauses with *who, where, whose,* or *that.*

1 The house ______ I grew up is next to a school.
2 A book ______ has lots of short chapters is perfect for the bus ride to school.
3 A person ______ knows a lot of jokes is usually a good public speaker.
4 We went to hear a lecture by a writer ______ books are always on the bestseller list.
5 The author ______ wrote the famous teen novel *The Outsiders* was only 16.

Look
In defining relative clauses, we use *that* to refer to things. In non-defining relative clauses, we can only use *which* to refer to things.

5 Check (✓) the sentences that contain non-defining relative clauses and add commas.

1 My brother is someone who just doesn't like listening to jokes. ☐
2 Fairy tales which were written for children are now being adapted for the big screen. ☐
3 The Brothers Grimm whose stories have fascinated millions of children lived in the 19th century. ☐
4 It's difficult to read in places where people are talking on cell phones. ☐

→ workbook page 46

4 Encourage students to refer to the rule to check their answers once they've finished.

1 where 2 that 3 who 4 whose 5 who

5 2 ✓ Fairy tales, which were written for children, are now being adapted for the big screen.
3 ✓ The Brothers Grimm, whose stories have fascinated millions of children, lived in the 19th century.

Workbook p46

Get it Right!
Relative pronouns

Student's Book p124

THINK more

Workbook
Grammar pp46–47, Ex.1–6

Worksheets
Grammar Worksheets 5
Grammar presentation: Defining and non-defining relative clauses

Language note Relative pronouns

The relative pronoun is sometimes the subject of the clause. We do not repeat the subject: *The woman who ~~[she]~~ plays guitar in that band ...*

The relative pronoun is sometimes the object of the clause. We do not repeat the object: *Do you remember the girl who we met ~~[her]~~ at the party?*

When the relative pronoun is the object of the clause, we can omit it from the sentence: *Do you remember the girl ~~who~~ we met at the party?*

6 Check/clarify: *harms.*
During feedback, focus on pronunciation as well as meaning. Pay attention to the /k/ sound at the beginning of *character*, the /v/ sound in *villain* /ˈvɪlən/, and the silent *ue* at the end of *dialogue* /ˈdaɪəlɒg/.
1 plot 2 character 3 ending 4 hero 5 villain 6 dialogue 7 opening 8 setting

7 Check/clarify: *disappointing.*
Students should work alone for this exercise.
Workbook p48

8 To help students, write phrases for agreeing and disagreeing on the board: *I totally agree with you; you're right; no way; I totally disagree.* Drill these phrases using emphatic intonation before students begin their discussions.

9 Write on the board: *Roald Dahl.* Ask students what they know about him and write their ideas on the board. Give them one minute to read the fact file.

10 5.02 Check/clarify: *pickpocket.*
For feedback, give students two minutes to discuss what they understood from the story.
A fingersmith steals things from people.

11 5.02 Encourage students to try to answer as many questions as they can from memory before they listen again to check.
1 Because she thinks he only wrote books for children.
2 A TV series from the 1970s.
3 He introduced the shows, and many of them were based on his stories.
4 A driver and a hitchhiker (who is also a thief).
5 Because the driver is driving too fast.
6 The names and addresses of the driver and his passenger.
7 He takes off the driver's belt.
8 Because he has stolen the police officer's notebook.

12 Invite students to share their answers with the rest of the class during feedback.

VOCABULARY
Elements of a story

6 Match the words with their definitions.

character	dialogue	ending	hero
opening	plot	setting	villain

1 the story of a movie, play, etc.
2 a person in a story
3 the last part of a story
4 the main (usually good) character in a story
5 a character who harms other people
6 the words that the characters say to each other
7 the beginning of a story
8 the time and place in which the action happens

7 Think about these things for two minutes. Make notes.
- a movie or book with a great plot
- the setting of the last movie you saw or story you read
- a movie or book with a great opening
- a good movie or book with a disappointing ending
- a movie or book with a memorable villain

→ workbook page 48

8 SPEAKING Work in pairs or small groups. Share your ideas.

I really enjoyed the latest Spider-Man movie – the plot was amazing!

I don't think the ending of the book is very good.

All the characters in the story are fascinating, but the villain is the best!

LISTENING

9 Find out how much your class knows about Roald Dahl. Then read the fact file.

Roald Dahl FACT FILE
- Dahl was born in 1916 in Cardiff, Wales.
- His parents were immigrants from Norway.
- He was a fighter pilot during the Second World War.
- His first children's book was *The Gremlins*, which was published in 1942.
- His most famous book, *Charlie and the Chocolate Factory*, has sold over 13 million copies.
- Many of his books have been made into successful Hollywood movies, including *Charlie and the Chocolate Factory*, *Fantastic Mr. Fox*, and *The BFG*.

10 5.02 Listen to two teenagers talking about a short story by Roald Dahl called *The Hitchhiker*. In the story, he uses an invented word: "fingersmith." What does a fingersmith do?

11 5.02 Listen again and answer the questions.
1 Why is Annie surprised that Lucy is reading Roald Dahl?
2 What was *Tales of the Unexpected*?
3 What was Roald Dahl's connection to it?
4 Who are the two main characters in *The Hitchhiker*?
5 Why does the police officer stop them?
6 What does the police officer write down in his book?
7 What does the hitchhiker do to show how good he is with his fingers?
8 Why isn't the hitchhiker worried about the police officer?

12 SPEAKING Compare your answers in pairs.

Activity idea Extension
Ask each group to come to an agreement on which book/movie has the best plot and which has the most disappointing ending. Groups should aim to reach unanimous agreement on each item. When they have decided, ask groups to report back to the class and to try to convince other groups to agree with them.

Homework
Ask students to keep a journal for two or three days and make a note of the books they read, or if they don't, what books their family reads, and whether they enjoyed them.

TH!NK more
Workbook
Vocabulary p48, Ex.1–3
Listening p52, Ex.1–5

Worksheets
Vocabulary Worksheets 5

Warmer

Do an internet image search on book covers before the class and choose a mix of different ones to display on the board. Ask students to guess the types of story from the images. Try to elicit some of the types of story included in Exercise 10 on page 53.

1 As feedback, hold a vote to find out if students generally thought the book or the movie was better in each case.

2 Set a two-minute timer to encourage students to read quickly and focus on the task rather than trying to understand every word.

Paragraph 1: for
Paragraph 2: against

3 🔊 **5.03 Check/clarify:** *spoil.*
Give students time to read the article and answer the questions. Encourage them to justify their answers.

1 She likes using her imagination.
2 Because the director's visions were amazing, even though they were different from what she had imagined.
3 Because she thought the characters were all wrong, and they had changed some of her favorite parts of the book.
4 It takes him too long to read a book, whereas watching a movie only takes 90 minutes and leaves him free to do other things.
5 He really enjoyed them.
6 Because knowing what the story is about helps him to understand books that can be difficult for him to read.

4 You may want to give your own answers as an example before hearing from the students.

5 If you are short on time, you could assign this for homework. Students should organize their work to follow the same format as the article in Exercise 2. Remind them to refer back to the model text if necessary.

THINK more

Workbook
Reading p50, Ex.1–4
Developing Writing p51

READING

1 **Look at the titles. Have you seen any of the movie versions of the books? What did you think of them?**

LORD OF THE FLIES
THE MAZE RUNNER
THE HUNGER GAMES
The Jungle Book
The Lord of the Rings

2 **Read the magazine article and title quickly. Decide which paragraph is *for* and which is *against* the argument.**

3 🔊 5.03 **Read and listen to the article. Answer the questions.**

1 What does Ellie like doing when she's reading a book?
2 Why wasn't she disappointed by the movie of *The Lord of the Rings*?
3 Why didn't she like the movie version of *The Maze Runner*?
4 Why does Ben prefer movies to books?
5 What did he think of *The Hunger Games* books?
6 Why does he try to watch movies of the books he has to read for school?

4 SPEAKING **Work in pairs. Discuss.**

1 Which do you prefer to do first: read the original book or watch the movie version of it?
2 Think of a movie that you think was much better or worse than the book. Say why.

WRITING
A short paragraph expressing an opinion

5 **Write a paragraph giving your ideas on the statement: "Books are always better than their movies."**

1 Say what your opinion is and why.
2 Give examples from books you've read and movies you've seen.

THERE ARE ALWAYS TWO SIDES TO AN ARGUMENT

BOOKS ARE ALWAYS BETTER THAN THEIR MOVIES.

When you read a book, you can imagine it all in your head: what the characters look like, where the action takes place – that sort of thing. Then when you see the movie, you can compare your ideas with those of the director, which is always interesting. If you see the movie first, you don't get to use your own imagination because you just see things the way they were in the movie. It's a shame and I don't really see the point in doing it. For example, I read *The Lord of the Rings* and had all these wonderful images in my head. When I saw the movies, which were directed by the great Peter Jackson, some of it was really different from how I had imagined it, but it didn't matter. His visions were so good and I wasn't disappointed. It doesn't always work like that, though. Sometimes the movie version can be a real disappointment. I saw *The Maze Runner* a few weeks ago. I loved that book, but the movie just wasn't right for me. In my opinion, the characters were all wrong and they'd changed some of my favorite parts. I didn't bother to see the other movies in the series. I didn't want to spoil my own personal memories of the books. *Ellie*

I hardly ever read books, so I nearly always see the movie first. I think it's probably because I'm a bit lazy. It takes me weeks to finish a book, whereas I can watch the movie in 90 minutes, which leaves me time to do other things. But sometimes I enjoy a movie so much that it makes me want to go and read the book. I love fantasy and science fiction stories, so I did that with *The Hunger Games* series. The movies were amazing, so I went out and bought the books. It took me a little time to get through them, but they were worth the time and effort. I really enjoyed them, even though I knew what was going to happen. It was also pretty interesting seeing where the movie and book were a bit different. When our teacher asks us to read books for school, I always see if I can get a movie of the book first. That helps me get into the books, which are often really difficult. If I already know what the story is about, it helps me understand better when I'm reading. I did this with *Lord of the Flies* and *The Jungle Book*. Seeing the movies first really helped me enjoy the books more. *Ben*

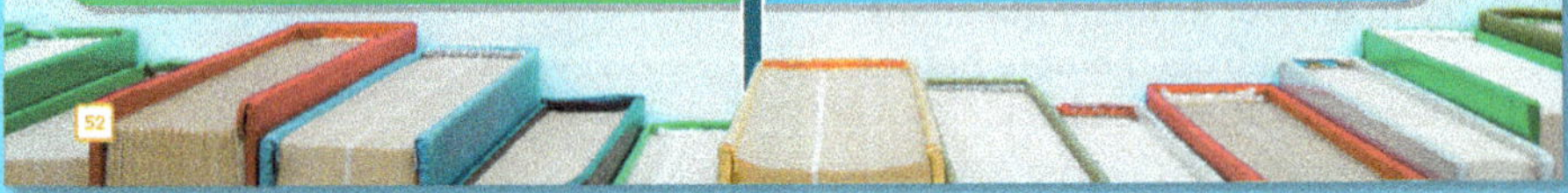

52

Culture notes

The Lord of the Rings is a three-part fantasy novel by J.R.R Tolkien. The trilogy has sold over 150 million copies, making it one of the best-selling novels ever written.

The Maze Runner is a 2009 novel for young adults by James Dashner. Although it is the first book in the *Maze Runner* series, it is the third in narrative order. Set in a post-apocalyptic world, the story begins when a teenage boy wakes up in an elevator, with no memory other than his name is Thomas. He meets other teenage boys who also have no memories. They try to solve the mystery of the maze to find a way out.

The Hunger Games is a series of three novels by Suzanne Collins. The first was published in 2008. The story is of a girl who takes part in the Hunger Games, in which young people have to fight to the death.

The Lord of the Flies by William Golding was first published in 1954. The book is about a group of boys who try to look after themselves after their plane crashes on a deserted island.

The Jungle Book is a collection of stories by Rudyard Kipling, published in 1894. Set in India, most of the characters are animals, although the main character is a boy named Mowgli who lives in the jungle with wolves.

Grammar; Vocabulary; Speaking

6 Ask students to try to complete the sentences from memory before referring back to page 52 to check.
1 which 2 which RULE: 3 which 4 which

7 Point out the use of the comma before *which* in the example. During feedback, ask students what *which* refers to in each sentence and clarify whether this is a clause or a noun (*which* refers to a clause in every case).
1 all her money, which means she'll be
2 learned the new words, which was frustrating
3 have been turned into successful teen movie, which has surprised
4 manages to write several books per year, which is
5 have been made into movies, which is

8 You may like to give an example of your own to get students started on this.

9 Monitor and prompt students to keep talking, but as this is a fluency activity, do not interrupt to correct mistakes. While monitoring, note down any common errors, focusing on relative pronouns, to review together as a class.

Workbook p47

10 🔊 **5.04**
A3 B6 C5 D4 E7 F1 G2

11 (auto)biography

12 As feedback, hold a vote to find out what the class' favorite book genre is.

Workbook p48

13 At the end of the exercise, listen to some of the students' ideas and encourage open class discussion.

14 If you are short on time, you could assign this for homework.

15 At the end of the exercise, listen to some of the students' ideas as a class and find out where the most popular places and times to read are.

GRAMMAR
Relative clauses with *which*

6 **Complete these sentences from the article on page 52. What does *which* refer to in each of the sentences? Complete the rule.**

1 I can watch the movie in 90 minutes, ______ leaves me time to do other things.
2 You can compare your ideas with those of the director, ______ is always interesting.

> **RULE:** The pronoun ³______ normally refers to a noun, but it can sometimes refer to the whole of the previous clause. We cannot use ⁴______ or *that* in the same way.
> *She was late, which made her nervous.*

7 **Join the pairs of sentences using *which*.**

0 I often play the drums on Sunday mornings. This annoys the neighbors.
I often play *the drums on Sunday mornings, which annoys* the neighbors.
1 She's lost all her money. This means she'll be in trouble.
She's lost __________________ in trouble.
2 Nobody in class learned the new words. It was frustrating for our teacher.
Nobody in class __________________ for our teacher.
3 Fairy tales have been turned into successful teen movies. This has surprised many people.
Fairy tales __________________ many people.
4 It's really amazing that the author manages to write several books per year.
She __________________ really amazing.
5 It's fascinating that most of his books have been made into movies.
Most of his books __________________ fascinating.

8 **Complete the sentences so that they are true for you.**

0 My favorite singer *is giving a concert in our town next month*, which is fantastic.
1 __________________ last year, which made me feel really proud.
2 I heard on the news that __________________, which I was really upset about.
3 __________________, which really isn't easy.

9 SPEAKING **Work in pairs. Share your sentences. How long can you keep each conversation going?**

My favorite singer Dua Lipa is giving a concert in our town soon.

Wow! I like her songs, too. Do you know when …?

→ workbook page 47

VOCABULARY
Types of story

10 🔊 5.04 **Match the types of story with the book covers. Write numbers 1–7 in the boxes. Then listen and check.**

1 crime novel
2 science fiction
3 historical fiction
4 horror story
5 (auto)biography
6 romance novel
7 fantasy

11 **Which books are nonfiction?**

12 SPEAKING **Which types of story do you like reading most?**

→ workbook page 48

SPEAKING

13 **Work in pairs. If you had to choose one of the books in the previous exercise, which would it be and why?**

I'd choose … because the cover looks / the title sounds (exciting / funny / interesting / …).

14 **Prepare a one-minute talk about reading. Think about the following points and take notes.**

- if you prefer articles, short stories, novels, etc.
- where and when you like reading

15 **Take turns giving your talks in small groups.**

Activity idea Mixed ability

In Exercise 14, weaker students can write a set of simple sentences. Stronger students should develop their ideas and attempt to present their information in an interesting way (perhaps using rhetorical questions to draw in the listener).

Activity idea Extension

If you are able to show videos in the classroom, this is a good opportunity to show some trailers from fantasy movies. Put students into A/B pairs. Ask As to turn their backs to the board/screen or cover their eyes. Bs watch a fantasy movie trailer with no sound. While watching, Bs describe what they see on the screen to A. When the trailer has finished, A has to guess which trailer was shown. This is a good fluency activity which requires students to speak quickly and clearly, as they have to keep pace with the trailer!

TH!NK more

Practice Extra
Unit 5 Practice it!

Workbook
Grammar p47, Ex.7–8
Vocabulary p48, Ex.1
Vocabulary Extra p49, Ex.1–3

Worksheets
Grammar Worksheets 5
Vocabulary Worksheets 5

Warmer

To review story genres, give students two minutes to think of as many different genres as they can. After two minutes, play a game of "vocabulary tennis," with each group taking turns saying one genre until one team runs out of ideas.

▶ 14 TH!NK

Storytelling in the Caribbean

1 Before students read the article, get them to cover it, look at the pictures, and answer the questions. Write their ideas on the board. When they read to check, set a three-minute timer to encourage them to skim the article quickly and not to focus on every word.

2 🔊 **5.05** Tell students not to worry about difficult vocabulary at this stage as this will come up later.
Paul Keens-Douglas is a famous storyteller in the West Indies. Tanti Merle is a character who appears in many of his stories.

3 **Check/clarify:** *ancestors, to perfect, material, originating.* Encourage students to think about the correct answer to the false statements.
1 F 2 F 3 T 4 T 5 F

4 Encourage students to express themselves in English and to use any vocabulary they have learned from the article. At the end of the exercise, listen to some of the students' ideas and encourage open class discussion.

Culture note

The Caribbean Islands is a massive archipelago of more than 700 islands located in the Caribbean Sea. Primarily located between North America and South America, the Caribbean stretches across 2,745,387 square kilometers. The main languages are Spanish, French, English, Dutch, and Haitian Creole.

TH!NK Storytelling in the Caribbean

Culture

1 Look at the photos and answer the questions.
1 What can you see in the photos?
2 What do you think the person is doing?
3 Would you like to visit this place? Why or why not?

2 🔊 5.05 **Read and listen to the article. Find out who Paul Keens-Douglas and Tanti Merle are.**

Storytelling in the Caribbean

Storytelling plays a big part in the childhood of most people growing up on the Caribbean Islands. It is a tradition that was brought over from Africa by their ancestors many years ago and is a way of keeping their shared culture alive. The stories are a way of remembering the past and making sure it's not forgotten in the future.

And despite the modern distractions of television and video games, many Caribbean families still gather on the steps outside their homes, with the full moon in the sky and the wind blowing gently through the palm trees, to hear stories that they have already heard many times before.

The storyteller has an important position in Caribbean society. But it is not an art that is learned quickly. Good storytellers take years to perfect their performances. First, they must collect a catalog of good stories that are short, simple and work well for people of all ages. They must then practice these on family members to test out their material before moving on to larger crowds in local community centers. From there they may choose to become traveling storytellers and move from town to town looking for new audiences to share their tales with. And the very best storytellers make it onto the international stage and travel the world. More recently many storytellers have started using movies to reach even more people.

With many Caribbean islands and people originating from many African countries, there are lots of types of stories to be told. One common feature though is the performance tradition known as "crick crack." Although this may differ a little in each country, the basic idea is that the audience participates in the storytelling. For example, in St. Lucia, where stories are usually told in French, the storyteller (known as the "conteur") announces that he or she wants to tell a story by shouting out "Crick!" and the audience shows they want to listen by responding "Crack!" Throughout the performance, the storyteller continues to involve the audience by inviting them to answer questions and riddles and to make comments. In this way, the storyteller and the audience become an almost equally important part of the whole experience.

But as well as the many traditional tales and myths there are to be told, storytellers also create their own characters, and the most successful of these have become part of cultural life. One of the most famous storytellers in the West Indies is Paul Keens-Douglas, who was born in Trinidad but grew up in Grenada. Probably his most popular character, Tanti Merle, is known throughout the region and appears in many of his stories. Tanti Merle is a woman who is not afraid to say what she thinks and Keens-Douglas uses her as a lovable comic figure to make comments on everyday life in the Caribbean.

3 Read the article again. Mark the sentences T (true) or F (false).
1 Children in the Caribbean don't use modern technology. ☐
2 Storytellers have to learn long detailed stories. ☐
3 Audiences play an important part in the storytelling. ☐
4 You should shout "crack" if you want to hear a story. ☐
5 Storytellers only tell traditional stories. ☐

4 SPEAKING **Work in pairs. Discuss these questions.**
1 How does the Caribbean storytelling tradition compare with storytelling in your country?
2 What stories are there about places near where you live?

54

Social Responsibilities
Understanding and describing own and others' cultures
Makes informed comparisons between their own society and other societies.

5 Before students do the exercise, write the highlighted words on the board. Tell students to find the words in the article as quickly as possible. When they have seen them being used in context, ask them to try to work out the meaning of the phrases. Compare their meanings with the definitions in the book.
1 riddles 2 crowds 3 appears 4 culture 5 participates 6 catalogue 7 everyday 8 distractions

6 Tell students that there is no specific correct order. Nominate pairs to share their stories with the rest of the class but do not comment on how close they are to the actual story at this stage.

7 **5.08** In pairs, encourage students to discuss similarities and differences.

Pronunciation
The schwa /ər/ in word endings
Student's Book p120

8 **5.08** To help students get an overall understanding, ask: *What happened to Annie the other day?* (a song she couldn't stop singing all day was on the radio when she got home) *Why was this strange?* (because it wasn't a current song that you'd expect to hear on the radio)
1 The strangest thing happened to me the other day. 2 That was the annoying thing. 3 Well, let me finish … 4 you'll never believe what 5 What are the chances?

9 You may like to give an example from your own experience to get students started on this exercise.

Homework
Ask students to use the notes they made in Exercise 9 to write the story at home.

5 VOCABULARY There are eight highlighted words or phrases in the text. Match the words with these meanings. Write the words.
1 short word puzzles
2 lots of people together
3 is present
4 the art, stories, and history of a place
5 takes part in something
6 a collection of something
7 normal
8 things that take your attention from what you are doing

SPEAKING

6 Look at the pictures. Put them in order and use them to tell a story.

A

B

C

7 5.08 Listen and compare your story to the one you hear.

PRONUNCIATION
The schwa /ər/ in word endings Go to page 120.

FUNCTIONS
Telling a story

8 5.08 Annie uses these expressions to bring her story to life. Match them with the correct places in the conversation. Then listen again and check.
- [ ] you'll never believe what
- [ ] The strangest thing happened to me the other day.
- [ ] Well, let me finish …
- [ ] That was the annoying thing.
- [ ] What are the chances?

Annie [1] ____________
Mac What?
Annie I woke up with this song in my head and I couldn't stop singing it all day long. It was really annoying.
Mac What was it?
Annie [2] ____________ It was a song I knew, but I couldn't remember what it was. I even sang it to a few of my friends, but they didn't know what it was either.
Mac So what was so strange about that?
Annie [3] ____________ I got home from school (with the song still in my head) and I went upstairs to do my homework. I decided to turn on the radio to try to forget the song and [4] ____________ they were playing!
Mac Go on.
Annie They were playing the song that I'd been singing all day!
Mac So you'd just been singing a pop song that you'd forgotten the name of.
Annie Yes, but the strange thing is that it wasn't a pop song from now. It was some obscure song from the 1980s that you never hear any more. It was a song that my dad used to play when I was really little. I hadn't heard it for years. And they were playing it on the radio! [5] ____________
Mac Yes, that is pretty weird.

9 Think of a strange story that happened to you or to someone else.
- Write down the main events in note form.
- Think how you can use some of the expressions.
- In groups, tell your stories.

55

Activity idea Extension
To extend the speaking activity, ask students, in pairs, to try to retell the story they heard on the audio.

THINK more
Practice Extra
Unit 5 Master it!
Workbook
Pronunciation p119
Tests
Unit, extension, and skills test 5

Warmer

If you have access to the internet, do a video search for magic tricks and choose a suitable one to show in class. Ask students to discuss how they think the tricks were done. If you don't have the internet, perform this simple magic trick: ask a student to give you a number between 1 and 100. Write the number on a small piece of paper and fold it up. (Do not let them see what you are writing!) Ask another student for a number, but write the first number again and fold up the piece of paper. Do the same with eight other students, always writing the first number. Put the ten pieces of paper into a cup and ask a student to take out a piece of paper and look at it. Pretend that you are mind-reading and say the number on the paper! Ask students to guess how the trick was done.

▶ 15 Get TH!NKing

Play the video and discuss the question with your class.

1 During feedback, invite students to perform a trick for the class (you may like to take a deck of cards to class for this activity).

2 Set a three-minute time limit to encourage students to read quickly and focus on finding the three tricks rather than trying to understand every word.
The Great Wall, The Statue of Liberty, Lucky 13

3 🔊 **6.01 Check/clarify:** *illusions, silhouette, screens, to be staged, column, volunteers, flashlights, cage.*
1 d 2 f 3 e 4 g 5 b 6 a

6 THAT'S IMPOSSIBLE

OBJECTIVES

FUNCTIONS: talking about sequence; explaining how things are done

GRAMMAR: present and past passive (review); *have something done*; future and present perfect passive (review)

VOCABULARY: extreme adjectives and modifiers; *make* and *do*

Get TH!NKING
Watch the video and think:
what is your favorite magic trick?

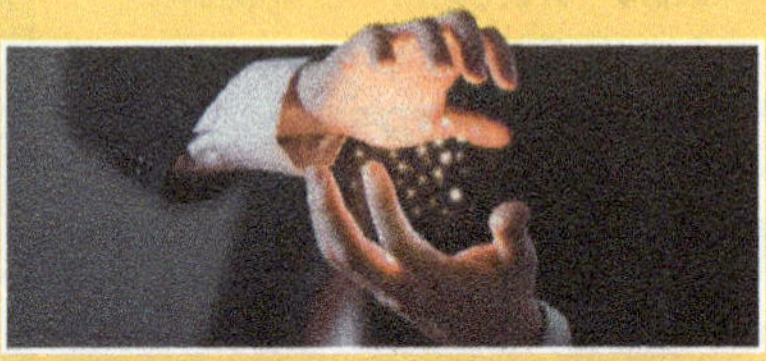

READING

1 SPEAKING **Work in pairs. Discuss these questions.**
1 What magicians can you name?
2 What magic tricks have you seen?
3 Can you do any tricks yourself? What are they?

2 **Read the article about David Copperfield quickly. Which three of his tricks does it mention?**

3 🔊 6.01 **Read and listen to the article again and match the sentences (a–g) with the spaces (1–6). There's one extra sentence that doesn't belong in the text. Check your answers.**
a It was very dark and he fell. ☐
b The audience is absolutely amazed. ☐
c Where had he gone? ☐
d Time and time again, people have wondered: ☐
e There was nothing there. ☐
f He walked in one side and out the other. ☐
g People who catch one are invited to come up onto the stage. ☐

56

Train to TH!NK

Understanding what's relevant

To write a good text, a writer must make sure that each sentence is linked to what comes before it. Understanding how this is done will help you to do tasks like Exercise 3.

4 **Choose the sentence that *doesn't* have any relevance to the first.**
David Copperfield made the Statue of Liberty disappear.
A He was watched by millions on TV.
B He performed in front of a live audience.
C People from all over the world visit the Statue every year.
D He used a large sheet to hide the Statue.

5 SPEAKING **Work in pairs. Use this sentence to make a similar task for your partner.**
Gavin Cox was injured in one of David Copperfield's magic tricks.
A ______ C ______
B ______ D ______

4 During feedback, point out the use of the pronoun *he* – elicit that this refers to "David Copperfield" and that it works to link the sentences. *C*

5 While students are writing, monitor to see how they're doing and steer them in the right direction on this potentially challenging activity.

Collaboration
Taking personal responsibility for own contribution to a group task
Makes relevant suggestions based on the current topic of conversation. Introduces new ideas and links them to prior knowledge during the task. Makes contributions that are on task and explains them fully.

Objectives

Functions and speaking Talking about sequence; explaining how things are done
Grammar Present and past passive (review); *have something done*; future and present perfect passive (review)
Vocabulary Extreme adjectives and modifiers; *make* and *do*
Fiction *The Mind Map*
Train to TH!NK *Understanding what's relevant*

Resources for this unit

All available online

Videos
- Get **TH!NK**ing: *What is your favorite magic trick?*
- Grammar rap!: Present and past passive (review)

Tests
- Unit, extension, and skills test 6
- End of term test 2

Worksheets
- Grammar and vocabulary: Basic, Standard, and Extension Worksheets
- Project: Magic tricks
- Communication: How do they do it?
- Get **TH!NK**ing and Grammar rap! video Worksheets

6 Monitor to help with any difficulties, but do not interrupt as this is a fluency activity. You might also offer ideas if students have none. At the end of the exercise, listen to some of the students' ideas and encourage open class discussion.

Pronunciation

The /ʒ/ phoneme

Student's Book p120

Homework

Ask students to write a short paragraph summarizing their discussion in Exercise 6.

Culture notes

David Seth Kotkin, known professionally as David Copperfield, is a highly successful American illusionist and magician. Born in New Jersey in 1956, Copperfield has acquired 11 Guinness World Records and a knighthood from the French government during his 40-year career.

The Great Wall of China is a military construction in China. Spanning the historical northern borders, some parts were built as early as 7th century BCE and joined together at various points throughout history. Its exact route is difficult to determine as it is not complete in places. The idea that the wall can be seen from space is a myth.

The Statue of Liberty (official name: *Liberty Enlightening the World*) is a large neoclassical copper sculpture on Liberty Island, New York Harbor in the United States. It was a gift from the French people to the US population and was dedicated in 1886. It was designed by the French sculptor Frédéric Auguste Bartholdi and built in part by Gustave Eiffel. The statue is of a Roman goddess of liberty holding a torch above her head with her right hand. Her left hand carries a tablet with the date of the US Declaration of Independence. A broken shackle and chain lie at her feet, to commemorate the abolition of slavery.

HOW ON EARTH DOES HE DO IT?

Perhaps the world's most famous magician, David Copperfield has entertained his audiences for years with his fantastic magic tricks and thrilling illusions. [1]_____ "How did he do that?"

The Great Wall

In a 1986 TV special, Copperfield appeared to walk *through* the Great Wall of China. [2]_____ First, he stepped into a box and the audience could see his silhouette on the white screens around the box. Then, he appeared to enter the wall. Minutes later his silhouette could be seen pushing out through the wall into a similar box on the other side. The white screens were lifted and there stood the magician on the other side of the wall.

The Statue of Liberty

A live TV event was staged in April of 1983. A huge audience sat on Liberty Island in New York Harbor, facing the Statue of Liberty. There was a column on each side of the stage and the Statue was visible between the two columns. A white screen was raised and the Statue was hidden from view. Minutes later, the screen was lowered, and to the amazement of the audience, the Statue had disappeared. [3]_____ Then, as the stunned audience watched, the screen was raised again. But this time, when it was lowered, the Statue of Liberty was there again.

Lucky 13

Imagine the scene at one of David Copperfield's shows. From the stage, 13 soft balls are thrown into the audience. [4]_____ These 13 volunteers enter a cage, which is raised above the stage. The people inside are given flashlights to shine at the audience, and then a cover is lowered over them. When the magician lifts the cover, the cage is empty – but then, moments later, the 13 people reappear at the back of the theater, still holding the flashlights they were given. [5]_____ This is David Copperfield's famous Lucky 13 trick, which he performed for nearly 20 years. How did he do it?

The secret revealed

Normally, magicians guard their secrets, but this time, we know the answer. In 2013, 55-year-old chef Gavin Cox was at one of Copperfield's shows in Las Vegas. He was called up to the stage by the magician to take part in the Lucky 13 illusion. As soon as the cage was covered, he and the other 12 volunteers were pushed quickly into a secret passage and outside the theater. In the confusion, Mr. Cox was injured. "They were shouting, 'Hurry! Run, run, run,'" he said. He didn't know where he was going. [6]_____ After the accident, there was a court case and Copperfield had to reveal the trick and the technique of his famous "disappearing audience" illusion.

SPEAKING

6 Work in pairs. Discuss these questions.

1 What other magic tricks can you think of?
2 How do you think the Great Wall and the Statue of Liberty tricks were done?

PRONUNCIATION
The /ʒ/ phoneme Go to page 120.

Activity idea Extension

If you have access to the internet, do a video search for *walking on water revealed*. During feedback, ask students how they think the trick was done before showing the video to explain it.

TH!NK more

Workbook
Pronunciation p119

Worksheets
Project Magic tricks
Communication How do they do it?
Get TH!NKing *What is your favorite magic trick?*

Warmer

In pairs, ask students to test each other on their irregular past participles.

▶ 16 Grammar rap! Present and past passive (review)

1 Ask students to try to answer the questions from memory before referring back to page 57 to check.
1 was 2 are 3 were 4 is
RULE: 5 be 6 past participle 7 by

2 Ask: *Do you know how this trick is done?* Invite students to volunteer ideas. Ask students to check by reading the sentences for the gist, ignoring blank spaces.
1 hides / is hidden 2 gets 3 holds; pushes 4 is cut 5 are pulled

Workbook p54

3 Do the first sentence together.
1 very surprised 2 very large
3 very good; very exciting

4 During feedback, say the words for students to repeat and check pronunciation. Pay attention to the pronunciation of *minute* /maɪˈnuːt/ (very small), as compared to *minute* /ˈmɪnɪt/ (sixty seconds).
1 e 2 a 3 f 4 c 5 g 6 h
7 d 8 b

5 Refer students to the *Look* box to help them.
1 ✓ 2 ✓ 3 ✓ 4 ✗ 5 ✓ 6 ✗

6 Encourage students to first read the text for overall understanding by asking the questions: *What trick did the writer see? Did he/she enjoy the show?*
1 fantastic/wonderful/brilliant/amazing 2 funny/hilarious
3 enormous 4 tiny/minute
5 happy/delighted

Workbook p56

Grammar rap!

GRAMMAR
Present and past passive (review)

1 **Complete these sentences from the article on page 57. Use the correct form of *be*. Then complete the rule with *by*, *be*, and *past participle*.**

1 Gavin Cox ______ called up to the stage by the magician.
2 Thirteen soft balls ______ thrown into the audience.
3 The white screens ______ lifted.
4 The cage ______ raised above the stage.

> **RULE:** We form the passive with a form of the verb [5]______ and the [6]______.
> We use the preposition [7]______ to say who or what does the action, but only if this is important.

2 **Complete the instructions with the correct active or passive forms of the verbs.**

cut | get | hide | hold | pull | push | ~~use~~

0 A long box *is used* for this trick.
1 One woman ____________ at one end of the box.
2 A second woman ____________ into the box.
3 She puts her head out of one end and ____________ her legs to her chest with her arms. At the same time, the first woman ____________ her legs out of the other end.
4 The box ____________ in half by the magician.
5 The ends of the box ____________ apart to show that it has been cut in two.

→ workbook page 54

VOCABULARY
Extreme adjectives and modifiers

3 **Look at these phrases from the article on page 57. What do the adjectives in bold mean?**

1 As the **stunned** audience watched, the screen was raised again.
2 A **huge** audience sat on Liberty Island.
3 David Copperfield has entertained his audiences for years with his **fantastic** magic tricks and **thrilling** illusions.

4 **Match the gradable adjectives (1–8) with the extreme adjectives (a–h).**

1 good	a hilarious
2 funny	b fascinating
3 happy	c huge / enormous
4 big	d freezing
5 small	e great / fantastic / wonderful / brilliant / amazing
6 bad	f delighted
7 cold	g tiny / minute
8 interesting	h terrible

> **Look**
> We use:
> - *very* with gradable adjectives.
> - *extremely* with extreme adjectives.
> - *really* with gradable and extreme adjectives.

5 **Look at these examples of adjectives with the modifiers *very*, *really*, and *extremely*. Which combinations are correct and which are incorrect? Mark them ✓ or ✗.**

1 really good ☐	4 very hilarious ☐
2 really amazing ☐	5 extremely small ☐
3 very funny ☐	6 extremely tiny ☐

6 **Complete the text with adjectives from Exercise 4. Sometimes more than one answer is possible, but don't use each adjective more than once.**

> Last night, we went to a magic show. It was very good – in fact, it was extremely [1]______. The magician was really [2]______ – we couldn't stop laughing. In one trick, he had two hats: a really small one and an [3]______ one. But from the big hat he pulled out an absolutely [4]______ rabbit and from the small hat he pulled out a huge one. It was great fun and I left feeling really [5]______.

→ workbook page 56

58

Get it Right!
absolutely vs. *very*

Student's Book p124

Language note Present and past passive (review)

When forming questions in the passive, *by* comes at the end of the question. For example: *Who were the photos taken by? Who was the man pulled into the boat by?*

Activity idea Extension

Write on the board: *gorgeous, frightening, ugly, pretty, hideous, terrifying, silly, ridiculous*. Ask students to work with a partner and decide which of the adjectives are gradable and which are extreme. They should then match each gradable adjective to an extreme adjective.

(Answers: gradable: *pretty, ugly, frightening, silly*; extreme: *gorgeous, hideous, terrifying, ridiculous*)

TH!NK more

Workbook
Grammar p54, Ex.1–4
Vocabulary p56, Ex.1–3

Worksheets
Grammar rap! Present and past passive (review)
Grammar Worksheets 6
Vocabulary Worksheets 6

7 6.04 Tell students not to focus on understanding every word for now, but to focus on listening for the answer.
It's in the shape of a lizard.

8 6.04 Before playing the audio again, ask students to answer as much as they can from memory.
2✓ 3✓ 5✓

9 *1 a work of art 2 a disaster 3 center of attention 4 must be joking 5 furious*

10 *1 I 2 I 3 I*
We don't know who is performing the action.
RULE: 4 someone 5 us

11 In weaker classes, write the base form of the verbs needed on the board.
1 has … cooked 2 have … done 3 has … bought 4 have … driven 5 have … organized 6 have … looked after

12 Draw attention to the question form (*have* + object + past participle)
1 Where can you have/get a/your wedding cake made?
2 Where can you have/get your car repaired?
3 Where can you have/get a tattoo done?
4 Where can you have/get your teeth cleaned?

Workbook p54

13 Before students do the exercise, elicit the verbs that are illustrated in the photos (*pierce*, *get a tattoo*, *dye*).
A 3 B 2 C 1

14 Invite students to share their answers with the rest of the class during feedback.

15 At the end of the exercise, listen to some of the students' ideas and encourage open class discussion.

Homework

Students write a list of things that they or their parents never do themselves, e.g., *We never clean our windows, Mr. Smith does it. I never cut my hair; I go to the hairdresser*, and so on. Students exchange sentences with each other and at home, rewrite the sentences using *have something done*, e.g., *We have our windows cleaned by Mr. Smith. I have my hair cut at the hairdresser.*

LISTENING

7 6.04 Listen to two people talking about a haircut. What is unusual about James' haircut?

8 6.04 Listen again. Check (✓) the reasons why Mia is so upset about James's haircut.

1 It was expensive. ☐
2 He'll spoil his sister's wedding photos. ☐
3 It looks silly. ☐
4 He missed his date with her. ☐
5 His parents will be angry. ☐
6 It was done poorly. ☐

9 Replace the underlined words or phrases with the words below from the dialogue.

center of attention | furious | a work of art | must be joking | a disaster

1 It's <u>a brilliant creation</u>.
2 It's <u>extremely bad</u>.
3 She should be the <u>person everyone is looking at</u>.
4 You <u>can't be serious</u>.
5 They will be <u>very angry</u>.

12 Use the words to write questions.

car | clean | ~~cut~~ | do | ~~hair~~ | make | repair | tattoo | teeth | wedding cake

0 *Where can you have your hair cut* ?
At the To Dye For salon.
1 ______________________ ? At Derek's Bakery.
2 ______________________ ? At Bridge Street Mechanics.
3 ______________________ ? At Body Art.
4 ______________________ ? At the Northgate Dental Center.

→ workbook page 54

GRAMMAR
have something done

10 Underline the subject in each sentence. Do we know who is performing the action? Then complete the rule with *us* and *someone*.

1 I've had my hair cut.
2 I can have the lizard shaved off.
3 I'm going to have my arms tattooed.

RULE: We often use the structure *have* + object + past participle when we arrange for [4]_____ to do something for [5]_____. In less formal contexts, *get* often replaces *have*.

11 Complete the sentences. Use *have* + object + past participle.

Lord Uppity doesn't do anything himself.
1 He never cooks. He _____ his meals _____ by chefs.
2 He and his wife never do any housework. They _____ it _____ by cleaners.
3 He never goes into stores. He _____ everything _____ by his assistant.
4 Neither he nor his wife drives. They _____ their car _____ by an ex-racing driver.
5 They never organize parties. They _____ them _____ by party planners.
6 They don't look after their children. They _____ them _____ by a nanny.
Life is boring. There's simply nothing to do!

SPEAKING

A

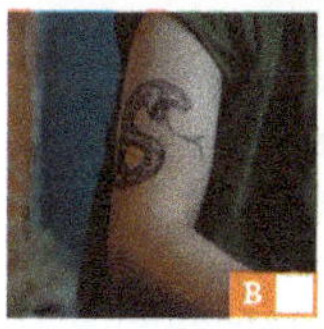
B

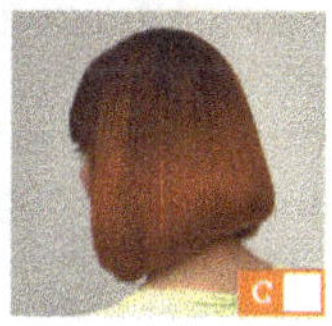
C

13 Match the photos with 1–3.

1 "My parents won't let me have my hair dyed."
2 "Dad was right. What a bad idea it was to get a tattoo!"
3 "I'm not allowed to get my ears pierced."

14 Work in pairs. Think of possible reasons for these teenagers' parents' attitudes.

15 How do you feel about these issues? Tell your partner.

Language note *have something done*

The person doing the activity is usually paid.

I have my dinner made by my mother. ✗
My mother makes my dinner. ✓

I have my car repaired by my father. ✗
I have my car repaired by Mr. Barry, the mechanic. ✓

Activity idea Extension

Divide the class into A/B pairs. Tell students they are going to do a role-play in which a parent and a teenager discuss the issues in Exercise 13. As are teenagers who want to do the three things. Bs are parents and should respond negatively to their child. Tell students they must try to convince their partner to change their mind.

TH!NK more

Workbook
Listening p60, Ex.1–6
Grammar pp54–55, Ex.5–6

Worksheets
Grammar Worksheets 6

Reading

Warmer

Write on the board: *make* and *do*. Split the class into two groups. Give students three minutes to brainstorm collocations with *make* and *do*. One group can think of phrases with *make*, the other phrases with *do*. (Examples: make: *fun of (someone), a difference, an effort, a mess, room for something, a mistake*; do: *your best, some good, damage, homework, a job*) During feedback, give a point for each correct answer and write it on the board for later in the lesson.

1 Set a two-minute timer to encourage students to read quickly and focus on the task, rather than trying to understand every word.
A 3 B 4 C 1 D 2 E 5

2 6.05 **Check/clarify:** *enthusiastic, graphics, episode, hold their breath, feel guilty, touchscreen, put on weight, pretend, box set.*
Before students read the blog entry again, get them to read the questions through.
1 They travel the world to find answers to questions that are asked on the shows.
2 Eight.
3 One eye looks in front and the other looks behind.
4 Because he/she couldn't really understand the explanation given by the show.
5 They can freeze without dying.
6 Because you learn the answers to lots of fascinating questions, and you can appear to be very smart.

3 Encourage students to justify their answers.
1 The body 2 Famous buildings
3 Around the house
4 Natural wonders 5 Magic

4 You may like to give an example of your own to get students started on this.

READING

1 Read the blog entry quickly and number the photos in the order they are mentioned 1–5.

BIG QUESTIONS BIGGER ANSWERS!

I just discovered a fantastic new show called *Big Questions – Bigger Answers!* It's one of the best online shows at the moment! The idea is simple: take a topic – like dolphins, for example – and then think of lots of little mysteries that can be explained. How do dolphins communicate? How do baby dolphins stay awake for a whole month? How can dolphins hear sounds that are so far away? That sort of thing. Then get two young, enthusiastic hosts to travel the world and find answers to these questions, add some cool graphics to explain the rest, and there's your show. Get the idea?

Each episode looks at a different subject. In addition to the *Dolphins* episode, topics that have already been covered include *Famous Buildings, The Body, Around the House, Natural Wonders*, and *Magic* – my favorite so far. Still to come are *Sports* and *Travel*. But back to dolphins. I really learned a lot of fascinating facts about them. Here's one I liked: how can dolphins look in two different directions at the same time? The answer: one eye looks in front and the other looks behind – amazing! And what about this? Dolphins replace their skin every two hours. Yes, every two hours! Also, did you know that dolphins can dive 550 meters underwater and hold their breath for 12 minutes? These are just a few of the things I learned on this great new show. And yes, I think you've guessed that I love dolphins!

What I like best about the show is that it's fun and you learn something at the same time, so you don't feel guilty about spending 60 minutes in front of a screen. We've been shown how birds make their way back to the exact same place each summer (they use the stars) and how a touchscreen works (that one didn't really make much sense to me). We haven't been shown how to eat chocolate without putting on weight yet, but I'm still hoping they might include that!

In future episodes, secrets like how top athletes can run so fast and why elephants can't jump will be revealed. The one I'm personally looking forward to the most is how frogs can freeze without dying.

So if you aren't already watching *Big Questions – Bigger Answers!* I strongly recommend that you make time to. It gives you facts that you can use to pretend that you're actually very smart for a while – as long as you can remember them, of course. Why not log in and watch this week's show now or download the box set at the end of the season? Many fascinating questions will be answered. So get watching and start learning!

2 6.05 **Read and listen to the blog. Answer the questions.**
1 What do hosts on the show do?
2 How many different topics are mentioned?
3 How can dolphins see in two different directions?
4 Why couldn't the writer tell you how a touchscreen works?
5 What amazing thing can frogs do?
6 How can watching this show make you more knowledgeable?

3 **In which episode are these questions probably answered?**
1 Why do we sneeze?
2 Why is the Eiffel Tower 15 cm taller in the summer?
3 How can solar heating work when it's raining?
4 How does Aurora Borealis (the Northern Lights) work?
5 How do you make a rabbit come out of a hat?

4 SPEAKING **Work in pairs. Choose four of the episodes from the text and think of a question you would like to see answered in each episode.**

60

Homework

Extend Exercises 3 and 4 into a homework research task with different students researching the answers to different questions to feed back to the group in a subsequent class.

Activity idea Extension

In pairs or small groups, students discuss the answers to each of the things in Exercise 3. Monitor to keep them on task and to ensure they're using English. Listen to some of their answers in open class.

TH!NK more

Workbook
Reading p58, Ex.1–3

5 Ask students to try to answer the questions from memory before referring back to page 60 to check.
1 been covered 2 been shown
3 be revealed 4 be answered
RULE: 5 be 6 past participle
7 present perfect 8 past participle

6 To check why we'd want to use the passive in these sentences (to emphasize the object of each sentence), ask students to decide what *they/people/someone* refer to in each one.
1 The match will be shown live on TV.
2 The next Olympic city will be chosen in April.
3 The match will be watched (by people) all over the world.
4 All the tickets for the show have already been sold.
5 The decision has already been made.
6 That money has already been spent.

7 Numbers 2 and 9 are also possible in active voice, but point out that students should use the future passive form.
1 will be filmed 2 will be shown
3 will be hosted 4 won't (will not) be joined 5 will be chosen
6 will … be joined 7 will be covered
8 won't (will not) be shown 9 'll (will) be moved 10 'll (will) be watched

8 A place for the party has already been found.
The invitations have already been sent.
The drinks haven't been bought yet.
The food hasn't been prepared yet.
A DJ has already been hired.
The music hasn't been chosen yet.

Workbook p55

9 **Check/clarify:** *make your way, make sense, make time, do time.* Encourage students to say the collocations aloud and think about whether the collocation sounds right or wrong. Encourage students to add their collocations from the beginning of the lesson.
make: money, sense, time, your way
do: an experiment, housework, time, well

10 1 doing 2 make 3 make 4 doing
5 makes 6 made

Workbook p56

GRAMMAR

Future and present perfect passive (review)

5 **Complete the sentences from the blog on page 60 with the words in the list. Then complete the rule with past participle (x2), *be*, and present perfect.**

been shown | been covered
be answered | be revealed

1 … topics that have already ______ include *Famous Buildings* …
2 We haven't ______ how to eat chocolate without putting on weight yet …
3 In future episodes, secrets like how top athletes can run so fast … will ______.
4 Many fascinating questions will ______.

RULE:
- To make the **future passive**, we use *will* + [5] ______ + the [6] ______.
- To make the **present perfect passive**, we use the [7] ______ form of *to be* and the [8] ______.

6 **Rewrite the sentences using the passive.**
1 They will show the match live on TV.
2 They will choose the next Olympic city in April.
3 People all over the world will watch the match.
4 They have already sold all the tickets for the show.
5 They have already made the decision.
6 Someone has already spent that money.

7 **Complete the text with the future passive form of the verbs.**

Good news for fans of
How Do They Do That?

A new season [1] ______ (film) over the next three months and the new episodes [2] ______ (show) in the new year. They [3] ______ (host) by Helen, but she [4] ______ (not join) by Liam this time. A new host [5] ______ (choose) in the next few weeks – watch this space! The hosts [6] ______ also ______ (join) by Spike the robot dog, but we aren't sure exactly what he'll do. Topics that [7] ______ (cover) include *Buildings, Space,* and *Food.* There'll also be a new time for the show. It [8] ______ (not show) at the old time of 9 p.m. on Tuesdays. It [9] ______ (move) to Sunday afternoons at 3 p.m. and the producers are hoping it [10] ______ (watch) by a bigger audience. I know one person who will be watching for sure – me!

8 **Look at the list and write sentences. Use positive and negative present perfect passive forms and *already* or *yet*.**

Mom and Dad's anniversary party – things to do

arrange a date for the party	✓
buy decorations	✗
find a place for the party	✓
send invitations	✓
buy drinks	✗
prepare food	✗
hire a DJ	✓
choose music	✗

A date has already been arranged for the party.
The decorations haven't been bought yet.

→ workbook page 55

VOCABULARY

make and *do*

9 **Write the words in the correct columns. Use page 60 to help you.**

an experiment | housework | money | sense | time | well | your way

make	do

10 **Complete the sentences with the correct form of *make* or *do*.**
0 I really need to <u>do</u> well on this test. I'm going to study hard tonight.
1 I've been ______ housework all day. I'm exhausted.
2 It's a really good exhibition. You should ______ time to see it.
3 Sorry I can't meet you at the station, but I'm sure you can ______ your own way to my house.
4 Don't go in there. They're ______ a dangerous experiment.
5 The movie is very long, so it ______ sense to have something to eat first.
6 He ______ a lot of money in banking and retired when he was 50.

→ workbook page 56

Activity idea Extension

Ask students to write the negative and question forms of each of the sentences in Exercise 6.

TH!NK more

Practice Extra
Unit 6 Practice it!

Workbook
Grammar p55, Ex.7–9
Vocabulary p56, Ex.4–5
Vocabulary Extra p57, Ex.1–3

Worksheets
Grammar Worksheets 6
Vocabulary Worksheets 6

Warmer

Write these story "clues" on the board: *gold pendant; grandmother; computer; library; Hotel Continental; magic.* In pairs, students discuss what the story might be about. Tell them they should try to use all of the items on the board to create a possible story. Monitor and help with vocabulary and ideas. Listen to their ideas in open class, but do not comment at this stage.

1 Get students to cover the extract and just look at the picture. Give them a minute to discuss the question in pairs.
Suggested answer: It's a diagram used to organize words or ideas around a central topic.

2 🔊 **6.06** Tell students not to focus on understanding every word for now, but to focus on listening for the answer.
The mind map in his notebook has words in it that he didn't write. Then red words appear on his computer screen saying "TAKE IT BACK."

Culture notes

The Kogi, also known as the Cogui or the Kágaba, are an indigenous ethnic group who live in the Sierra Nevada de Santa Marta mountains in the north of Colombia. They are descended from the Tairona culture, which thrived before the Spanish conquest. The Tairona were an advanced civilization, which made stone constructions and created paths through the jungle. In order to preserve their traditional way of life, the Kogi rarely interact with the modern world.

Fiction

1 What is a "mind map"? What do people use them for?

2 Read and listen to the extract. What two things surprise Lucho very much?

THE MIND MAP

BY DAVID MORRISON

Lucho and Eva are classmates at a school in Salvador. Their teacher tells them to make a mind map together. Lucho starts one at home, around the word *guaca*, which are special gold objects made by South American tribes. At home Lucho has a gold pendant that his grandmother gave him. Here, Lucho and Eva go to a computer to find more information for the mind map Lucho started.

Eva typed "Kogi" and pressed Enter. […] Soon [she] had found the web page she was looking for.

"OK." Eva started reading. "The Sierra Nevada mountains are home to the Kogi tribe. The ancestors of the Kogi were the brave Tairona …," she continued. "Like their ancestors, the Kogi still make things from gold."

"Should I write this down?" asked Lucho.

"Of course or we will forget it," Eva answered.

Lucho put his notebook on the table next to the computer and looked at the screen, where there was a photograph of a Kogi chief. The chief was wearing a jaguar skin and he had jaguar teeth on a piece of gold string round his neck. He seemed to be looking straight at Lucho from the screen. […]

"What are you waiting for, Lucho? Write these things on your mind map!" Eva said.

[Lucho] opened his notebook and turned to the page where he had drawn his mind map, but when he saw what had happened, he almost fell off his chair.

"Eva, something's wrong!" Lucho shouted.

"Shh!" said Eva. "We're in the library!"

"The mind map has changed, Eva. Look!"

He showed her the mind map. There were words now in the four circles he had drawn with the pendant. The words were, "Nebtashi," "Hotel Continental," "Esmeralda," and "Ichua."

"I don't even write like that, Eva!"

"Lucho," said Eva, "this is not the time for silly jokes. We don't have much time before the next class."

"Eva, I promise. All I did last night was to draw the circles and the lines and write 'guaca' in the centre circle. Something amazing has happened!"

Eva stood up.

"I'm sorry, Lucho." Her voice was very serious now. "I don't think you're a bad person, but you are a little strange. I will do the mind map alone. You can tell your story to Mr. Parra on Monday."

Eva walked out of the library. Lucho didn't know what to think. How had the words appeared on the mind map? Something strange, something very strange, was happening.

Quickly, he typed "Ichua" into the computer, but couldn't find any information. He now knew that "Nebtashi" meant "jaguar" and "Esmeralda" was his grandmother's name. He looked for information about the "Hotel Continental," but could only find pages about hotels in places he had never heard of.

"I must show Eva that I'm not lying!" he said to himself as he put his notebook and pen into his bag and stood up. Suddenly, he sat down again. Big red letters had started to appear on the computer screen and slowly the letters became words, three words:

"TAKE IT BACK."

Lucho could not believe his eyes.

3 **Check/clarify:** *pendant, Kogi, tribe, Tairona chief, jaguar, skin.* Encourage students to underline the language in the extract that helped them choose their answers.
1 They make things from gold.
2 To write information about the Kogi tribe in his mind map.
3 Because he's astonished to see the new words in his mind map.
4 Because she thinks Lucho is playing silly jokes and doesn't want to go on working with him.
5 He looks for information about the words "Ichua" and "Hotel Continental" which have appeared in his mind map.
6 He wants to prove that he hasn't been lying.

4 Encourage students to express themselves in English and to use any vocabulary they have learned from the extract. At the end of the exercise, listen to some of the students' ideas and encourage open class discussion.

5 **Check/clarify:** *powered up, pulled up, lifted into, taken off, turned around, lined up.* Encourage students to use the phrases in the speech bubbles. Do not give students the answers yet.

1 Give students two minutes to read quickly to check their answers to Exercise 5.
A 2 B 5 C 4 D 3 E 6 F 1

2 During feedback, go through the explanation, eliciting which parts refer to theory (these are described with active forms) and which describe procedure (these are described with passive forms).

3 Divide the class into small groups so that they can share ideas and make notes in preparation before writing individually (they could do this for homework). Prompt students to use sequence markers (from the *Functions* section) and the passive in their compositions.

3 **Read the extract again. Answer the questions.**
1 What do the Kogi people still do now that they did in the past?
2 Why does Lucho open his notebook?
3 Why does Lucho almost fall off his chair?
4 Why does Eva leave the library?
5 What does Lucho look for after Eva leaves?
6 What does Lucho want to prove to Eva?

4 SPEAKING **Work in pairs and answer the questions.**
1 What do you think "it" could be in the message on Lucho's screen?
2 What might the words in the mind map mean?
3 Why has he been told to "take it back"?

FUNCTIONS
Talking about sequence

5 SPEAKING **Work in pairs. In what order do these things happen when an airplane takes off? Number the boxes. Discuss your ideas.**

First, I think ... *After that, ...* *Next, ...* *Finally, ...*

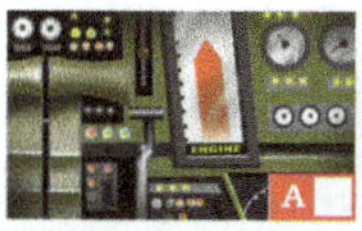
A *The engine is powered up.*

D *The brakes are taken off.*

B *The wheels are pulled up.*

E *The plane is turned around in the air.*

C *The nose is lifted into the air.*

F *The plane is lined up on the runway.*

WRITING
Explaining how things are done

1 INPUT **Read the explanation and check your answers to the last exercise.**

HOW DO PLANES
TAKE OFF?

To get an airplane into the air, you need the correct airspeed. Airspeed is not the speed of the plane, but how fast the air is moving over it. If the plane is facing a strong wind, the airspeed is already very high. That's why planes are usually lined up to take off facing into the wind.

The engines are turned up to a certain power. Then the brakes are released and the plane speeds down the runway. As it does this, air passes over the wings. The wings are curved on the top, so the air has farther to travel over the wings than under the wings and has to travel faster. This creates a force that pushes upwards. When that force is great enough, the nose of the plane is pushed into the air and when the correct airspeed is reached, the whole plane takes off.

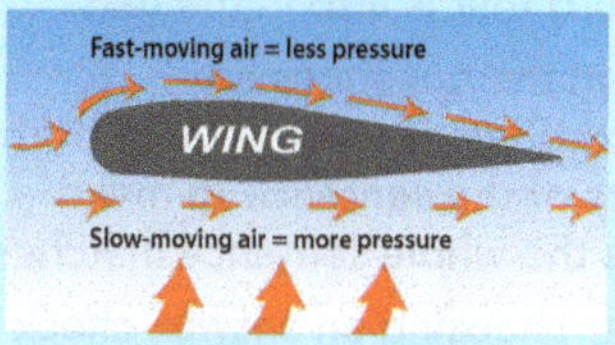

When the plane is high enough in the air, the wheels are pulled up and the plane continues on its way, leaving space for the next one to take off.

2 ANALYZE **Read the explanation again. Then make two lists for:**
- the procedure (what happens and in what order).
- the theories (explanations of why things happen).

3 PRODUCE **Choose an activity from the list or your own idea. Write an explanation of how to do it (150 words).**
- how to play the guitar
- how to play your favorite computer game
- how to do a headstand

Think about:
- the procedure and the sequence.
- whether you need to explain any theories.
- how to explain any difficult vocabulary.

63

Homework
If you are short on time, students can do Writing Exercise 3 for homework. If you have done this in class, ask students to exchange their explanations with another student for them to read and give feedback on content and structure. Students could check that the explanation uses the same structure as the template. They should also decide which the most/least interesting part of the explanation is.

Activity idea Extension
Perform a sequence of activities in front of the students, for example: open your bag, look at your phone, open the window, say "Hello", close the window, leave the room. Review sequence markers: *first, after that, next, finally* and write them on the board. Ask students to work with a partner and describe what you just did. Monitor and listen to how they sequence the activities. During feedback, write the sequence.

TH!NK more
Practice Extra
Unit 6 Master it!

Workbook
Developing Writing p59

Tests
Unit, extension and skills test 6
End of term test 2

In B2 First for Schools Reading and Use of English Part 5, candidates have to read a text followed by six four-option, multiple-choice questions (NB: On page 64 there are only four questions.) This part of the exam tests understanding of content and text organization.

Encourage your students to do the following when they approach this task:

- Skim the text to find out the topic and general meaning.
- Read each question carefully.
- Check that the meaning of the option is reflected in the text.
- Do not assume an option must be correct simply because it contains a word that is also in the text.
- When the questions are incomplete sentences, read both parts of the sentence to make sure the whole sentence matches.
- After choosing an answer, check the other three options and decide why they are wrong.

1 D 2 B 3 C 4 C

Workbook p61

TOWARDS B2 First for Schools

READING AND USE OF ENGLISH

Multiple choice

workbook page 61

1 You are going to read a text about urban legends. For questions 1–4, choose the answer (A, B, C or D) which you think fits best according to the text.

People have been telling stories for as long as they have been walking the Earth. And from cave paintings to Shakespeare's Globe Theatre to Hollywood blockbusters, the methods of telling them have got more and more sophisticated.

In the 1960s, a new storytelling art form emerged – the urban legend. Even if you've never heard the term, you've certainly heard an urban legend. What about the story of the unwanted pet alligators that were flushed down the toilet and are now living in the sewers of New York City? Or the man who woke up in a bathtub full of ice and saw a note informing him that one of his kidneys had been taken out?

One of the key features of the urban legend is its lack of an author. The stories appear mysteriously and are then passed on by word of mouth. And although we know these mini-tales of horror, humour and embarrassment are almost certainly not true, part of us wants to believe them.

Then the internet, which is packed with fiction (everything from jokes to the latest releases from top-selling authors), helped create and spread urban legends. Before the internet, urban legends went around quite slowly. They took time to reach a larger audience. The internet changed all that almost overnight.

The internet is the perfect vehicle for the urban legend, for it not only allows the stories to spread much faster but also allows for greater anonymity, too – a lot of what we read online doesn't have an author's name attached to it. This anonymity adds to the overall mystery.

Of course, the internet also allows you to check the truth of a story more easily. Over time, a number of sites have appeared which collect stories, investigate their origins and report the results. Often there isn't any truth to the story at all. But sometimes the urban legend grew from something that did actually happen. Thanks to the internet, learning about the origins of an urban legend can be as interesting and entertaining as the story itself.

1 What do we learn about stories from the first paragraph?
A They've never been as popular as they are now.
B They have their origins in the days of Shakespeare.
C They were much longer in the past.
D Ways of telling them have changed over time.

2 What does the author suggest about urban legends?
A Everyone knows the term 'urban legend'.
B Everyone knows an example of one.
C They appeared at the same time as the internet.
D They're always about horrific events.

3 What does the author mean when he says 'the internet … is packed with fiction'?
A You can find every story written online.
B You can get most fiction for free online.
C There are lots of stories on the internet.
D There are too many stories on the internet.

4 What does the author suggest about urban legends in the last paragraph?
A They're generally mystery stories.
B They're usually short.
C Nowadays it's easier to discover if they're true or not.
D Some include the author's name.

64

1 1 hero 2 hilarious 3 ending 4 tiny 5 freezing 6 character 7 terrible 8 fascinating 9 delighted 10 villain

2 1 that 2 have been taken 3 who 4 have it removed 5 are pulled 6 where

3 1 ~~done~~ made 2 ~~make~~ do 3 ~~will have shown~~ will be shown 4 ~~what~~ which 5 ~~allowed have~~ allowed to have 6 ~~who~~ whose

4 1 believe; What; chances 2 annoying 3 is; that 4 joking

TEST YOURSELF UNITS 5 & 6

VOCABULARY

1 **Complete the sentences with the words in the list. There are four extra words.**

character | delighted | ending | enormous | fascinating | freezing
hero | hilarious | opening | plot | setting | terrible | tiny | villain

1 The ________ of the movie is an amazing doctor who can travel through time and save people.
2 The show that we saw in the theater last night was ________. I couldn't stop laughing.
3 I just read the last page of the book and I don't like the ________.
4 I couldn't read all the words very well because the letters were ________.
5 He dove into the ________ water.
6 There is one ________ in the movie who is really funny. He makes everybody laugh.
7 I haven't done my homework. I had a ________ headache last night.
8 I can't put this book down – it's ________. I'm learning so much!
9 I'm ________ that you can come and see the show. The other actors will be happy, too.
10 The ________ of the story is an evil vampire.

/10

GRAMMAR

2 **Complete the sentences with the words/phrases in the list. There are two extra words/phrases.**

are used | have it removed | have been taken | whose | where | who | that | are pulled

1 It's a story ________ has been passed down from generation to generation.
2 Hundreds of photos of the magician ________.
3 She's an actor ________ has a great talent for storytelling.
4 Jack had a tattoo done a few years ago, and now he wants to ________.
5 Two rabbits ________ out of a hat in this trick.
6 He still lives in the city ________ he was born.

3 **Find and correct the mistake in each sentence.**

1 The decision will be done by the judges tonight.
2 I didn't make very well on the test.
3 The marathon will have shown live on TV.
4 I won a medal for swimming last semester, what made me feel proud.
5 I'm not allowed have my hair dyed.
6 Mrs. Jones, who son I went to school with, is my piano teacher.

/12

FUNCTIONAL LANGUAGE

4 **Choose the correct words.**

1 **A** You'll never *know* / *believe* what happened just now.
B *What* / *Really*?
A I guessed all the answers in the TV game show correctly. What are the *chances* / *opportunities* of that?
2 **A** What's that song you keep singing?
B That's the *annoying* / *angry* thing! I can't remember what it's called or who sings it.
3 **A** How does this machine work, then?
B First, the engine *is* / *was* turned on. After *it* / *that*, the handbrake is released.
4 **A** My dyed hair is a work of art!
B A work of art? You must be *laughing* / *joking*.

/8

MY SCORE /30
22–30 | 10–21 | 0–9

65

The Cambridge Life Competencies Framework

Collaboration
Setting measurable objectives
Watch this video for tips on how to help your students develop their collaborative skills. Scan the QR code here.

Reading; Train to TH!NK

Warmer

Write on the board: *men's jobs; women's jobs*. Give groups two minutes to think of five examples of each. Tell students to think in general terms / historically and not say that every job can be done by both. Say some more jobs, like *teacher, nurse, bus driver, ballet dancer* and ask them to decide which list to put them in.

▶ 17 Get TH!NKing

Play the video and discuss the question with your class.

7 BREAKING AWAY

OBJECTIVES

FUNCTIONS: talking about permission; talking about habits; invitations

GRAMMAR: *make / let* and *be allowed to*; *be / get used to*

VOCABULARY: phrasal verbs (1); personality; phrases with *all*

Get TH!NKING

Watch the video and think: who is the oldest person you know?

READING

1 **Look at the photos. What can you see? Use these words to help you.**

ironing | rugby | surfing

2 **Answer the questions.**

1 Do any of the photos make you laugh? If so, why?
2 Do you think any of the photos are strange? If so, why?
3 Do you think the photos have anything in common?

3 **Read the text that your teacher tells you to read (A or B). Answer the questions.**

1 Who is the text about?
2 In what way did the person do something different?
3 Who tried to stop the person from doing what they wanted to do?
4 Who (if anyone) helped the person?
5 What long-term effect did the person's actions have?

4 SPEAKING **Work in pairs. Using your answers to Exercise 3, tell your partner about your person.**

5 🔊 7.01 **Now read and listen to both texts. Answer the questions.**

1 How did Kathrine Switzer usually write her name?
2 What happened to Switzer after the race?
3 How much slower was Switzer 50 years later?
4 Why did Hogan not go to medical school?
5 Why did Hogan choose to go to MUW?
6 Why did MUW have to accept Hogan as a student?

Train to TH!NK

Thinking outside the box

In problem-solving, it can be useful to think really imaginatively, trying to avoid obvious or standard ideas. We call this "thinking outside the box." Sometimes thinking of very different possible answers to a problem helps us find the best solution.

It isn't a question of intelligence, just of thinking freely and creatively. The more you try it, the easier it is.

6 **Complete the table with as many ideas as you can think of.**

Questions about the texts	My "outside the box ideas"
1 Why did Semple want to stop Switzer?	*He wanted to get his photo in the newspaper.*
2 Why were a lot of women at MUW against letting Hogan in?	

7 **How many "outside the box" answers can you think of for these questions?**

1 What weighs more than it did half a year ago?
2 What are things money can't buy?
3 What can you do at school but not at home?

56

1 Put a copy of the photos on the board before students open their books.

2 Invite reactions in open class.

3 *A 1 Kathrine Switzer 2 She ran in a marathon, which normally only men took part in. 3 A race official called Jock Semple 4 Her friend Tom Miller 5 The organizers of the Boston Marathon changed their policy, and now women compete in all marathons.*
B 1 Joe Hogan 2 He enrolled in a college that normally accepted only women. 3 MUW leaders 4 No one 5 MUW changed their admissions policy, and now men are allowed to enroll in all its programs.

4 Ask students to make a note of their partner's answers.

5 🔊 **7.01 Check/clarify:** *marathon, registered, initials, grabbed, banned, campaigner, enroll, went to court, judges.*
1 K.V. Switzer 2 She was banned from entering competitions. 3 She was 24 minutes slower. 4 Because he couldn't afford it. 5 Because it offered a course in nursing, and it was close to his home. 6 Because he went to court, and the judges finally ruled that MUW had to accept him.

6 Tell students that there are no wrong answers and they should try to be as imaginative as possible.

7 Divide the class into small groups. When students have discussed some ideas, regroup students into new groups to share ideas.

Creative Thinking

Participating in creative activities

Actively participates in activities that require creative thinking with others (e.g., exercises that challenge firmly-held assumptions about a situation and require looking at an issue from many different perspectives).

Objectives

Functions and speaking Talking about permission; talking about habits; invitations
Grammar *make / let* and *be allowed to; be / get used to* **Vocabulary** Phrasal verbs (1); personality; **WordWise:** phrases with *all*
Life Competencies Getting along with others
Train to TH!NK Thinking outside the box
Values Stereotypes

Resources for this unit

All available online

Videos

- Get **TH!NK**ing: *Who is the oldest person you know?*
- Grammar rap!: *be / get used to*
- Vlog: Getting along with others

Tests

- Unit, extension, and skills test 7

Worksheets

- Grammar and vocabulary: Basic, Standard, and Extension Worksheets
- Project: People who changed the world
- Communication: All the same?
- Grammar presentation: *make / let* and *be allowed to*
- Get **TH!NK**ing, Grammar rap!, and Life Lessons video Worksheets

Culture notes

Kathrine Switzer, born 1947 in Germany, is an American marathon runner, writer, and television personality. In 1967, she became the second woman to run the Boston Marathon and the first as a numbered entrant. (Bobbi Gibb had run unregistered in 1966.) In 1974, she was the women's winner of the New York City Marathon. Her personal best time for a marathon was at Boston in 1975, when she ran it in 2:51:37. In 1968, Switzer married Tom Miller, the man who had come to her help while running the Boston Marathon in 1967, although they later divorced.

The Boston Marathon is an annual marathon race that was established in 1897 with just 15 participants. It is the world's oldest annual marathon and one of the world's best-known road racing events. It is always held on Patriots' Day – the third Monday of April – and now attracts an average of 30,000 participants each year. In 2015, about 46% of the entrants were female.

The Mississippi University for Women was established in 1884 in Columbus, Mississippi, USA. During the 2005–06 academic year, MUW's student body was about 15% male.

Mississippi University for Women v. Hogan (1982) is a legal case in which the US Supreme Court ruled (5–4) that the single-sex admissions policy of MUW, a publicly funded women's university, violated the equal protection clause of the 14th Amendment to the United States Constitution.

8 At the end of the exercise, listen to some of the students' ideas and encourage open class discussion.

Homework

Ask students to research someone who has tried to change a situation they thought was wrong. As a follow-up, students can present this person to the class in the next lesson.

CHANGING THE RULES

A CHANGING THE MARATHON

In 1967, runner 261 was just one of hundreds of competitors in the Boston Marathon – K.V. Switzer. But something was different. The race started and soon spectators and photographers realized that K.V. Switzer was … a woman.

Back then, there was no rule that women couldn't run official long-distance races – they simply didn't and many thought they wouldn't want to. When Kathrine Switzer registered for the marathon, she wrote her initials as she always did, so no one found out she was a woman. When she showed up for the race, none of the race officials noticed, so when the starter fired the gun, she set off.

But after about six kilometers, an official named Jock Semple wanted to make her stop. He ran out, grabbed her, and tried to pull her off the road. Switzer's friend Tom Miller pushed Semple away and Switzer kept on running. She finished the race in 4 hours 20 minutes.

After the race, Switzer was banned from entering other competitions because she had run with men. However, newspaper reports of her run made many people question their ideas about women and running. In 1972, public opinion forced the organizers of the Boston Marathon to let women compete. One of them was Switzer. Later, she went on to play an important role as a campaigner, which led to the first ever women's Olympic marathon in the 1984 Games.

In 2017, Switzer ran the Boston Marathon again at age 70. She finished in 4 hours 44 minutes. And the organizers retired number 261 – no one will use that number again.

B A MALE STUDENT AT AN ALL-WOMEN'S COLLEGE

Joe Hogan took up nursing as a young man. He didn't have many qualifications, but he started working at a community hospital in Mississippi, US. In 1981, he decided that he wanted to get higher qualifications. He didn't have enough money to go to medical school, so he applied for a course in nursing. One option he had was to enroll at the University of Mississippi, but that was almost 200 km away from his home. He didn't want to move or to travel that far every day – so he applied to the Mississippi University for Women (MUW).

MUW leaders turned him down – as a college for women only, it did not allow men to study there. But Joe didn't give up. He went to court, but he lost the first time. He went to court again and in 1982, after a year of arguments, a panel of nine judges decided that MUW had to accept Joe as a student. The president of MUW (a man) was furious and many of the students (women) thought the decision was wrong and that the college should not let Hogan enroll. But the college, in the end, had no choice – and Hogan enrolled. MUW ended up accepting men in all its programs (not just nursing) and now a small number of men study there. The college has not changed its name, however.

SPEAKING

8 **Work in pairs. Discuss these questions.**

1 If you could meet either Switzer or Hogan, which one would you choose? What questions would you ask her or him?

2 Do you know any stories about someone who tried to change a situation they thought was wrong? Tell your partner.

Activity idea An interview

Students could act out an interview with either Kathrine or Joe. Divide the class into four groups: A (Kathrine), B (Joe), C (Reporter to Kathrine), and D (Reporter to Joe). Ask groups C and D to look at the relevant text again and write down five questions to ask Kathrine/Joe. Ask group A to look at the texts again and find key information about Kathrine and group B about Joe in preparation for an interview. Monitor to make sure all the students are making notes and help with ideas if necessary. Put the students in A/C and B/D pairs and give them time to act out the interview.

TH!NK more

Worksheets

Project People who changed the world
Communication All the same?
Get **TH!NK**ing *Who is the oldest person you know?*

Grammar; Vocabulary

Warmer

In pairs, ask students to list rules at their school and at home. Set a three-minute timer and ask them to make notes. Discuss as a class.

1 Ask students to complete the sentences before referring back to page 67 to check.
1 make 2 made 3 let 4 did not allow 5 let RULE: 6 let 7 be allowed to 8 make

2 Suggested answers:
1 We aren't allowed to eat food in the classroom. 2 My parents let me sleep late on Sundays.
3 The teacher makes us read a book every week. 4 I'm allowed to listen to music in my bedroom.
5 The school lets us wear our own clothes. 6 Mom doesn't let us play soccer in the yard.
7 My parents don't make me go to bed early on Saturday.

Workbook p64

Get it Right!
make vs. *let*

Student's Book p124

3 Remind students that phrasal verbs usually have a different meaning from the verb they contain.
1 set off 2 ended up 3 carried on 4 took up 5 found out 6 showed up 7 give up 8 turned (him) down

4 As well as underlining the phrasal verbs, ask students to work out the meaning and think of different ways of saying each of them, using context to help them.
1 take care of 2 takes off 3 came over 4 hang out

GRAMMAR
make / let and *be allowed to*

1 Complete these sentences from the texts on page 67. Then complete the rule with *make*, *let*, and *be allowed to*.

1 Jock Semple wanted to ____________ her stop.
2 Newspaper reports of her run ____________ many people question their ideas.
3 Public opinion forced the organizers of the Boston Marathon to ____________ women compete.
4 As a college for women only, it ____________ men to study there.
5 Many of the students … thought … that the college should not ____________ Hogan enroll.

RULE: We can use [6] ______ *(someone do something)* and [7] ______ to talk about permission. We can use [8] ______ *(someone do something)* to talk about forcing someone to do something that they don't really want to do.

2 Rewrite the sentences. Use each of the three structures at least once.

0 I have to study every night. Dad says so.
Dad makes me study every night.
1 We can't eat food in the classroom.
____
2 I can sleep in on Sundays. My parents say so.
____
3 We have to read a book every week. The teacher says so.
____
4 I can listen to music in my bedroom. My dad says so.
____
5 We can wear our own clothes. The school says so.
____
6 We can't play soccer in the yard. Mom says so.
____
7 I don't have to go to bed early on Saturday. My parents say so.
____

→ workbook page 64

VOCABULARY
Phrasal verbs (1)

3 Look at the underlined phrasal verbs in the texts on page 67. Match them with the definitions.

1 began a journey
2 finally was in a situation or place (after some time or effort)
3 continued, didn't stop
4 started doing (a new activity)
5 got information or learned about (something new)
6 arrived or appeared at a place (usually late or unexpectedly)
7 quit (doing something)
8 refused, said "no" (to someone or something)

Look! The verbs in Exercise 3 are examples of phrasal verbs. These are usually formed with an ordinary verb (for example, *take*) and a particle (for example, *up*): *take up*. Together, they have a meaning that is often very different from the meaning of the verb alone.

4 Underline the phrasal verbs in the sentences.

1 I can't come tonight – I have to take care of my little brother at home.
2 Do you know what time the plane takes off tomorrow?
3 I had fun last night – my friends came over and we watched a movie.
4 She likes to hang out with her friends at the shopping mall.

5 Complete the sentences with phrasal verbs from Exercises 3 and 4. Use the correct forms of the verbs.

1 When we go on vacation, my friend ____________ my pet rabbit.
2 They offered Mom a job, but it was too far away, so she ____________ it ____________.
3 She said she'd meet me at six o'clock, but she didn't ____________ until seven.
4 Would you like to ____________ to my house tonight?
5 I started learning Russian, but it was very difficult, so I ____________ after six months.
6 I don't know what her name is, but I'm going to ____________!
7 She hurt her foot, but she ____________ playing until the end of the game.
8 I need to do more exercise, so I'm going to ____________ running and cycling.

→ workbook page 66

66

5 During feedback, encourage students to explain why each option is correct.
1 takes care of 2 turned … down 3 show up 4 come over 5 gave up 6 find out 7 carried on 8 take up

Workbook p66

THINK more

Workbook
Grammar pp64–65, Ex.1–6
Vocabulary p66, Ex.1–2
Vocabulary Extra p67, Ex.1–3

Worksheets
Grammar Worksheets 7
Grammar presentation: *make / let* and *be allowed to*
Vocabulary Worksheets 7

Language note *make / let* and *be allowed to*

Students may produce statements like **My dad makes me to help him in the garden*. In English, we don't use *to* after *make*. The structure is *make* + someone + base infinitive (something). The negative form is auxiliary + *not make* + someone + base infinitive. Students might also say **My parents don't allow to watch TV all the time*. Or **I'm not allow to watch TV all the time*. The structure is *am/is/are (not) allowed* + *to* + infinitive, so we would normally say *I am allowed to watch TV all the time*. However, *My parents allow me to watch TV all the time* is also possible.

Activity idea Fast finishers

Ask students to write three sentences of their own using phrasal verbs from this page.

6 🔊 **7.02** Tell students not to focus on understanding every word for now, but to focus on listening for the answers.
A people B curry C Hindi

7 🔊 **7.02** Before playing the audio again, ask students to answer as much as they can from memory. During feedback, you could play the audio again and encourage students to think about the correct answer to the false statements.
1 F 2 T 3 T 4 T 5 F

8 You could ask pairs to discuss a possible context for each sentence before choosing an expression.
1 after all 2 all the time 3 first of all 4 All the same

9 *1 all the time 2 First of all 3 after all 4 All the same*

Workbook p66

▶ 18 Grammar rap!
be / get used to

10 During feedback, draw students' attention to the *Look* box and be prepared to clarify the difference between *be* and *get used to*.
1 'm used to 2 aren't used to 3 get used to 4 got used to RULE: 5 gerund

11 Before students complete the exercise, they can discuss in pairs what a Brazilian who moves to London might have to *get used to*.
0 looking 1 weather; sunshine 2 coats and sweaters; wearing 3 British money; going 4 speaking; different accents

Workbook p65

Homework

Ask students to imagine they are living in another country, but they must keep this country a secret from the rest of the class. Students write down a list of things they *are* and *aren't used to doing* because these things are different in their home country. As a follow-up in the following class, ask students to read their sentences to a partner who should try and guess where they are living. For example: A *I'm not used to the long nights, and I'm not used to wearing a spacesuit.* B *You're living on the moon!* Monitor and make a note of any nice contributions to praise at the end of the activity.

LISTENING

6 🔊 7.02 **Listen to a speaker talking to some students about his trip to India. Which of the things in the photos does he mention?**

A

B

C

7 🔊 7.02 **Listen again. Mark the sentences T (true) or F (false).**

According to the speaker, …
1 he loved India immediately. ☐
2 India is a good place for people who don't eat meat. ☐
3 his Hindi is not very good. ☐
4 you need an open mind when you go abroad. ☐
5 everyone in a country is the same. ☐

WordWise: Phrases with *all*

8 Complete these sentences from the listening with the expressions.

all the time | after all | all the same | first of all

1 I mean, ____________, people are people – there are a variety of people all over the world.
2 Did you have to eat spicy food ____________?
3 So, ____________ I want to say that I think traveling is a great thing.
4 People aren't used to seeing foreigners. ____________, I thought everyone was really warm and kind.

9 Replace the underlined phrases with expressions from Exercise 8.

1 In England, it seems like it rains every day.
2 Welcome, everybody! To begin, I'd like to introduce myself.
3 Of course I like Italian food – as an example to prove my point, I eat pasta, don't I?
4 I know you don't like dentists. Nevertheless, if you're in pain, you should go and see one.

→ workbook page 66

GRAMMAR
be / get used to

10 Complete these sentences from the listening. Use the phrases in the list. Then complete the rule with *infinitive* or *gerund*.

aren't used to | 'm used to
gotten used to | get used to

1 I ____________ exploring and meeting new people.
2 In some places, people ____________ seeing foreigners.
3 I can't ____________ spicy food.
4 The trains are very crowded, but I soon ____________ that.

RULE: *be / get used to* is followed by a noun or noun phrase, or by a verb in the [5]______ form. We use *be / get used to (doing) something* to talk about experiences and habits.

Look
Be used to refers to a state – something that is normal or familiar. ***Get used to*** refers to a process – something unusual *becomes* normal or familiar.

11 João is Brazilian, but he's living in London. Complete the sentences with the words.

British money | coats and sweaters
different accents | going | looking | speaking
sunshine | ~~traffic~~ | wearing | weather

0 I'm from Rio, so I'm used to *traffic*, but I'm not used to ____________ right before I cross the street!
1 I haven't gotten used to the ____________ yet. It rains a lot here. In Brazil, I was used to ____________.
2 It's hard to get used to all the ____________! I'm not used to ____________ so many clothes.
3 I'm used to ____________ now. But most stores close at 5:30. I'm not used to ____________ home so early.
4 I was used to ____________ English before I arrived. But I'll never get used to all the ____________ here.

→ workbook page 65

69

Language notes *be / get used to*

Students may have difficulty forming negative sentences with *get / be used to*. There are two possible negatives with different meanings. For example:

I am not used to waking up early.
(I don't often wake up early, and it is strange for me.)

I am used to not waking up early.
(I usually wake up late.)

Also *be / get used to* is different from the structure *used to* + infinitive which refers to repeated past actions or states that no longer happen, e.g., *I used to play the violin, but I gave up a few months ago.*

TH!NK more

Workbook
Listening p70, Ex.1–4
WordWise p66, Ex.5
Grammar p65, Ex.7–8

Worksheets
Grammar rap! *be / get used to*
Grammar Worksheets 7

Reading

Warmer

Write on the board: *prison*. Ask students to imagine they are in prison and discuss the following in pairs: *How is your life different? Describe a typical day. What was difficult to get used to when you first went to prison?*

1 **Check/clarify:** *prison warden.* Before students do the task, get them to cover the article and just look at the title and photos. In pairs, give students two minutes to think about the answer to the question. Encourage them not to focus on every word for now.

2 Tell students to read quickly and not worry about understanding every word, but just focus on checking their answer to Exercise 1.
C

3 🔊 **7.03** Once students have finished, it is a good idea to read the article with their answers to check it sounds correct.
1 politics 2 future 3 color 4 short 5 all the people in the room 6 friend

4 Ask students to try to answer as many of the questions as they can from memory before reading again to check.
1 He spent his childhood on a farm in South Africa.
2 Brand was told he was going to work with the biggest criminals in South African history, including political prisoners and that some of them would be dangerous.
3 They had both grown up on a farm.
4 Because close relationships between prisoners and wardens weren't allowed by the prison authorities.
5 He got Brand a job.

READING

1 **Look at the photos and the title. What do you think the article is about?**
A two men who built a prison
B a man whose father went to prison and became president
C a friendship between a prisoner and a prison warden
D a friendship between two prisoners

2 **Read the article quickly. Check your answer to Exercise 1.**

3 🔊 7.03 **Read the article again. At each point 1–6, choose the best answer. Then listen to check your answers.**

4 **Answer the questions.**
1 Where did Brand spend his childhood?
2 What kind of prisoners was Brand told he was going to work with?
3 What did Brand and Mandela have in common?
4 Why did Mandela and Brand have to keep their friendship secret?
5 What did Mandela do for Brand when he became president?

MY PRISONER, MY FRIEND, MY PRESIDENT, AND MY FATHER

In 1978, Christo Brand joined the prison service. He was an 18-year-old white South African boy who had grown up on a farm. Now he was being sent to work as a warden in the famous prison on Robben Island. There, he was told he was going to work with the biggest criminals in South African history, including political prisoners. Brand didn't know very much about [1]*politics / prisoners* – he just knew that he was going to work with some dangerous people.

And then he met prisoner 46664, a quiet 60-year-old black man who started to talk to Brand and ask him questions – questions about his family, his education, his plans for the [2]*future / prison*. Prisoner 46664 was Nelson Mandela, who would one day become the first black president of South Africa.

"There was no [3]*language / color* barrier between us," said Brand, who later worked as a guide showing tourists around Robben Island. "Like me, Mandela came from a farm. We understood that we shared the same sky and the same air." The two men got along well and became really close, although this wasn't allowed by the prison authorities. They had to keep their friendship secret and their conversations had to be [4]*short / fascinating*. Brand found that Mandela was a warm and thoughtful person, even a little shy sometimes.

Mandela was also a generous man and he never forgot his friend. When he became president, he got Brand a job. One day, at a meeting of important politicians, Brand was in the room and was putting documents on the table. When Mandela came in, he saw Brand, went to him and hugged him. Mandela looked at [5]*Brand / all the people in the room* and said, "This person was my warden. This person was my [6]*friend / teacher*." Brand says that he felt very proud at that moment.

Nelson Mandela died in December of 2013, at age 95. Like so many people around the world, Brand was very sad when he heard the news. He said at the time, "Mandela was my prisoner, my friend, my president, and my father."

Culture notes

Nelson Rolihlahla Mandela (1918–2013) was a South African anti-apartheid activist, political leader, and humanitarian. In 1944 he joined the African National Congress (ANC) – a political group that strived for equal rights for whites and blacks. His activism made him very unpopular with the authorities and in 1962, he was arrested and sent to prison. Mandela served 27 years as a political prisoner. He was released in 1990 and became president of the ANC a year later. In 1994, in the first fully representative democratic election, he became President of South Africa and was the country's first black head of state, serving until 1999. His government focused on breaking down the legacy of apartheid (institutionalized racial segregation). Nelson Mandela is widely regarded as an icon of democracy and social justice. Over the course of his life, he was given over 250 awards in recognition of his political achievements, including the Nobel Peace Prize in 1993.

TH!NK more

Workbook
Reading p68, Ex.1–4

5 1 warm and kind 2 cold and unfriendly 3 generous and thoughtful

6 Encourage students to use English–English dictionaries to complete the exercise as there may not be a direct translation in their own language. During feedback, work on pronunciation by saying the adjectives for students to repeat. Check that they're placing stress on the correct syllable (on the first in all cases except for *polite* and *unfriendly*, where the second syllable is stressed).
Positive (+): warm, kind, polite, generous, thoughtful
Negative (–): selfish, rude, cold, unfriendly
Neutral (0): shy, lively

7 You could stage the task by first asking students whether a positive, negative, or neutral adjective is required.
1 selfish, rude, unfriendly 2 shy 3 thoughtful, kind, warm 4 kind 5 rude, unfriendly, cold

8 1 rude 2 lively 3 generous/kind 4 polite 5 cold 6 thoughtful/kind/generous

9 Monitor and help as required.

10 Students could compare in pairs before swapping partner and comparing again.

Workbook p66

VOCABULARY
Personality

5 Read the sentences about the listening on page 69 and the article on page 70. Choose the correct words.

1 Everyone in India was *shy and rude / warm and kind*, even when we didn't understand each other well.
2 Some people can be *cold and unfriendly / lively and polite*, but everyone I met was really nice.
3 The writer describes Mandela as a *lively and selfish / generous and thoughtful* man.

6 Which adjectives in Exercise 5 are positive, negative, and neutral? Mark them +, –, or 0. Use a dictionary to check the meaning of any of the words that you are unsure of.

7 Which adjectives describe each person? You can choose more than one for each person.

1 *No, it's mine. You can't use it.*
2 *I don't want to go to the party, thanks. I'm not comfortable with strangers.*
3 *Jack got some bad news. Let's go and talk to him. Perhaps he needs a friend.*
4 *Don't worry. There's a problem, but everything's going to be all right, OK?*
5 *Go away! I'm working. I don't want to talk to you now.*

8 Complete each response with an adjective. There may be more than one possible answer.

1 A Hey, you! Get out of my way!
B What a ______ boy!
2 A The children aren't tired at all.
B Yes, they're very ______ tonight.
3 A Let's all go and have a hamburger. I'll pay.
B Wow! That's very ______ of you.
4 A He always says "please" and "thank you."
B Yes, he's very ______.
5 A She never laughs or cries or anything.
B I know. She's a bit ______ sometimes.
6 A Mandy always thinks about other people.
B Yes, she's a really ______ person.

9 Write four sentences about people you know. (You don't need to use their names!) Use adjectives from Exercise 5 and give reasons.
I know someone who I think is rude because he/she never says hello at the bus stop.

10 SPEAKING Compare your sentences with the class.

→ workbook page 66

TH!NK values
Stereotypes

11 SPEAKING Work in small groups. Discuss these questions.

1 Think about your own country, or a region of your country. Do people from other places have fixed ideas about the people who live there?
Some people think the British are very polite but not very friendly.
2 Why do you think people have these ideas?
3 Do you think there is any truth in the stereotypes of your country or region?

12 Some stereotypes are about nationalities. What other groups of people are there stereotypes about? Write a list. Then compare your ideas.
People who live in small towns ...

13 SPEAKING In your groups, discuss stereotypes that you think people have about teenagers.

WRITING
An article about stereotypes

14 Write an article (80–120 words) for a school magazine about a national stereotype. Think about:

- a culture that some people in your country see as a stereotype.
In Britain, a lot of people think that Americans talk very loudly, only eat fast food, and wear colorful clothes.
- why you think the stereotype exists.
I think it's because some American tourists in Britain are like that sometimes, and in some movies, too.
- why this stereotype is wrong.
My friend went to the US last year. She said she ate excellent food and the Americans she met were quiet and fashionably dressed!

11 You could also ask: *Do you think any of the stereotypes used to be true, but aren't now?*

12 You could give an example of your own to get students started.

13 At the end of the exercise, listen to some of the students' ideas and encourage open class discussion on people's attitudes towards teenagers.

14 Students should organize their work to follow the same format as the example in Exercise 14.

Activity idea Extension

Write on the board: *Is there any truth in the stereotypes in Exercise 13? What are the impacts of stereotypes on teens or different nationalities? What can be done to change stereotypes?* Ask students to work in small groups to discuss the questions. Monitor and encourage students to try to express their real ideas and opinions in English. Avoid error correction unless it really hinders comprehension. Invite students to share their ideas in open class.

Social Responsibilities
Understanding and describing own and others' cultures
Accepts others and shows respect for cultural difference, challenging prejudice, and discriminatory views.
Makes informed comparisons between their own society and other societies.

Critical THINKing
Evaluating ideas, arguments, and options
Distinguishes between fact and opinion.
Identifies evidence and its reliability.

Critical THINKing
Understanding and analyzing links between ideas
Compares points and arguments from different sources.

TH!NK more

Practice Extra
Unit 7 Practice it!

Workbook
Vocabulary p66, Ex.3–4
Developing Writing p69

Worksheets
Vocabulary Worksheets 7

Developing Speaking; Phrases for fluency; Functions; Pronunciation

Warmer

Ask students to think about how they spent their last birthday. In small groups, students share their ideas and respond with *So did I*, *Neither did I*, etc. Hold a vote to find out which are the most common birthday celebrations.

1 7.04 Tell students to cover the dialogue and discuss the question in pairs before listening to check their answers.
The teenagers are angry with each other.

2 7.04
1 Because their birthdays are on the same day. / Because Mom won't let them.
2 He should try to get along with Harry for one evening. / He should be more flexible.
3 She doesn't like her.
4 Jackie, Luke, and Mom

3 Encourage students to use the language from the dialogue when giving their answers.

4 During feedback, say the sentences for students to repeat. Drill sentences to ensure correct pronunciation.

5 As an alternative, you could ask students to cover the phrases in the dialogue and get them to guess what the alternative expressions are.
1 Don't mention it 2 good point
3 Well yeah 4 Give it a rest
5 Don't get me wrong
6 I'm with you on this one

DEVELOPING SPEAKING

1 7.04 **Look at the photo. How do you think the people feel about each other? Listen and read to check.**

Jackie: Well, I think you're being unfair. Just because he likes different music than you do…
Luke: It's not just that and you know it! Harry's boring and there's no way I want him there.
Mom: Give it a rest, you two. Please! I'm tired of this endless arguing. What is it now? Let me guess. That's who you're going to invite.
Jackie: Well yeah, Mom. The thing is, we don't have the same friends, so it's hard when we're having just one party!
Luke: I'm with Jackie on this one, Mom. Can't we have two parties?
Mom: How is that going to work? You're twins, so your birthdays are on the same day. And we live in one house. One house, one day, one party. You can invite thirty people – end of story.
Jackie: So, Luke, we have to find a way to do this. Don't get me wrong, but I think you could be more … well, flexible, you know? I know you don't like Harry, but can't you get along with him for one evening?
Mom: Good point, Jackie.
Luke: Well, I suppose you're right.
Jackie: And listen, I promise you can invite Mary Tanner and I won't complain. OK?
Mom: That's more like it. A little bit of give-and-take.
Luke: Thanks for helping us sort it out, Mom.
Mom: Don't mention it. Now, let's all go out and buy some decorations.

2 7.04 **Listen and read the dialogue again. Answer the questions.**
1 Why can't Luke and Jackie have separate parties?
2 What does Jackie say Luke should try to do?
3 How does Jackie feel about Mary Tanner?
4 Who is going to buy decorations?

3 SPEAKING **Discuss the statements in pairs. What do you think?**
1 Luke and Jackie should have their parties on two different days.
2 Jackie's right to ask Luke to be nice to Harry.
3 Their mother sorts out their problem.

Phrases for fluency

4 **Find the underlined expressions in the dialogue. How do you say them in your language?**

5 **Replace each underlined part with an expression from the dialogue.**
1 A Thanks for your help.
B You're welcome.
2 A If we don't leave now, we'll be late.
B Yes, I think you're right. Let's go!
3 A You look happy. Good exam results?
B Yes, of course I did! I got 95%.
4 A Dad, Alex won't let me use the computer.
B Arguing again? Stop it now, before I get angry!
5 A You're always looking at your phone. Don't be offended, but I think you should use it less.
6 A It's raining. I suggest we watch a movie inside.
B I agree with you. Which movie should we watch?

FUNCTIONS
Invitations

KEY LANGUAGE
Making invitations
Why don't you (join us)? / How about (coming with us)? Do you want to (go to the movies with me)?
Accepting invitations
That'd be (great). / I'd love to. / Yes, of course, thank you.
Declining an invitation
Sorry, I can't. / You'll have to count me out.

6 **Complete the sentences with the words in the list.**

about | count | course
don't | want | love | would

1 Why ______ you come along?
2 How ______ bringing some friends along with you?
3 Do you ______ to come along?
4 That ______ be fantastic. I'd ______ to.
5 Yes, of ______. It's a great idea.
6 You'll have to ______ me out.

ROLE PLAY **Work in pairs. Student A: turn to page 127. Student B: turn to page 128.**

PRONUNCIATION
Intonation – inviting, accepting, and refusing invitations Go to page 121.

72

6 You could move on to pronunciation at this stage prior to doing the role-play. Allow students six to eight minutes to prepare their role-plays. Monitor to make sure all students are on task. If students have access to a recording device (their mobile devices, for example), they could record their conversation and play it back to check their own pronunciation and intonation. They can then repeat the exercise and listen for improvements.
1 don't 2 about 3 want 4 would; love 5 course 6 count

Pronunciation
Intonation – inviting, accepting, and refusing invitations
Student's Book p121

TH!NK more
Workbook
Pronunciation p120

Life Competencies

Warmer

Write *getting along with others* on the board and elicit the meaning in this context (able to be friends with people easily). Ask students to give themselves a mark out of ten for their ability to get along with people. Does ability to do this change depending on who they are interacting with?

▶ 19 Life Lessons: Getting along with others

1 ▶ **19 Check/clarify:** *difficult, jail.* Ask students to compare their ideas with a partner.

2 ▶ **19** Ask students to try to answer the questions from memory before watching the video again to check.
a He plays music loudly; he borrows his sister's phone charger and forgets to put it back; he teases her about a boy she likes.
b She's usually in a bad mood; she shouts at Leo; she says his music is bad; she doesn't help around the house; she thinks she's better than anyone else.

3 As a follow-up, ask students to rank their list in Exercise 2a from the most to the least annoying. Discuss as a class and come up with a definitive list.

4 You could put students in two groups and give each one of the situations to read and share ideas on.

5 Give students three or four minutes to think about their answers before discussing.

6 Monitor and prompt students to keep talking, but as this is a fluency activity, do not interrupt to correct mistakes. While monitoring, note down any common errors to review as a class at the end.
A 1 and 3 B 2 and 4

7 You may want to talk about or make up someone you don't get along with as an example.

BREAKING AWAY UNIT 7

LIFE COMPETENCIES

Getting along with others is important. We don't always agree with other people or like the way they do things. However, even when we disagree with them, we ought to be friendly and respect them.

1 ▶ 19 **Watch the vlog. How would you describe the situation at home between Leo and his sister?**

2 ▶ 19 **Watch the vlog again and make notes on:**
a three annoying things Leo does.
b three annoying things his sister does.

3 **Compare your notes with a partner.**

4 **Read the situations. Make notes about what you would do in each situation.**

A You are working on a project with a group of students in your class. You have a lot of good ideas that you want to use, but one person is difficult to work with. She also has lots of ideas for the project, but the problem is you don't think her ideas are very good. She says that you are too bossy and that you won't listen to anyone else, because you think your ideas are the best.

B You have always been good at English, particularly in creative writing, and you usually get good grades. You used to have a good relationship with your teacher, but recently, he has started to be pretty negative about your work and has even criticized it in front of the class. Last week, you got a really bad grade on your homework and you don't know why. When you tried to speak to your teacher about it, he seemed annoyed.

5 **Compare your answers with a partner. Do you agree? Have you ever been in a similar situation? What did you do?**

6 SPEAKING **Work in pairs. Match the solutions 1–4 to situations A and B in Exercise 4. Then discuss. Which solutions do you think are the best? Which would you *not* recommend?**

1 Suggest everyone in the group votes on which ideas to use. Both of you will have to be prepared to accept that it may not be your ideas that are chosen.
2 Confront your teacher again and ask for an explanation. Explain that your work won't improve unless he gives you clear feedback on exactly what the problem is. Refuse to leave until it is resolved.
3 Listen to your friend's ideas and think about how they could work with your own. Maybe you could use some of your ideas and some of hers, too.
4 Try talking to another teacher. Ask him/her for advice on how to deal with the situation.

Me and my world

7 **Think of someone you don't get along well with. Write down:**
1 three reasons why you don't get along.
2 three things you could do to change things.

TIPS FOR GETTING ALONG WITH OTHERS

- **Take a bit of time to stop and think about what someone has said or done. Don't respond or react in anger. This could make the situation worse.**
- **Be positive. Think of solutions to your problem before you speak to the person.**
- **Try to feel empathy. There may be a reason why the person is behaving a certain way. Ask how they are feeling.**

73

Homework

Ask students to write two short texts describing their relationship with someone they get along with and someone they don't get along with in their family.

Have the students keep a journal for two or three days, with a record of how they got along with their family – who they got along with, who they didn't get along with, and what they did or could have done to get along better.

Activity idea Extension

Students write five sentences describing the people that they get along with best.

TH!NK more

Practice Extra
Unit 7 Master it!

Worksheets
Life Lessons: Getting along with others

Tests
Unit, extension, and skills test 7

Emotional Development
Empathy and relationship skills
Showing understanding of other people's perspectives and feelings.
Stating opposing opinions in a respectful way.
Negotiating conflict constructively.

Warmer

To assess students' current knowledge, draw two circles on the board and write the word *Crimes* in one and *Criminals* in the other. Ask pairs of students to write a list of crimes and a list of criminals. Set a three-minute timer. During feedback, create two mind maps on the board.

▶ 20 Get TH!NKing

Play the video and discuss the question with your class.

1 Ask concept-check questions such as: *Does a pickpocket steal from a person or place?* (a person); *Does a robber steal from a house, a person, or a bank?* (a bank)

2 Point out that stress falls on the first syllable of these words.
A4 B1 C6 D2 E5 F3

3 Give a couple of examples before students work in pairs.

4 🔊 **8.01** Before students read the news stories, get them to cover them and just look at the photos and answer the question.
It's about poachers in Africa.

5 **Check/clarify:** *get rid of, evidence, possessions, facing charges, agents, arrested, poisoned, weapon, caught red-handed, illegal item, horn, dye, poisonous.*
Before students read the news stories again, get them to read the questions through.
1 rhino 2 lion 3 lion 4 rhino
5 rhino 6 lion 7 lion 8 rhino

6 **Check/clarify:** *pride, regret, guilt.*
1 a 2 b

8 CRIME AND PUNISHMENT

OBJECTIVES

FUNCTIONS: reporting what someone said, asked, or requested; giving and reacting to news

GRAMMAR: reported speech (review); reported questions, requests, and imperatives

VOCABULARY: crime; reporting verbs

Get TH!NKING
Watch the video and think:
do you always pay for the music you listen to?

READING

1 **Look at the words for different types of criminals. How do you say them in your language?**

1 burglar	3 poacher	5 bank robber
2 con artist	4 pickpocket	6 shoplifter

2 **Match the pictures with words from Exercise 1.**

3 **Think of examples of these criminals from the news, books, TV, or movies.**

4 🔊 8.01 **Look at the photos and headlines on the next page. Guess what the news stories are about. Then read and listen to check.**

5 **Read the news stories again. In which stories do these things happen? Write *lion* or *rhino*.**
1 The criminals tried to get rid of the evidence. ____
2 The criminals were caught as they tried to kill the animal. ____
3 The criminals attacked the agents. ____
4 The criminals were caught after a car chase. ____
5 It was not the first time the criminals had gotten into trouble. ____
6 The agents found important evidence among the criminals' possessions. ____
7 The criminals are facing charges for three different crimes. ____
8 Agents believe their work is starting to make a difference. ____

Train to TH!NK

Thinking about empathy
To understand another person's feelings, you need to "put yourself in their shoes" – try to imagine how you'd feel in their situation.

6 **Read the first story again. Who do you think felt these emotions? Match 1–2 with a–b.**
1 the agents ☐
2 the poachers ☐
a excitement and pride
b regret and guilt

7 **Why do you think they might have felt these things? What other emotions do you think they might feel?**

8 **How do these stories make you feel? Tell your partner.**

74

7 Elicit or give the meaning for as many relevant adjectives as possible. Some language is high level, so accept L1 if students are struggling to come up with words in English.

8 At the end of the exercise, listen to some of the students' ideas and encourage open class discussion.

Emotional Development
Empathy and relationship skills
Shows understanding of other people's perspectives and feelings.

Objectives

Functions and speaking Reporting what someone said, asked, or requested; giving and reacting to news
Grammar Reported speech (review); reported questions, requests, and imperatives
Vocabulary Crime; reporting verbs
Culture Famous prisons
Train to TH!NK Thinking about empathy
Values Respecting the law

Resources for this unit

All available online

Videos
- Get **TH!NK**ing: *Do you always pay for the music you listen to?*
- Grammar rap!: Reported speech (review)
- Culture: Famous prisons

Tests
- Unit, extension, and skills test 8

Worksheets
- Grammar and vocabulary: Basic, Standard, and Extension Worksheets
- Project: Making the rules
- Communication: It's a crime
- Literature Worksheets: *The Hound of the Baskervilles*; *The Wonderful Wizard of Oz*
- Get **TH!NK**ing and Grammar rap! video Worksheets

Culture notes

Limpopo, a province in the north of South Africa, is named after the Limpopo River, which forms its borders to the north and west. The name Limpopo means "strong gushing waterfalls." The capital is Polokwane.

Letaba is a main rest camp within the Kruger National Park in South Africa. It sits along the Letaba River, which runs in a southeasterly direction about halfway up the game reserve. The name Letaba means "sandy river." The area around Letaba had been settled for thousands of years before Kruger Park was created, but tribes were removed during the park's creation and now live just outside the perimeter.

CRIMES!

POACHERS *ARRESTED*

Anti-poaching agents in Limpopo, South Africa caught two poachers as they tried to kill lions at the Letaba River Wildlife Reserve Park last Sunday evening.

The agents had received information about the planned attack and made plans of their own to catch the criminals in the act.

Under a full moon, the poachers broke into the park where the agents were waiting. They jumped on the poachers as they approached the cages where the lions were kept for their own protection. After a short fight in which one of the poachers used a knife, the agents were able to arrest the two men.

One of the agents said that they had searched the men's bags and had found poisoned dead chickens and wire cutting equipment. He explained how poachers throw the chickens to the lions, wait for the lions to eat the chickens, and then return when the animals are dead. He also said that the poachers could sell the dead animals for over $3,500.

The poachers are now in jail awaiting trial. The prisoners are facing charges of attempted poaching, possession of a dangerous weapon, and attempted murder. If found guilty, they could go to prison for up to ten years. An anti-poaching agent said he hoped this would be a warning to other poachers and help in their fight against one of their country's most serious problems.

CAUGHT *RED-HANDED*

In another part of Limpopo, three rhino horn smugglers have been caught red-handed by members of the Limpopo Endangered Species Unit. The agents had received information the men were trying to sell the illegal item. As they approached the men's car, it drove away quickly and a large item was thrown from the window. While one agent got the item, which turned out to be the horn, others chased and caught the three men. Two of the men, who are brothers, were already known to the agents. They had been arrested in 2014 for rhino poaching but had not been sent to prison and were let go. This time agents are hoping they will finally be sent to prison. They believe the horn comes from a rhino that was shot dead a week ago in a nearby area. Agents said they were going to send the horn for testing to see if they are right.

Rhino poaching continues to be a huge problem in many southern African countries as the demand for their horns increases around the world. But South African law officers are determined to protect the animals and are spending more money to catch those committing the crimes. An official from the department of environmental affairs said that the situation was improving and that the number of rhino deaths in 2016 had fallen since the record number of over 1,200 in 2014. They also said they are using modern technology in their fight. One technique is to put a dye into the rhino's horns, which is poisonous for humans but perfectly safe for the rhinos.

SPEAKING

9 SPEAKING **Work in pairs. Discuss these questions.**

1 What punishment do you think these men should get?
2 What other animals do you know that are in danger from poachers?

9 Monitor and prompt students to keep talking, but as this is a fluency activity, do not interrupt to correct mistakes. While monitoring, note down any common errors to review as a class at the end. At the end of the exercise, listen to some of the students' ideas and encourage open class discussion.

Homework

Write on the board *lion, elephant, shark, tiger, panda, Amur leopard, orangutan, Mekong river dolphin.* Ask students to choose one of the animals and research a success story about it (the World Wide Fund for Nature has some information). They can upload a picture with details of the success story in English. As a follow-up, students can bring the picture to the next lesson and present their success story to the class.

Activity idea Extension

Ask students to find the names of the crimes that correspond to each of the criminals in Exercise 1. burglar – *burglary*; con artist – *fraud*; poacher – *poaching*; pickpocket – *pickpocketing*; robber – *robbery*; shoplifter – *shoplifting*.

Activity idea Extension

Ask students to discuss these questions in small groups: *Why do people commit crimes like those in Exercise 1? What are some of the possible effects on the victims? What do you think society should do with each of the different types of criminal?* Monitor, but avoid error correction. The focus of this task is on fluency, not on practice of structures or lexis. Instead, make a note of common errors. Write a mix of correct and incorrect sentences on the board, ensuring anonymity, and ask students to identify and correct the mistakes during feedback.

TH!NK more

Worksheets
Project Making the rules
Communication It's a crime
Get **TH!NK**ing *Do you always pay for the music you listen to?*

Warmer

Write on the board: *What are the punishments if you get into trouble in school? Do you think that some of the punishments are too strict?* Students discuss their answers in pairs.

▶ 21 Grammar rap! Reported speech (review)

1 1 had searched 2 could sell 3 hoped; would 4 were going to send 5 was improving 6 had fallen

2 a 4 b 3 c 6 d 2 e 1 f 5
RULE: 1 past continuous 2 past perfect 3 past perfect 4 could 5 would 6 was/were going to

3 1 The manager said (that) he/she would be happy to put cameras all over the park.
2 The reporter said (that) the agents couldn't wait for the DNA report.
3 The woman told the police (that) they had seen the men from across the street.
4 The manager said (that) they were thinking of having a new alarm installed.
5 One of the brothers said (that) they hadn't done anything.
6 The agent told the poachers (that) they would get a long time in jail for this.

Workbook p72

Get it Right!

say vs. *tell*

Student's Book p125

4 Draw attention to the long vowels in *murder* /'mɜ:rdər/, *murderer* /'mɜ:rdərər/ and *caught* /kɔ:t/.
1 commit a crime 2 go to prison 3 arrest 4 murder 5 a fine 6 break in 7 a murderer 8 get caught 9 get into trouble 10 a prisoner

Grammar rap!

GRAMMAR
Reported speech (review)

1 **Complete the sentences with suitable verbs. Then check your answers in the news stories on page 75.**

1 One of the agents said that they ____________ the men's bags.
2 He also said the poachers ____________ the dead animals for over $3,500.
3 An anti-poaching agent said that he ____________ this ____________ be a warning to other poachers.
4 Agents said they ____________ the horn for testing.
5 An official from the department of environmental affairs said that the situation ____________.
6 He said that the number of rhino deaths in 2016 ____________ since the record number of over 1,200 in 2014.

2 **Match what was said (direct speech) with the reported sentences in Exercise 1. Underline the verb forms which are different. Then complete the rule.**

a "We're going to send the horn for testing."
b "I hope this will be a warning to other poachers."
c "The number of rhino deaths in 2016 has fallen since the record number of over 1,200 in 2014."
d "The poachers can sell the dead animals for over $3,500."
e "We searched their bags."
f "The situation is improving."

RULE:

Direct speech		Reported speech
simple present	→	[0] *simple past*
present continuous	→	[1] ____________
present perfect	→	[2] ____________
simple past	→	[3] ____________
past perfect	→	*past perfect*
would	→	*would*
can	→	[4] ____________
will	→	[5] ____________
am / is / are going to	→	[6] ____________

3 **Rewrite these sentences in reported speech.**

1 "I'll be happy to put cameras all over the park," the manager said.
2 "The agents can't wait for the DNA report," the reporter said.
3 "We saw the men from across the street," the woman told the police.
4 "We're thinking of having a new alarm installed," the manager said.
5 "We haven't done anything," one of the brothers said.
6 "You'll get a long time in jail for this," the agent told the poachers.

→ workbook page 72

VOCABULARY
Crime

4 **Match the words with the definitions.**

murder | break in | arrest | a fine
commit a crime | go to prison | a murderer
get into trouble | get caught | a prisoner

1 to do something illegal
2 to be made to live in a special building for criminals
3 to take (a suspected criminal) to the police station
4 to kill (a person) intentionally
5 money that you have to pay if you break a law
6 to enter by force (usually to steal something)
7 someone who intentionally kills another person
8 to be found while committing a crime
9 to have a problem because of something that you did wrong
10 a person who is in prison

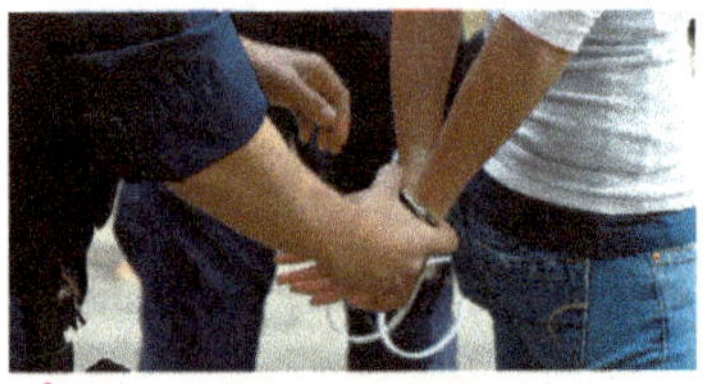

5 SPEAKING **Work in pairs. Use these questions to help you invent a crime story. Make notes and then tell your partner your story.**

- Where and when did it happen?
- Who was involved?
- What happened?
- What crime was committed?
- How did the police react?
- What happened to the criminal?

→ workbook page 74

76

5 Allow students six to eight minutes to prepare their stories. If students have access to a recording device (their mobile devices, for example), they could record their conversation and play it back to check their own pronunciation and intonation.

Workbook p74

Language notes Reported speech (review)

Most languages report speech, but it can be useful for students to compare how it is done in L1 with how we do it in English. In addition to tenses, some time phrases may need to be changed in reported speech, e.g., *last night/the night before*, *next week/the following week*. Pronouns also change, e.g., *these/those*, *this/that*, *here/there*, *my/his* or *her*, *we/they*. The two main verbs used to report speech are *say* and *tell*. These have the same meaning but are different in use (*tell* is immediately followed by an object – someone).

Activity idea Mixed ability

Ask stronger students to cover Exercise 2 and transform each sentence in Exercise 1 into direct speech before looking at Exercise 2 to check their answers. Weaker students proceed directly to matching the direct speech in Exercise 2 with the (reported) sentences in Exercise 1.

TH!NK more

Workbook
Grammar p72, Ex.1–3
Vocabulary p74, Ex.1–3
Vocabulary Extra p75, Ex.1–3

Worksheets
Grammar rap! Reported speech (review)
Grammar Worksheets 8
Vocabulary Worksheets 8

Listening; Grammar; TH!NK Values

6 Check/clarify: *to mug, to suffer.*

7 8.02
Restoring Justice is a program that instead of punishing criminals, tries to help them to change. They meet their victims and try to see the situation from their point of view. It is for people who have committed crimes and would normally go to prison.

8 8.02
1 He didn't know what to say. / He didn't want to meet the woman again, but didn't want to go to prison. 2 For criminals to see the consequences of their actions 3 Terrified / mixed feelings 4 Unsure / frightened 5 He wanted some money to spend. 6 Jason's parents

9 1 d 2 b 3 c 4 a
RULE: 5 if; whether 6 asked 7 told

10 Encourage students to check if the sentences are *yes/no* questions, requests, or imperatives.
1 The presenter asked if/whether the victims were scared of meeting their muggers.
2 Ken's wife asked if/whether he had seen the article about Restoring Justice in the newspaper that morning.
3 The presenter asked him to tell them more about the ideas behind the program.
4 Ken's manager told him not to include other criminals in the program.

11 Students could write questions in pairs and swap with another pair for the second stage.

Workbook p72

12 1 e 2 a 3 c 4 b 5 d 6 f

13 Hold a class vote to decide which they feel are the most and the least serious.
1 4 2 1 3 2 4 6 5 3 6 5

14 Listen to some of the students' ideas and encourage open class discussion.

LISTENING

6 SPEAKING **Imagine a young person mugged somebody. Discuss these questions.**

1 Why might someone mug a person?
2 Who might suffer as a result?
3 What would be the best punishment?

7 8.02 **Listen to a radio interview. What is Restoring Justice and who is it for?**

8 8.02 **Listen again and make notes on these topics.**

1 Jason's initial reaction to Restoring Justice
2 the main idea behind Restoring Justice
3 how Jason felt about meeting his victim
4 how Mrs. Schwartz felt about meeting her mugger
5 the reason Jason gave for mugging Mrs. Schwartz
6 the people Mrs. Schwartz feels suffered most

GRAMMAR
Reported questions, requests, and imperatives

9 Match 1–4 with a–d. Then complete the rule with *asked, if, told,* and *whether.*

1 She asked me if I knew who'd suffered ☐
2 [The judge] asked me whether I wanted ☐
3 [She] asked me to look at the other side ☐
4 He told me to ☐

a think carefully about my choices.
b to go to prison.
c of the table, where my mom and dad were sitting.
d most from what I'd done.

RULE:
- In reported *yes / no* questions, we use *asked* + [5]______ or ______ and the same word order as in a statement.
- In reported requests, we use [6]______ + object + infinitive with *to.*
- In reported imperatives, we use [7]______ + object + infinitive with *to.*

10 These are things people have said to Ken, the social worker. Rewrite them in reported speech.

0 Reporter: "Have you had much success with the program so far?"
The reporter asked if he'd had much success with the program so far.
1 Reporter: "Are victims scared of meeting their muggers?"
2 Ken's wife: "Did you see the article about Restoring Justice in the newspaper this morning?"
3 Reporter: "Could you tell us more about the ideas behind the program, please?"
4 Ken's manager: "Don't include other criminals in the program."

11 Write four to six more questions that Mrs. Schwartz might ask Jason. Use direct speech. Then put your partner's questions into reported speech.

"How do you see your future?"
She asked him how he saw his future.

→ workbook page 72

TH!NK values
Respecting the law

12 Match the punishments (1–6) with the sentences (a–f).

1 He got a fine. ☐
2 He got community service. ☐
3 He got a life sentence. ☐
4 He got a warning. ☐
5 He got the death penalty. ☐
6 He got a prison sentence. ☐

a He has to spend 80 hours cleaning the streets.
b But he'll be in serious trouble if he does it again.
c It means at least 20 years in prison.
d But it will be years before they carry it out.
e He had to pay $100.
f He'll be locked up for two years.

13 Number the punishments in Exercise 12 from 1 (least serious) to 6 (most serious).

14 SPEAKING **Work in pairs. Read these newspaper headlines. What crimes have been committed? What punishment (if any) would be fair?**

- Hungry student steals chocolate bar from store
- Man steals TV from old couple's home
- Speeding driver kills family of four
- Bank robber escapes with thousands

Language note Reported questions, requests, and imperatives

Students sometimes apply the rules for *yes/no* questions to open-ended questions such as *What have you been doing?* When there is a question word, we use it in the reported question, but we do not use the auxiliary verb. The word order is like an affirmative sentence, but we change the tense as with reported statements. For example:

He asked me if I had been doing. ✗

He asked me what had I been doing. ✗

He asked me what I had been doing. ✓

Reported questions and requests do not have a question mark at the end.

Social Responsibilities
Understanding personal responsibilities as part of a group and in society – including citizenship
Is aware of positive behavior in different groups (e.g., class, home, and with friends). Understands the rights and responsibilities of individuals in society at local and national levels.

TH!NK more

Workbook
Listening p78, Ex.1–5
Grammar pp72–73, Ex.4–7

Worksheets
Grammar Worksheets 8

Warmer

Write *ranatruest* in the center board. Ask students: *Which word has been mixed up?* Elicit *restaurant*. Ask: *What are the characteristics of a good restaurant?* Hold a brainstorming session. Write some of their ideas on the board.

1 To encourage quick skimming, get students to race to find and circle all five numbers in the article. Then get them to find out what the numbers refer to.
a The average number of Clink prisoners who commit crimes in the year after they are released
b The average number of other adult prisoners who commit crimes in the year after they are released
c The number of prisoners who were trained in Clink restaurants in 2018
d The number of Clink ex-prisoners who found jobs when they were released in 2018
e The number of restaurants who said they were happy to take on graduates from the Clink program

2 8.03 During feedback, encourage students to think about the correct answer to the false statements.
1 F 2 F 3 T 4 T 5 T 6 F

3 At the end of the exercise, listen to some of the students' ideas and encourage open class discussion.

READING

1 Read the article quickly. What do these numbers refer to?
a 16% b 25% c 361 d 78 e 250

EATING OUT

BEHIND BARS

Next time you're looking for a special evening out, why not invite someone special to eat out with you at one of the Clink restaurants? They offer delicious, beautifully cooked dishes, but this is fine dining with a difference, because these are no ordinary restaurants. The Clink restaurants are found inside four of the UK's most famous prisons: High Down, Brixton, Cardiff, and Styal, so your waiter might be a burglar and your food might have been cooked by a robber. Because the restaurants are actually inside the prison walls, anyone wanting to eat out in one of the Clink prisons has to agree to go through a special security check first.

The man behind the idea is Chef Alberto Crisci, who was looking for a way to help prisoners make the most of their time inside by studying for professional cooking qualifications. He also wanted to offer members of the public a chance to eat out somewhere truly different, so he set up the Clink charity to make all this happen. The idea is to encourage prisoners to learn how to do a new job while they are in prison. When they are released from prison with their newly earned qualifications, they can persuade restaurant owners to give them a job. Many hope that then they will be less likely to commit crimes in the future.

Supporters of the restaurants claim that it really works. They explain that only 16% of prisoners who have worked in the Clink restaurants commit crimes in the year after they are released – compared to the national average of 25% of adult prisoners. Some critics refuse to accept these figures. They say that only the prisoners who are not likely to return to crime are chosen to work in the restaurants. But the organizers of the charity are not worried by this argument. They have plenty more evidence to show how successful they are. In 2018, 361 prisoners were trained in the Clink restaurants and 142 earned a professional qualification; 78 out of 112 ex-prisoners who had worked in Clink found jobs on release and 250 restaurants said they were happy to take on graduates from the training program. One graduate even made a successful appearance on the TV cooking show *Bake Off: The Professionals*.

So if you're looking for a great meal out and like the idea of helping a criminal make a new start, one of the Clink restaurants might just be the place you're looking for. But I'd recommend that you book early. The restaurants are extremely popular.

2 8.03 Read and listen to the article and mark the sentences T (true) or F (false).
1 The food in the Clink restaurants is not particularly good. ☐
2 Alberto Crisci wanted to improve the quality of meals in prisons. ☐
3 You can't just walk into a Clink restaurant. ☐
4 Prisoners with Clink qualifications are less likely than other prisoners to go back to prison. ☐
5 Not everyone agrees that the program is really successful. ☐
6 It's easy to get a table at one of the Clink restaurants. ☐

3 SPEAKING Work in pairs. Discuss these questions.
1 Would you like to visit a Clink restaurant? Why (not)?
2 What other useful skills could prisoners learn in prison?

TH!NK more

Workbook
Reading p76, Ex.1–4

4 Ask students to try to complete the sentences by using the context before referring back to the article to check.
1 claim 2 explain 3 agree
4 invite 5 recommend 6 refuse
7 encourage 8 persuade

5 1 c 2 e 3 a 4 b 5 d

6 Tell students that they should think about these structures when they learn any new reporting verbs to ensure they are using them correctly.
RULE: 1 claim, refuse 2 persuade, encourage, invite 3 recommend, explain, agree 4 recommend

7 You may like to do the first item with the whole class as an example.
1 to meet 2 for forgetting
3 to help 4 me to go 5 having
6 me to enter 7 that we read
8 to drive

8 If you're short on time, students can finish this for homework.
Suggested answers:
1 They apologized for forgetting to inform us.
2 The mayor said/explained/claimed that they were going to introduce a new system to reduce crime.
3 The reporter asked the official to give / if he/she could give them more information about the plan.
4 The man said/claimed / told me that if I worked for them, I'd be very rich soon.
5 The woman refused to buy the watch because it was too expensive.
6 The teacher told the class to study the text carefully.
7 The man offered to help me with my work.
8 The principal invited my parents to go to his office the following morning.
9 Jack agreed to go to the movies with Olivia, but only if she paid.

Workbook p74

9 Tell students to make notes before expanding their notes into a report.

VOCABULARY
Reporting verbs

4 **Complete the sentences with the correct forms of the verbs. Then check your answers in the article on page 78.**

agree | claim | encourage | explain | invite | persuade | recommend | refuse

1 Supporters of the restaurant ______ that it works.
2 They ______ that only 16% of prisoners who have worked in the Clink restaurants commit crimes in the year after they are released.
3 Anyone wanting to eat out in one of the Clink prisons has to ______ to go through a special security check first.
4 Why not ______ someone special to eat out with you at one of the Clink restaurants?
5 I'd ______ that you book early.
6 Some critics ______ to accept these figures.
7 The idea is to ______ prisoners to learn how to do a new job.
8 They can ______ restaurant owners to give them a job.

5 **Match the verbs (1–5) with the definitions (a–e).**

1 agree ☐
2 claim ☐
3 explain ☐
4 persuade ☐
5 refuse ☐

a make something clear
b try to get someone to do or believe something
c accept an idea or a suggestion
d say no
e say that something is true

6 **Complete the rule with reporting verbs from Exercises 4 and 5. Some verbs can go in more than one list.**

RULE:
We use different structures with different reporting verbs.
1 verb + (*not*) infinitive with *agree*, *offer*, ______, ______
2 verb + object + (*not*) infinitive with *ask*, *tell*, ______, ______, ______
3 verb + *that* + clause: *say*, *claim*, ______, ______, ______
4 verb + gerund: *apologize for*, *suggest*, ______

7 **Complete the sentences with the correct forms of the verbs and any other necessary words.**

1 Liam agreed ______ (meet) me at nine o'clock.
2 Lucy apologized ______ (forget) my birthday.
3 Jack refused ______ (help) us.
4 Bobby persuaded ______ (me / go) to the party with him.
5 Dad suggested ______ (have) dinner at a restaurant.
6 My mom encouraged ______ (me / enter) the singing competition.
7 Mr. Jones recommended ______ (we / read) the book before we saw the movie.
8 Liz offered ______ (drive) me home after the game.

8 **Rewrite the sentences in reported speech. Use suitable reporting verbs. Sometimes more than one verb is possible.**

1 "We forgot to inform you. We're really sorry," they said.
2 "We're going to introduce a new system to reduce crime," the mayor said.
3 "Can you give us more information about the plan?" the reporter said to the official.
4 "If you work for us, you'll be very rich soon," the man said.
5 "I don't want to buy the watch because it's too expensive," the woman said.
6 "Study this text carefully!" the teacher said to the class.
7 "I can help you with your work," the man said.
8 "Come to my office tomorrow morning, please," the principal said to my parents.
9 "Oh, all right. I'll go to the movies with you, but only if you pay," Jack said to Olivia.

→ workbook page 74

WRITING
A report of a crime

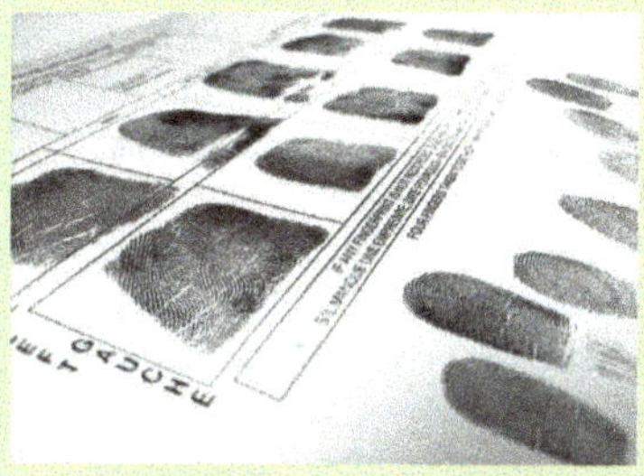

9 **Write a newspaper report about a crime (100–150 words).**
- Give a description of the crime (what happened).
- Include what one witness said.
- Say what the investigators think.

Homework

If you are short on time, students can do Exercise 9 for homework. If you did this in class, ask students to exchange their reports with another student for them to read at home and give feedback on content and structure. Students could check if the report uses the same structure as the bullet points. They should also decide which is the most/least interesting part of the report.

Activity idea Extension

Ask students to look back at the news stories on page 75 and use some of the reporting verbs to write sentences reporting what was said or what might have been said by the people in the stories. Monitor to ensure students are using reporting verbs correctly.

THINK more

Practice Extra
Unit 8 Practice it!

Workbook
Vocabulary p74, Ex.4
Developing Writing p77

Worksheets
Vocabulary Worksheets 8

Warmer

Write on the board: *Have you or your family ever been the victim of a theft? What was stolen? What can we do to stop people from breaking into our homes? If you were the victim of a theft, what would you do?* Students discuss in pairs.

▶ 22 TH!NK Famous prisons

1 Give students two minutes to read the article and write the names. Encourage them not to focus on every word for now. Do not give the answers yet.

2 🔊 8.04
1 Nelson Mandela 2 Al Capone / Robert "Birdman" Stroud
3 King Henry VI / Anne Boleyn / Catherine Howard 4 Edmond Dantès
5 Henri Charrière

3 Before students read the text again, get them to read the questions through. Tell students not to worry about difficult vocabulary at this stage as this will come up later.
1 Alcatraz, Château d'If, Devil's Island
2 Robben Island 3 Robben Island, Alcatraz, the Tower of London, Devil's Island 4 The Tower of London
5 The Tower of London 6 Château d'If, Devil's Island

4 At the end of the exercise, listen to some of the students' ideas and encourage open class discussion.

TH!NK
Famous prisons

Culture

1 Scan the article and find one famous prisoner from each prison.

2 🔊 8.04 Read and listen to the article to check your answers.

FAMOUS PRISONS

1 ROBBEN ISLAND, SOUTH AFRICA

Robben Island is known all over the world because of one of its former prisoners. From 1964 until 1982, this island prison, 11 km off the coast of Cape Town, was home to perhaps the most famous prisoner in the world, Nelson Mandela, who in 1994 became the first black president of his country. Robben Island was used mainly for political prisoners and more than 3,000 of them spent time there before it was finally closed in 1996. These days it is a museum and it is visited by thousands of tourists each year.

2 ALCATRAZ, US

Another island that was home to a prison is Alcatraz, which is situated 2 km off the coast of San Francisco. Probably America's most well-known prison, Alcatraz had many famous inmates, such as the gangster Al Capone and Robert "Birdman" Stroud, a murderer who was also one of the country's biggest experts on birds. Alcatraz closed in 1963 and in its 29 years of being a prison, no one ever escaped, although 36 prisoners tried. These days it is open to the public and tourists can take a short boat ride across the San Francisco Bay to visit it.

3 THE TOWER OF LONDON, UK

The Tower of London, which was built in the 11th century, is now one of the city's most popular tourist attractions, with people coming from all over the world to see the Crown Jewels that are kept inside it. However, up until the mid 20th century, it was a prison and home to many famous prisoners, including King Henry VI and two of King Henry VIII's wives, Anne Boleyn and Catherine Howard, who were also both executed in the Tower. Visitors see the cells and enjoy interactive displays that show what life was like in this ancient prison.

4 CHÂTEAU D'IF, FRANCE

Although Château d'If is a real island, most people know of it because of a fictional prisoner. The island prison, which is situated off the coast of Marseilles in the south of France, was home to many criminals from the mid 17th century to the end of the 19th century, but it is really famous for one prisoner who was never actually there. In his novel *The Count of Monte Cristo*, French author Alexandre Dumas tells the story of Edmond Dantès, an innocent man who is sent to the prison for a crime he did not commit. In the book, Dantès manages to escape, something that no prisoner was ever able to do in real life.

5 DEVIL'S ISLAND, FRENCH GUIANA

Devil's Island is off the coast of French Guiana in the Caribbean. For the hundred years that it was open, it was known as one of the toughest prisons in the world and fewer than 25% of all prisoners who went there left the island alive. The prison was set in the middle of a jungle and the waters around it were full of man-eating sharks, which made escape almost impossible. One man who managed to escape and write a book about his experiences was Henri Charrière and the movie *Papillon* tells his story. Since it was closed in 1953, Devil's Island has become a tourist attraction for passengers on the many cruise ships that pass nearby.

3 **Answer the questions.**

According to the texts, which prison or prisons …

1 was impossible to escape from?
2 was home to a future politician?
3 can now be visited by members of the public?
4 is not on an island?
5 contains really valuable objects?
6 appeared in a book?

4 SPEAKING **Work in pairs. Discuss these questions.**

1 What other famous prisons do you know of either in real life or in movies/books?
2 Would you like to visit any of these prisons? Why or why not?

80

Culture notes

Nelson Mandela – see Culture Notes in Unit 7, page 70.

Henry VI became King of England in 1422 at the age of nine months when his father, Henry V, died. He reigned until 1461 when he was deposed during the War of the Roses (a civil war in England). He was restored to the throne again in 1470 and remained king until his imprisonment and death in 1471.

Anne Boleyn was King Henry VIII's second wife. She was Queen of England from 1533 to 1536. Their marriage, and the annulment of his first one, began the breaking of the Catholic Church's power in England and made Anne a key figure in the disorder that instigated the English Reformation. In 1533, she gave birth to the future Queen Elizabeth I, but Henry was disappointed not to have a son. Anne was imprisoned and then executed in the Tower of London in 1536.

Catherine Howard was Henry VIII's fifth wife. She was a teenager, and he was 49 at the time of their marriage. They were married for just over a year when she was executed on the king's orders.

The Crown Jewels of the United Kingdom, kept in the Tower of London, are 142 royal ceremonial objects. They contain 23,578 gem stones including *Cullinan I* – the largest clear, cut diamond in the world.

Social Responsibilities
Understanding personal responsibilities as part of a group and in society – including citizenship
Understands various aspects of society.

5 Before students do the exercise, write the highlighted words on the board. Tell students to find the words in the article as quickly as possible. When they have seen them being used in context, ask them to try to work out the meaning of the phrases. Compare their meanings with the definitions in the book.
1 cells 2 executed 3 jewels
4 tourist attraction 5 former
6 experts 7 innocent 8 inmates

6 🔊 8.05 Before students listen, ask them to look at the photos and predict words they might hear in relation to each photo in pairs.
A 3 B 2 C 1 D 4

7 🔊 8.05 Before playing the audio again, ask students to answer as much as they can from memory.
Conversation 1: burglar; nothing
Conversation 2: pickpocket; phone
Conversation 3: con artist; the lady's life savings / money
Conversation 4: shoplifter; clothes

8 During feedback, elicit/explain that these expressions are used as a way of introducing a story.
1 You'll never guess what happened.
2 You won't believe what happened to me last week.
3 I heard a really sad story about an old lady.
4 There was a scary story in the paper the other day.

9 1 Tell me. 2 What? 3 Really?
4 That's awful! 5 No way!

10 You could move on to the pronunciation exercise at this stage prior to doing Exercise 10.

Allow students six to eight minutes to prepare their dialogues. Monitor to make sure all students are on task. Encourage students to use the phrases in Exercises 8 and 9.

Pronunciation
Intonation – expressing surprise
Student's Book p121

5 VOCABULARY There are eight **highlighted** words or phrases in the article. Match the words with these meanings. Write the words.
1 rooms in prison where prisoners are kept
2 killed as a legal punishment
3 valuable stones
4 place visited by people on vacation
5 at an earlier time
6 people who know a lot about something
7 not guilty
8 people who are kept in prison

LISTENING

6 🔊 8.05 Listen to the conversations and match them with the photos.

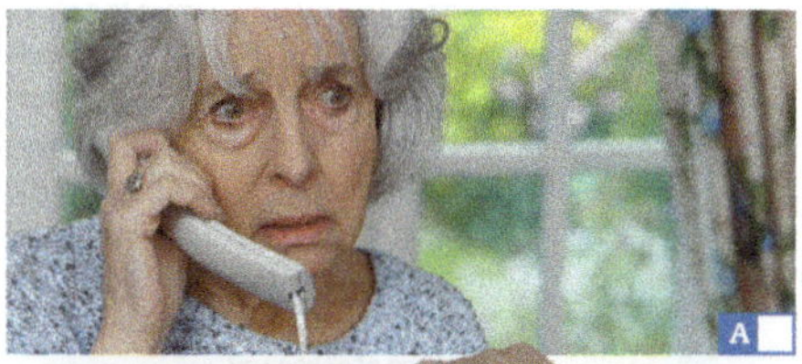

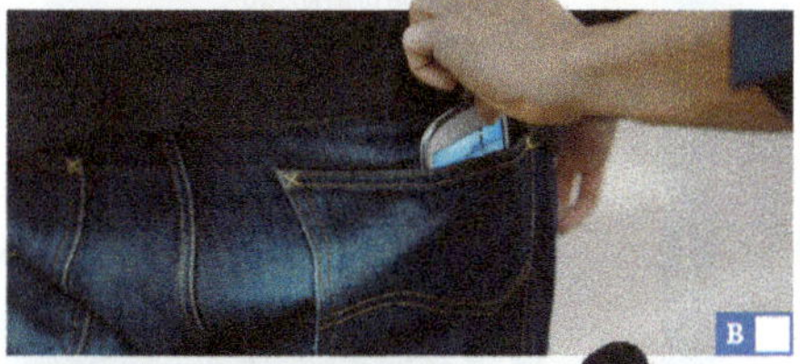

7 🔊 8.05 Listen again and complete the notes.

Conversation 1
Criminal: ______ What was taken: ______
Conversation 2
Criminal: ______ What was taken: ______
Conversation 3
Criminal: ______ What was taken: ______
Conversation 4
Criminal: ______ What was taken: ______

FUNCTIONS
Giving and reacting to news

8 Put the words in order to form expressions for giving news from the conversations.
1 never / You'll / happened / what / guess
2 believe / won't / to / week / what / You / happened / last / me
3 about / a / really / an / sad / lady / story / heard / I / old
4 paper / a / scary / story / There / the / was / other / in / day / the

9 Complete the reactions to news.
1 T _ l l m _ .
2 W h _ t?
3 R _ _ l l y?
4 T h _ t's _ w f _ l!
5 N _ w _ y!

10 SPEAKING Work in pairs. Make conversations using the expressions from Exercises 8 and 9.
- Think of (or make up) a piece of news.
- Take turns to give your news.
- React and ask for more details.

PRONUNCIATION
Intonation – expressing surprise
Go to page 121.

81

Homework
Ask students to research a prison from their country and write a few sentences. As a follow-up, students could present it to the class.

Activity idea Mixed ability
In Exercise 5, weaker students can complete the exercise in pairs.

TH!NK more
Practice Extra
Unit 8 Master it!
Workbook
Pronunciation p120
Tests
Unit, extension, and skills test 8

1 In B2 First for Schools Reading and Use of English Part 3, candidates have to read a text containing eight blank spaces. At the end of some of the lines, there is a stem word in capital letters. Candidates need to form an appropriate word from the given stem word to fill each space. This part of the exam tests understanding of structure, lexis, and more specifically how prefixes, suffixes, and compounds are used.

Encourage your students to do the following when they approach this task:

- Skim the text to have a sense of the topic and general meaning.
- Read the text more carefully. Think of a possible word which makes sense in each space.
- Check which part of speech is needed and if the word needs to be singular or plural, positive, or negative.
- Check if the word fits the meaning and grammar of the sentence and the whole text.
- Check that the spelling is correct.
- Read the completed text again to check that it makes sense.

1 scientist 2 entered 3 various 4 valuables 5 apology 6 unlucky 7 criminals

Workbook p71

TOWARDS B2 First for Schools

READING AND USE OF ENGLISH
Word formation

→ workbook page 71

1 For questions 1–7, read the text below. Use the word given in capitals at the end of some of the lines to form a word that fits in the gap in the same line. There is an example at the beginning (0).

A thief who kissed his victim after a 0 *robbery* in a	**ROB**
French jewellery shop has been caught after a forensic	
1 ________ matched his DNA with that left on the	**SCIENCE**
hand of his victim.	
The thief 2 ________ the Parisian shop late in the	**ENTRY**
afternoon, as the owner was preparing to close for the	
evening. After tying the woman to a chair, he smashed	
open 3 ________ display cabinets and loaded	**VARY**
4 ________ worth more than 20,000 euros into	**VALUE**
a bag. Before leaving the shop, he kissed the owner's	
hand and made an 5 ________ for his crime.	**APOLOGISE**
However, the 6 ________ thief could never have	**LUCK**
imagined that the kiss would lead to his arrest.	
Police used the DNA and ran it through a	
database of all known 7 ________ .	**CRIME**

WRITING
An informal email

→ workbook page 79

2 You have received an email from an English-speaking penfriend.

To: Mike
mike_2000@mail.com
Subject: Any suggestions?

Hey Mike,
How are things? Listen, I'm writing because a friend of mine is coming to spend a few days in your town. She asked me to write to you to see if you could suggest some of the things she should do while she's there. She also wanted to know what the weather's like and what clothes she should bring with her. She leaves on Friday. Sorry for the short notice, but can you help?
Hope to hear from you soon.
Best,
Angie

Write your email in 140–190 words.

82

2 In B2 First for Schools Writing Part 2, candidates are given a choice of four tasks, one of which is to write an email of 140–190 words. For the email, they are given a short text and must write a response. This part of the exam tests the candidates' ability to write well-organized texts with a real communicative purpose and a good range of language.

Encourage your students to do the following when they approach this task:

- Candidates should read all the tasks and consider the topic and the language that is needed in each before choosing the task that best suits them.
- For the chosen task, identify what is required, who it is for, and what kind of information is needed.
- Make a plan, referring closely to the question.
- Look for opportunities to develop ideas and show a range of language.
- Write a rough draft before writing the final answer. Make sure that it is well-organized and has a range of tenses, expressions, and vocabulary.
- Read the work again to check that it makes sense and that all the content points have been included. Check the spelling.

Workbook p79

1 1 give up 2 selfish 3 set off 4 got into trouble 5 burglar 6 find out 7 generous 8 after all 9 arrested 10 polite

2 1 encouraged 2 would 3 'm not used to 4 going to 5 gotten used to 6 had been

3 1 ~~has taken~~ had taken 2 ~~let~~ made 3 ~~persuaded me report~~ persuaded me to report 4 ~~won't make~~ won't let 5 ~~explained me that~~ explained that / explained to me that 6 ~~make me to clean~~ make me clean

4 1 along; about 2 want; count 3 heard; That's 4 believe; Tell

TEST YOURSELF UNITS 7 & 8

VOCABULARY

1 Complete the sentences with the words / phrases in the list. There are four extra words / phrases.

give up | got into trouble | unfriendly | generous | find out | after all
commit a crime | polite | selfish | set off | burglar | shy | arrested | end up

1 Don't ____________ now. You're a great player. I'm sure you'll get on the team next time.
2 That was very ____________ of you to eat all those cookies and not leave any for us.
3 We ____________ very early in the morning because we wanted to arrive before it got dark.
4 Tim ____________ for not doing his English homework again.
5 The ____________ broke into the house when everybody was asleep.
6 I hope they ____________ who stole Amanda's purse.
7 It was very ____________ of James to pay for all your concert tickets.
8 It rained a lot that day, so we didn't go on the school trip ____________ .
9 The police finally ____________ the con man and he went to prison.
10 Emma's very ____________ . She always says "please" and "thank you."

/10

GRAMMAR

2 Complete the sentences with the words / phrases in the list. There are two extra words / phrases.

get used to | would | 'm not used to | going to | encouraged | is | had been | gotten used to

1 My mom ____________ me to do well in school.
2 The police officer told me that the robber ____________ get a prison sentence.
3 I ____________ taking my shoes off before I go into a house, but here in Japan, it's what everyone does.
4 She says she is ____________ report the crime to the police.
5 At home, I always have dinner at six o'clock, so I haven't ____________ eating at nine o'clock here in Spain.
6 She said the con artist ____________ sentenced to two years in prison.

3 Find and correct the mistake in each sentence.

1 She asked me if I knew who has taken the bike.
2 My mom let me do all the dishes for a week because I was late home one night.
3 He persuaded me report the incident to the police.
4 I really want to go on the school trip, but my dad won't make me.
5 The reporter explained me that the mugger would get community service.
6 My parents make me to clean my bedroom.

/12

FUNCTIONAL LANGUAGE

4 Choose the correct words.

1 **A** We're going camping this weekend. Why don't you come *along* / *on*?
B I'd love to. How *for* / *about* asking Mike to come, too?
2 **A** We're going swimming. Does anyone *feel* / *want* to join us?
B You can *call* / *count* me out. I hate swimming.
3 **A** The other day, I *hear* / *heard* a really sad story about an old man whose house was broken into.
B *That's* / *It's* awful.
4 **A** You'll never *believe* / *understand* what happened to me last week!
B Go on. *Say* / *Tell* me!

/8

MY SCORE /30

22–30 | 10–21 | 0–9

83

The Cambridge Life Competencies Framework

Creative Thinking

Making problems for your students

Watch this video for tips on how to develop your students' creative thinking skills. Scan the QR code here.

Reading; Train to TH!NK

Warmer

Do an internet image search for *unexplained mysteries* and show a variety of strange images on the board. Ask students to work in pairs to describe the images and discuss what they have in common.

▶ 23 Get TH!NKing

Play the video and discuss the question with your class.

1 You may like to put a copy of the four photos up on the board before students open their books.
A2 B1 C3 D4

2 You may like to give your own example to get students started.

3 Give students 30 seconds to scan the text under the title and find the answer. Encourage them not to focus on every word for now.
They aren't the author's favorite unexplained mysteries.

4 🔊 **9.01 Check/clarify:** *rock pool, senses, population, spheres, diameter, extraterrestrial, camera flash, manuscript, code, code breakers.*
1S 2Sp 3V 4O 5Sp 6V 7O 8S

5 Encourage students to underline the parts of the article that helped them decide.
1F 2O 3F 4O

6 Do the first one as an example, making sure students understand the difference between fact and opinion.
Students' own answers

9 IT'S A MYSTERY!

OBJECTIVES

FUNCTIONS: making deductions

GRAMMAR: modals of deduction (present); *should(n't) have*; modals of deduction (past)

VOCABULARY: mysteries; expressions with *go*

Get TH!NKING
Watch the video and think: are there any unexplained mysteries from your country?

READING

1 Look at the photos and match them with the mysteries.

1 Stonehenge | 2 the Loch Ness Monster
3 the yeti | 4 UFOs

2 SPEAKING Work in pairs. Compare your answers. What do you know about these mysteries?

3 Read the article on the next page quickly. Why *isn't* the author writing about any of the mysteries in Exercise 1?

4 🔊 9.01 Read and listen to the article. Write Sp (spheres), O (octopuses), S (spaceman), or V (Voynich) in the boxes to answer the questions.

Which mystery …
1 is about the appearance of a mysterious character? ☐
2 is about things that were difficult to make? ☐
3 is a challenge to language experts? ☐
4 is about the unusual behavior of some creatures? ☐
5 involves huge stone objects? ☐
6 involves a book written centuries ago? ☐
7 can perhaps be explained by the weather? ☐
8 is about a family and a photograph? ☐

Train to TH!NK

Fact or opinion?

A fact is something that can be proven to be true.
An opinion is a personal belief. It's important to be able to see the difference.

5 Read about the octopuses again. According to what is written in the text, mark the sentences F (fact) or O (opinion).
1 The population of the octopuses is bigger now than before. ☐
2 The octopuses needed to travel to find food. ☐
3 There were storms not long before they were seen walking on the beach. ☐
4 The octopuses had a disease. ☐

6 Complete the table with two facts and two opinions for each mystery according to the article.

	Facts	Opinions
1 Giant stone spheres		
2 Solway spaceman		
3 Voynich manuscript		

84

Critical THINKing
Evaluating ideas, arguments, and options
Distinguishes between fact and opinion.

Objectives

Functions and speaking Making deductions
Grammar Modals of deduction (present); *should(n't) have*; modals of deduction (past)
Vocabulary Mysteries; expressions with *go*
Fiction *Wild Country*
Train to TH!NK Fact or opinion?
Values Thinking carefully before you act

Resources for this unit

All available online

Videos
- Get **TH!NK**ing: *Are there any unexplained mysteries from your country?*
- Grammar rap!: Modals of deduction (present)

Tests
- Unit, extension, and skills test 9
- End of term test 3

Worksheets
- Grammar and vocabulary: Basic, Standard, and Extension Worksheets
- Project: Mysterious events
- Communication: What happened?
- Literature Worksheets: *The Hound of the Baskervilles; Yukki-Onna*
- Get **TH!NK**ing and Grammar rap! video Worksheets

Culture notes

The Loch Ness Monster is a mysterious animal that some people believe lives in Loch Ness, a lake in Scotland. The famous photograph of it from 1934 (on page 84 of the Student's Book) was revealed to be a fake in 1994. There have been several searches of the lake, most recently in 2018, which have found nothing.

Stonehenge is a prehistoric monument in Wiltshire, England. It is made up of a ring of standing stones, each about four meters high and two meters wide. The monument is believed to have been constructed between 3000 and 2000 BCE. It is regarded as a British cultural icon, has been legally protected as an Ancient Monument since 1882, and the site and the surrounding area became a UNESCO World Heritage Site in 1986. Stonehenge was produced by a culture that left no written records and so many aspects of it remain unclear. What *is* known is that some of the stones originally came from a town in Wales, over 230km away.

The Yeti (or Abominable Snowman) is an apelike creature which is said to live in the Himalayas. In 1921, a British Royal Geographical Society expedition found footprints in the snow and there have been frequent reports of sightings ever since. It is generally believed that the "Yetis" are actually bears.

The term UFOs (Unidentified Flying Objects) refers to any flying object that cannot be explained, but is usually used to refer to spaceships with aliens on board. The number of sightings has increased greatly since the advent of science fiction movies in the 1950s. Some believe that there are government conspiracies to suppress information of alien visitations. However, there is still no conclusive evidence to prove their existence.

7 Tell students they should look back at the article to find any evidence to support their answers. At the end of the exercise, listen to some of the students' ideas and encourage open class discussion.

Pronunciation
Moving word stress
Student's Book p121

IT'S A MYSTERY! UNIT 9

THE TRUTH IS OUT THERE

There are many unexplained mysteries in the world. How was the Great Pyramid at Giza built? Are there yetis in the Himalayas? Is there a monster in the depths of Loch Ness? Here are our favorites.

A The octopuses that walked on land

You might see an octopus hop from one rock pool to another, but in late October of 2017, more than 20 octopuses were seen coming out of the water and moving along a beach in Wales. "No one has ever seen anything like this before," said one local. "It's very odd behavior." So, why did it happen? Different experts have different opinions. One is that the octopuses were sick. Another is that two big storms a few days earlier had confused the octopuses and affected their senses. A third expert said, "There's been an increase in the octopus population, so perhaps the octopuses needed to travel further to find food."

B The giant stone spheres

There are hundreds of large stone spheres in the Costa Rican jungle. Evidence shows that they must be at least 600 years old and some could date back to 200 BCE. The objects are up to 2.4 meters in diameter and are almost perfectly round. They are also very heavy, with some of them weighing 16 tons. The stone itself comes from miles away, so it took a huge effort to move them. It's thought they probably had a religious purpose and some people suggest a connection with the sun. Others have even suggested that the spheres were created by an alien life form. But no one really knows and the mystery continues.

C The Solway spaceman

In 1964, Jim Templeton from Carlisle took a photo of his daughter Elizabeth and was surprised to see in the photo a strange figure behind her that looked like an extraterrestrial spaceman. Jim took the photo with the mysterious figure to the police, and soon afterwards it appeared in the newspapers. Then one day, Jim was visited by two men who said they were government officials. They asked him to take them to the scene of the photograph. Who were they? Why were they interested? Some people say the figure in the photo must be Templeton's wife – the camera flash made her dress look bright white. Most people agree that the image is real but can't be a spaceman. What do you think?

D The Voynich manuscript

In 1639, Georgius Barschius from Prague told a friend that he had a mysterious book that might be about science or medicine. It was full of puzzling pictures and diagrams, and it was written in an unknown language. Today, the Voynich manuscript is over 600 years old and still no one can read it. It has been suggested that the mysterious writing could be based on an Arabic or Roma or Aztec language. Others say it must be a secret code, and many expert codebreakers have tried to crack it. Every year people think they have solved the mystery, but no one ever has.

SPEAKING

7 **Work in pairs. Discuss these questions.**
1 Which of these mysteries do you think is the most interesting? Why?
2 What other mysteries do you know of?

PRONUNCIATION
Moving word stress Go to page 121.

85

Homework

Ask students to research a mystery from around the world. They can upload a picture with a description of the mystery in English. If students do not have access to the internet, they can create their own ideas. As a follow-up, students can bring the picture to the next lesson and present their mystery to the class.

Activity idea Extension

Ask students to read paragraphs B, C, and D again and try to work out if the author believes any of the mysteries are true. Monitor and guide weaker students towards the parts of the article which hint at the author's opinion. Get students to discuss their findings in pairs. Nominate one or two students to share their ideas in open class and invite reactions from the rest of the class.

TH!NK more

Workbook
Pronunciation pp120–121

Worksheets
Project Mysterious events
Communication What happened?
Get **TH!NK**ing *Are there any unexplained mysteries from your country?*

Warmer

Draw a line on the board with *I always think very carefully before doing things* on the far right and *I never think carefully before doing things. I just do it!* on the far left. Ask students to copy the line and put a mark on the line to show how much they think before acting. Divide the class into small groups and ask students to compare and give examples to explain the positioning of their mark. Come back to this later in the lesson.

▶ 24 Grammar rap! Modals of deduction (present)

1 Ask students to try to complete the sentences from memory before referring back to the article to check. Encourage them to underline the sentences in the reading text.
1 might 2 could 3 can't 4 must
RULE: 5 must 6 can't 7 might, could

2 You may like to do the first item with the whole class as an example.
1 might/may/could 2 must
3 can't 4 might/may/could
5 must 6 might/may/could
7 can't 8 can't

Workbook p82

Get it Right!
Modals of deduction in the present

Student's Book p125

3 During feedback, focus on pronunciation. Draw attention to the word stress in *unexplained*, *mysterious*, and *extraterrestrial*.
1 unexplained 2 odd 3 alien
4 strange 5 extraterrestrial
6 mysterious 7 puzzling 8 secret

Grammar rap!

GRAMMAR
Modals of deduction (present)

1 **Complete the sentences from the article on page 85. Use *must, can't, could,* and *might*. Then complete the rule.**

1 You ___ see an octopus hop from one rock pool to another.
2 Some of the giant stone spheres ___ date back to 200 BCE.
3 Most people agree that the image ___ be a spaceman.
4 Others say that it ___ be a secret code.

RULE:
When we're sure something is true, we use [5] ___.
When we're sure something isn't true, we use [6] ___.
When we think something is possibly true, but aren't sure, we use [7] ___ or ___.

2 **Complete the sentences with suitable modal verbs. Sometimes there's more than one possible answer.**

1 They're speaking Spanish, so they ___ be from Argentina, I suppose.
2 She ___ love cats – she has 20.
3 You ___ want more – you've already eaten two whole pizzas!
4 I'm not sure, but I think that man ___ need our help. I don't think he can swim.
5 You've been working all day. You ___ feel really tired.
6 He's a little older than John, but he ___ know him. I think they went to the same school.
7 Tim ___ be happy. He studied really hard, but he still failed the test.
8 It's the world's oldest mystery. You ___ know the answer.

→ workbook page 82

VOCABULARY
Mysteries

3 **Add the missing vowels to make adjectives related to mysteries.**

1 _ n _ x p l _ _ n _ d mysteries
2 _ d d behavior
3 _ l _ _ n life form
4 s t r _ n g _ figure
5 _ x t r _ t _ r r _ s t r _ _ l spaceman
6 m y s t _ r _ _ _ s writing
7 p _ z z l _ n g pictures
8 a s _ c r _ t code

4 **Answer the questions about the words from Exercise 3.**

1 Which two words mean "from another world"?
2 Which word means "known by very few people"?

5 **Complete the text with the adjectives from Exercise 3.**

I left for school at the usual time, but something seemed wrong. The streets were empty and there was a [1]m ___ feeling in the air. I passed a few people, but they all seemed rather [2]o ___ . I didn't see anyone from school on the way. When I got to school, the gates were closed. Why were they closed? I looked at my watch – 9 a.m. The gates should be open. This was extremely [3]p ___ .

I pushed the gates open and walked inside. Where was everyone? Had they been transported away by some [4]e ___ beings and taken to an [5]a ___ planet? Had they all been taken away as part of some [6]s ___ government experiment? What should I do? Run away? No, this was one mystery that couldn't be left [7]u ___ . I had to find out where everyone was.

I opened the school door and walked inside. I saw a man – it was Mr. Barnes, who looked after the school. I ran up to him. "Thank goodness!" I cried. "Where is everyone?" He gave me a [8]s ___ look.

"At home, probably," he replied. "It's Saturday morning."

→ workbook page 84

---

4 1 extraterrestrial, alien 2 secret

5 Ask students to read the text quickly, ignoring the blank spaces, to answer the question: *Why was no one at school?* (It was Saturday.)
1 mysterious 2 odd 3 puzzling 4 extraterrestrial 5 alien 6 secret
7 unexplained 8 strange

Workbook p84

Language note Modals of deduction (present)

The opposite of *must be* when making deductions is *can't be*, not ~~*mustn't be*~~. *Could/might* have similar meanings when used to make deductions. It is also possible to use *may* in this context.

Activity idea Fast finishers

Students use modal verbs of deduction to write sentences about the four mysteries in the article on page 85.

TH!NK more

Workbook
Grammar p82, Ex.1–2
Vocabulary p84, Ex.1–2
Vocabulary Extra p85, Ex.1–4

Worksheets
Grammar rap! Modals of deduction (present)
Grammar Worksheets 9
Vocabulary Worksheets 9

6 Put a copy of the four pictures up on the board before students open their books.
A 4 B 2 C 1 D 3

7 9.04 Before playing the audio, ask students to predict what happens in the story based on the title and the pictures from Exercise 6. Encourage them to use modal verbs of deduction.
It's mysterious because it isn't clear who or what will fall.

8 9.04 **Check/clarify:** *cheat death.* Stress that a statement is only *false* if there is information in the text explicitly contradicting it. If there is no information, the answer is *doesn't say*.
1 F 2 F 3 T 4 T 5 DS 6 T

9 1 a No b Yes 2 a Yes b No
RULE: 3 have 4 past participle

10 If you want to focus on students' pronunciation, draw their attention to the elision of /t/ and the weak *have* in *shouldn't have* by saying the first sentence and getting students to notice these features. Say the rest of the sentences for students to repeat.
Suggested answers:
1 We shouldn't have played with a ball in the house. 2 You shouldn't have bought those jeans. 3 You should have studied harder. 4 He should have invited you to his party. 5 You should have paid less for the tickets.

11 Give a couple of your own ideas before students begin.

Workbook p82

12 Give students 30 seconds to reflect before they discuss in pairs. Encourage them to try to persuade their partner that the response they chose was the right one, where they have different answers.

13 During feedback, students could swap partners and compare ideas with a different person.
Suggested answers:
1 He should have put on some sunscreen. 2 She should have cleaned her shoes before she came in. 3 He should have left home earlier. 4 She should have taken the cake out of the oven earlier.

Critical THINKing
Evaluating ideas, arguments, and options
Analyzes causes and effects of problems.

IT'S A MYSTERY! UNIT 9

LISTENING

6 **Match the pictures with the words.**

1 fortune teller 2 rope 3 housekeeper 4 chandelier

7 9.04 **Listen to a story called *The Case of the Mysterious Fall*. Why is the fall mysterious?**

8 9.04 **Listen again. Mark the sentences T (true), F (false), or DS (doesn't say).**

1 Mr. Huntingdon was friendly and sociable. ☐
2 He only spoke to one person each week. ☐
3 He thought of a plan to try to cheat death. ☐
4 Mr. Huntingdon tried to call Mrs. Crabtree back to the house after she'd left. ☐
5 Mrs. Crabtree always started work at 8 a.m. ☐
6 The fortune teller's prediction came true. ☐

GRAMMAR
should(n't) have

9 **Look at these sentences from the listening. Answer the questions. Then complete the rule.**

1 Maybe [Mrs. Crabtree] should have asked why.
a Did Mrs. Crabtree ask why?
b Would it have been a good idea to?
2 He shouldn't have sent Mrs. Crabtree home.
a Did Mr. Huntingdon send Mrs. Crabtree home?
b Was it a good idea to?

RULE: To criticize actions in the past, we use *should / shouldn't* + [3] ______ + the [4] ______ form of the verb.

10 **Write replies to the statements. Use *should have* or *shouldn't have* and suitable verbs. Then practice reading them out in pairs.**

0 "I had five slices of pizza! Now I feel sick."
"You shouldn't have eaten so much pizza!"
1 "We've broken the TV. Quick! Put the ball away!"
2 "I bought these jeans yesterday, but now I don't have enough money to buy Mom a birthday present."
3 "I failed the test!"
4 "Joey didn't invite me to his party."
5 "You only paid $100 for those tickets? I paid $250!"

11 SPEAKING **Work in pairs. Write three sentences about famous people using *should have* or *shouldn't have*. Then read them out without saying the names. Your partner tries to guess who the people are.**

→ workbook page 82

TH!NK values
Thinking carefully before you act

12 SPEAKING **Work in pairs. Which do you think was Mr. Huntingdon's biggest mistake?**

A He should have thought about his plan more carefully.
B He should have told Mrs. Crabtree about the fortune teller's prediction.
C He shouldn't have gone to see the fortune teller.

13 SPEAKING **Look at the pictures. What mistake did each person make? What should they have done?**

Homework

Ask students to make up a new plot for a movie which includes Mr. Huntingdon, the housekeeper, the fortune teller, and a rope. Encourage them to include other characters and objects if they wish. As a follow-up, students could present their stories to the class to decide which would be the best movie.

Activity idea Extension

Students write three true sentences and one false one about themselves and their family. Give examples of your own first. Divide the class into small groups. Students read their sentences for the others to decide which one is not true. Students should say: *That must / might / could / can't be true because …* They report back on something they learned about their partners during feedback in open class.

TH!NK more

Workbook
Listening p88, Ex.1–5
Grammar pp82–83, Ex.3–5

Worksheets
Grammar Worksheets 9

Reading

Warmer

Look up some less well-known optical illusions online and present them to the class. Can students say what they see and how they work?

1 **Check/clarify:** *optical illusion.*

2 🔊 **9.05** Tell students not to try to understand every word, but to focus on getting a general understanding of the article.

3 1e 2d 3f 4b 5c 6a

Culture note

The dress is a photograph that went viral on February 26, 2015. The photo was taken by Cecilia Bleasdale and the color scheme, as seen in the photo, caused so much discussion at her daughter's wedding that friend Caitlin McNeill reposted the image on Tumblr along with the question about what color people thought it was. Within hours, Tumblr had crashed, and at its peak, the image was getting 14,000 views a second. Twitter also kept crashing because of the high volume of traffic. Many celebrities joined in the discussion, even brands that had nothing to do with clothing turned their social media to the topic. Although over two-thirds of BuzzFeed users thought that the dress was white and gold, the retailer, Roman Originals, confirmed that it was actually blue and black. They experienced a major surge in sales as a result of the incident and eventually also produced a one-off version of the dress in white and gold for charity.

READING

1 SPEAKING **Look at the pictures. What do you see in them? Discuss your answers in pairs.**

2 🔊 9.05 **Read and listen to the article. Why do you think the photo of the dress went viral?**

3 **Read the article again. Find and match 1–6 with a–f.**

1 ☐ started a family argument
2 ☐ sold the dress
3 ☐ became an internet sensation
4 ☐ set up a study
5 ☐ studied the photo
6 ☐ makes decisions about colors

a the brain
b researchers
c scientists
d the retailer
e the dress
f the photo of the dress

THE DRESS

It goes without saying that people love optical illusions – they've always been popular in books and pictures. Now, with social media, we've gone one step further and everyone is sharing these puzzling illusions. Here's one that was a smash hit with people all over the world.

Is it blue and black **or** white and gold? Which two colors would you go for? This is the story of how an ordinary dress became an internet sensation. You couldn't have missed it!

The mother of a bride sent her daughter a photo of a dress that she was planning to wear to the wedding and it started an argument between the daughter, her fiancé, and their friends. Some of them saw the dress as white and gold while others saw it as blue and black. How weird is that?

One friend posted the photo on the internet and the social media world went crazy. Within a week, the photo went viral and more than 10 million tweets mentioned the dress, using hashtags such as #thedress, #whiteandgold, and #blueandblack. The retailer confirmed that the actual color of the dress was blue and black, but the debate went on.

So why did people see the dress so differently? After reviewing the photo, scientists had some answers. The photo wasn't very clear, so when it was taken the dress could have been in shadow or in the light. And the lighting may have been natural daylight (which is blueish) or from an electric light (which is yellowish). That's important, because our brain depends on the light to decide what color things really are.

A group of researchers set up an online study to find out more. The study went well, as 8,000 people responded and the results were interesting. There was a big difference between "larks," who get up early and spend a lot of time in daylight, and "owls," who stay up late and are more used to artificial light. Larks usually saw the dress as white and gold and owls usually saw it as blue and black.

However, the researchers say that there might have been other reasons for the difference. The study showed that it wasn't important where people lived or what time of day they viewed the photo. But the size of their screen made a difference – people who saw the dress on a bigger screen were more likely to see it as white and gold. Also, women were a bit more likely than men to see it as white and gold. It seems there's still a lot to learn about how we see colors!

One thing is certain. As a result of all this attention on social media, sales of the dress went up dramatically. The retailer produced the dress in white and gold as well as blue and black and they must have made a lot of money!

88

TH!NK more

Workbook
Reading p86, Ex.1–4

Grammar; Functions; Vocabulary

4 1 c 2 b 3 a RULE: 1 rule 2 2 rule 1 3 rule 3

5 Ask students to quickly read the conversation and answer the question: *Who ate the cake?* (Matt) They should ignore the blanks at this point and just focus on gist understanding.
1 must have been 2 can't have eaten 3 might/may/could have taken 4 can't have been 5 must have jumped 6 can't have got/gotten 7 might/may/could have eaten 8 must have been

Workbook p83

6 **Check/clarify:** *meteorite, metal screw.*
Look at the picture and ask students to read the text to find out what's strange. They then complete the sentences with their own opinions.

7 Challenge students to try to convince their partners that their opinion is the "right" one.

8 Encourage students to use the context of the text to help them complete the exercise.
1 g 2 a 3 e 4 b 5 c 6 h 7 d 8 f

9 Tell students to be careful to put *go* into the correct tense.
1 going well 2 goes without saying 3 went crazy 4 went for 5 went viral 6 went one step further 7 go up 8 went on

Workbook p84

Homework

Ask students to research another mystery from around the world. They can upload a picture with a description of the mystery in English. If students do not have access to the internet, they can create their own ideas. As a follow-up, students can bring the picture to the next lesson and present their mystery so the class can make deductions about it.

Language note Modals of deduction (past)

Students may use **It mustn't have been* ... when they want to say something is definitely not true. We need to say *It can't have been* or *It couldn't have been* ... in this case.

GRAMMAR
Modals of deduction (past)

4 Match 1–3 with a–c. Check your answers in the article on page 88. Then match sentences 1–3 with the rules.

1 You can't have
2 The dress could have
3 The retailer must have

a made a lot of money!
b been in shadow or in the light.
c missed it!

RULE:
To say something was possibly the case in the past, we use *might / could / may + have +* past participle. ☐
To say something was definitely not the case in the past, we use *couldn't / can't + have +* past participle. ☐
To say something was definitely the case in the past, we use *must + have +* past participle. ☐

5 Complete the conversation. Use suitable modals and the correct forms of the verbs in parentheses.

"The Case of the Missing Cake"

Oliver What?! My cake! It's gone!
Matt Really?
Oliver Yes, it was here an hour ago and now it isn't. Who took it?
Matt What about Dad? I heard him saying how hungry he was. In fact, I'm sure it [1] ______ (be) Dad.
Oliver No, he [2] ______ (eat) it. It was chocolate. Dad doesn't like chocolate.
Matt That's true I suppose, Mom. [3] ______ (take) it, maybe?
Oliver No, it [4] ______ (be) Mom. She's been out all morning.
Matt The dog! He [5] ______ (jump) onto the table and eaten it. That dog's always doing things like that.
Oliver Are you crazy? The cake was in the fridge. The dog [6] ______ (get) into it.
Matt Are you sure it wasn't you? I mean, you [7] ______ (eat) it and forgotten.
Oliver I'm pretty sure it wasn't me. So if it wasn't me, Mom, Dad, or the dog, that leaves one person. It [8] ______ (be) you, Matt!
Matt What?! Me?
Oliver Yes, and that explains why you have chocolate all around your mouth!

→ workbook page 83

FUNCTIONS
Making deductions

6 Read the text and complete the sentences with your opinions. Use *can't, must,* or *might*.

In 1998, Russian scientists found a meteorite with a metal screw in it. The rock is at least 300 million years old. At that time, there weren't even any dinosaurs on the planet.

1 It ______ be fake.
2 There ______ have been intelligent life on Earth 300 million years ago.
3 I think someone ______ have made it as a joke.
4 It ______ be from another planet.
5 The scientists ______ have lied about it.

7 SPEAKING Work in pairs. Discuss your ideas.

VOCABULARY
Expressions with *go*

8 Find expressions 1–8 in the text on page 88. Match them with the definitions.

1 go for
2 go one step further
3 go viral
4 go well
5 go crazy
6 go up
7 go without saying
8 go on

a do something extra
b be satisfactory
c become very excited about something
d be obvious
e be shared by many people on the Internet
f continue
g choose
h increase

9 Complete the sentences with the correct forms of the expressions in Exercise 8.

1 The party's ______, I think. Everyone's having fun.
2 It ______ that your mom and I will support you in your decision!
3 The soccer fans ______ when their team won the game.
4 I ______ the red one. It's cool.
5 He posted the photo and within days it ______!
6 I drew a picture of my dream house. My brother ______ and built it.
7 The price of bread has continued to ______.
8 It was raining, but we still ______ playing. We didn't stop.

→ workbook page 84

Activity idea Extension

Draw a picture of a sad man on the board as follows: draw the first line of the picture (perhaps his chin) and ask students to guess what the drawing is. Encourage them to use modals of deduction: *might, could, must*. Elicit that *might* and *could* have similar meanings in this context but *must* indicates that you are sure. Add a few more lines (an eyebrow, part of his ear) to the drawing and prompt students to speculate a bit more. Continue until you have nearly finished the drawing and invite them to comment again.

Next, ask students to speculate why the man is sad. Listen to some of their ideas. Elicit/remind students that if we want to use a modal verb to describe the past, we use: modal + *have* + past participle, for example *he might have failed a test*.

TH!NK more

Practice Extra	Workbook	Worksheets
Unit 9 Practice it!	Grammar p83, Ex.6–8 Vocabulary p84, Ex.3–4	Grammar Worksheets 9 Vocabulary Worksheets 9

Warmer

Review collocations with *go* by giving students a definition from Exercise 8 on page 89 and eliciting a verb which collocates. Once you've demonstrated this with one or two examples, pairs take turns testing each other in the same way.

1 Ask students to cover the extract, look at the picture, and answer the questions. Write their ideas on the board.

2 **9.06** Before listening, you could set a three-minute timer to encourage students to read quickly and focus on the question rather than trying to understand every word.

Activity idea Review

To review narrative tenses, ask students which three past tenses are used in the extract. Elicit simple past, past continuous, and past perfect. In open class, elicit the rules for the usage of all three tenses, referring to the grammar rules in Units 1 and 2 if necessary. Tell students they are going to do a reading race. Write on the board: *Read the extract and find at least …*

10 irregular past tense verbs (were/was, did, had, found, began, drew, forgot, knew, stood, felt, said, bit, flew, held)

3 examples of the past continuous (was holding, was moving, was smelling, were talking and laughing)

2 examples of the past perfect (I'd gotten up, had disappeared, had done)

Instruct students to find the items as quickly as possible.

Fiction

1 Look at the picture. Make some predictions.

- What do you think will happen to spoil this beautiful scene?
- What will happen to the woman in the red dress?
- Why will the flower seller get angry?

2 9.06 Read and listen to the extract. Were your predictions correct?

Wild Country by Margaret Johnson

Chapter 1 *The flower market mistake*

The woman in the red dress was holding some large yellow flowers to her face. Behind her, there were lots more flowers – big flowers, small flowers, flowers of every possible color. I was very pleased I'd got up early to see Nice's famous flower market. It was beautiful, and it helped me to forget that I wasn't going to have a nice day. Or a nice ten days. Grant Cooper! Grant Cooper! I couldn't believe I was going to work with that man for ten days. It was going to be horrible. But I wouldn't think about it until I had to. And here, in the market, I could almost forget. There was color all around me – not just the flowers, but also the people buying them in their summer clothes. Even the buildings behind the market were colorful – red and orange with blue windows. What a lovely picture it would make, if I only had my paints with me. But I did have a pencil somewhere. I could do a quick drawing. I still had a few minutes before I had to leave for the airport. I found the pencil in the bottom of my shoulder bag, together with an old letter. Soon my pencil was moving quickly over the back of the letter as I began to draw the woman in the red dress. She was smelling some red flowers now, and her hair was very blonde in the sunshine. As I drew what I saw, I quickly forgot about everything else. The woman buying the flowers obviously knew the flower seller. They were talking and laughing together, and I had lots of time to work on my picture.

I don't know how long I stood there. I only know that the next time I looked at my watch, it was nine o'clock. Nine o'clock! I only had thirty minutes to get to the airport. Oh no, I was going to be late. Again. But before I could put the pencil and paper back into my bag, I felt something soft against my legs. It was a small brown dog, and he was on his own. "Hello, boy," I said. "Are you lost?" The dog seemed to smile up at me, and I reached out to touch it. The dog smiled again, and then … it bit me! I screamed and jumped quickly back from the dog. Too quickly. There was a very loud crash behind me. "Mademoiselle!" shouted an angry voice. I turned round to see flowers all over the ground. "I'm sorry," I said. "That dog – it bit me!" "What dog?" asked the angry flower seller. "Well, that one," I said, but when I looked down, the dog had disappeared. "It was here a minute ago," I said, turning to look. Unfortunately, I turned so quickly that my shoulder bag flew through the air and crashed into some more flowers. "Mademoiselle!" shouted the flower seller again. "I'm sorry," I started to say, but then I noticed that things were about to get even worse. A river of dirty water from the flowers was moving very quickly towards the blonde woman's expensive white summer shoes. "Madame!" I shouted, but it was too late. "My shoes!" cried the blonde woman. "My flowers!" cried the flower seller. I held my hand up to show what the dog had done. "My finger!" I cried, but neither the flower seller nor the blonde woman was interested in my hurt finger.

90

Reading; Writing

3 🔊 **9.06**

1 That she was going to have a horrible time working with Grant Cooper for the next ten days.
2 The back of a letter.
3 Because she only had 30 minutes to get to the airport.
4 Because a dog bit her.
5 Her bag flew through the air and knocked them over.
6 Because her expensive white shoes were covered with dirty water.

4 Monitor and prompt students to keep talking, but as this is a fluency activity, do not interrupt to correct mistakes. At the end of the exercise, listen to some of the students' ideas and encourage open class discussion.

3 🔊 9.06 **Read and listen to the extract again. Answer the questions.**

1 What did the flowers help the woman to forget?
2 What did she draw the picture on?
3 Why did she stop drawing?
4 Why did the woman jump backwards?
5 How did she knock over the second lot of flowers?
6 Why was the blonde woman upset?

4 SPEAKING **Work in pairs. Discuss these questions.**

1 Was the woman really bitten?
2 Will she find out more about the dog?
3 What will she find out?

WRITING
Explaining a mystery

1 INPUT **Read the article on the right. Who does the writer think is responsible for the crop circles?**

2 **Write the underlined expressions in the correct columns.**

I'm sure	I'm reasonably sure	I'm not sure

3 ANALYZE **The article has three paragraphs. What does the writer talk about in each one?**

4 PLAN **Read about a mystery. Then write three sentences about it. Use a different expression from Exercise 2 in each sentence.**

MISSING
HELICOPTER

An army helicopter with a pilot, co-pilot, and twelve soldiers on board has disappeared off the north coast of Scotland. The last contact with the helicopter was more than 12 hours ago, when the pilot radioed that everything was OK. No distress signal was received and despite a huge search over sea and land, no sign of the helicopter has been found. What happened to army helicopter 487?

5 PRODUCE **Write a blog entry (200 words) explaining what you think happened to the missing helicopter.**

Mysterious patterns
appear in local field overnight

1 This isn't the first time something like this happened and it probably won't be the last time either. For decades, crop circles have been fooling experts who are still asking, "What exactly causes these patterns?"

2 Some people say aliens might create this phenomenon. They suggest that aliens come to Earth at night and leave these patterns in our fields. These people are definitely wrong. Even if aliens from other planets existed, how could they land a huge spaceship without anyone noticing? It would be impossible, of course.

3 Humans must have made these crop circles, just as they must have made all the others, but I'm not certain how they did it. Obviously, it couldn't have been done by just one person; it must have been a group and more than likely, a really big one. Also, it's clear that the person or people behind the design must be extremely intelligent because these patterns are extraordinarily complex. It was most probably organized by a group of math students from a university. It's the kind of thing that students like to do as a joke. But whoever did it, they certainly got people talking.

1 Write on the board *1 Where might you see this text? 2 What is the purpose of the text?* Give students two minutes to read the article quickly and think about the answers.
The writer thinks that some math students were responsible for the crop circles.

2 **Check/clarify:** *reasonably.*
Draw students' attention to:

- Word order: *be* + *definitely/most probably* + adjective.
- *Obviously* is followed by a comma and appears at the beginning of the sentence.
- *More than likely* is followed by a comma and appears in the middle of the sentence.

I'm sure: definitely, of course, must have, Obviously, can't have, it's clear, certainly
I'm reasonably sure: more than likely, most probably
I'm not sure: might, not certain

3 Point out that in a well-structured piece of writing, each paragraph should have its own purpose.
Paragraph 1: How long the mystery of crop circles has been around
Paragraph 2: The idea that crop circles are created by aliens
Paragraph 3: The writer's opinions, supported by reasons, about who made these crop circles

4 You could divide the class into small groups so that they can share ideas before writing individually (they could do this for homework).

5 Encourage students to organize their writing as outlined in Exercise 3 and to use modals of deduction.

Activity idea
Peer correction

On completion of the writing task, ask students to exchange their blog entries with another pair for them to read and evaluate on the basis of content (How interesting were the ideas?); organization (Did each paragraph include a clear and distinct idea like the model answer?); communicative purpose (Were you convinced by it?); and language (Were past modals used correctly?) They should avoid focusing solely on accuracy.

TH!NK more

Practice Extra
Unit 9 Master it!

Workbook
Developing Writing p87

Tests
Unit, extension, and skills test 9
End of term test 3

Warmer

Write on the board: *How often do you save money? Where do you save it – in a bank or a piggy bank? Have you ever lost any money? How did you lose it? Have you ever found any money? What did you do with it?* Ask students to discuss in pairs.

▶ 25 Get TH!NKing

Play the video and discuss the question with your class.

1 Before students discuss, you could write the following on the board for them to match with the pictures: *coins, bills, check, debit card, smartphone, smartwatch* plus a few extra words: *contactless card, credit card, bitcoin.*

2 **🔊 10.01 Check/clarify:** *undeniably, wristbands, registered, refund, check-out, fraud, fingerprint, invade our privacy.*
Before playing the audio, give students two minutes to scan the article and find as many of the "money" words as possible. Encourage students to think about the correct answer to the false statements.
1 T 2 T 3 F 4 F 5 F 6 T

3 Write on the board: *an exaggeration* and try to elicit reasons why people exaggerate (e.g., for dramatic effect).
1 undeniably 2 By far the most

4 It will help students if they identify the words in each of the sentences which express exaggeration in order to find the one sentence which isn't an exaggeration.
Sentence 2 isn't an exaggeration.

10 MONEY

OBJECTIVES
FUNCTIONS: talking about future events; sympathizing
GRAMMAR: future continuous; future perfect
VOCABULARY: money and value; jobs and work; by

Get TH!NKING
Watch the video and think: do you think it would be possible to live without money?

READING

1 **Look at the photos and answer the questions.**
1 Which of the payment methods do you recognize? Where are they used?
2 Which of them do you or your family use?

2 **🔊 10.01 Read and listen to the article. Mark the sentences T (true) or F (false) according to the article.**
1 Paper money was invented because of the weight of coins. ☐
2 In Sweden, cash is disappearing. ☐
3 Supermarkets will never use invisible payments. ☐
4 It's good to have computers looking after money systems, because they are 100% reliable. ☐
5 Security measures aren't a concern when thinking about privacy issues. ☐
6 In the future, there might be payment systems we haven't thought of yet. ☐

Train to TH!NK

Exaggeration

Sometimes writers exaggerate to create dramatic effect. Of course, this doesn't mean that what they're saying is completely true.

3 **Look at these sentences from the article. Which words show that they're exaggerations?**
1 The answer is undeniably "no."
2 By far, that's the most important question.

4 **Read the sentences. Which *isn't* an exaggeration? Write the words that help you decide.**
1 There's no way that credit cards will exist in ten years.
2 I found this subject really interesting.
3 It's the best article that has ever been written.

5 **Rewrite these sentences so they contain an exaggeration.**
1 It was a really boring movie.
2 Justin Timberlake is a great singer.
3 Brian's good at math.

92

5 During feedback, say the sentences for students to repeat together with appropriately exaggerated stress and intonation.
Possible answers:
1 It was the most boring movie I've ever seen. 2 Justin Timberlake is by far the greatest singer in the world. 3 Brian is a math genius.

Communication
Using appropriate language and register for context
Uses language for effect (e.g., exaggerations or cleft sentences).

Objectives

Functions and speaking Talking about future events; sympathizing
Grammar Future continuous; future perfect
Vocabulary Money and value; jobs and work; **WordWise:** Phrases with *by*
Life Competencies Being determined
Train to TH!NK Exaggeration

Resources for this unit

All available online

Videos
- Get **TH!NK**ing: *Do you think it would be possible to live without money?*
- Grammar rap!: Future continuous
- Vlog: Being determined

Tests
- Unit, extension, and skills test 10

Worksheets
- Grammar and vocabulary: Basic, Standard, and Extension Worksheets
- Project: All about money
- Communication: Money
- Literature Worksheets: *One Thousand Dollars*
- Grammar presentation: Future continuous and future perfect
- Get **TH!NK**ing, Grammar rap!, and Life Lessons video Worksheets

6 Monitor and prompt students to keep talking, but as this is a fluency activity, do not interrupt to correct mistakes. While monitoring, note down any common errors to review as a class at the end by writing a mix of correct and incorrect sentences on the board, ensuring anonymity. Ask students to identify and correct the mistakes during feedback.

Homework

Ask students to keep a journal for two or three days and make a note of the money they spend, what they spend it on, and whether they could have saved the money instead.

Activity idea Extension

The article includes several time expressions which refer to periods of time or points in time. Point out the first example to students (*Thousands of years ago* in line 1). In pairs, students race to underline at least four more time expressions in the article. Answers: *now, by about 2025, Twenty years from now, in 20 years' time.*

MONEY: PAST, PRESENT, AND FUTURE

Thousands of years ago, people started using metal coins as money to buy and sell things. But the coins were heavy, so paper money was invented. Different payment systems evolved through time and now we also use credit and debit cards. These cards often have to be put into a machine and then a PIN has to be entered – but that practice is disappearing with contactless cards and smartphone apps becoming more and more popular. So, cash has mostly been replaced by alternative payment methods. And things don't stop there; it's possible that some countries will soon be completely cashless. For example, it's predicted that no one in Sweden will be using cash at all by about 2025.

So, what is the future of money? Twenty years from now, will we still be using cash? The answer is undeniably "no." And it's highly likely that bank cards are on their way out as well. This is happening already: the use of smartphones, smartwatches, and electronic wristbands has allowed people, in many situations, to avoid using cash or cards. Some apps let us transfer money from phone to phone like a text message, which makes it a quick and easy way to repay a friend if you owe them money. Increasingly, people are making "invisible" payments for things like car rides – you choose a car, you take the ride, the money automatically comes out of your registered card. You can even include a tip for your driver this way! Perhaps we will soon be doing this in places like supermarkets, too – you'll get your goods, a reader will record the details of what you've bought as you leave and the amount will be taken automatically from your account. And if you need a refund, the money is put back in your account as easily as it was taken out. Worry-free shopping. No machines or long check-out lines. No more heavy wallets or purses. This all sounds very positive, but there are possible disadvantages, too. Technological advancement, as we all know, brings many positives but also forces us to consider other matters. Will fraud, especially online, get easier? And as our money systems become more dependent on computers, how can we make sure that the computers don't fail? Security might get better as we increase our use of things like fingerprint and facial recognition, but will they be used to invade our privacy by gathering information about our movements? By far, that's the most important question.

Questions like these won't go away easily. We are in a state of change, and there are many different future possibilities. Perhaps unimagined payment methods will be developed. It will be interesting to see how things move forward, but one thing is for sure – in 20 years' time, we won't be buying, selling, or paying for things the same ways we do now.

SPEAKING

6 **Work in pairs. Discuss these questions.**

1 Do you think a cashless society would be a good idea? Why or why not?
2 Do you think there will still be coins and bills in 30 years' time? Why or why not?

TH!NK more

Worksheets
Project All about money
Communication Money
Get **TH!NK**ing *Do you think it would be possible to live without money?*

Warmer

Review money words. Present images to represent different payment forms from page 92 and ask students to name them.

▶ 26 Grammar rap! Future continuous

1 Ask students to try to complete the sentences from memory before referring back to the article to check.
1 we … be using 2 will … be doing
3 won't be RULE: 4 a specified

2 During feedback, you may like to point out that while *have* when referring to ownership is a state verb, e.g., *I have a new phone*, it is not used in a stative sense here – it is used in its dynamic sense. *Enjoy* is a dynamic verb.
1 'll be sitting 2 'll be enjoying
3 'll be working 4 will … be doing
5 'll be playing 6 'll be having

3 Ask students to explain why they chose the simple future or the future continuous in each case (5–7 refer to routine activities in the future).
1 won't be working 2 won't be traveling 3 'll be lying 4 'll be drinking 5 'll wake up 6 'll have
7 'll put on 8 will … be paying

4 You may like to give an example from your own experience to get students started.

Workbook p90

Get it Right!
Future continuous vs. simple future
Student's Book pp125–126

GRAMMAR
Future continuous

1 **Complete the sentences from the article on page 93. Then choose the correct words to complete the rule.**
1 Twenty years from now, will ____________ still ____________ cash?
2 Perhaps we ____________ soon ____________ this in places like supermarkets, too.
3 In 20 years' time, we ____________ buying, selling, and paying the same way that we do now.

RULE: We use **the future continuous** to talk about things that will be in progress at [4]*a specified / an unspecified* time in the future.

2 **Complete the sentences with the correct forms of the verbs.**
1 Tomorrow at ten o'clock, I ____________ (sit) on a train.
2 Lucky you! This time next week, you ____________ (enjoy) your vacation.
3 Susan is still in college, but a year from now, she ____________ (work) in her dad's company.
4 What ____________ I ____________ (do) three years from now? I have no idea.
5 Talk to Sam now. Tonight he ____________ (play) tennis, so you won't be able to reach him.
6 Tomorrow afternoon, we ____________ (have) a coffee in a café next to the river.

3 **Complete the text. Use the simple future or future continuous form of the verbs.**

not travel | drink | wake up | put on
not work | pay | lie | have

I know where I'll be ten years from now. I [1]____________ 50 hours a week in a small office. I [2]____________ two hours every day to get to and from work. No, I [3]____________ on a beautiful Caribbean beach! I [4]____________ coconut water and reading a good book. Every day will be the same. I [5]____________ late and I [6]____________ a long, lazy breakfast. Every morning I [7]____________ my shorts and walk down to the beach to meet my friends. And how [8]____________ I ____________ for all of this? That's an excellent question!

4 SPEAKING **Work in pairs. Discuss what you will be doing at these times.**
1 an hour from now
2 at eight o'clock tonight
3 this time next week
4 on January 1st

An hour from now, I'll be having lunch.

→ workbook page 90

VOCABULARY
Money and value

5 **Match the words with the definitions.**

a tip | $(X) off | a reward | a bargain
owe | a refund | be worth
not good value for money | valuable | on sale

1 money that you get for doing something helpful (for example, finding something that was lost)
2 money that's paid back to you (for example, if you return something to a store)
3 extra money to thank someone (for example, a waiter) for a service
4 to need to pay someone
5 available at a good price (usually for a short time)
6 money taken away from the original price
7 something you get at a really good price
8 not worth its price
9 having a very high value
10 to have a value of

6 **Complete the sentences with the words from Exercise 5.**
0 I'm not buying the shoes in this store. There's another one nearby where they're *on sale*.
1 I ______ Kylie $20. I mustn't forget to repay her.
2 Mr. Brown offered a big ______ for any information that would help him to find his cat.
3 The taxi driver was very helpful, so we gave him a good ______.
4 Have a look at this old coin. Do you think it's ______ much?
5 I bought this expensive laptop last week. Today I saw it in the store for $100 ______.
6 The tablet didn't work, so I took it back to the store and they gave me a ______.
7 I paid $50 for this toy and it broke after a week. It really was ______.
8 I waited until after the holiday and got the bike for half price. It was a real ______.
9 This vase is 3,000 years old and very ______.

94

5 During feedback, check pronunciation and the short vowels in *bargain* /ˈbɑrɡɪn/ and *valuable* /ˈvæljəbl/.
1 a reward 2 a refund 3 a tip 4 owe 5 on sale 6 $(X) off 7 a bargain
8 not good value for money 9 valuable 10 be worth

6 During feedback, point out these verb–noun collocations: ***to be** on sale*; ***to offer** a reward*; ***to give** a tip*; ***to give** a refund*.
1 owe 2 reward 3 tip 4 worth 5 off 6 refund 7 not good value for money
8 bargain 9 valuable

THINK more

Workbook
Grammar p90, Ex.1–3
Vocabulary p92, Ex.1–2
Vocabulary Extra p93, Ex.1–3

Worksheets
Grammar rap! Future continuous
Grammar Worksheets 10
Grammar presentation: Future continuous and future perfect
Vocabulary Worksheets 10

Language note Future continuous

We do not use continuous tenses with state verbs, so we can say *I will be happy* and *He won't understand you* but not **I will be being happy* or **He won't be understanding you.*

7 At the end of the exercise, listen to some of the students' ideas and encourage open class discussion.

Workbook p92

8 Invite students to share their answers with the rest of the class during feedback.

9 🔊 **10.02** During feedback, ask: *Which fact was the most interesting/surprising?*
1 C 2 C 3 A 4 D 5 B

10 During feedback, point out the frequent use of *by* followed by the gerund as in item 2, *by* followed by a noun, as in items 1 and 3 and *by* with a time phrase and with the future continuous as in item 4. The future continuous will come up later.
1 d 2 c 3 a 4 b

11 During feedback, extend this by asking students to say if each sentence uses a gerund, a noun, or a time phrase with *by*.
1 by the end of class 2 by the French teacher 3 by the bus station 4 by washing

Workbook p92

Pronunciation
Short and long vowel sounds: /ɪ/ – /iː/ and /ɒ/ – /oʊ/

Student's Book p121

Homework
Ask students to write five sentences describing what they'll be doing in ten years' time.

Activity idea Extension
In pairs, students make predictions for what other students will be doing in 20 years' time. Give some examples of your own to get them started: *I think Frank will be playing soccer for Barcelona. I think Martha will be working for the United Nations.* Students should write at least five sentences for a positive future. Listen to some of their sentences in open class and encourage students to react to predictions made about them.

7 SPEAKING **Work in pairs. Discuss the questions.**
1 What's the most valuable thing that teenagers usually own?
2 What are some good ways to get a bargain?
3 In what situations might you give someone a reward or a tip? Have you ever received one?
4 Have you ever had to ask for a refund? What for?

→ workbook page 92

LISTENING
8 **Look at the questionnaire and try to guess the answers. Then compare with a partner.**

9 🔊 10.02 **Listen to an extract from the quiz show *Moneyspinners*. Check your answers.**

WordWise: Phrases with *by*
10 **What do the phrases in bold refer to? Match 1–4 with a–d.**
1 Cash has mostly been replaced **by alternative payment methods.** ☐
2 She won $1,000 **by answering** questions about money. ☐
3 You can get money from the cash machine **by the entrance** to the supermarket. ☐
4 No one in Sweden will be using cash at all **by 2025.** ☐

a a location
b a time in the future
c a way to do something
d the person / people / thing(s) that do something

11 **Complete the sentences with the phrases.**

by the bus station | by the end of class | by the French teacher | by washing

1 Please finish Exercise 2 ________________.
2 I was made to stay after class ________________.
3 Meet me tomorrow ________________ downtown.
4 I made some money ________________ people's cars.

→ workbook page 92

PRONUNCIATION
Short and long vowel sounds: /ɪ/ – /iː/ and /ɑ/ – /oʊ/ Go to page 121.

ODD FACTS ABOUT MONEY

1 Some coins in … have holes in the middle.
A Britain
B Iceland
C Japan
D South Africa

2 More people take money out of automatic teller machines (ATMs) on … than any other day.
A Mondays
B Thursdays
C Fridays
D Saturdays

3 Of all the money in the world, only … is actual cash (coins and bills).
A 8%
B 12%
C 20%
D 50%

4 The first country to make plastic bills was …
A Sweden.
B Germany.
C the US.
D Australia.

5 The world's first known coin is called the …
A Egyptian Lira.
B Lydian Lion.
C Ying Yuan.
D Saxon Shilling.

TH!NK more
Workbook
Listening p96, Ex.1–3
WordWise p92, Ex.5–6
Pronunciation p121

Warmer

Ask students to work in pairs to make a list of jobs with high salaries. Write these on the board. Next, students work in pairs to rank the jobs from what they believe to be the highest to the lowest paid. Give students five minutes or so for this and ask pairs to report back to the class on which they think are the top three highest paid jobs.

1 You may like to put a copy of the three photographs up on the board before students open their books. Students can work in pairs. During feedback, draw three columns on the board and write one of the three names at the top of each. Ask the pairs to come up and write how much they think each earns. When all the numbers are in, set a challenge for the first student to work out the average salary that the class thinks each person earns.

2 Give students two minutes to read the texts and choose the title. Encourage them not to focus on every word for now.
D

3 🔊 **10.05 Check/clarify:** *wealthy, billions, salaries, bonuses, real estate, taxes.*
1 B 2 A 3 C 4 B 5 D 6 A

Activity idea Extension

Before the lesson, do an internet search to find the highest paid actors and actresses. Write these questions on the board: *Can you name the three highest paid actors and the three highest paid actresses in 2020? How much did they earn?* Students could answer the questions in pairs or small groups. Ask: *Do you think actors deserve to be paid so much money? Why (not)?* Listen to their ideas as a class.

READING

1 Look at the people in the photographs. If Margaret Phelps earns $95,000 a year, how much do you think the other two get?

Margaret Phelps: doctor

Andy Wilson: delivery man

2 Read the article and posts quickly. Choose a suitable title.

A Inequality isn't only about money
B A new kind of inequality
C Equality is impossible
D Continued inequality

3 🔊 10.05 **Read and listen to the article and posts. Which writer thinks …**

1 it's not always ability that determines who gets rich and who doesn't?
2 people can get good jobs because of who they know?
3 high salaries are OK because earners contribute to society?
4 differences in salaries are just part of life?
5 healthcare managers shouldn't earn more than medical professionals?
6 it's possible to earn a lot of money before you're very old?

Graham Hargreaves: company director

MONEY**MATTERS** HOME BLOG LOGIN

It's said that the easiest way to be really rich is to be born into a really rich family. That aside, undoubtedly the best way to become truly wealthy is to get a good idea for a product, make it, and sell it, then sit back and watch the money come in. Throughout history, many people have become incredibly wealthy that way.

There's nothing new in this – for centuries people have had ideas, made things, and become very rich. But questions are increasingly being asked about the way we're going. How fair is it for one person to have a personal fortune of billions of dollars? Is it right for big company bosses to be paid huge salaries and often to receive large bonuses on top of that? In just one year, the head of a real estate company in the US received $29 million in bonuses. Is that acceptable? In 1965, bosses in the US's biggest companies earned on average about 20 times an ordinary employee's salary – in 1978 it was 30 times, but by 2020, this had increased to 70 times. However, some CEOs make more than 400 times what their employees make.

We'd like to hear your comments on this subject. 5 20 9

A I finished high school with a guy I know and we went to work in a finance company. His father's one of the directors, so now he has a very well-paid job, earning five times as much as me. By the time he's 30, he'll have earned millions – and he does everything he can to avoid paying taxes. It's sickening.
GBarker95

B I'm not sure what the problem is. It's just how the world is. Like the article says, there's nothing new here. Some people get lucky, some don't. Look at writers – lots of people get an idea and write a book or books – and sometimes thousands of people buy the book and the writer gets rich. They're not even always the best writers. That's just how it is.
Thatcherman

C One time, I heard a politician say, "It's fine for people to be extremely rich – as long as they pay their taxes." I agree. A top boss, after ten years of work or so, will have given millions of dollars back in taxes to help the country. And that benefits everyone, right?
Arguer123

D My mom's a doctor and she'll be working until she's 60 – 35 years of work – and when she stops, she won't have made a tenth of what some of these people make in a year. And there are people who manage the hospitals she works in who earn five times what she does. Who contributes more to healthcare – a doctor or someone who works in management? It's disgraceful.
Aliboy

96

TH!NK more

Workbook
Reading p94, Ex.1–3

Grammar; Vocabulary; Writing

4 Ask students to try to answer the questions from memory before referring back to page 96 to check.
1 will have given 2 won't have made RULE: 3 will 4 have 5 past participle

5 If you're short on time, assign this exercise for homework.
1 will have built 2 'll have worked 3 'll have done 4 won't have finished 5 'll have bought 6 'll have visited

6 Before they start speaking, encourage students to think about their answers and make notes. Tell them they should think of at least one thing they will have done and one thing they won't have done for each question and they should use the future perfect when telling their partner.

Workbook p91

7 You could put students in small groups and give each group five words. Students then sit with someone who has different words and peer teach them.
1 qualifications 2 public service 3 management 4 education 5 employer 6 finance 7 salary 8 law 9 healthcare 10 employee

8 **Check/clarify:** *degree.*
1 healthcare 2 finance 3 public service 4 education 5 management 6 employer 7 qualifications 8 law 9 salary 10 employee

9 Encourage students to put the items in order of importance. Hold a class vote to decide which are the most and least important.

Workbook p92

10 If you are short on time, you could assign this for homework.

Homework

If you are short on time, students can do Exercise 10 for homework. If you have done this in the class, ask students to exchange their texts with another student for them to read at home and give feedback on content and structure. Students could check if the text uses the same structure as the bullet points. They should also decide which the most/least interesting part of the text is.

GRAMMAR
Future perfect

4 **Complete the sentences from the comments on page 96. Then read the rule and complete it with the words in the list.**

1 A top boss, after ten years of work or so, ______________ millions of dollars back in taxes.
2 When she stops, she ______________ a tenth of what some of these people make in a year.

have | past participle | *will*

RULE: We use the future perfect to talk about actions that will finish at some time between now and a specified time in the future.

now ——— $1 million ——— $2 million ——— $3 million ——— end of the year

By the end of the year, he'll have made more than $3 million.

- We form it with [3]____ + [4]____ + [5]____.
- We often use it with *by* + a point in time or *by the time* + a time clause.
  By 2050, …
  By the time I'm 50, …

5 **Complete the sentences with the future perfect form of the verbs.**

1 The government ______________ (build) lots of new houses here by 2030.
2 By the time I'm 35, I ______________ (work) in IT for over ten years.
3 If I work really hard, I ______________ (do) my homework by the time the game starts on TV.
4 The test is from 9 to 12 tomorrow morning. So at ten o'clock, I ______________ (not finish) it.
5 By that time, I ______________ (buy) my first house.
6 I hope that three years from now, I ______________ (visit) one or two other countries.

6 SPEAKING **Work in pairs. Look at the questions and make notes. Then compare your ideas.**

1 Which tasks will / won't you have finished by 6 p.m. tomorrow?
2 What will / won't you have done by the end of the year?
3 Which goals will you have achieved six years from now?

→ workbook page 90

VOCABULARY
Jobs and work

7 **Match the words with the definitions.**

education | employee | employer | finance | healthcare | law | management | public service | qualifications | salary

1 abilities or experience needed for a particular job
2 jobs paid for by the government
3 people who make the big decisions in a company
4 teaching and learning
5 a person or organization that people work for
6 an area of work related to managing money
7 the money a person is paid for doing a job
8 an area of work related to the legal system
9 an area of work related to medicine
10 someone who's paid to work for someone else

8 **Complete the sentences with words from Exercise 7.**

1 Her dad works in ______. He's a nurse.
2 Margaret Bourne is the director of ______ for a big company. She decides on all the investments.
3 Joanna was a police officer and now she's a teacher. She's been in ______ all her professional life.
4 Larry is a teacher. He works in ______.
5 The company suffered years of bad ______.
6 This tech company is the biggest ______ in the Seattle area.
7 A degree and some experience in IT are necessary ______ for this job.
8 James works in the ______. He's a judge.
9 Allan got a new job with a higher ______.
10 She's been an ______ of this company for 25 years.

9 SPEAKING **Work in pairs. Discuss these questions.**

1 Which of the areas of work in Exercise 7 would you be most / least interested in? Why?
2 Would you rather be an employer or an employee? Why?

→ workbook page 92

WRITING
My life in the future

10 **Write about your life 30 years from now (150–200 words). Think about the things that you:**

- will be doing.
- won't have done.
- will have done.
- will still want to do.

Language note Future perfect

The future perfect is frequently used with *by* + time expression. For example: *The movie will have finished by seven o'clock.*

TH!NK more

Practice Extra
Unit 10 Practice it!

Workbook
Grammar pp90–91, Ex.4–8
Vocabulary p92, Ex.3–4
Developing Writing p95

Worksheets
Grammar Worksheets 10
Grammar presentation: Future continuous and future perfect
Vocabulary Worksheets 10

1 10.06 Tell students to cover the dialogue and discuss the questions in pairs before listening to check their answers.
They're in a café. They're talking about money.

2 10.06 **Check/clarify:** *strapped for cash, I'm broke, What a shame, material things, as far as I'm concerned.*
1 Because she had to fix her bike last week. 2 Because they have spent their lives without having much money, whereas she is determined to be rich. 3 $50 4 Mark

3 Encourage students to use the language from the dialogue when giving their answers.

4 During feedback, say the sentences for students to repeat. Drill sentences to ensure correct pronunciation.
1 don't look at me; I'm broke; are on me 2 same as usual 3 It's not my fault; that's all

5 As an alternative, you could ask students to cover the Key Language box and try to guess which key words complete the sentences. Write the phrases on the board and ask students for an L1 translation.
1 What a shame 2 Never mind 3 That's too bad

6 Allow students six to eight minutes to prepare their role-plays. Monitor to make sure all students are on task. If students have access to a recording device (their mobile devices, for example), they could record their conversation and play it back to check their own pronunciation and intonation. They can then repeat the exercise and listen for improvements.

DEVELOPING SPEAKING

1 10.06 **Look at the photo. Where are the three people? What do you think they're talking about? Read and listen to check.**

Josh: That was a delicious cookie. I wish I could buy another one – but I'm really strapped for cash, same as usual.
Tanya: Don't look at me. Sorry, but I only have enough for my ice cream. Last week, I had to fix my bike. So I'm broke.
Josh: What a shame. Never mind, though, you'll get some spending money soon, won't you?
Tanya: I hate not having money to do the things I want. My grandparents have spent their whole lives like that. Not me. I'm determined to be seriously rich when I'm older.
Josh: Your grandparents seem really happy to me. Maybe they never worried about material things.
Tanya: So I'm wrong to want to be rich?
Josh: No, I'm saying not everyone wants to be, that's all. You can be happy without a lot of money.
Tanya: I'm just ambitious. It's not my fault.
Mark: Hi, guys! All right?
Josh: Not bad, Mark. We're talking about money – or rather, not having it. We're both broke, basically.
Mark: That's too bad. But good news. I've had some luck. I sold my tablet online for $50. The food and drinks are on me! What do you guys want?
Tanya: An ice cream please – and another cookie for Josh?
Josh: No, I'm fine thanks. You should keep your money.
Mark: No, money's for spending as far as I'm concerned. OK, then: one ice cream for Tanya and two for me!

2 10.06 **Listen and read the dialogue again. Answer the questions.**
1 Why doesn't Tanya have any money?
2 Why doesn't she want to be like her grandparents?
3 How much did Mark sell his tablet for?
4 Who is going to buy food and drinks?

3 SPEAKING **Discuss the statements in pairs. Which do you agree with (if any)?**
1 I'm determined to be seriously rich when I'm older.
2 You can be happy without a lot of money.
3 Money's for spending as far as I'm concerned.

Phrases for fluency

4 **Find the underlined expressions in the dialogue. How do you say them in your language? Use the expressions to complete the dialogues.**
1 A I don't have enough money for lunch.
B Well, ______________! I can't pay because ______________ – again!
C It's OK. I'll pay for the food. Lunch and drinks ______________!
2 A Hi, Jack. How are you?
B Oh, ______________, really. Nothing changes a lot, does it?
3 A Wow, this room is really messy!
B Hey! ______________! Julie made the mess, not me.
C OK, calm down. I didn't say it was you. I just said it was messy, ______________.

FUNCTIONS
Sympathizing

KEY LANGUAGE
I'm really sorry (to hear that).
That's too bad.
How awful.
What a shame.
Never mind.

5 **Look back at the dialogue. Complete the extracts with some phrases from the Key Language box.**
Tanya So, I'm broke.
Josh 1______________!
2______________ though, you'll get some spending money soon.
Josh We're both broke, basically.
Mark 3______________!

6 SPEAKING **Work in pairs. Write two-line conversations like the one in Exercise 5 about each of these situations. Then act them out.**
You tell your friend that …
- your exam results are very bad.
- you lost some money.
- you broke your smartphone.

98

Activity idea Extension

Write out one of the dialogues on the board. Make A/B pairs. Students practice the conversations. Cover a small section of the dialogue, beginning from the right-hand side of the screen or board. Students repeat the dialogues in their same A/B pairings trying to remember the whole thing, including the parts they can no longer see. Cover more and more of the dialogue, with students practicing at each stage, until eventually nothing is left on the board. Ask for volunteers to perform for the class or have all As and all Bs perform in unison. This activity involving lots of repetition is a fun way for students to memorize useful chunks.

Life Competencies

Warmer

Write *being determined* on the board and elicit what it might mean. Encourage students to try and clarify its meaning through examples or explanation, rather than through a translation. Ask students to read the introductory paragraph to check their ideas. Elicit examples of people being determined in Unit 10.

▶ 27 Life Lessons: Being determined

1 ▶ **27** Ask students to compare their answers with a partner.
1 c 2 a 3 b

2 ▶ **27** Ask students to try to answer the questions from memory before watching the video again to check.
1 She's going to cut down on the time she spends in front of a screen. 2 He taught himself to draw and paint and has made a success of it. 3 She advised Serena to learn an instrument / the guitar while she's young. 4 She's going to form a band with them.

3 **Check/clarify:** *cancer, half marathon, raise money.*
Give students one minute to read the text and find the answer. Encourage them not to focus on every word.
To raise money for a cancer charity by running a half marathon

4 *1 He isn't very good at running, and he hurt his ankle. It was often cold when he started training. 2 His aunt had cancer, and he is determined to finish the race for her. 3 He has raised $400. 4 His mother encouraged him and ran with him, and his aunt is proud of him.*

5 You may like to give your own example to get students started on this.

6 Monitor to help with any difficulties, but do not interrupt as this is a fluency activity.

LIFE COMPETENCIES

Being determined is a positive quality to have and it's good to want to achieve things in life.

1 ▶ 27 **Watch the vlog. Match these people with the roles they play in Serena's dream of learning the guitar?**

1 her dad	a her mentor
2 her music teacher	b her motivation
3 her friends	c her inspiration

2 ▶ 27 **Watch the vlog again and answer the questions.**
1 How is she going to find the time to learn the guitar?
2 How did her dad inspire her?
3 What advice did her teacher give her?
4 What is she going to do with her friends?

3 Read the text. What is Harry's goal?

Last year, my aunt got sick with cancer. She has spent a year getting treatment and she's recovering now, but I felt that I wanted to do something for her and other people who are sick. So, in two months' time, I am doing a half marathon to raise money for a cancer charity. I'm not very good at running and during the first month of training, I hurt my ankle. My training also started in January when it was cold and often dark. It's been tough sometimes, but I'm so grateful to my mom, who encouraged me and ran with me on the cold mornings. So far I've raised $400 and I'm hoping to raise $500. My aunt is really proud of me, so I'm determined to finish for her.
Harry

4 Answer the questions about the text.
1 What difficulties has Harry had to overcome to try to reach his goal?
2 What kind of special motivation does he have for being determined?
3 How much money has he raised?
4 How are other people helping him to achieve his goal?

Me and my world

5 Think of a time you were determined to do something and make notes.
- What did you want to do?
- Why did you want to do it?
- Were you successful?
- How did the experience make you feel?

6 Talk to your friend about the experience.

TIPS FOR BEING DETERMINED

- **Try not to get discouraged – don't give up if things don't work out for you at first.**
- **Being determined isn't the only thing that counts. Remember to think about how your actions might affect the people around you.**
- **It's OK to accept help even when you were determined to complete a task alone.**

Homework

Ask students to interview a family member about a time when they were determined. As a follow-up, students can present this to the class in the next lesson.

Activity idea An interview

Students could act out an interview with either Harry or Harry's aunt. Divide the class into four groups: A (Harry), B (Harry's aunt), C (Reporter to Harry), and D (Reporter to Harry's aunt). Ask groups C and D to look at the text again and write down five questions to ask Harry / Harry's aunt. Ask group A to look at the text again and find key information about Harry and group B about Harry's aunt in preparation for an interview. Monitor to make sure all the students are making notes and help with ideas if necessary. Put the students in A/C and B/D pairs and give them time to act out the interview.

Emotional Development
Identifying and understanding emotions
Describes strategies for dealing with difficult situations.

TH!NK more

Practice Extra	Worksheets	Tests
Unit 10 Master it!	Life Lessons: Being determined	Unit, extension, and skills test 10

1 🔊 10.07 In B2 First for Schools Listening Part 2, candidates have to listen to a monologue and complete ten sentences. This part of the exam tests candidates' ability to listen for specific and detailed information. It also checks the spelling of common words.

Encourage your students to do the following when they approach this task:

- Read and listen to the instructions carefully.
- Read the sentences, think about the context, and predict the language and information.
- During the first listening, find and write down single words, numbers, or short noun phrases to complete the information. Use the order of the information on the page to follow the recording.
- During the second listening, check that the answers are correct and make sense. There will only ever be a maximum of three words to write in each space. If the word was spelled in the recording, the answer must also be spelled correctly.

1 coins 2 biggest 3 banknotes 4 King Alfred 5 stops 6 week 7 60 8 blank 9 (London) Olympics 10 visit

Workbook p89

2 In B2 First for Schools Writing Part 1, candidates have to write an essay of about 140–190 words. There will be a statement or question, which students have to give their opinion about, and some prompts to help give students some ideas. This part of the exam tests the candidates' ability to write well-organized texts with a real communicative purpose.

TOWARDS B2 First for Schools

LISTENING
Sentence completion

→ workbook page 89

1 🔊 10.07 You will hear Conner talking about the Royal Mint, where coins are made. For questions 1–10, complete the sentences with a word or short phrase.

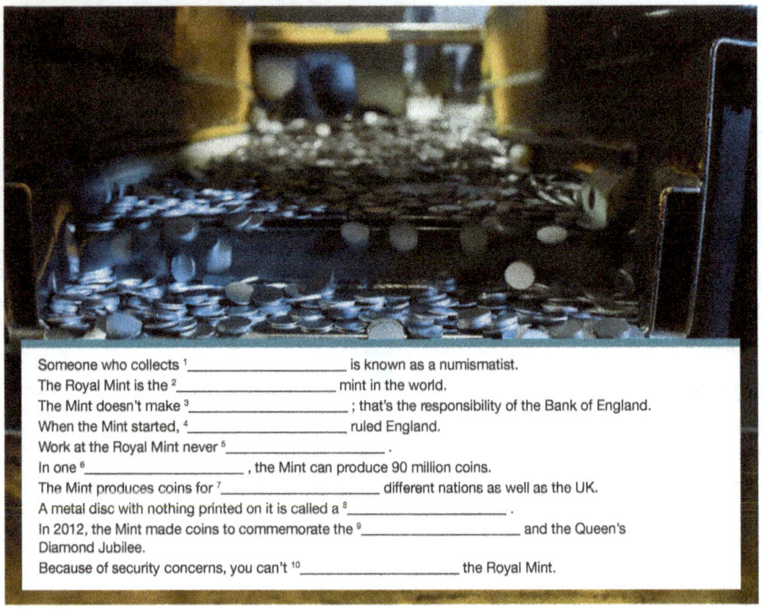

Someone who collects [1]__________ is known as a numismatist.
The Royal Mint is the [2]__________ mint in the world.
The Mint doesn't make [3]__________ ; that's the responsibility of the Bank of England.
When the Mint started, [4]__________ ruled England.
Work at the Royal Mint never [5]__________ .
In one [6]__________ , the Mint can produce 90 million coins.
The Mint produces coins for [7]__________ different nations as well as the UK.
A metal disc with nothing printed on it is called a [8]__________ .
In 2012, the Mint made coins to commemorate the [9]__________ and the Queen's Diamond Jubilee.
Because of security concerns, you can't [10]__________ the Royal Mint.

WRITING
Essay

→ workbook page 97

2 **In your English class, you have been talking about money. Now your English teacher has asked you to write an essay for homework.**

Write your essay using all the notes and giving reasons for your point of view. Give your opinion (for or against) in the last paragraph.

Is it more important to enjoy your job or to earn a lot of money?

Notes – write about:
1 material possessions
2 happiness and job satisfaction
3 __________ (your own idea).

Write your essay in 140–190 words.

100

Encourage your students to do the following when they approach this task:

- Read the question/statement and the two prompts carefully to identify what is required, who it is for, and what kind of information is needed.
- Plan the answer and respond to both prompts.
- Students will need to think of a third idea of their own which is different from the two given prompts. Brainstorm some ideas for this.
- Write a rough draft of the essay before writing the final answer. Make sure that it is well-organized and has a range of tenses, expressions, and vocabulary.
- Read the essay again to check that it makes sense and that all the content points have been included.

Workbook p97

1 1 employee 2 unexplained
3 went on 4 owe 5 bargain
6 worth 7 go very well 8 going for
9 on sale 10 refund

2 1 should have 2 might have
3 will be living 4 won't be working
5 couldn't have 6 will have written

3 1 ~~shouldn't has~~ shouldn't have
2 ~~might like~~ might have liked
3 ~~will have working~~ will be working
4 ~~will you living~~ will you be living
5 ~~must be finished~~ must have finished
6 ~~will have climb~~ will have climbed

4 1 can't; might 2 really; mind
3 on; usual 4 saying; awful

TEST YOURSELF UNITS 9 & 10

VOCABULARY

1 Complete the sentences with the words / phrases in the list. There are four extra words / phrases.

unexplained | went on | bargain | mysterious | worth | employer | on sale
employee | alien | refund | go very well | owe | going for | salary

1 He's worked for that company for 25 years now. He's their oldest ______________ .
2 Nobody knows what happened to him. The mystery of his disappearance is still ______________ .
3 The rain was terrible, but the race ______________ despite it.
4 Michael lent me some money last month. I still ______________ him 75 cents.
5 I bought this camera for half price. It was a real ______________ !
6 You paid too much for it. It isn't ______________ that much money.
7 I'm afraid the exam didn't ______________ . I'm sure I failed it.
8 He's been training all year. He's ______________ a gold medal.
9 You know those sneakers you like? They're ______________ at the moment! You should buy them.
10 It's broken. I think you should take it back and ask for a ______________ .

/10

GRAMMAR

2 Complete the sentences with the verbs in the list. There are two extra verbs.

might | should have | won't be working | must have | might have
will be living | will have written | couldn't have

1 She hurt her head when she fell off her scooter. She ______________ worn a helmet.
2 She's a really good runner. If she'd entered the race, she ______________ won it.
3 By the time I'm 25, I ______________ on a Greek island!
4 In ten years' time, I ______________ for anybody. I'll have my own company.
5 He got there too late. He ______________ prevented the accident.
6 By the time I'm 30, I ______________ my first novel.

3 Find and correct the mistake in each sentence.

1 He shouldn't has left the window open. That's how the burglar got in.
2 She might like the movie if she had come.
3 In ten years' time, I hope I will have working in London.
4 Where will you living in 20 years' time?
5 He must be finished his homework by now.
6 In five years' time, I will have climb Mount Everest.

/12

FUNCTIONAL LANGUAGE

4 Choose the correct words.

1 **A** No way! This piece of rock *can't / mustn't* be from another planet.
B I don't agree with you. I think it *can / might* be.
2 **A** I'm *many / really* sorry I can't come to the soccer game with you.
B Never *mind / know*. You can come with me next week.
3 **A** Hi, guys. What would you like to eat? The food's *on / with* me!
B Great! Same as *normal / usual*, please!
4 **A** It goes without *seeing / saying* that Peter can't come on Saturday. He crashed his scooter.
B How *shameful / awful*!

/8

MY SCORE /30

22–30 | 10–21 | 0–9

101

The Cambridge Life Competencies Framework

Communication
Using appropriate language and register for context
Watch this video for tips on how to develop your students' communication skills. Scan the QR code here.

Reading

Warmer

Write the word *dangerous* on the board. In pairs, ask students to make a list of as many dangerous activities as they can. Give them four or five minutes for this and then elicit a few ideas. Ask students what would happen if they had an accident during one of the activities and elicit *emergency services*.

▶ 28 Get TH!NKing

Play the video and discuss the question with your class.

1 Give pairs two or three minutes. Accept all feasible suggestions.

2 **Check/clarify:** *rescuers, victim, first aid, emergency services, rescue operation, treatment.*
1 B 2 A, B, C 3 A 4 A, B, C

3 Create a master list on the board. Students should copy the whole list into their notebooks.

4 Before students read the report, get them to cover it, look at the photos, and answer the question. Write their ideas on the board. When they read to check, set a three-minute timer to encourage them to skim the report quickly and not to focus on every word.
It's about the rescue of 12 boys and their soccer coach who were trapped in a cave.

5 🔊 **11.01 Check/clarify:** *coach, flashlights, network of chambers, narrow passages, tunnels, open to the public, failed (to do something), trapped, divers, supply of oxygen, flooded, ropes, stretchers, miracle.*

11 EMERGENCY!

OBJECTIVES

FUNCTIONS: expressing purpose; emphasizing

GRAMMAR: verbs followed by gerund or infinitive; *to / in order to / so as to; so and such*

VOCABULARY: danger and safety; adjectives with negative prefixes

Get TH!NKING
Watch the video and think: have you ever been in a dangerous situation? What happened?

A

B

C
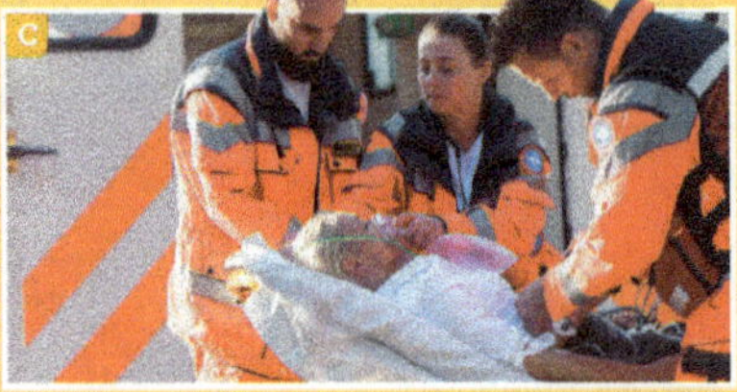

READING

1 **Look at the photos. What is the same about all of them? What is different in each one?**

2 **Read the sentences. Which photo(s) might each one refer to?**
1 It took the rescuers a long time to bring the victim down. ☐
2 The victim was given first aid before going to the hospital. ☐
3 The helicopter emergency services managed to pull the victim out of the water. ☐
4 After the rescue operation, the victim was taken to the hospital for treatment. ☐

3 **Make a list of people and things that can help in an emergency. Compare your ideas with others in the class.**

Things	People
ambulance	*police officer*

4 **Look at the photos on the next page and the title of the news report. What do you think it's about? Read the report quickly and check your ideas.**

5 🔊 11.01 **Read and listen to the report. Mark the sentences T (true) or F (false).**
1 The boys had just finished playing a soccer game. ☐
2 There is no complete map of the caves. ☐
3 You can get a guided tour of the beginning of the cave all year round. ☐
4 It was two days before the police knew where the boys were. ☐
5 The rescue quickly turned into an international mission. ☐
6 The boys had been missing for two weeks before contact was made with them. ☐
7 The divers knew they had to get the boys out quickly. ☐
8 The boys had to dive through the tunnels to get to safety. ☐

102

Complete question 1 as a class. Encourage students to think about the correct answer to the false statements.
1 F 2 T 3 F 4 F 5 T 6 F 7 T 8 F

Objectives

Functions and speaking Expressing purpose; emphasizing
Grammar Verbs followed by gerund or infinitive; *to / in order to / so as to; so and such*
Vocabulary Danger and safety; adjectives with negative prefixes
Culture The Great Escape
Train to TH!NK Understanding cause and effect

Resources for this unit

All available online

Videos
- Get **TH!NK**ing: *Have you ever been in a dangerous situation? What happened?*
- Grammar rap!: *so* and *such*
- Culture: The Great Escape

Tests
- Unit, extension, and skills test 11

Worksheets
- Grammar and vocabulary: Basic, Standard, and Extension Worksheets
- Project: Survival
- Communication: Help!
- Grammar presentation: Verbs followed by gerund or infinitive
- Get **TH!NK**ing and Grammar rap! video Worksheets

Culture notes

Wild Boars FC, called *Moo Pa* in Thai, was established in 2015 as a small, regional club to play in local tournaments. It has squads for players under 13, 16, and 19. The majority of the players are from poor and ethnic minority backgrounds and come from an area that extends across Thailand, Myanmar, Laos, and China. At the time of the cave rescue, members of all the squads were trapped in the cave, so the whole club was unable to play in competitions.

Tham Luang Nang Non (the Great Cave of the Sleeping Lady) is a cave system in the north of Thailand. It lies under the Doi Nang Non mountain range, on the border with Myanmar. Winding through 10.3 km of limestone, it has a permanent stream inside. It was first surveyed in 1986.

The Kingdom of Thailand (previously known as Siam) is a country in Southeast Asia. It is the world's 50th largest country by area and the 21st most populous. Thailand shares borders with Myanmar, Laos, Cambodia, and Malaysia, and its coastline runs along the Gulf of Thailand and the Andaman Sea. The capital and biggest city is Bangkok.

Miracle UNDERGROUND

It was June 23rd, 2018. Twelve members of the Wild Boars soccer team and their coach stood in front of the entrance to the Tham Luang cave in northern Thailand. The boys, aged between 11 and 16, had finished training for the day and they decided to explore the cave. They left their bikes outside and took their flashlights and some snacks inside with them. It would be more than two weeks before the group saw daylight again.

The Tham Luang cave stretches 10 km into the mountain with a network of chambers, narrow passages, and tunnels. Parts of the cave have been explored, but much of it hasn't. Inside, there is no phone signal, so contact with the outside world is impossible. The first kilometer is open to the public, but only until June. In the rainy season from July to November, it becomes extremely dangerous because the whole system quickly fills with water. And in June of 2018, the rain came early.

When the boys failed to come home that evening, their parents contacted the police. Finding the bikes outside the cave, the police soon realized where they were, but they also knew that rainwater had flooded the caves. The boys and their coach were trapped somewhere inside and were in great danger.

At 4 a.m. the next morning, Thai divers tried to start searching the cave, but it was soon clear that they did not have the equipment or experience they needed. News of the emergency soon spread. Within days, experts from countries all over the world had arrived at the cave hoping to help rescue the group.

For days, an international team of divers searched deep into the caves, but found no sign of the group. Then, at last, on the tenth day, two British divers arrived in a new chamber where they saw 13 figures sitting on a shelf of rock above the water. The boys and their coach were very thin and weak, but they were alive. The celebrations, though, were short. The divers knew the boys weren't out of danger yet and that the rescue would be extremely difficult. They had 13 young people with no diving experience to bring to safety through 4 km of dark, narrow passages. Furthermore, heavy rain was predicted and water levels would soon be rising. If they weren't brought out soon, it would be impossible to save them.

A team of experts worked night and day to plan the rescue. Each boy, dressed in a wetsuit and with a supply of oxygen, was taken underwater by a diver through the flooded chambers. The divers were guided by ropes to avoid losing their way and they kept checking the air bubbles to make sure the boys were breathing. In other parts of the cave, the boys lay on plastic stretchers, which were pushed with great difficulty through the narrow spaces.

It took three days to get everyone to safety and the last person was brought out just as the water levels in the cave started to rise quickly. It was a miracle – all 13 members of the Wild Boars had survived.

Train to TH!NK

Understanding cause and effect

There is a cause-and-effect relationship between two ideas only if we can show that one thing leads to another.

6 **Match the causes (1–5) with the effects (a–e). Then check your answers in the article.**

1 The boys didn't come home. ☐
2 The police found the boys' bikes. ☐
3 It had rained a lot overnight. ☐
4 News of the emergency spread. ☐
5 The boys had been missing for ten days. ☐

a Experts from all over the world arrived to help.
b Most people thought they were dead.
c The caves were flooded.
d They knew the boys were in the cave.
e The parents contacted the police.

7 **Complete 1–3 with a cause or an effect.**

1 The flooding became worse, so the divers …
2 … , so we decided to call the emergency services.
3 … Therefore, the victim was taken to the hospital.

SPEAKING

8 **Work in pairs. Discuss these questions.**

1 Do you think the divers were heroes? Why or why not?
2 Do you know any stories of ordinary people being heroes?

103

6 You may like to do the first question with the whole class as an example.
1e 2d 3c 4a 5b

7 Encourage students to brainstorm possible answers before they start writing. During feedback, draw attention to the punctuation in each sentence (*so* comes after a comma in the middle of a sentence, and *therefore* begins a new sentence).

8 Encourage students to speak at length and to try to use vocabulary from the article in their answers.

Homework

Ask students to research another story of ordinary people being heroes. They can upload a picture with a description in English. If students do not have access to the internet, they can create their own ideas. As a follow-up, students can bring the picture to the next lesson and present their story to the class.

TH!NK more

Worksheets
Project Survival
Communication Help!
Get TH!NKing *Have you ever been in a dangerous situation? What happened?*

Critical THINKing
Evaluating ideas, arguments, and options
Analyzes causes and effects of problems.

Warmer

Write on the board: *danger*. Ask students to brainstorm adjectives to describe how they might feel if they were in danger or involved in a rescue. Make a list on the board.

1 Ask students to try to answer the questions from memory before referring back to page 103 to check.

1 to explore 2 to come 3 to help

2 Point out that the verbs in 1–3 can be followed by a noun, e.g., *I finished my homework at 10 o'clock*, but if they're followed by a verb, the verb must be a gerund.

1 training 2 losing 3 checking
RULE: 4 gerund 5 *to* + infinitive

3 Point out that *hope* followed by an infinitive expresses a future meaning when used in the simple present tense. For example: *I hope to do well on the test on Friday.*

1 ('ve) decided to buy 2 hope to see
3 feel like going 4 avoid speaking
5 finish watching

Workbook p100

Get it Right!
Verb patterns

Student's Book p126

Pronunciation
Strong and weak forms: /tuː/ and /tə/

Student's Book p121

4 Before tackling this exercise, students work in pairs and categorize the words in the box according to whether they refer to *safety* or *danger*.

GRAMMAR
Verbs followed by gerund or infinitive

1 **Complete the sentences from the news report on page 103. What do the verbs have in common?**

1 They decided ______ the caves.
2 The boys failed ______ home.
3 They hoped ______ rescue the group.

2 **Now complete these sentences from the report. What do these verbs have in common? Then complete the rule. Label the columns with *to* + *infinitive* or *gerund*.**

1 The boys, aged between 11 and 16, had finished ______ for the day.
2 The divers were guided by ropes to avoid ______ their way.
3 Divers kept ______ the air bubbles.

RULE:

Followed by [4] ______	Followed by [5] ______
avoid, enjoy, feel like, finish, imagine, keep, (don't) mind, miss, practice, (can't) stand, suggest	afford, choose, decide, expect, fail, hope, learn, offer, promise, want

3 **Complete the sentences. Use a verb from A followed by a verb from B in each sentence.**

A avoid | ~~choose~~ | decide | feel like | finish | hope
B buy | go | see | speak | ~~stay~~ | watch

0 I can't believe you *chose to stay* at home last night rather than come to the movies with us.
1 After a lot of thought, I ______ a new bike.
2 Bye! I ______ you again soon.
3 I'm so tired. I just ______ to bed.
4 I really don't like him, so I ______ to him.
5 I'll help you. I'll just ______ this video first.

→ workbook page 100

PRONUNCIATION
Strong and weak forms: /tuː/ and /tə/
Go to page 121.

VOCABULARY
Danger and safety

4 **Replace the underlined phrases with the words and phrases in the list.**

rescued | dangerous | in danger | to safety
survived | recover | save his life | out of danger

1 He was in a terrible accident, but he didn't die.
2 Don't go into that room! There might be something that could hurt you in there.
3 She went to the hospital to get better.
4 The firefighter took the baby away from a dangerous situation.
5 The doctors managed to prevent him from dying.
6 People who lived near the volcano moved away so they were not going to be harmed.
7 People who drive really fast sometimes put their lives in a situation where they are likely to be harmed.
8 The helicopter took him to a place where he wasn't going to be harmed.

5 **Choose the correct words.**

1 Thank you so much – you *rescued* / *saved* my life!
2 We can go in here. It isn't *safe* / *dangerous* at all.
3 We were lucky to *survive* / *save* the accident.
4 The boat sank, but all the passengers were *recovered* / *rescued* by another boat.
5 Fortunately, he *recovered* / *saved* from his injuries.
6 No one died. All the passengers *rescued* / *survived*.
7 She was badly hurt in the accident, but fortunately she's *in* / *out of* danger now.
8 The helicopter flew the survivors *in danger* / *to safety*.

6 SPEAKING **Work in pairs or small groups. Discuss these questions.**

1 In which sports and activities are people in danger? Do you do them? Would you like to? Why or why not?
2 Do you know of someone who has been in a bad accident and survived? How did he/she survive?
3 Do you know anyone who's saved another person's life? Who was it? What happened?

→ workbook page 102

1 survived 2 dangerous 3 recover 4 rescued 5 save his life 6 out of danger
7 in danger 8 to safety

5 **Check/clarify:** *passengers, harm*.

1 saved 2 dangerous 3 survive 4 rescued 5 recovered 6 survived
7 out of 8 to safety

6 Focus attention on the picture. Elicit or pre-teach *kayaking*. Ask: *Have you ever been kayaking? How dangerous is it? Why?* Give students some time to discuss the subjects in small groups and then hold a class vote to decide which sports/activities they feel are the most and the least dangerous.

Workbook p102

Activity idea Extension

Students write four sentences about themselves using verbs from the Rule box – two from each column.

TH!NK more

Workbook
Grammar p100, Ex.1–3
Vocabulary p102, Ex.1–2
Vocabulary Extra p103, Ex.1–3
Pronunciation p121

Worksheets
Grammar Worksheets 11
Grammar presentation: Verbs followed by gerund or infinitive
Vocabulary Worksheets 11

Listening; Grammar; Functions

7 Check/clarify: *arena, emperor, paw, slave, thorn.*
arena: A, D emperor: A gate: D master: C paw: B, D slave: A, B, C, D thorn: B

8 🔊 **11.04** Listen to students' ideas and write a few of their suggested orders on the board, but do not comment until after listening to the audio.
A 4 B 2 C 1 D 3

9 🔊 **11.04 Check/clarify:** *execute, moral.*
Ask students to answer as many of the questions as they can before they listen again.
1 Because the lion was making strange noises and showed no interest in harming him.
2 To punish him for running away.
3 Because he recognized him as the friend who had helped him in the forest.
4 He decided to set Androcles free because he was amazed by what he had seen in the arena.
5 A true friend never forgets.

10 Invite students to share their answers with the rest of the class during feedback.

11 Allow students time for pairs to discuss and put the items in order of importance. Hold a class vote to decide which they agree with most/least.

12 Encourage students to underline the phrases in the sentences.
RULE: 4 so as to 5 in order to

13 You may like to do the first item with the whole class as an example. Remind students to use the correct verb tense.
1 c The divers used ropes so as to avoid losing their way.
2 d The international divers went to Thailand in order to help save the boys.
3 a The boys needed oxygen to breathe underwater.
4 b The lion was put into the arena in order to kill Androcles.

Workbook p100

14 1 e 2 a 3 d 4 b 5 c

15 Monitor and check that students are using *so as to / in order to* correctly.

LISTENING

7 In which picture can you see these things?

arena | emperor | gate | master | paw | slave | thorn

8 🔊 11.04 You're going to hear a story called *Androcles and the Lion*. Put the pictures in the order you think tells the story. Then listen and check.

9 🔊 11.04 Listen again. Answer the questions.
1 Why didn't Androcles run from the lion in the forest?
2 Why did his master want to execute Androcles?
3 Why didn't the lion attack Androcles?
4 What did the emperor do and why?
5 What does the host think the moral is?

10 SPEAKING Work in pairs or small groups. What do you think the moral of the story is? Do you know any other stories with morals?

11 SPEAKING Mark these statements 1–5 (1 = I strongly agree; 5 = I strongly disagree). Then discuss your answers in small groups.
1 Helping someone else makes me feel good. ☐
2 I only help someone when they ask me to. ☐
3 You can always help another person. ☐
4 I only help people when I think they can also help me. ☐
5 I try to do something myself before I ask for help. ☐

GRAMMAR
to / in order to / so as to

12 Look at the sentences from the listening. Then complete the rule.
1 Androcles managed to escape and went to the forest to hide.
2 Androcles took it in his hand so as to see what the problem was.
3 The lion was kept in a cage for days without food in order to make him as hungry as possible.

RULE: We can use *to* + infinitive to talk about purpose. In more formal language or in writing, we can also use [4]_____ or [5]_____ + infinitive.

13 Think about the stories in the unit so far. Match 1–4 with a–d. Then rewrite each pair as one sentence using the words in parentheses.
0 Why did Androcles pull the thorn from the lion's paw? [e]
Androcles pulled the thorn from the lion's paw to help the lion.
1 Why did the divers use ropes? ☐
2 Why did the international divers go to Thailand? ☐
3 Why did the boys need oxygen? ☐
4 Why was the lion put into the arena? ☐

a help the boys breathe underwater. (to)
b kill Androcles. (in order to)
c avoid losing their way. (so as to)
d help save the boys. (in order to)
e ~~help the lion.~~ (to)

→ workbook page 100

FUNCTIONS
Expressing purpose

14 Match 1–5 with a–e.
1 Why did she send you a card? ☐
2 Why did you get up early yesterday? ☐
3 Why did you go into town? ☐
4 Why did he save his money for so long? ☐
5 Why did they move? ☐

a to watch the sun come up
b in order to get a new guitar
c so as to have more room
d to get a present for my mom
e to say thank you

15 SPEAKING Work in pairs. Think of three *Why do / did you ... ?* questions to ask your partner. Ask and answer each other's questions.

Activity idea Extension

Tell students a story of your choice or write the title of a famous story that your students will know on the board, e.g., *The Tortoise and the Hare*. Ask students to work in pairs and retell the story in their own words.

Language note *to / in order to / so as to*

To form a negative, we use *so as not to* or *in order not to*: *He left home early in order not to be late. He left home early so as not to be late.* We cannot say: *He left home early not to be late.*

TH!NK more

Workbook
Listening p106, Ex.1–5
Grammar pp100–101, Ex.4–5

Worksheets
Grammar Worksheets 11

Reading

Warmer

Write on the board: *small problem; big problem; very big problem.* Elicit three examples of each from the class. Students work in pairs or small groups to decide what to do if they have each kind of problem. For feedback, nominate students to share their solutions with the class and elicit *call the police.*

1 If your class is all from the same country, you could ask if they know any emergency numbers for countries they've been to / are going to on vacation. It could be an important thing to know!

2 11.05 Before playing the audio, give students just two minutes to scan the article quickly. Encourage them not to focus on every word for now, but just to find the answers.
A6 B3 C8

3 **Check/clarify:** *footage, password, squirrel, irresponsible, illegal.*
1 Being in a car accident, seeing a crime happening 2 It's irresponsible and illegal.

4 Allow students time for pairs to discuss and put the items in order of craziness. Hold a class vote to decide which they feel are the most and the least crazy.

Culture note

In the UK, the number for emergency services is 999, but you can also call 112, which is the same number as in many other European countries, or 911, which is the same as the US.

READING

1 In the US, you dial 911 for the emergency services. What number do you call in your country? Does it depend on the type of emergency?

2 11.05 Read and listen to the article. Which of the "emergency" calls do pictures A–C show?

A

B

C

EMERGENCY? What emergency?

An emergency service should be exactly that: a service that you call in an emergency. You might need to call an ambulance if you're in a car accident or the police if you see a crime happening. But some people call emergency services for such unimportant reasons that it's hard to believe these calls are real. Then again, there are some strange people out there, so maybe it isn't really so surprising that the emergency services get some unusual calls.

1 One soccer fan was so angry that his team, Manchester United, had lost an extremely important game that he called emergency services after the match and demanded to speak to the team's manager, Sir Alex Ferguson.

2 There was also a man who called the police after his son refused to get off his video game console late at night. He said they'd had such a bad argument that he wanted them to come and put the boy to bed.

3 One woman couldn't find her glasses and thought the emergency services might help. She complained that she was trying to peel potatoes, but her eyesight was so bad that she couldn't see what she was doing.

4 Once, a man dialed 911 when he found that his snowman had gone missing. He had left his house for five hours to find that it was gone when he returned. He said he was really angry and wanted the police to check security camera footage of the area.

5 The emergency services received a call from a woman to tell them that she had such a bad memory that she couldn't remember the password for her computer. She was so disappointed when they explained that they couldn't help her.

6 When one man's friend threw his shoes onto a supermarket roof as a joke, he called 911 and asked if the fire engine could come and help him get them down. He even offered to climb up to the roof himself if they could just bring a ladder.

7 One woman called up to complain that her husband was such a lazy man because he wouldn't bring her her dinner while she sat and watched TV.

8 Finally, one time a woman was so upset about a squirrel in her yard that didn't have any nuts that she called to say she wanted emergency services to find someone to bring it some food. She was worried it would starve.

These calls are amusing to read about, but they can have very serious consequences. "It's such a waste of time! Every call takes about a minute," said one man who works in the call center for the emergency services. "Maybe that doesn't sound a very long time, but in that one minute, other people are calling who really have an emergency. And for them, a minute might be extremely important."

So let's get serious: please THINK before you call emergency services. And, of course, remember that you should never call them with information that's untrue – it's irresponsible and it's also illegal.

3 Read the first and last paragraphs again. Answer the questions.

1 What examples are given of real emergencies?
2 Why should you never call emergency services with untrue information?

4 SPEAKING Work in small groups. Which of the calls do you think was the craziest?

106

Activity idea Extension

Ask students to work with a partner and think of possible responses the police might give to each of the calls. Tell them they should be polite and offer suggestions to help the caller. Listen to some of the best examples in open class and write them on the board. Put students into different pairs for variety. One student is the caller, and one is the police officer. Ask students to create dialogues using some of the ideas on the board or others of their choice.

THINK more

Workbook
Reading p104, Ex.1–3

Grammar; Vocabulary

▶ 29 Grammar rap!
so and *such*

5 Ask students to try to answer the questions from memory before referring back to page 106 to check. Ask: *How do* so *and* such *change the sentences in Exercise 5?* (They emphasize or intensify the meaning of the adjectives that follow.)
1 so 2 such RULE: 1 so 2 such

6 1 such a bad memory 2 so bad 3 such a bad argument 4 so angry RULE: 5 that

7 Weaker students could start by identifying the cause (adjective or noun) and then deciding whether *so* or *such* is appropriate before they write sentences in full.
1 It was such a bad accident that two people had to go to hospital.
2 It was so windy that it was dangerous to walk there.
3 The music was so loud that I couldn't fall asleep.
4 The road was so icy that it was dangerous to drive on (it).
5 They were such careless people that they always forgot to lock the door to their house.

Workbook p101

8 During feedback, say the adjectives with negative prefixes for students to repeat. Elicit which is the stressed syllable in each adjective. Also draw attention to these spelling anomalies: the double "r" in *irresponsible* and the double "l" in *illegal*.
1 impossible 2 unhappy 3 unsurprising 4 unimportant 5 unnecessary 6 untrue; irresponsible; illegal

9 Ask students to read the adjectives and underline any they don't know. Clarify meaning by giving example sentences.
un-: unafraid, uncomfortable, unconcerned, unhealthy, unhelpful
im-: impatient, impolite, impossible
in-: inexpensive, informal
ir-: irregular, irresponsible
il-: illegal, illogical

10 1 unhealthy 2 unconcerned 3 impatient 4 irresponsible 5 inexpensive

11 Write the word *Why?* on the board in large letters to encourage them to give reasons and examples to support their answers.

Workbook p102

GRAMMAR
so and *such*

5 **Complete the sentences from the article on page 106. Then complete the rule.**

1 She was ______ disappointed when they explained that they couldn't help her.
2 One woman called up to complain that her husband was ______ a lazy man.

> **RULE:** We can use *so* or *such* to emphasize adjectives, adverbs, nouns, and noun phrases:
> [1]______ + adjective / adverb
> [2]______ (+ *a* / *an*) (+ adjective) + noun

6 **Now complete these sentences from the article and complete the rule.**

1 She had ______ that she couldn't remember the password for her computer.
2 Her eyesight was ______ that she couldn't see what she was doing.
3 They'd had ______ that he wanted the police to come and put the boy to bed.
4 One man was ______ that his team, Manchester United, had lost an extremely important game that he called emergency services.

> **RULE:** We also use *so* or *such* to show how one thing is a result of another. The clause with *so* or *such* is followed by ______ + a result clause.

7 **Join the pairs of sentences. Use *so* / *such* ... *that*.**

0 We were very late. We had to take a taxi.
We were so late that we had to take a taxi.
1 It was a very bad accident. Two people had to go to the hospital.
2 It was very windy. It was dangerous to walk there.
3 The music was very loud. I couldn't fall asleep.
4 The road was very icy. It was dangerous to drive on it.
5 They were careless people. They always forgot to lock the door to their house.

→ workbook page 101

VOCABULARY
Adjectives with negative prefixes

8 **Replace the underlined words with one word.**

0 The divers were not concerned about their own safety.
unconcerned
1 It was not possible to get the boys out together.
2 The Manchester United fan was not happy because his team had lost.
3 It's not surprising that the emergency services get so many crazy calls.
4 Some people call 911 for not important reasons.
5 These not necessary calls take up a lot of time.
6 You should never call with information that's not true – it's not responsible and it's also not legal.

9 **Which negative prefixes do these adjectives take? Write them in the correct columns.**

afraid | comfortable | concerned | expensive | formal | healthy | helpful | legal | logical | patient | polite | possible | regular | responsible | ~~surprising~~

un-	im-	in-	ir-	il-
unsurprising				

10 **Complete the questions. Use adjectives from Exercise 9 with negative prefixes.**

0 Do you think it's very *impolite* to talk with food in your mouth?
1 Do you think it's ______ to eat fried food?
2 Do you worry about exams, or are you ______ ?
3 Do you sometimes get a little ______ when you have to wait for things?
4 Do your parents think you're too ______ to be at home alone all weekend?
5 Do you think that ______ clothes are always bad quality?

11 SPEAKING **Work in pairs. Discuss the questions in Exercise 10.**

→ workbook page 102

Homework

Ask students to write five sentences explaining the results of some of the things that happen to them at home, e.g. *It was so hot that I took a cold shower to cool down.* They can share these in the next lesson.

Activity idea Fast finishers

In Exercise 7, ask students to rewrite the *so* sentences with *such* and vice versa.

TH!NK more

Practice Extra
Grammar: *so* and *such*
Vocabulary: Adjectives with negative prefixes

Workbook
Grammar p101, Ex.6–8
Vocabulary p102, Ex.3–5

Worksheets
Grammar rap! *so* and *such*
Grammar Worksheets 11
Vocabulary Worksheets 11

Warmer

Nominate a student to give you the name of a job. If they can't think of a job immediately, move on to the next student. After a few examples, ask students to name a dangerous job and continue around the class. Write these on the board and elicit reasons why each of them is dangerous.

▶ 30 TH!NK
The Great Escape

1 You may like to put a copy of the two photos up on the board before students open their books.

2 🔊 **11.06** Tell students not to worry about difficult vocabulary at this stage as this will come up later.
The men in photo A escaped from a mine where they were trapped. Rescue teams drilled a hole to get them out.
The picture is of open water; should this be changed?

3 Ask students to locate and circle the numbers in the article. Point out that the numbers may be in word or numerical form and that one of the numbers refers to two different things.
1 The date in October when the miners were brought above ground. / The number of crew members on the *Jascon-4*.
2 The number of days that had passed before the rescue mission received the miners' note.
3 The age of Harrison Okene, the ship's cook.
4 The number of meters below the surface of the water where the ship was lying.
5 The number of miners trapped underground / rescued from the mine.
6 The number of hours that had passed since the ship had gone down when Okene heard knocking.

4 At the end of the exercise, listen to some of the students' ideas and encourage open class discussion.

TH!NK The Great Escape

Culture

1 Look at the photos. What type of survival stories do they suggest?

2 🔊 11.06 Read and listen to the article. Check your answers.

The Great ESCAPE

After many tragedies, there are always stories of people who have shown an amazing ability to survive. Here are two stories that remind us that miracles can happen.

On August 5th, 2010, the San José copper and gold mine in the Atacama Desert in Chile collapsed and 33 miners were trapped underground. The mine had a poor safety record and there were fears that the missing men wouldn't come out alive. A rescue team immediately began drilling into the ground where it was thought the men might be. On Day 17, when the drill was brought out of the ground, there was a note taped to it. In bright red letters it read: "We are alive and well in the shelter, all 33 of us." It was the news the whole country had been waiting for and the Chilean government promised to bring them out alive. For the next seven weeks, rescue teams from all over the world worked together to drill a hole big enough to bring out the men, who were waiting 700 meters below the ground. It was a long, difficult, and dangerous job, but on October 13th, more than a billion people around the world watched live on TV as the first of the miners was finally brought above ground. Twenty-four hours later, the last miner, number 33, was reunited with his family and friends.

A

B

In June of 2013, a rescue diver was swimming through the wreck of the tugboat *Jascon-4* when he got an enormous shock: a hand reached out and grabbed his leg. The ship had sunk two and a half days earlier and was now lying 30 meters below the surface of the water. The diver, who was part of a team looking for the bodies of the 13 crew members, hadn't expected to find anyone alive. But one man had managed to survive. Twenty-nine-year-old Harrison Okene from Nigeria was the ship's cook. When the ship got into trouble in rough seas and started turning over, Okene found an air pocket and put his head in it. As the ship sank towards the ocean floor, he expected the pocket to fill with water, but it didn't. Despite the freezing water and having nothing to eat or drink, Okene had enough air to breathe. There was nothing he could do except wait. Sixty hours after the ship went down, Okene heard knocking and knew that rescue teams had entered the ship. He still wasn't safe and a complicated plan was needed to bring him slowly to the surface. Unfortunately, none of the other crew members survived. But for one man, the tragedy had ended with a miracle.

3 **Read the article again. What do these numbers refer to?**
0 7 *The number of weeks the miners were trapped underground.*
1 13 2 17 3 29
4 30 5 33 6 60

4 SPEAKING **Work in pairs. Discuss these questions.**
1 What do you think these people did while they were waiting to be rescued?
2 These people had accidents at work. Do you think people should be rescued when they are doing dangerous things for pleasure, like climbing mountains? Why or why not?

108

Culture notes

In the twelve years before the San José copper mine collapse, there had been several accidents at the San José mine, and eight people had died. The miners were found 17 days after the collapse. Their emergency supplies had just run out. It took another 52 days before all 33 were free. Almost all the miners were in good physical condition but had lost an average of 8kg. When the mine first collapsed, they had tried to reach the surface via escape ladders, but the mining company had not installed the ladders.

The *Jascon-4* tugboat capsized and sank off the Nigerian coast in late May 2013. Lone survivor Harrison Okene spent sixty hours trapped in an air pocket at the front of the boat. As he had spent so long at pressure underwater, Mr. Okene would have had a heart attack if he had been brought quickly to the surface. He had to be brought up slowly in a diving helmet and put into a decompression chamber. He thought he had been underwater for only twelve hours.

Social Responsibilities
Understanding and discussing global issues – environmental, political, financial, and social
Is aware of different global issues.

Culture; Writing

5 During feedback, focus on pronunciation by saying the words and asking students to repeat them. Encourage them to notice the silent "w" in *wreck*.
1 air pocket 2 safety record 3 sunk 4 tragedy 5 miracles 6 drill 7 wreck

1 Ask students to quickly read the story and answer the question: *Why did the boy need to be rescued? (He got stuck in mud.)* They should ignore the spaces at this point and just focus on gist understanding. Check answers and make sure students understand *mud*.
1 To save time and get home more quickly.
2 It took around half an hour.
3 Because he was cold, he was in shock, and his legs were very sore because of the pressure of the mud.
4 She was grateful to the people who had worked hard and put themselves in danger to save her son.

2 Point out that these are linking words, which are used to join ideas together in a text.
1 after 2 that 3 and 4 because 5 where 6 but 7 later

3 Ask students to give examples from the text to support their answers.
a 2 b 4 c 1 d 3

4 The planning for this exercise can be done in class and the writing assigned for homework. Tell students that their rescue story can be true or made up. Students should organize their writing by following the plan in Exercise 3.

Homework

You could assign the writing for homework.

Activity idea Extension

On completion, ask pairs to swap stories and read and evaluate each other's writing on the basis of content (How interesting was the story?); organization (Did the story follow the structure of the model text?); and language (Did they use a variety of linking words?).

5 VOCABULARY **There are seven highlighted words or phrases in the article. Match the words with these meanings. Write the words.**

1 a space where water doesn't get in
2 the history of accidents at a place
3 gone down in the water
4 a terrible event that often kills many people
5 amazing events that almost seems impossible
6 an instrument that makes a hole in the ground
7 what's left of a car, ship, plane, etc. after a crash

WRITING
A story about a rescue

1 INPUT **Read the story. Answer the questions.**

1 Why did the boy and his friends walk across a vacant lot?
2 How long did the rescue take?
3 Why did he need to go to the hospital?
4 How did his mother feel about the rescue?

2 **Complete the story with the words.**

after | and | because | but
later | that | where

3 ANALYZE **The story has four paragraphs. Which of them ...**

a gives details about how the accident happened? ☐
b gives people's reactions to the accident? ☐
c gives a summary of the whole event? ☐
d describes how the accident was dealt with? ☐

4 PRODUCE **Think of a rescue that you know about or invent one. Write your story (200 words). Think about:**

- who was involved in the accident and the rescue.
- any special words that you will need to talk about the accident. (Use a dictionary to help you.)
- how to organize the information into paragraphs.
- how to make the story dramatic.

1 In March of 2014, 14-year-old Za'Quan Clyburn from North Carolina, USA, was rescued [1]_____ he got trapped in mud.

2 Za'Quan was walking home with some friends. To save time, they walked across a vacant lot [2]_____ was being prepared for a building. Za'Quan walked down a hill towards a large pool of water. He thought the ground was solid [3]_____ that he could walk across it, but it was mud. He sank into it and couldn't get out. The mud went up to his chest and then almost to his chin.

3 One of his friends called 911. Firefighters arrived and started to work to get Za'Quan out. It took 24 people about half an hour to free him. Za'Quan was extremely cold and in shock, and his legs were very sore [4]_____ of the pressure of the mud. An ambulance took him to the hospital, [5]_____ he was kept for two days.

4 One of the firefighters said, "The outcome could have been much worse, [6]_____ fortunately he came through it OK." The boy's mother said [7]_____ that she was really grateful to the people who had worked so hard and risked their lives to save her son.

TH!NK more

Practice Extra
Unit 11 Master it!

Workbook
Developing Writing p105

Tests
Unit, extension, and skills test 11

Warmer

Draw a river across the center of the board and write *My childhood* above it. Write 0 at the left end and 12 at the right. Draw Xs along the line to represent important moments in your childhood, e.g., when you started school, but do not explain what each X refers to. Ask students to guess. Write correct guesses on the board. Explain any unexplained Xs. Also elicit further important moments in childhood.

▶ 31 Get TH!NKing

Play the video and discuss the question with your class.

1 Encourage students to use the structures in the example sentences.

2 All three recall stressful moments.

3 🔊 **12.01 Check/clarify:** *spaghetti spoon, broth, spiral it around, fork, stains, knock (yourself) out, ward, wisdom teeth, curtain, offstage, lines, stage, audience.* 1 eating spaghetti 2 tomato sauce 3 Because he had fallen while he was ice skating and had hit his head on the ice. 4 Because it was his first night away from home, and he felt miserable. 5 The actor who shared the scene with her didn't come on stage when he was supposed to. 6 She said, "I wonder where my husband is," and he heard her.

4 To show the difference between a logical and an illogical conclusion, write on the board:

I can speak Spanish. Therefore I am Spanish. (illogical) *She was born on the same day as her sister. Therefore they are twins.* (logical)

No, it isn't logical because she has no evidence and there are other possible reasons to explain why she didn't reply.

12 LIFE'S FIRSTS

OBJECTIVES

FUNCTIONS: expressing regret; talking about fears

GRAMMAR: phrasal verbs; *I wish / If only* + past perfect

VOCABULARY: phrasal verbs (2); nervousness and fear

Get TH!NKING

Watch the video and think: what is your earliest memory? How old were you?

READING

1 SPEAKING Look at the photos. Which of these first experiences do *you* remember? Tell your partner. What other things can you remember doing for the first time?

I remember my first day of school. I was six and I cried.

I think I can remember the first time I ...

2 Read the blog posts on the next page quickly. Which posts recall stressful moments?

3 🔊 12.01 Read the posts again and listen. Answer the questions.

1 What did Emma find difficult at dinnertime?
2 What did Emma splash all over herself?
3 Why did Paul go to the hospital?
4 Why couldn't he sleep well there?
5 What was the problem that Susie had during the play?
6 How did she get the other actor to come on stage?

110

Train to TH!NK

Logical conclusions

Pay attention to conclusions in a text. Look at the ideas and arguments carefully. Do they logically lead to the conclusion?

4 Here is a conclusion from one of the posts. Is it a logical conclusion? Why or why not?

It was really strange that she never wrote back, but I'm sure she never got my emails.

5 Look at the underlined conclusions. Which aren't logical? Why?

1 Some Bradley Cooper movies are excellent. He's in *Avengers: Endgame*. It must be a good movie.
2 The chef of the restaurant around the corner is famous for his steak. Jane often eats there. Therefore, Jane often eats steak.
3 Apples are very healthy fruit. I often eat apples. I have a healthy diet.
4 Tina has fair skin and burns very easily. She's going to Brazil for a beach vacation. She needs to protect her skin from the sun.

5 1, 2, and 3 aren't logical.
1 Not all Bradley Cooper movies are good.
2 Jane doesn't necessarily order steak.
3 I might eat and drink lots of unhealthy things as well as eating apples.

Critical THINKing
Evaluating ideas, arguments, and options
Identifies evidence and its reliability.

Objectives

Functions and speaking Expressing regret; talking about fears
Grammar Phrasal verbs; *I wish / If only* + past perfect
Vocabulary Phrasal verbs (2); nervousness and fear
Fiction *Bullring Kid and Country Cowboy*
Train to TH!NK Logical conclusions
Values Breaking new ground

Resources for this unit

All available online

Videos

- Get TH!NKing: *What is your earliest memory? How old were you?*
- Grammar rap!: *I wish / If only* + past perfect

Tests

- Unit, extension, and skills test 12
- Final test

Worksheets

- Grammar and vocabulary: Basic, Standard, and Extension Worksheets
- Project: Life's firsts
- Communication: A first time for everything
- Literature Worksheets: *Yukki-Onna*
- Grammar presentation: Phrasal verbs
- Get TH!NKing and Grammar rap! video Worksheets

6 Monitor, but avoid error correction. The focus of this task is on fluency, not on practice of structures or lexis. Instead, make a note of common errors. Write a mix of correct and incorrect sentences on the board, ensuring anonymity, and ask students to identify and correct the mistakes during feedback.

Homework

Ask students to write a few sentences based on their "childhood river" in the Activity idea Extension.

Activity idea Extension

Ask students to draw their own "river" as in the warm-up (see page T110). They should include at least three Xs. Put students into small groups for them to guess what the Xs refer to. Tell them they can think of approximate ages if they're unsure exactly when the events occurred. Write these stems on the board as prompts: *Is that when you … for the first time? Were you [five] when you … for the first time?* Monitor to help with any questions and to check students' use of narrative tenses. (These are commonly used in telling anecdotes.) Make a note of any students describing particularly interesting events and call on these students to share them with the class during feedback. Also go through any common errors with narrative tenses.

THE FIRST TIME I…

We asked readers to tell us some of their "first times" and here are three that we liked.

My first time eating spaghetti – Italian style

My best friend in my first year at school was Italian. Her name was Caterina Ricci. We were very different, but we got along really well and went everywhere together. The first time I went to her house, we had spaghetti for dinner. I asked for a spoon, because that's how we eat spaghetti at home. When Caterina started giggling, I knew I had made a mistake. Italians only eat pasta with a spoon when it's in a broth, she told me. No big deal – watching Caterina, I tried to [1]figure out how to twirl the pasta around my fork, but all I managed to do was to splash tomato sauce all over myself. I guess I finished ten minutes later than everyone else. Nobody said anything, but I must have looked great in my white shirt covered in tomato stains! Caterina and her parents [2]moved away soon afterwards. I wrote to her a couple of times, but she didn't reply. It was really strange that she never wrote back, but I'm sure she never got my emails.

Emma

My first time in the hospital

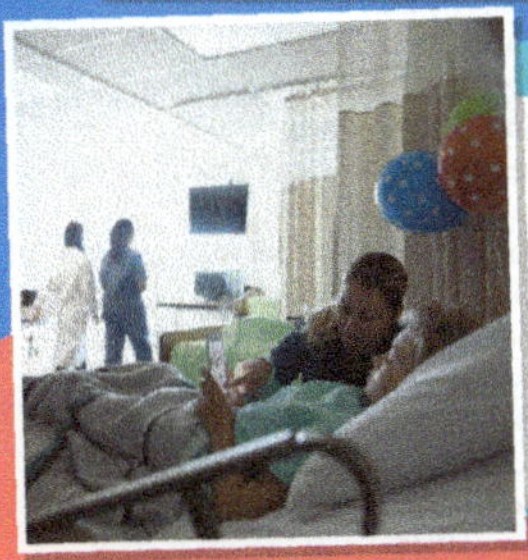

One winter day, I went ice skating with some friends. I fell down, hit my head on the ice, and knocked myself out. My friends were worried, but I quickly [3]came to. When I told my mom and dad what had happened, they took me to the hospital. The doctor decided to keep me in overnight for some tests. There were other patients in the ward with me. One of them had had his wisdom teeth taken out. It was the first time I'd heard the words "wisdom teeth" and it sounded strange to me. I remember that I tried to talk to him, but when he spoke, I couldn't make out the words, so I couldn't understand what he was saying. I felt miserable, even though the nurses [4]took care of me and tried to [5]cheer me up. I didn't sleep well at all. It was my first night away from home and I've never forgotten it.

Paul

My first time on stage

I remember the excitement as everyone [6]put their makeup on and got into their costumes. I also remember how nervous I felt just before the curtain went up. I thought I wouldn't remember any of my lines. But in the end I didn't really have to worry about that. Everything started off well, but in the middle of the play, I [7]ran into a problem. It was in a scene with the actor who played the role of my husband. He was supposed to come on stage, but I could see him offstage talking to someone. I knew he was going to miss his entrance. He didn't come on stage, so I had to [8]make some lines up and try not to panic! It seemed like hours, although it was probably only a few seconds. Then I said, "I wonder where my husband is?" He heard me, came on stage, and we carried on with the scene. I don't think the audience noticed anything wrong.

Susie

SPEAKING

6 **Work in pairs or small groups. Discuss these questions.**

1 How did the various people feel about their first-time experiences?
2 Would you have felt the same in their position?
3 What personal experiences did the stories remind you of?

111

TH!NK more

Worksheets
Project Life's firsts
Communication A first time for everything
Get TH!NKing *What is your earliest memory? How old were you?*

Vocabulary; Grammar

Warmer

Divide the class into four teams. To review phrasal verbs that students already know, say a verb for students to race to add a particle, for example: *give* – *give up*. The team must then say what the meaning is in order to get a point.

1 Before students do the exercise, write the underlined words from page 111 on the board. Tell students to find the words in the blog posts. When they have seen them being used in context, ask them to try to work out the meaning of the phrases. Compare their meanings with the definitions in the book.
a 6 b 2 c 3 d 8 e 4 f 5 g 7 h 1

2 Remind students to be careful to put the main verb into the correct tense.
1 cheer … up 2 ran into 3 figure out 4 take care of 5 came to 6 move away 7 put on

Workbook p110

3 Encourage students to circle the objects within the sentences.
Sentences 1 and 3 RULE: 4 separated 5 together 6 separated 7 between 8 between

4 Tell students to write sentences out in full.
1 I'm taking part in a competition.
2 We have to take care of them.
3 She made up an excuse.
4 I told him a joke to cheer him up.
5 It was so cold that she put on her jacket. / It was so cold that she put her jacket on.

VOCABULARY
Phrasal verbs (2)

1 Find the phrasal verbs in the blog posts on page 111. Match the verbs (1–8) with the definitions (a–h).

a place (clothing, makeup) on your body so as to wear it ☐
b go to live in a different town or place ☐
c become conscious again ☐
d invent, create ☐
e watch and care for ☐
f make someone feel happy ☐
g meet a person or a problem without expecting to ☐
h understand, find the answer to ☐

2 Complete the sentences with the correct forms of the phrasal verbs from Exercise 1.

0 It isn't a true story – I *made* it *up*.
1 He is often very sad. I find it difficult to ______ him ______.
2 Yesterday, I ______ my best friend from elementary school.
3 This question is really difficult. I can't ______ the answer.
4 We're going on vacation – can you ______ our cats while we're away, please?
5 When he fell, he was knocked unconscious, but luckily, he ______ again after a minute.
6 I don't like this place any more. I think we should ______.
7 If you don't have a hat, please ______ some sunscreen at least.

→ workbook page 110

GRAMMAR
Phrasal verbs

3 Look at these sentences from the text on page 111. In which ones does the object go between the two parts of the phrasal verb? Then complete the rule with the words.

1 I had to make some lines up.
2 The nurses took care of me.
3 They tried to cheer me up.

between (x2) | separated (x2) | together

RULE: With some phrasal verbs, the two parts can't be [4]______. They have to be [5]______.
*They **took care of** me.*
Other phrasal verbs can be [6]______. We can put an object [7]______ the two parts or after the second part.
*I **put** my makeup **on**.*
OR
*I **put on** my makeup.*
When we use a pronoun (*him*, *it*, etc.) with a phrasal verb that can be separated, it must go [8]______ the two parts of the verb.
I worked it out.
I put it on.
How do you know if a phrasal verb can be separated?
Use a dictionary to look it up!
look sth *up* → it can be separated
look into sth → it can't be separated

4 Put the words in order to make sentences. When there are two possible orders, write both.

0 ago / moved / three / They / away / years
They moved away three years ago.
1 part / I'm / a / competition / in / taking
2 take / We / them / care / have to / of
3 excuse / made / an / She / up
4 joke / cheer / I / him / a / to / up / him / told
5 put / cold / It / she / jacket / was / so / her / on / that

5 SPEAKING Complete the questions with the correct forms of the phrasal verbs. Then discuss them in small groups.

take care of | figure out | move away
put on | run into | cheer up

1 When do you ______ nice clothes?
2 Have you ever ______ a friend in the street?
3 How do you ______ a friend if they're sad?
4 How do you ______ difficult problems?
5 Do you enjoy ______ animals or small children?
6 How would you feel if your best friend ______?

→ workbook page 108

5 As an alternative, you could ask students to cover the list and try to guess what key words complete the sentences.
1 put on 2 run into 3 cheer up 4 figure out 5 taking care of 6 moved away

Workbook p108

Get it Right!
Phrasal verbs

Student's Book p126

Activity idea Extension

In pairs, students write a short dialogue using three of the phrasal verbs from the lesson.

TH!NK more

Workbook
Grammar p108, Ex.1–4
Vocabulary p110, Ex.1–2
Vocabulary Extra p111, Ex.1–3

Worksheets
Grammar Worksheets 12
Grammar presentation: Phrasal verbs
Vocabulary Worksheets 12

Listening; TH!NK Values

6 Check/clarify: *the English Channel, hot-air balloon.*
Give students time to discuss the quiz questions. Invite students to share their ideas with the rest of the class, but do not give the answers yet.

7 🔊 **12.02**
1 A 2 B 3 A 4 B 5 C

8 🔊 **12.02**
1 Germany, 1886 2 French, 1909
3 Russian, 1961 4 France, 1783
5 1863, Metropolitan Line

9 Refer students to the quiz for question 1. To encourage students to use modals of deduction in their discussions, write on the board: *It might / It will (probably/ definitely); It (definitely/probably) won't* + base infinitive. Ask students to rank this list from most to least likely to happen in the near future. At the end of the exercise, listen to some of the students' ideas and encourage open class discussion.

10 Ask students to raise their hands and say *finished* as soon as they have completed the exercise. During feedback, ask the first person to finish: *How did it make you feel to be the first to finish?*
1 b 2 e 3 d 4 a 5 c

11 At the end of the exercise, listen to some of the students' ideas and encourage open class discussion.

LIFE'S FIRSTS UNIT 12

LISTENING

6 SPEAKING Work in pairs. Read the quiz questions. What do you think the answers are?

QUIZ: TRANSPORTATION FIRSTS

1 Who built the first car?
A Karl Benz B Henry Ford C Gottlieb Daimler
2 Who was the first pilot to fly across the English Channel from France to England?
A Amelia Earhart B Louis Blériot C Amy Johnson
3 Who was the first person to travel into space?
A Yuri Gagarin B Neil Armstrong C Valentina Tereshkova
4 The first hot-air balloon to carry passengers, over 200 years ago ... how far did it travel?
A 9 meters B 9 km C 19 km
5 Where was the first subway line built?
A Paris B Istanbul C London

7 12.02 Listen to the same quiz on a radio show. Check your answers.

8 12.02 Listen again. Complete the notes.

1 The first car
Where? ___
When? ___
2 First flight across the English Channel
Nationality of pilot? ___
When? ___
3 First person in space
Nationality? ___
When? ___
4 First hot-air balloon flight
Where? ___
When? ___
5 Oldest subway line
Opened when? ___
Name of first line? ___

9 SPEAKING Work in pairs. Answer the questions.
1 Which of the "transportation firsts" do you think is the most important?
2 Do you think these "transportation firsts" will ever happen? If yes, when?
☐ passenger travel to the Moon
☐ non-stop flights from New York City to Sydney, Australia
☐ trains that travel at 1,000 kph

TH!NK values
Breaking new ground

10 Match the people (1–5) with their achievements (a–e).
1 Neil Armstrong ☐
2 Nelson Mandela ☐
3 Charles Lindbergh ☐
4 Kathryn Bigelow ☐
5 Marie Curie ☐
a was the first female director to win an Oscar.
b was the first man on the Moon.
c was the first woman to win a Nobel Prize.
d was the first man to fly alone across the Atlantic.
e was the first black president of South Africa.

11 SPEAKING Work in small groups. Discuss these questions.
1 Is it important to be the first person to do something? Why or why not?
2 What's more important: coming first (like in a competition) or just taking part?

113

Homework

Ask students to write three more questions for the quiz, each with A, B, and C answer options. They can bring them to the next lesson for partners to read and respond to.

Activity idea Extension

Ask students to research a person from around the world for the series on *World Firsts*. They can upload a picture with a description of the person and what they did in English. If students do not have access to the internet, they can create their own ideas. As a follow-up, students can bring the picture to the next lesson and present their person to the class. If students are struggling to think of someone, you could give them the following people to research and find out what their *World First* is: *Serena Williams* (first to win 23 Grand Slam tennis titles), *Shakira* (first to have 100 million likes on Facebook), *Tim Berners-Lee* (first to invent the world wide web), *Psy* (first to have a YouTube clip watched a billion times), *Walt Disney* (first to win 22 Oscars).

TH!NK more

Workbook
Listening p114, Ex.1–5

Social Responsibilities
Taking active roles including leadership
Encourages others to participate and contribute in projects.

Warmer

Check/clarify: *phobia.*
Write the following phobias on the left-hand side of the board and the causes on the right-hand side, mixed up: *xanthophobia* (yellow), *globophobia* (balloons), *pogonophobia* (beards), *somniphobia* (falling asleep), *turophobia* (cheese), *bibliophobia* (books), *dentophobia* (dentists), *zoophobia* (animals), *hydrophobia* (water). Ask students to try to match the phobias with their causes.

1 Write *arachnophobia* on the board and see if students can guess what the cause of the fear for people with this condition is. Before students open their books, you should check that none of your students has a fear of spiders. This can be quite seriously debilitating and is one of the most common phobias. Students with this condition should cover the picture on page 114 or keep their books closed.
It means extreme fear of spiders.

2 **Check/clarify:** *nervous, frightened, petrified.*
Elicit some reactions and write the vocabulary on the board. Check it by asking students to make appropriate facial gestures.

3 **12.03 Check/clarify:** *panic, arachnophobes.*
You could get students to read the story and answer the questions before listening to the audio version. Encourage students to think about the correct answer to the false statements.
1 T 2 F 3 T 4 F 5 T 6 F 7 F 8 F

4 Elicit answers from students based on the last few sentences.

5 If students are struggling with ideas, remind them of the phobias from the beginning of the lesson. At the end of the exercise, listen to some of the students' ideas and encourage open class discussion.

READING

1 From looking at these pictures, what do you think *arachnophobia* means?

2 SPEAKING Discuss in pairs or small groups how you or people you know react when seeing a spider?

3 12.03 Read and listen to the story. Mark the sentences T (true) or F (false).

1 Over ten percent of people in the US are afraid of spiders. ☐
2 Allen thinks spiders can harm him. ☐
3 Allen didn't play the game alone. ☐
4 When he saw "Itsy" for the first time, he didn't want to continue the game. ☐
5 Allen expected that the game would not be fun. ☐
6 When Allen let the spider down, he didn't feel sorry at all. ☐
7 Allen thinks people with other fears won't find the app useful. ☐
8 Allen's sister went to the psychologist with him. ☐

4 Do you think Allen's sister will use the app, too? Why or why not?

THE FIRST TIME I MADE FRIENDS WITH A SPIDER

Allen was one of the 15 percent of teenagers in the US to have an extreme fear of something – also called a phobia. Allen's problem was arachnophobia: the fear of spiders. His phobia was so bad he couldn't be in a room with a spider. I asked him what he thought made spiders so terrifying. "It's the quick movement, the dark color, the legs," he said. "I couldn't look at them. I trembled if I saw one and I'd start to panic." He knew that the spiders in his house weren't dangerous and couldn't hurt him, so there was no real reason to be scared of them, but he just couldn't control his reaction.

When Allen went to see a psychologist, she told him about the Virtual Reality app *Phobia Free*. He decided to give it a try.

Allen sat with the psychologist while he played the game. I asked him how it worked. "I was asked to sit at a computer," he told me. "Then the psychologist told me I was going to meet a spider named Itsy. It felt a bit scary at first and I was glad the psychologist was with me. But when Itsy – a cartoon style animated spider – appeared, I couldn't help but smile. Itsy is fun and friendly and supports the person who has the phobia by making them kind of forget about the fear they want to overcome. And I must say I hadn't expected I would be playing an interactive game with a spider that would be so much fun! First, I was asked to help Itsy and its friends survive in difficult situations. For example, I had to help them avoid a vacuum cleaner. The game works like any computer game, but I soon noticed that I was developing an emotional link with the spiders. I really wanted to help them and when I couldn't, I felt sorry for them!"

"If I do start to feel stressed or panicky, the app has relaxation and breathing exercises that really help to calm me down. They're not just for arachnophobes like me – people who have any kind of fear or phobia will find these exercises useful."

"What's more, there's a real difference now in how I react to spiders in the real world. So, for the first time in my life, I recently touched a real spider. I saw it on my desk just in front of me. I kept really calm. I stretched out my hand and let it run over it. Wow! It wasn't as much fun as playing with Itsy, my virtual friend, but I was amazed that I was OK with it. If only I'd tried this program earlier! I might have avoided all that panic whenever I saw a spider. My sister has the same phobia and I wish she'd started this program with me, but she said the thought of it was just too frightening. Now, though, she wants to try it."

5 SPEAKING Work in pairs or small groups. Choose a different fear and design an app for it with four or five different kinds of activities. What would they be like?

PRONUNCIATION
Different pronunciations of *ea* Go to page 121.

114

Pronunciation
Different pronunciations of *ea*

Student's Book p121

Culture note

Arachnophobia is a strong and illogical fear of spiders and other arachnids. It is one of the most common phobias and affects 3.5 to 6.1% of the world's population. Symptoms can include screaming, crying, sweating, increased heart rate, fainting, and/or panic attack. In some extreme cases, even a picture or a realistic drawing of a spider can trigger the phobia. It can be treated by systematic desensitization / exposure therapy. The use of virtual reality spiders in such treatment has been proven to be effective.

TH!NK more

Workbook
Reading p112, Ex.1–3
Pronunciation p121

▶ 32 Grammar rap!
I wish / If only + past perfect

6 For each example, ask: *Is the situation in the past or the present?* (past). Elicit or explain that the sentences are showing the person imagining how things might have been different in the past.
1 'd tried 2 'd started RULE: 3 only 4 past perfect

7 During feedback, focus on students' pronunciation of *wish*.
1 I wish / If only I'd gone to bed early.
2 I wish / If only I'd asked her for her phone number.
3 I wish / If only I'd studied last weekend.
4 If only Dad / Dad wishes he hadn't forgotten (had remembered) Mom's birthday.
5 If only my friends / My friends wish they hadn't fallen asleep.

8 You may like to give an example from your own experience to get students started on this exercise. If this is too personal a subject for your students, they can make up some regrets.

Workbook p109

9 Check answers and draw attention to the advice given by Oliver (*you should lie down*). Remind students that we can use *should* + infinitive to give advice.
3, 1, 5, 4, 6, 2

10 This exercise can be done as a mingle activity with students changing partners after each conversation.

11 A 2 B 1 C 4 D 3

12 Put students into pairs and get them to race to list another ten fears that people commonly have.
Fear of flying, fear of snakes, fear of heights

13 Encourage them to include examples of specific times when they or people they know have been afraid.

Workbook p110

Grammar rap! ▶32

GRAMMAR
I wish / If only + past perfect

6 **Complete the sentences from the text on page 114. Use the correct form of the verbs. Then complete the rule.**

start | try

1 If only I ______ this program earlier.
2 I wish she ______ this program with me.

RULE: To express regret about the past, we can use *I wish* or *If* [3] ______ + the [4] ______ tense.

7 **Write sentences with *I wish* … or *If only* … .**

0 I didn't eat breakfast. Now I'm hungry.
I wish I'd eaten breakfast.
1 I didn't go to bed early. Now I'm tired.
2 I didn't ask her for her phone number.
3 Only 12 percent?! I didn't study last weekend.
4 Dad feels bad because he forgot Mom's birthday.
5 My friends are annoyed about missing the end of the movie. They fell asleep!

8 **Think of three things you've done recently that you now regret. Write sentences with *I wish* … and *If only* … .**

family | friends | vacations
money | school | shopping

→ workbook page 109

FUNCTIONS
Expressing regret

9 **Put the lines in order to make a conversation.**

☐ **Oliver** I'm sorry to hear that.
☐ **Oliver** What's the matter, Amelia?
☐ **Oliver** Maybe you should lie down for a few minutes.
☐ **Amelia** It was that third piece of cake. I wish I hadn't eaten it.
☐ **Amelia** That isn't a bad idea. I think I will.
☐ **Amelia** I ate too much. I feel sick.

10 SPEAKING **Work in small groups. Discuss your regrets from Exercise 8 above. Make suggestions using expressions from the conversation in Exercise 9.**

VOCABULARY
Nervousness and fear

11 **Look at the words and phrases in bold in sentences 1–4. Match them with the pictures.**

1 I was so **terrified** that I started **biting my nails.**
2 I was really **sweating.** In the end, I just **panicked** and ran out of the room.
3 When I saw the crowd in front of me, my mouth **got dry** and I started to breathe hard.
4 I started to **tremble.** In fact, I was **shaking** for about 15 minutes.

12 SPEAKING **Work in pairs. What fears do the photos represent? What other things are some people afraid of?**

13 **Write sentences about your fears or those of people you know. Use words and phrases from Exercise 11. Then compare with a partner.**

My uncle is afraid of heights. He starts to sweat, even if it's just in a movie!

→ workbook page 110

115

Activity idea Extension

Ask students to scan the story on page 114 and find at least five words or phrases connected to fear (*extreme fear, phobia, terrifying, trembled, panic, dangerous, scared, stressed, panicky, fear, frightening*). Once they're ready, nominate students to call out their answers and write them on the board.

Activity idea Extension

Write these categories on the board: *Movement*; *Physical reaction*; *Feeling*. Ask students to sort the words in bold in Exercise 11 into these categories. Tell them that some of the words could go into more than one category.

Movement: biting my nails, tremble, shaking
Physical reaction: sweating, mouth went dry, tremble, shaking
Feeling: terrified, panicked

Homework

Have the students keep a journal for two or three days with a record of what made them nervous, for how long, and how they overcame their nervousness.

TH!NK more

Practice Extra
Unit 12 Practice it!

Workbook
Grammar p109, Ex.5–7
Vocabulary p110, Ex.3–4

Worksheets
Grammar rap! *I wish / If only* + past perfect
Grammar Worksheets 12
Vocabulary Worksheets 12

Warmer

To review simple past verb forms, give students a verb in the infinitive and ask students to say the past tense to score a point. Do this two or three times with different verbs and then get students to play *Past forms tennis*. In pairs, one student says an infinitive, and the other person must reply with the correct past form as quickly as possible.

1 **🔊 12.06** Before students listen and read, get them to cover the text on page 116 and just look at the title and pictures. In pairs, give students two minutes to think about the answer to the question. Before students read and listen to the introduction, tell them to focus on checking their answer.

It's a very small island with not many people and no cars.

2 **🔊 12.07 Check/clarify:** *jewelery, jugs, counter, chewing gum, judo, admitted defeat.*

For stronger classes, you could ask them to try to complete the text with the time expressions before listening to check.

1 c 2 f 3 d 4 b 5 e 6 g 7 a 8 h

Fiction

1 🔊 12.06 **Look at the picture. What kind of place is this? Read and listen to the introduction to check your ideas.**

Bullring Kid and Country Cowboy by Louise Clover

"So are you looking forward to our holiday, Fizza?" asked her dad.
"No," thought Fizza.
"Yes, she is!" interrupted her mom. "Aren't you, darling?"
Fizza smiled falsely […].
Fizza McIntyre is a city girl from Birmingham, UK. One year her parents hire a holiday cottage on the very small island of Sark, where there are no cars. Fizza goes along, to keep her parents happy. She doesn't know that a big adventure is going to start.

2 🔊 12.07 **Read and listen to the rest of the extract. Complete the text with the missing time expressions (a–h) below.**

a Then, lifting her nose into the air
b Later, after supper
c By the time you get back
d As she began the climb back up the hill
e For over an hour
f In five minutes
g Eventually
h For a moment

And so it was that Fizza found herself on "the island that time forgot" with absolutely nothing to do.
Her mom's voice brought her out of her dream and back to the present moment.
"Why don't you go and explore, Fizza?" said her mom. "[1] ________________, I'll have supper ready. Oh! And get your dad a newspaper, please."
Fizza went down the hill towards the little village at the bottom. [2] ________________ she had discovered two bicycle hire shops, three shops that sold jewelery and jugs, and a tiny post office which was also a supermarket. Fizza went up to the counter.
"Do you sell newspapers?" she asked a small grey-haired lady.
"Sorry," she said, "they haven't arrived from Guernsey today. Try tomorrow."
"What is this place?" thought Fizza. "There aren't even any newspapers!"
She thanked the lady and left the shop.
[3] ________________, she passed a group of girls of about her age. They were chewing gum and wearing short skirts. They looked just like the "cool" girls from school, which made Fizza smile.
"Some things never change," she thought, "wherever you go." And she began to run back towards the cottage.
[4] ________________, Fizza and her dad practiced judo in the field behind the cottage.
[5] ________________, they threw one another onto the grass until Imran admitted defeat and went inside to play a game of cards with Rubel.
As the sun began to drop down from the sky like a great big orange, Fizza continued to practice her judo moves. [6] ________________, she got tired and stopped. She looked out at the dark grey sea and breathed in deeply. And for the first time since she had arrived on Sark, she found herself listening. She could hear the birds singing goodnight to each other, and the sound of sheep bells and a boat in the distance.
[7] ________________, she breathed in deeply and she found that the evening air of Sark smelled sweet. It was completely different from the heavy city smell of her much-loved Birmingham. Such beauty suddenly made Fizza McIntyre feel alive and she decided to show the island how good she felt.
"Goodnight, Sark!" she shouted as she jumped high in the air and then fell on the grass.
Laughing at herself for being silly, she picked herself up and turned to go indoors, but immediately she came to a stop.
Sitting in a tree beside the cottage was a red-haired boy who looked about the same age as her.
[8] ________________ they stared at one another until her attention was taken by a small brown rabbit that ran past her. She took her eyes away from the boy for just a few seconds and during this time he completely disappeared.

116

3 Complete question 1 as a class. Encourage students to think about the correct answer to the false statements.
1 F 2 T 3 T 4 F 5 T 6 F

4 Give a couple of your own ideas as examples before students work in pairs.

1 **Check/clarify:** *to run a store, homesick.*
Ask students to quickly read the story and answer the question.
Her bad decision was to go to college to please her parents.

2 Encourage students to underline the language in the story.
If necessary, refer back to the rules of *wish* / *if only* + past perfect to express past regrets and *should have* + past participle to criticize past actions.
1 Pauline wished she hadn't gone 2 If only you'd told 3 I wish she'd told 4 Pauline should have made

3 Draw students' attention to the fact that each paragraph is about a distinct point and that the order is typical for a story.
a 2 b 1 c 4 d 3

4 This exercise can either be assigned for homework or done as a collaborative writing activity in class with pairs of students working together. Encourage students to organize their writing as outlined in Exercise 3 and to use narrative tenses.

3 **Read the rest of the extract again. Mark the statements T (true) or F (false).**

1 The store on the island never has newspapers. ☐
2 Fizza sees some girls who remind her of her school. ☐
3 Fizza and her father do judo together. ☐
4 Fizza thinks that the air on the island is like the air at home. ☐
5 She shouts, "Goodnight, Sark" because the island made her feel good. ☐
6 The boy she sees is chasing a rabbit. ☐

4 SPEAKING **Think about these questions. Then discuss your answers with other students.**
Imagine you can travel somewhere that's completely different from where you live.
1 Where would you choose to go? Why?
2 What would you miss most about where you live now?

WRITING
A story about a bad decision

1 INPUT **Read the story. What was Pauline's bad decision, according to the writer?**

2 **Find sentences in the story with these meanings. How are the underlined phrases expressed in the story?**
1 Pauline regretted the fact that she'd gone to the big university.
2 It's a shame that you didn't tell us.
3 I think it's a shame that she didn't tell her parents.
4 It isn't good that Pauline didn't make her own decision.

3 ANALYZE **The story has four paragraphs. Which of them …**
a is about a decision that the person made?
b gives background information about the person?
c gives the writer's thoughts about the whole situation?
d explains the effects of the decision?

4 PRODUCE **Think of a (true or invented) story about a bad decision. Write your story (200 words).**
Think about:
- who the person is / was.
- the situation the person was in which meant that he/she had to make a decision.
- the decision that the person made.
- what happened after making the decision.
- what you or the person felt about it all afterwards.

ABOUT BLOG LATEST POSTS ARCHIVES

LEARNING FROM EXPERIENCE?

We asked readers to tell us stories about bad decisions they or people they know have made.

Here's this week's story.

1 A friend of mine has a sister, Pauline, who's six years older than him. She was always good at school, but all she really wanted to do was to help her parents in their small store and then perhaps take it over when they were too old to run it.

2 Pauline's parents, however, really wanted her to go to college, so she spent two years at community college working incredibly hard, studying for an exam so that she could go to a big university in another city. She passed and a few months later she left home to start studying there.

3 From the beginning, Pauline wished she hadn't gone to the university. She hated it. She'd been a good student in high school and did well at the community college, but the courses at the university were much harder. She didn't make many friends either, so she was lonely and homesick. After six months, she asked her parents to let her leave and come home. They were very surprised when she said that she'd never wanted to go to college. "If only you'd told us!" they said. "But I didn't want to disappoint you," was her answer.

4 Now Pauline is working at the store and she's very happy. I wish she'd told her parents that college wasn't what she wanted – then she wouldn't have wasted six months of her life. Pauline should have made her own decision.

Activity idea Extension

This might be a good opportunity to review prepositions as there are several of them in the extract. Tell students they are going to do a memory test. Ask them to work with a partner and give them five minutes to read the extract on page 116 again. Get them to focus on the prepositions and the words before and after them. To help weaker students, tell them you are focusing on these prepositions: *towards, up to, past, behind, down, beside*. When the time is up, ask students to close their books. Write these sentences on the board.

1 Fizza went … the hill … the little village at the bottom.
2 Fizza went … the counter.
3 She began to run back … the cottage.
4 Fizza and her dad practiced judo in the field … the cottage.
5 The sun began to drop … from the sky.
6 Sitting in a tree … the cottage was a red-haired boy.
7 Her attention was taken by a rabbit that ran … her.

1 down … towards 2 up to 3 towards 4 behind 5 down 6 beside 7 past

TH!NK more

Practice Extra
Unit 12 Master it!

Workbook
Developing Writing p113

Tests
Unit, extension, and skills test 12
Final test

1 In B2 First for Schools Reading and Use of English Part 6, candidates have to read a longer text with six numbered spaces, then decide which of the seven sentences provided belongs in each blank space.

This part of the exam tests whether candidates can follow the narrative of a text, the development of ideas, and understand how a well-structured text is formed.

Encourage your students to do the following when they approach this task:

- Read the whole text to understand the narrative.
- Look at each numbered space and choose one of the sentences to complete each space.
- After choosing a sentence, check the other six options and decide why they are wrong.
- Read the completed text again to make sure it makes sense.

1 G 2 F 3 A 4 B 5 D 6 C

Workbook p115

TOWARDS B2 First for Schools

READING AND USE OF ENGLISH

Gapped text

→ workbook page 115

1 **You are going to read about someone travelling abroad for the first time. Six sentences have been removed from the text. Choose from the sentences (A–G) the one that fits each gap (1–6). There is one extra sentence that you do not need to use.**

I've never really enjoyed travelling very much. The idea of leaving the comfort of my own bed to sleep somewhere else has never appealed to me. And when you add in things like the food and not being understood, the thought of leaving my hometown fills me with terror. I did go away on a school trip once, when I was eight, for two nights. My mother tells me I quite enjoyed the experience. [1]_____ There must be a reason why I can't remember anything positive about it.

So for 28 years I'd managed to lead a life that kept me happily at home. A few nights in hotels for work had been the worst I'd had to go through. Then, one day, my boss called me in. He shook my hand. He was smiling from one ear to the other. [2]_____ 'Paul!' he announced. 'You've been promoted.' I should have been happy, I suppose, but something in the back of my mind was telling me this wasn't 100 percent good news. [3]_____ 'Of course, you'll need extra training. I've booked you on a course at head office in Linz. Your flight's on Monday.'

I started to feel dizzy. I had to hold on to the table to stop myself from falling. My boss patted me on the back.

'Great news, eh?' he smiled. Then he left the room.

So that was it. Just when my professional life had got better, the rest of my life was over. No one had ever survived an aeroplane flight, had they? [4]_____ I wasn't so sure. I spent the weekend making my final farewells as Monday morning got closer.

[5]_____ Before I knew it, my taxi had left me at the airport. Somehow I made my way to the check-in desk. I lifted my suitcase onto the conveyor belt and walked through airport security to the lounge. I have no idea how I knew what to do. I guess that because I'd seen it so many times in films, it was programmed into my mind.

The flight was only two hours. [6]_____ I tried to read a book, but I couldn't. I tried listening to my MP3 player – I'd chosen some relaxing music especially – but it sounded like it was being played by an orchestra of three-year-olds. Every sound the plane made sent my imagination spinning out of control. Was that the sound of the wing falling off? Was that a bird being sucked through an engine? Was that the noise of wheels hitting the runway? Yes, it was. We had landed.

Somehow we'd arrived. I wanted to grab my fellow travellers and celebrate the fact that we were still alive, but they were all busy getting their luggage from the overhead lockers. So I celebrated on my own.

But then I remembered: unless I wanted to spend the rest of my life in Austria, I still had to fly back!

A What wasn't right about this?
B My family and friends tried to assure me that of course they had.
C I thought that it was never going to end.
D And then the day I had been dreading arrived.
E Would I ever see my wife again?
F It wasn't long before I found out why.
G That certainly isn't what my memory tells me.

118

1 1 coming to 2 afraid 3 rescued 4 panicked 5 survived 6 impatient 7 made up 8 figure out 9 irresponsible 10 run into

2 1 such 2 in order to 3 feel like 4 afford 5 only 6 I wish

3 1 ~~figure out it~~ figure it out 2 ~~decided going~~ decided to go 3 ~~such~~ so 4 ~~so to~~ to / so as to / in order to 5 ~~so bad a movie~~ such a bad movie 6 ~~promised wearing~~ promised to wear

4 1 to; such 2 matter; hadn't 3 in; idea 4 so; that

TEST YOURSELF UNITS 11 & 12

VOCABULARY

1 Complete the sentences with the words / phrases in the list. There are four extra words / phrases.

survived | afraid | illogical | figure out | rescued | panicked | informal | dangerous | hang out | run into | coming to | irresponsible | impatient | made up

1 After she hit her head, she slowly started ______ .
2 I can't come climbing with you. No way! I'm ______ of heights.
3 The firefighter ______ the cat from the tree.
4 The show didn't go very well – I ______ when I walked on stage, and then I forgot what I wanted to say.
5 Luckily, everyone ______ the plane crash last night.
6 Don't be so ______ . It'll be your turn soon.
7 They ______ that story. There is no way that it is true.
8 I can't ______ the answer to this question. Can you help me?
9 It was very ______ of you to go swimming during the storm.
10 When I'm in town, I often ______ people I know.

/10

GRAMMAR

2 Complete the sentences with the words / phrases in the list. There are two extra words / phrases.

I wish | if | only | such | feel like | afford | so | in order to

1 It was ______ a loud noise that everybody in the street heard it.
2 He jumped into the lake ______ rescue the boy.
3 I don't ______ going swimming. It's too cold.
4 He can't ______ to buy that computer game. He owes Tom some money.
5 Everyone laughs at my hair. If ______ I hadn't dyed it green!
6 ______ you'd waited for me. Then this wouldn't have happened.

3 Find and correct the mistake in each sentence.

1 It's a complicated problem. We need to figure out it.
2 I decided going out this evening.
3 I'm such hungry! I'll have to eat something now.
4 They're going to cover the hole so to prevent future accidents.
5 It was so bad a movie that we left before it had finished.
6 After the accident, my dad promised wearing a seat belt in the future.

/12

FUNCTIONAL LANGUAGE

4 Choose the correct words.

1 **A** The police want to increase the fine to $1,000 *for / to* stop people from driving so fast.
B I think that's *so / such* a good idea.
2 **A** What's the *shame / matter*, Erika?
B I'm feeling a bit sick. I wish I *hadn't / haven't* eaten all that cake.
3 **A** Let's have a book sale *in / on* order to make some money for the school.
B That's not a bad *matter / idea*.
4 **A** His headache was *so / such* bad that he couldn't concentrate on the exam.
B I'm sorry to hear *this / that*.

/8

MY SCORE /30

22–30 | 10–21 | 0–9

119

The Cambridge Life Competencies Framework

Social Responsibilities
Reflecting on roles
Watch this video for a tip on how to encourage your students' awareness of social responsibilities. Scan the QR code here.

Get it Right!

Unit 1
Simple present vs. present continuous
1 I think I am the person you're looking for.
2 I play tennis on Tuesdays.
3 At the moment, I'm writing a letter to a friend.
4 I like what you're wearing today.
5 I know what you mean and appreciate your help.
6 We play soccer during most school breaks.

Unit 2
Present perfect vs. simple past
1 I haven't seen the new Hobbit movie yet.
2 Have you ever been to Spain?
3 John took his exam last week.
4 Nina got here a few minutes ago.
5 They haven't eaten at this restaurant before.
6 I haven't eaten breakfast so I'm really hungry, and it's two hours until lunchtime!

Past continuous vs. simple past
1 When she arrived, I was cooking dinner so I was a little distracted.
2 correct
3 As usual, we arrived at about 6 p.m., and then we had dinner.
4 My teacher came to see how our project was going.
5 I'll never forget the time I spent in Nepal.
6 The police saw the men and asked them what they were doing there.

Unit 3
have to* vs. *had to
1 I'm sorry, I can't attend class tomorrow because I have to go to the doctor.
2 My dad was going to work for another company so we had to move.
3 correct
4 If I had to choose between going to a small school or a large one, I would choose a large one.
5 correct
6 correct

don't have to* vs. *mustn't
1 You don't have to finish your essay now. Mr. Jenkins said that we can hand it in next Friday.
2 You don't have to bring anything to the party – just bring yourself!
3 You mustn't eat food in class – it's against the rules!
4 You mustn't talk during exams.
5 You don't have to study every unit. The exam only includes units 1 to 3.
6 You mustn't use your phone in class. It'll be confiscated.

Unit 4
if* vs. *when
1 when
2 if
3 when
4 if
5 If
6 when
7 if

Unit 5
Relative pronouns
1 which
2 that
3 that
4 which
5 that
6 that

Unit 6
absolutely* vs. *very
1 absolutely
2 absolutely
3 very
4 absolutely
5 very
6 very

Unit 7
make* vs. *let
1 Let
2 made
3 made
4 let
5 make
6 let

Unit 8
say* vs. *tell
1 say
2 tell
3 Tell
4 say
5 said
6 say
7 was telling

Unit 9
Modals of deduction in the present
1 Well, I think another route could be better.
2 It could be. The man looks like he might be waving for us to stop.
3 It could be because it's so light. Just a guess!
4 correct
5 correct
6 It can't be Nick – he didn't think there was a problem.

Unit 10
Future continuous vs. simple future
1 This time next year, we'll be in college, and we'll be living away from home.
2 correct
3 This time next week, I'll be taking my final exam.
4 correct
5 I'll be playing hockey when you arrive at the station tomorrow, but Chloë can meet you.
6 correct

Unit 11
Verb patterns
1 Do you need more time to finish your work?
2 Lately, I've been spending a lot of time watching TV.
3 correct
4 It was an intense movie, but we enjoyed learning about history.
5 It's best to study new vocabulary regularly.
6 correct

Unit 12
Phrasal verbs
1 Our family has agreed to put up a foreign student for a month during the summer.
2 One advantage of taking the train is that you don't have to put up with traffic jams.
3 I don't get to exercise so much any more, and I'm worried about putting on weight.
4 Good news! We're going to have to put off today's test until next Friday.
5 We put up posters to advertise the event.

Pronunciation

Unit 1

Linking words with *up*

1.04 & 1.05 Students learn to identify and produce linking words ending in consonants followed by *up*. Ask students to read the dialogue and listen to the recording, focusing on the words in blue. Ask students to say what happens to those words (they are linked – the final consonant sound is connected to the vowel sound in *up*). Then ask students to listen and repeat the dialogue.

Unit 2

Initial consonant clusters with /s/

2.02 & 2.03 Students learn to identify and produce different consonant clusters beginning with /s/ correctly. Ask students to read the tongue twisters and listen to the recording. Then ask them to say the words with blue letters in them. Finally, ask them to listen again to the tongue twisters and repeat them.

Unit 3

Strong and weak forms: /ɒv/ **and** /əv/

3.05 & 3.06 Students learn to identify and produce the weak and strong form of *of* as well as distinguish between the two. Ask students to read the dialogue and listen to the recording. Then ask them to focus on the word *of* and how it is pronounced in each case. Then ask them in which cases *of* is stressed (when it is not followed by another word) and in which cases it is unstressed (when it is followed by a noun or an adjective and a noun). Finally, ask them to listen and repeat the whole dialogue.

Unit 4

Consonant-vowel word linking

4.05 & 4.06 Students learn to identify and produce linking sounds between words ending in a consonant and words starting with a vowel. Ask students to read the dialogue and listen to the recording. Then ask them to focus on words ending in a consonant followed by a word starting with a vowel (*was only, wish I, said it, was unkind, believe I, should I, I'd apologize, prefer it, looks amazing*). Then ask them what happens in these cases (the words are linked). Finally, ask them to listen and repeat the whole dialogue.

Unit 5

The schwa /ər/ **in word endings**

5.06 & 5.07 Students learn to identify and produce the schwa sound /ər/ in word endings. Ask students to read the tongue twisters and listen to the recording. Then ask them to say the words with blue letters in them. Ask them what sound these syllables all have in common (the schwa sound). Finally, ask them to listen again to the tongue twisters and repeat them.

Unit 6

The /ʒ/ **phoneme**

6.02 & 6.03 Students learn to identify and produce the /ʒ/ phoneme. Ask students to listen to the recording and read the dialogue. Ask them to say the words with an *s* in blue. Ask them how the *s* is pronounced in each of these words (as /ʒ/). Finally, ask them to listen and repeat the whole dialogue.

Unit 7

Intonation – inviting, accepting, and refusing invitations

7.05 & 7.06 Students learn to identify and produce correct intonation when issuing, accepting, and refusing invitations. Ask students to listen to the recording and read the dialogue. Then, ask students to focus on Gina's intonation when she accepts Max's invitation and when she turns it down. Which one has rising intonation? (accepting the invitation) Which one has falling intonation? (refusing the invitation) Then ask students to listen and repeat the whole dialogue.

Unit 8

Intonation – expressing surprise

8.06 & 8.07 Students learn to identify and produce sentence intonation for expressing surprise. Ask students to listen to the recording and read the dialogue. They then listen again and write down the words Maryanne stresses (*Tell, What, awful, Really*). Then ask them to listen and repeat the whole dialogue.

Unit 9

Moving word stress

9.02 & 9.03 Students learn to identify and produce words with moving word stress. Ask students to listen to the recording and read the dialogues. They then listen again and say the words in blue. Ask students which syllable is stressed in each of the word pairs (**mys**tery – mys**te**rious, **pho**tograph – pho**to**graphy, navi**ga**tion – **na**vigate). Students then listen and repeat the dialogues.

Unit 10

Short and long vowel sounds: /ɪ/ – /iː/ **and** /ɒ/ – /oʊ/

10.03 & 10.04 Students learn to identify and produce the /ɪ/ - /iː/ and /ɒ/ - /oʊ/ vowel sounds, as well as distinguishing between the two. Ask students to listen to the recording and read the dialogues. They then listen again and say the words with the /ɪ/ (*it, Tim, It*), /iː/ (*we, need, esteem, mean, Green, really, feel, be, we*), /ɒ/ (*copy, pop, Ross, f**o**llow, pop, not*), and /oʊ/ (*So, clothes, Rose, foll**ow**, don't, clothes, clone*) vowel sounds. Ask students what position their mouth is in when producing each sound (/ɪ/: the mouth is small and slack, /iː/: the mouth is stretched into a wide smile, /ɒ/: the lips are pushed out in a circle, /oʊ/: the mouth starts in a large circle shape and turns into a small one). Students then listen and repeat the whole dialogue.

Unit 11

Strong and weak forms: /tuː/ **and** /tə/

11.02 & 11.03 Students learn to identify and produce strong and weak forms of *to* in connected speech, as well as distinguishing between the two. Ask students to listen to the recording and read the dialogue. Then ask them to say the words in blue (*to* in its weak form) and in red (*to* in its strong form) and focus on the difference in pronunciation. Students then listen and repeat the whole dialogue.

Unit 12

Different pronunciations of *ea*

12.04 & 12.05 Students learn to identify and produce the different pronunciations of *ea*. Ask students to listen to the recording and read the dialogue. Then ask students to say the words in each of the different colors and ask them which sounds they are (/e/ *read, healthy*; /ɜː/ *research, learned, early*; /ɪə/ *appear, year, ideas*; /iː/ *Eating, really, Heath*; /eɪ/ *Great, break*). Students then listen and repeat the whole dialogue.

Welcome Unit

W.01

Sara Hey, Karl, what are you looking at?

Karl My history book. Can't you see I'm busy?

Sara I'm just asking. Sorry.

Karl No, *I'm* sorry. I don't feel great today.

Sara You don't look very happy. What's the matter?

Karl My dad makes me so angry.

Sara That doesn't sound so good. Why?

Karl He says I'm not allowed to be in the band.

Sara What?! So he won't allow you to play in the talent show on the weekend?

Karl No. He says no music until after my exams.

Sara But that's four weeks from now!

Karl I know. He wants me to study and forget about writing songs. He won't even let me practice the guitar.

Sara But you need some time to relax.

Karl I know. I get so angry when I think about it. It just isn't fair.

W.02

Conversation 1

Man 1 There's so much litter on the streets. It's disgusting.

Woman 1 I agree. There's trash everywhere you look.

Man 1 Why can't people just throw it away? There are plenty of trash cans around.

Woman 1 I guess they're just lazy, aren't they?

Man 1 Not everyone does it, of course.

Woman 1 But it only takes a few people to ruin everything, doesn't it?

Man 1 Yes, unfortunately you're right.

Conversation 2

Woman 2 The smog in our city is getting worse and worse.

Man 2 Yes, it's all those fumes from the factory, isn't it?

Woman 2 That factory is nothing but trouble. They didn't ask us if we wanted it here, did they?

Man 2 No, they never ask us what we want.

Woman 2 Do you think all this pollution's monitored?

Man 2 Well, I hope so. I mean, there are people who check on these things.

Woman 2 Even if they do, it doesn't make our lives any better, does it?

Man 2 I think we should do something.

Woman 2 So do I, but what?

Conversation 3

Man 3 Did you see all that flooding on the news?

Woman 3 Yes. Hundreds of homes were damaged, weren't they?

Man 3 It's such a shame.

Woman 3 And the politicians aren't really doing anything to help, are they?

Man 3 It isn't the sort of thing you'd expect to see here, is it?

Woman 3 No, it isn't. But then all this rain we've been having is really unusual.

Man 3 Do you think it's because of climate change?

Woman 3 No, I don't really believe in all that.

Man 3 Neither do I. Still, it is strange.

W.06

Conversation 1

Girl 1 I have a problem here. I want to send Mandy a message.

Girl 2 Well, go ahead. What's the problem?

Girl 1 Well, I've written one, but I can't send it. I mean, I click "Send," but it doesn't work.

Girl 2 Let me see. Oh, right. There's no network coverage here.

Girl 1 Really? Oh wait – I remember now. The network is being repaired out here.

Girl 2 So you'll have to wait until we get to the town.

Girl 1 OK. It isn't so important anyway.

Conversation 2

Man 1 John Martin.

Woman 1 Hi, John. Did you get the email I sent you?

Man 1 No. When?

Woman 1 I sent you an email with an attachment. It's a great photo I found today. The photo was taken on a safari trip.

Man 1 Look, my email isn't working properly. Can you upload the photo? Then I can go online and see it.

Woman 1 Sure. I'll call you again when it's been uploaded, OK?

Man 1 Great – thanks.

Conversation 3

Man 2 Sarah, you know the email that was sent to me?

Woman 2 The one with the form to fill out?

Man 2 That's right. Well, I've downloaded it, but I can't open it.

Woman 2 Oh, right. I know what the problem is. You need to install a program that opens the file.

Man 2 OK. How do I do that?

Woman 2 I'll send you a link. Just click on it, and the program will be installed automatically.

Man 2 Great. Thanks a lot.

Unit 1

1.02

Becky Hey, Alan, how are things?

Alan Hi, Becky. Not too bad, thanks.

Becky Listen, we're having a party at our place tomorrow night. Come along.

Alan Maybe. Thanks. Well, actually, no thanks.

Becky Why? Are you doing something tomorrow?

Alan No. I just don't want to go to a party.

Becky What's up, Alan? You seem really down these days.

Alan Just worried, you know, about my future. You know I really want to be an actor.

Becky Yes.

Alan Well, three drama schools have said they don't want me. If I can't get into acting, I don't know what I'm going to do.

Becky Well, keep trying. They just haven't seen your talent yet. Are you going to apply to other drama schools?

Alan Maybe. I don't know. But I can't really see the point. They'll probably just say "no," too.

Becky Hey, don't be like that! I read somewhere about that actress Carey Mulligan …

Alan Yeah …

Becky Well, she said that all the drama schools she applied to when she was young said "no." And now she's a big star. All those really good movies! And she can't be the only actor who struggled at first.

Alan I guess.

Becky You can't just give up – if you have a dream, you have to fight for it.

Alan Yes, but it's hard.

Becky Sure. But think of Walt Disney – his first businesses failed; someone told him he wasn't creative enough!

Alan Wow. How wrong can you be!

Becky Then he was hugely successful. Started a film studio. Successful films. Disneyland. Mickey Mouse!!

Alan OK, I get the point. You have to keep trying. Know any more examples?

Becky Well, there's Van Gogh. He painted for years, and no one recognized his art. He only sold one painting during his lifetime – one painting! – and that was just before he died. But he didn't stop painting.

Alan And he was always poor and unhappy, wasn't he?

Becky Well, yes. True. But that's not why I mentioned him.

Alan No, I know. Actually I know another thing about Van Gogh.

Becky What's that?

Alan Well, he only kept going because his friends encouraged him. Just like you, Becky. So, you know, yes, I'm going to apply to other schools.

Becky And I'm sure one of them will say yes. Meanwhile – how about tomorrow's party?

Alan Sure. Why not?

Becky Great!

Unit 2

2.04

Sarah They once ruled the skies of the Eastern United States. People reported huge flocks of up to a billion, making the sky above darker for hours as they flew by. In the mid-1800s, the passenger pigeon was perhaps the most numerous bird in the world. Little more than 50 years later, just one remained, a female named Martha, who died all alone in 1914 at the Cincinnati Zoo. To tell us more about the tragic story of the passenger pigeon, we are joined by bird expert Chris Oddie.

Chris Thank you, Sarah.

Sarah So what happened to the passenger pigeon? How could a species go from being so numerous to none in around half a century?

Chris Well, what happened to the passenger pigeons was, in a word – us. Humans had always hunted these birds, but in the 19th century the number of killings exploded. They were also the victim of advances in technology. First, the telegraph, which allowed people to get messages across the country quickly, allowed people to report where the pigeons were, and secondly, the new railway system allowed hunters to get to these places easily and start killing the birds.

Sarah But why did they want to do that?

Chris Well, passenger pigeons were big business. The dead birds were sent all over the US by train and sold to restaurants or in markets.

Sarah Didn't anyone try to stop this?

Chris There was some concern, and it led to the US government making one of its first environmental laws to protect animal species. It actually became law in 1900 – the last year a passenger pigeon was seen in the wild.

Sarah So it was too late for the passenger pigeon.

Chris Yes, sadly.

Sarah So is there anything we can learn from this story?

Chris Well, if there is anything good to have come out of this, it's that the passenger pigeon has become a symbol of the damage humans are capable of doing. I hope it would be impossible for such a disastrous event to ever happen again. Though sadly, we do still see species that are threatened with extinction because of human activity. We need to remember this Earth doesn't just belong to us, and we share it with billions of other life forms. It is our responsibility to make sure we protect others.

Unit 3

3.02

Paul What do your friends call you? Do you have a nickname?

Alexandra Well, my family calls me Sandy. It's short for Alexandra.

Paul Oh, I didn't know that. I knew Alex was short for Alexandra but not Sandy. I like it. Maybe I can call you that, too, can I?

Alexandra Sure. I don't mind. What's your nickname then?

Paul It's very boring. It's from my surname. My last name's Smith, so some people call me Smithy. But you'd better not tell anyone at school. I don't want everyone to start calling me Smithy.

Alexandra Don't worry, I won't. My best friend in elementary school got nicknamed Gummy. She hated it.

Paul Why did they call her Gummy?

Alexandra It was because she used to like that candy – called gummy bears.

Paul Well, that's not too bad. My brother found his nickname quite annoying. It was Buzz. I bet you can't guess why he was called that.

Alexandra No idea. Perhaps because he looks like a mosquito?

Paul No! It was because we used to live in a town called Leighton Buzzard. The Buzz came from Buzzard.

Alexandra Oh, right. That's clever. I quite like that one.

Paul Talking of names, I read an article recently about celebrity nicknames. Do you know how Sting got his name?

Alexandra No, how?

Paul Well there was a sweater he wore on stage. It had black and yellow stripes like a bee, and another guy in the band started calling him "Sting."

Alexandra That's cool!

Paul And here's another one. Do you know how the American singer, Miley Cyrus got her name?

Alexandra Isn't that her real name, then?

Paul No, her given name was Destiny. But she was a happy baby, always smiling, so her parents nicknamed her Smiley, and later it got shortened to Miley. She changed her name officially to Miley in 2008.

Alexandra Oh, right.

Paul I read about Lady Gaga, too. Apparently, her friend thought she sounded like Freddie Mercury from Queen, so every time she came into the studio, he started singing that Queen song "Radio Ga Ga." And then one day, they were texting about a stage name for her, and he suggested Radio Ga Ga … and the phone automatically corrected it to Lady Gaga.

Alexandra That's brilliant. Hey, look at the time. We'd better go now. We have P.E. in ten minutes and …

Unit 4

4.02

Stuart What time does Jenny's bus get here?

Mark It's supposed to be four o'clock, but it's delayed.

Stuart Delayed how long?

Mark I looked at the station sign just now, but it doesn't say.

Stuart What are you reading, Angie?

Angie *Lord of the Rings.*

Mark I'm so bored! Can't we play a game or something?

Stuart Oh, good idea, Mark. Let's play "I wish" – it's a game I made up.

Mark OK.

Stuart You think of a fictional character, but don't say the name. Then you say three things that the character wishes. The others have to guess who the character is. Do you want to play, Angie? I mean, I know you have your book to read.

Angie It's OK, this sounds like fun. You go first, Stuart. It's your game after all!

Stuart Oh, OK. Right. Umm. I've thought of someone. I wish I was human.

Mark Ah! Interesting. A non-human fictional character. A cartoon animal, perhaps? Give us another clue.

Stuart Right. I wish I wasn't so short.

Angie Hmm, so probably not an animal. Are you … that little man in *Harry Potter*? What's his name?

Stuart Dobby?

Angie Yes!

Stuart No.

Angie Oh.

Mark Third clue, please?

Stuart OK. If only I spoke Luke Skywalker's language.

Mark Oh – right. *Star Wars*. The robot, R2-D2.

Stuart Yep, you've got it! OK, your turn.

Mark Oh, fine. Give me a minute. It has to be a fictional person, right?

Stuart Right.

Mark OK, got one. First clue – if only I wasn't so ugly.

Angie No idea. Stuart?

Stuart Nope, next clue.

Mark If only I had more teeth.

Stuart Wow. I have no idea.

Mark Angie?

Angie No, me neither.

Mark Oh, come on – ugly, doesn't have enough teeth …. come on, Angie!

Angie Eh?

Mark No? OK, third clue. I wish I could get the ring back.

Stuart Ah, Gollum!

Mark Yes!

Stuart A bit slow there, Angie!

Mark Especially because you're reading the book right now. Hahaha!

Angie Oh yes, good job, boys.

Mark Do you want to have a go now, Angie?

Angie Must I? OK, here goes. I wish I could steal the moon. I wish I could borrow more money. I wish those three girls would go to sleep.

Mark Hang on, I know this. Vector in *Despicable Me*!

Angie No, you're close. Right story but the wrong character.

Stuart Ah! It's Gru. But he does steal the moon, doesn't he? So he can't say: "I wish I could steal the moon!"

Angie I don't know! Who cares? Oh, I really wish Jenny's bus would come!

Mark Look, here it is.

4.07

You will hear people talking in eight different situations. For questions 1–8, choose the best answer (A, B, or C).

One: You hear a boy talking about how he got his name.

Boy 1 Sometimes I'm surprised I ever got a name at all. You see, my dad's Portuguese, and my mum's English, and they had real trouble choosing a name. Of course, my dad wanted to go for a Portuguese name, and my mum wanted one that was more English. But they decided it was only fair to choose a name that was easy to say in both languages. The problem was that there aren't really that many options, and since they already had three boys, they were running out of names. I spent the first two weeks of my life nameless. And what did they come up with in the end? Bob!

Two: You hear a girl talking on her phone.

Girl 1 Well, the thing is that Mum says if I want a sleepover for my birthday, then I can only have two friends. So that would be you and Julia, but what about Lucy? I mean, she's not going to be happy, is she? I begged Mum to let me have three, but she says if I want to invite more friends, then it's got to be a party or a cinema trip. She says my room is not big enough for four of us to sleep in. I said we could sleep in the living room, but she said, "No way." I suppose I could have a party. It would probably be fun, but a sleepover's way more fun. I don't know. What do you think?

Three: You hear part of an interview with a footballer.

Interviewer So what's the hardest part of your job?

Footballer That's a tough question. I mean, there are a few things I suppose I find difficult. I guess most people might think it would be all the training, but I really like that. No, that's no problem at all. Um, the fans can be a bit cruel at times, especially if you've had a bad game. That can be difficult, but as long as you try your best, they're usually OK. They forgive you pretty quickly. I suppose it must be having to work every Saturday and not being able to spend time with the kids. That can be tough.

Four: You hear two friends talking about a camping trip.

Steve You do a lot of camping, don't you, Alan? Got any advice?

Alan Steve, you're not going camping, are you? I don't believe it. I never thought I'd see you …

Steve I know, I know. I thought I'd give it a go.

Alan You'll love it. It's brilliant.

Steve So what do I need, then? I mean, I've got nothing.

Alan OK, well, obviously you'll need a tent. You should go for something light and easy to put up. Then you'll need a sleeping bag and something to cook on. Again, go for something light. Remember, you've got to carry everything. Keep it light. That's the secret.

Steve Actually, my dad's going to take us to the campsite, so that's not such a problem.

Alan What?! You're getting a lift to the campsite? That's not camping!

Five: You hear a local news report.

Reporter When street cleaner Clive Roberts found a brown paper bag containing £10,000 inside one of the bins he was emptying, he didn't think twice about what to do with it. He walked straight to the nearest police station and handed it in. The thought that he might keep it never entered his mind. Clive, who's been praised by the local police for his actions, might still discover that honesty is the best way: if the money isn't claimed within the next 30 days, he'll find himself £10,000 richer.

Six: Two friends are talking about a party.

Chloë Josh, I'm so sorry I missed your party.

Josh That's all right, Chloë. Though everyone asked where you were. What happened?

Chloë You're not going to believe it. My dad made us all get up early to go on a really long bike ride. Anyway, I was already feeling tired because I hadn't slept well. It was the last thing I needed. But you know my dad.

Josh He wasn't taking no for an answer.

Chloë Exactly. So we got back at about two, and I thought I'd just watch a bit of TV before getting ready for your party and ...

Josh You dozed off in front of the TV.

Chloë That's right. When I woke up, it was already five. I was so cross with my dad. I tried to text you, but my phone was out of credit. Anyway, I feel really bad about it.

Josh Don't worry. So long as you've got me a nice big present ...

Seven: You hear a girl talking about a difficult decision.

Man So what's the most difficult decision you've ever made, Ally?

Ally It was probably when I had to choose which subjects to take at school. I was only 13, and I had to choose which nine subjects to study at exam level. The problem was that I wasn't really sure what I wanted to do with my life, so it was tricky knowing which exams I'd need. My dad was saying I should do all the sciences because that would lead to a good job – I should say that he's a scientist. Although I didn't want to let him down, I thought, "This is my life I'm making decisions about, and one thing I do know is that I don't like science."

Eight: You hear a book review on the radio.

Girl 3 *Wild Country* by Margaret Johnson is a short novel written for learners of English. My teacher recommended it to give me some extra reading practice. I was really happy to be able to read a book in English, so that made me feel good. I should say I'm not a big fan of romantic stories, but I really enjoyed it. It had quite a bit of adventure, too, to keep things exciting. But I think what really brought the story alive were the main characters, Tess and Grant. They were really convincing, and I loved the way that their relationship slowly grew stronger. I would highly recommend this book to all learners of English.

Unit 5

5.02

Annie Hey, Lucy. What are you reading?

Lucy Some short stories by Roald Dahl.

Annie The children's author? Aren't you a little old?

Lucy Yeah, but he didn't just write kids' books. He also wrote short stories for older people. Have you seen *Tales of the Unexpected*?

Annie What's that?

Lucy It was a TV series from the 1970s. Each episode was a short story, and they always had a surprise ending. Well, Roald Dahl introduced these shows, and a lot of them were based on his stories.

Annie So tell me one.

Lucy Are you sure?

Annie Yeah, I want to hear one.

Lucy OK, the one I just read is "The Hitchhiker." It's about this man who has a new sports car and he's driving down the road when he sees a hitchhiker asking for a ride.

Annie So he picks him up.

Lucy Exactly, and the two men start talking. The driver brags about how fast his car goes. The hitchhiker doesn't believe him, so the man starts driving really fast. Anyway, they get stopped by a police officer.

Annie Oh dear.

Lucy The policeman is mean and tells the driver he could put him in jail. He writes down the driver's name and address and gives him a speeding ticket. He also writes down the name and the address of the hitchhiker because he doesn't like the look of him and wants to check him out.

Annie OK.

Lucy So the police officer leaves, and they keep going. The hitchhiker doesn't seem worried at all. The driver asks him why he's so calm, and the hitchhiker explains he's a "fingersmith."

Annie A fingersmith?

Lucy Yes, it's a word invented by Dahl, and it means he's a pickpocket. But when the driver suggests he's a pickpocket, the man gets annoyed and says he's an expert with his fingers. To prove this he takes off the driver's belt without him even noticing. The driver says that when the policeman looks him up, he'll be in trouble. But the hitchhiker isn't worried.

Annie Why not?

Lucy Well, he says that policemen are known for having bad memories. The driver doesn't understand. Why would the policeman need a good memory? He wrote down everything in his book. That's when the hitchhiker proudly shows him the policeman's book that he took from his pocket.

Annie Cool.

Lucy Yes, it is. You should read some of these stories. They all have endings like that.

Unit 6

6.04

Mia James! What have you done?

James What? I've had my hair cut.

Mia You've had it cut and you've had it dyed.

James That's right. So do you like it?

Mia Do I like it? It looks awful! Your mom and dad are going to go crazy.

James Maybe. But it's great. It's just what I wanted.

Mia It's really not attractive. So how did they do it?

James It was pretty difficult. First, I chose the design.

Mia A lizard.

James Yes, a lizard. Either a lizard or a spider.

Mia I'm glad you didn't go for the spider. Then what?

James Then the hairdresser dyed the top of my hair green. And then he started to cut part of my hair. That took a long time because it's so thick. He had to be careful, too, to get the shape. And then he added a bit of blue and a bit of red. Magic! He's an artist. It's a work of art.

Mia A work of art? You must be joking. It's a disaster! And there's Emily's wedding on Saturday. She's your sister! You'll spoil her wedding photos.

James I'll make her wedding photos special.

Mia There isn't time for the hair to grow back, but we could change the color, and you could wear a hat.

James So you really don't like it?

Mia No, I don't. I think it was a really silly thing to do.

James Why?

Mia Because it looks terrible. And I repeat: your sister's wedding is coming up. It's her big day, and she should be the center of attention, not you.

James So you think Mom and Dad and Emily are going to be annoyed?

Mia Annoyed? I think they'll be furious!

James Well, I can have the lizard shaved off, I suppose.

Mia But what about the green?

James I can have it dyed brown or …

Mia What are you doing?

James I'm just taking it off.

Mia You mean …?

James Yes. It isn't my real hair. It's fake hair, just a kind of wig. How silly do you think I am? I don't want to ruin Emily's wedding.

Mia I can't believe you did that.

James Oh, look at the time. I have to go. I'm going to have my arms tattooed!

Mia What?!

James Just joking!

Mia Ha, ha!

Unit 7

7.02

Man … and so first of all, I want to say that I think traveling's a great thing … but of course a lot depends on you, the way you look at things and what you want to see. I'm used to exploring and meeting new people. I learn so much!

Student 1 Is there one place that you would really like to go back to?

Man Well, there's a special place in my heart now for India. I found the experience quite difficult at first … but after a while, I found it a magical place.

Student 2 Is it difficult to travel around?

Man It's a large country, so you need to use lots of different types of transport, like boats, buses, and trains.

Student 2 How did you get around?

Man By train, mostly. Trains are very crowded, but I soon got used to that, and the experience was incredible. Some really amazing scenery.

Student 1 What about the food, though? I'd love to go to India, but I can't get used to spicy food. Did you have to eat spicy food all the time?

Man Listen – just go and don't worry about the food. Indian food is wonderful, and it certainly is not always spicy. It's a great place if you're a vegetarian, like me. And different parts of India have very different, delicious food.

Student 1 Do people there speak English? I think I heard there are different languages spoken there.

Man That's right – for example, Urdu and Hindi. But also, a lot of people speak English there as it's an official language, but in some places, people aren't used to seeing foreigners. All the same, I thought everyone was really warm and kind, even when we didn't understand each other well.

Student 2 So the people were nice?

Man Oh, sure. I mean, in the end, people are people – there's a variety of people all over the world, right? Some, of course, can be a bit cold or unfriendly, but everyone I met was really nice. You have to go to a country with an open mind. One thing I've learned, I think, is that sometimes we get an idea about a country or a group of people, and then we start to think that everyone in that country is like that, and really, it's a stereotype – it isn't true. If you really get to know people …

Unit 8

8.02

Presenter This is Radio 24, and today we're looking at a program called Restoring Justice. It's an unusual way to try and help people change – people who would normally go to prison. Listen to one of them, Jason Wilkins. He's 17, and he got arrested for mugging somebody.

Jason Well, I was in court, and I knew I was gonna go to prison … and I was feeling awful about it. And then the judge said he'd give me a choice. I didn't understand what he meant. He asked me whether I wanted to go to prison for six months or join a special program called Restoring Justice. He said the program would last for six months, and it meant I'd have several meetings with the woman I'd mugged. He told me to think carefully about my choices. I was … I really didn't know what to say … um … I didn't want to meet her again … but then, of course, I definitely didn't want to go to prison, so I said I'd join the program.

Presenter Ken Simmons, you're a social worker on this program. Can you tell us more about it?

Ken The idea behind this program is that people who've stolen something or mugged somebody, but haven't attacked their victims physically … well, they get a chance to see what they've done through the eyes of their victim. We're hoping that this helps them to think more the next time they get into a similar situation.

Jason The first time I met Mrs. Schwartz – the woman I mugged – was very difficult. At the meeting, Ken, my social worker, was also there and then my mom and dad. I was terrified about meeting Mrs. Schwartz, but she kind of helped … um … the first thing she said was that she wasn't going to get angry with me.

Presenter Here's what she said when we spoke to her.

Mrs Schwartz I wasn't enthusiastic about the idea of meeting my mugger, I have to say. The experience had already been frightening enough. But then I thought, "Well, we'd all like a country with less crime, wouldn't we? And who knows? Maybe I can make a contribution to that." I was also pretty nervous, but I really felt I wanted to try to make a difference.

Jason Well, now I've met Mrs. Schwartz three times, and I've learned a lot from her. I can really say that. I'll never forget when she looked me in the eye and asked me why I'd done it. I told her that I wanted some money to spend. And the moment I said that, I thought how stupid I'd been to mug somebody because I wanted to buy some stuff. The second time, she asked me if I knew who'd suffered most from what I'd done. And I said to her, "You of course!" She just said that no, it wasn't her, and asked me to look at the other side of the table, where my mom and dad were sitting. I knew immediately what she meant.

8.05

Conversation 1

Man 1 You'll never guess what happened.

Woman 1 What?

Man 1 Someone broke into our house the other day.

Woman 1 No way!

Man 1 Yes, we'd just got back from the movies, and we saw the front door open. I knew what had happened immediately.

Woman 1 What did they take?

Man 1 They didn't take anything, but they left the house in a real mess.

Conversation 2

Man 2 You won't believe what happened to me last week.

Woman 2 Tell me.

Man 2 I was walking down the street when this man just took my phone out of my back pocket and ran away.

Woman 2 What?!

Man 2 Yes. He was gone before I could do anything.

Woman 2 Did you report it to the police?

Man 2 Yes. They said it's been happening a lot recently.

Conversation 3

Boy 3 I heard a really sad story about an old lady. She was conned and lost her life savings.

Woman 3 Really?

Boy 3 Yes. Someone called her up and offered her an amazing deal to buy property in London.

Woman 3 Right …

Boy 3 So she transferred all her money into this bank account and, of course, she never heard from the man again.

Woman 3 That's awful. Old people are very vulnerable.

Boy 3 I know. It makes me worry about my grandparents. It's just the sort of thing that could happen to them.

Conversation 4

Woman 4 There was a scary story in the paper the other day. It was about gangs of teenagers going into stores and stealing clothes.

Man 4 How?

Woman 4 Well, a couple of them start an argument in the store, and the others use this as a chance to take stuff.

Man 4 I'd better warn my uncle. He has a clothes store.

Woman 4 Yes, tell him to be extra careful right now.

Unit 9

9.04

The Case of the Mysterious Fall

Mr. Huntingdon was a strange man. He lived all alone in the huge ancient house that stood on the top of the hill. Apart from Mr. Huntingdon, only one other person ever went into that house: his cleaning lady and housekeeper, Mrs. Crabtree. Mr. Huntingdon wasn't a very nice man, and he treated Mrs. Crabtree like a slave:

"Close the curtains! People are always trying to look in, trying to watch me. I won't have it!"

"Shake out those carpets! They're full of deadly spiders."

"Don't move that chair! All chairs must face south!"

Mr. Huntingdon was also a very secretive man and spent most of his time in the house. The only time he ever left his house was on Friday mornings, when he would leave home to visit a fortune teller in town. Half an hour later, he'd leave there and return home. He never stopped to buy anything. He never spoke to anyone.

One Friday, the fortune teller had some terrible news for Mr. Huntingdon. "This weekend," she told him, "you will be killed by a fall." It was an odd thing to be told, for sure, but Mr. Huntingdon wasn't particularly worried. After all, this was why he visited the fortune teller – so that he could make sure nothing bad would ever happen to him.

Mr. Huntingdon hurried home. He had a plan. "How can I fall if I spend all weekend lying down?" he reasoned to himself. He got some rope and lay down in the middle of the floor of his enormous hallway. He called Mrs. Crabtree. "I want you to tie me to the floor," he told her. "I want you to tie me so that I can't move."

Mrs. Crabtree did as she was told. Maybe she should have asked why, but she didn't. Mr. Huntingdon would probably just have told her to mind her own business. When he was tightly tied to the floor, he told Mrs. Crabtree to leave the house and lock the door behind her. He didn't need her this weekend, and she wasn't to return until Monday morning. Mrs. Crabtree left, leaving Mr. Huntingdon smiling at how clever he was. He heard the door close, and the key turn in the lock.

Mrs. Crabtree was gone. There was nothing but silence … or was there? What was that sound? A sort of creaking – very quiet at first, but slowly getting louder. Mr. Huntingdon looked up. Above him hung a huge chandelier. It was slowly, very, very slowly, starting to move. He suddenly knew he shouldn't have sent Mrs. Crabtree home. He shouted out for her, screaming her name again and again. It was too late. She wouldn't be coming back for 48 hours. He tried to free his arms and legs, but it was no use. He wasn't going anywhere. All he could do was look up at the chandelier and wait …

Mrs. Crabtree arrived at eight o'clock on Monday morning. She opened the door and saw the body of Mr. Huntingdon lying under the huge chandelier.

"Oh dear," she sighed. "I should have had that fixed."

Unit 10

10.02

Host Welcome back to Moneyspinners. And our next contestant is Cindy Jones. Hello, Cindy, here's your first question, good luck. Which country has coins with holes in the middle? Is it Britain, Iceland, Japan, or South Africa?

Cindy Oh, I know this! It's Japan. For sure. I was there last year.

Host Yes, you're right. So you have $100 – well done. Just out of curiosity, which Japanese coins have holes?

Cindy Um, the five and the fifty yen coins, I think.

Host Absolutely right, but you still only get a hundred dollars. So, OK, here's your next question, for $250. Which day of the week is the one when most people use ATMs? Mondays, Thursdays, Fridays, or Saturdays?

Cindy Well, of course I don't know, but I'll guess. I think it's probably Fridays.

Host Why?

Cindy Well, it's the start of the weekend, isn't it, so I think that's when people most want some money to spend.

Host It's a good guess, Cindy, and it's correct! Around the world, more money is taken out of ATMs on Fridays than any other day of the week. OK, Cindy, you have $250, and here's your next question. We all know that most of the money in the world doesn't exist as actual coins and bills, it's just numbers, figures in computer records. But what percentage of all the money in the world is coins and bills? Is it 8 percent, 12 percent, 20 percent, or 50 percent?

Cindy It can't be as high as 50, and I think 20 percent is very high, too. So, 8 or 12? Well, I'm sure it's a low percentage, so I'll say ... 8 percent.

Host You say 8 percent, and that is ... absolutely right! That puts you at $500. Great job! How do you feel?

Cindy Actually, I'm pretty calm now!

Host Great! OK, question four! For one thousand dollars. We often talk about paper money, but many bills are made of plastic. Which country was the first country to produce plastic bills? Is it Sweden, Germany, the US, or Australia?

Cindy I know this! I read it somewhere, ages ago. It's Australia.

Host Sure? It's for one thousand dollars!

Cindy I'm sure. Australia.

Host And it's the right answer! And it got you $1,000. OK, this is where it gets serious. A wrong answer now and you'll leave here with nothing.

Cindy I know.

Host OK, so here's your next question. Remember, you don't have to answer it. What's the name of the world's first known coin – in other words, the oldest coin in the world that we know of? Is it the Egyptian Lira, the Lydian Lion, the Ying Yuan, or the Saxon Shilling?

Cindy No idea at all. It's probably Ying Yuan, but no, I really don't know. I'll take the thousand dollars please.

Host Fair enough. Cindy Jones, you have won $1,000! And Cindy, if you'd said Ying Yuan you would have ... lost your money! The correct answer is B, the Lydian Lion. Applause please, for Cindy Jones!

🔊 10.07

You will hear Conner talking about the Royal Mint, where coins are made. For questions 1 to 10, complete the sentences with a word or short phrase.

Conner: I'd like to talk to you today about the Royal Mint. I should explain that I'm a numismatist, which means my hobby is collecting coins. That's why I'm so interested in the Royal Mint: it's where all the UK's coins are made.

The headquarters of the Royal Mint is in South Wales in a town called Llantrisant. I've never been there, but I've seen photos, and it looks amazing. It's massive – there's no bigger mint on the planet – and it uses the most amazing technology to produce the coins.

One thing I should mention is that not all the UK's money is made here. The banknotes are made by the Bank of England, which is a different organisation altogether.

The Royal Mint is also extremely old. It was started during the reign of King Alfred in 886. That's more than 1,100 years ago. At that time, there were several mints all over the country, but in 1279, all coins were made in one place – the Tower of London. The Mint stayed in London until 1968, when it moved to its current site in Wales. The new buildings were opened by Queen Elizabeth II.

As I've already said, the Royal Mint is a really big place. It takes up 35 acres, which is about the size of 23 football pitches. It's also a huge employer, offering jobs to 900 people. As you can see, it's really important for employment in the area.

Work at the site goes on for 24 hours a day, seven days a week, 52 weeks a year – it literally never stops. So it's not surprising that it has the potential to produce 90 million coins a week, which means its yearly output is around 5 billion coins.

Of course, that's more coins than the UK needs each year. The Mint also makes coins for other countries – around 60 countries in all get their coins from the UK.

So far, I've only talked about coins. But the Royal Mint makes other products as well. One of the things it produces is something called a blank. A blank is a metal disc which is the size of a coin but doesn't have anything printed on it. Blanks can be made into coins somewhere else at a later date.

The Mint also produces medals and coins to celebrate special occasions. They're always limited editions and can become quite valuable. These are the coins that got me interested in the hobby. I started in 2012, which was a good year because the Mint made special coins to celebrate the Queen's Diamond Jubilee and also the London Olympics. I've got them both.

Talking of collecting, the Royal Mint has an amazing collection of its own, with examples of almost all the coins it's produced since the 16th century. It keeps them in the Royal Mint Museum, and you can see most of them on its online pages. Unfortunately, you can't visit the museum in person to see the collection. In fact, you can't visit the Mint at all. Until a few years ago, you could have a guided tour around the museum, but they stopped them because they were worried about safety. It's a real shame because a trip to the Royal Mint would be my dream day out.

Unit 11

🔊 11.04

We asked you, our listeners, to send us your favorite fables – you know, stories with a moral, where we learn a lesson about life. We've received some great fables from you, and now we're reading one every day as part of the podcast series.

Today's suggestion is from Jeff in Philadelphia. He has sent us the classic fable of *Androcles and the Lion*. So here it goes:

Once upon a time in ancient Rome, there was a slave called Androcles whose master was cruel and treated him badly. One day, Androcles managed to escape and went to the forest to hide. While he was walking through the trees, he came across a lion lying on the ground under some trees. His first thought was to turn and run, but then he noticed that the lion was making strange noises and showed no interest in harming him. Androcles walked closer to the lion who held out his paw to him. The paw was purple and swollen. Androcles took it in his hand so as to see what the problem was, and he discovered that there was a sharp thorn deep in the lion's paw. Very gently Androcles took hold of the thorn and pulled it out. The lion stood up and licked the hand of the man who had helped him. He then led Androcles to his cave. For days after, the lion looked after Androcles and brought him meat to eat.

Some time later, both Androcles and the lion were captured and taken to the town. Androcles was returned to his master, and the lion was kept in a cage for days without food in order to make him as hungry as possible. Androcles' master wanted to punish him for running away and decided to throw him to the lions.

On the day of the public execution, Androcles was led out into the arena. There were many people there to see the event, including the emperor himself.

The gates were opened, and the lion came running out into the arena towards Androcles. But instead of attacking the poor slave, the lion stopped and lay down on the ground in front of him – he had recognized his friend from the forest.

The emperor was amazed by what he had seen and asked for Androcles to be brought to him. When the slave told him his story, the emperor decided that Androcles should be a free man. And he also decided that the lion should be free to return to his cave in the forest.

So, there you are. And the moral of the story? I think it's that a true friend never forgets. What do you think of this story? Post your comments on our website ....

Unit 12

12.02

Quiz master Good evening, and welcome to the first in our new quiz series of First Things First. This evening the topic is Transportation. Now, let's meet today's contestants. Please welcome Belinda Nightingale from Hill High School in Columbus, Ohio and Steve King from Ashbury Charter School in Weirton, West Virginia.

Belinda Hello, everybody.

Steve Hi.

Quiz master So are you ready for my first question? It's about cars. Who built the first car? Was it a) Karl Benz from Germany, or b) Henry Ford from the US, or c) Gottlieb Wilhelm Daimler from Germany?

Belinda, what do you think? Was it a) Karl Benz, b) Henry Ford, or c) Gottlieb Wilhelm Daimler?

Belinda I think it was a) Karl Benz.

Quiz master Yes, that's the right answer. Karl Benz completed the first car in Germany in early 1886. It had three wheels. Daimler's car was built a little later, in 1886, and it had four wheels. That's five points for you, Belinda.

Now question number 2 goes to Steve. Who was the first pilot to fly across the Channel from France to England? Was it a) Amelia Earhart, b) Louis Blériot, or c) Amy Johnson?

Steve Was it c) Amy Johnson?

Quiz master No, I'm afraid that's the wrong answer. I must now give the question to Belinda.

Belinda I know this one. It was Louis Blériot.

Quiz master Yes, that's the right answer. Frenchman Louis Blériot flew across the Channel in 1909, and it made him famous all over the world. Here's question number 3. Who was the first person to travel into space? Was it a) Yuri Gagarin, b) Neil Armstrong, or c) Valentina Tereshkova? This question goes to Belinda.

Belinda I know it wasn't Neil Armstrong because he was the first man on the moon. I also know that Valentina Tereshkova was the first woman in space, but I think her space mission was later. I think it was a) Yuri Gagarin.

Quiz master Yes, that's correct. The Russian cosmonaut, Yuri Gagarin, completed one orbit of the Earth in his Vostok spacecraft in 1961, and he became the first man to travel into space. Now, question 4. The first hot air balloon to carry passengers, over 200 years ago ... how far did it travel? Was it a) 9 meters, b) 9 kilometers, or c) 19 kilometers? Steve?

Steve I really don't know this one. I'm pretty sure it's not a). So I'll guess. B) – 9 kilometres.

Quiz master And you're ... right. Way to go, Steve! It was 9 kilometers. Do you know where that first flight took place?

Steve In France, I think.

Quiz master Yes, in France, in 1783. Question number five goes to Belinda. Where was the first subway line built? Was it in a) Budapest, b) Istanbul, or c) London?

Belinda This is a difficult one. I want to say London, but then I think it could be Istanbul. I'm going to go with b) Istanbul.

Quiz master No, I'm afraid that's the wrong answer. Sorry, Belinda, but I must now give the question to Steve.

Steve It was London – c) London.

Quiz master That is the correct answer. The first London subway line was opened in 1863, and it's the oldest in the world. It's known as the Metropolitan Line. The one in Istanbul wasn't built until 1875. Steve, you have 10 points and ...

Acknowledgements

The authors and publishers acknowledge the following sources of copyright material and are grateful for the permissions granted. While every effort has been made, it has not always been possible to identify the sources of all the material use or to trace all copyright holders. If any omissions are brought to our notice, we will be happy to include the appropriate acknowledgements on reprinting and in the next update to the digital edition, as applicable.

Key: WL = Welcome; U = Unit.

All third party texts are reused from *Think Second Edition British English Student's Book 3*; **WL–U12:** All photographs are reused from *Think Second Edition British English Student's Book 3*.

Cover photography by Mustafagull/E+/Getty Images; George Pachantouris/Moment/Getty Images

Teaching Tip videos produced by Honest ideas Ltd.

Adaptation by Zoltan Rezmuves